UNIVERSITIES, SOCIETY, AND THE FUTURE

© Edinburgh University Press 1983
22 George Square, Edinburgh

Set in Linoterm Melior by
Speedspools, Edinburgh, and
printed in Great Britain by
Redwood Burn Limited, Trowbridge

British Library Cataloguing
 in Publication Data
Universities, society, and the future
1. Universities and colleges—
Great Britain—History
I. Phillipson, Nicholas
378'.103'0941   LC 191
ISBN 0 85224 461 4

1983

UNIVERSITIES, SOCIETY, AND THE FUTURE

Edited by Nicholas Phillipson and published by the University Press, Edinburgh

A CONFERENCE

HELD ON THE

400TH ANNIVERSARY

OF THE UNIVERSITY OF

EDINBURGH, 1983

SPEAKERS

Dr Tessa Blackstone
Deputy Director, Inner London Education Authority
Lord Briggs
Provost, Worcester College, Oxford
Professor Anthony Grafton
Princeton University
Professor Ian Gregor
University of Kent
Professor F.S.L. Lyons
Trinity College, Dublin
Dr James McConica
All Souls College, Oxford
Dr Patrick Nuttgens
Director, Leeds Polytechnic
Dr Nicholas Phillipson
University of Edinburgh
Dr Harold Silver
Principal, Bulmershe College of Higher Education
Professor Lawrence Stone
Princeton University
Professor Gareth Williams
University of Lancaster

DISCUSSANTS

Sir Kenneth Alexander
Principal, University of Stirling
Dr Robert D. Anderson
University of Edinburgh
Sir Stuart Hampshire
Wadham College, Oxford
Dr Andrew McPherson
University of Edinburgh
Professor Berrick Saul
Vice-Chancellor, University of York
Peter Scott
Times Higher Education Supplement
Dr Richard Tuck
Jesus College, Cambridge

CONTENTS

Preface, *by John H. Burnett* p.vii
Introduction, *by the Editor* p.ix

ONE. The Early Modern University.
Social Control and Intellectual Excellence:
Oxbridge and Edinburgh 1560–1983
   Lawrence Stone p.1
      Comments *by Sir Stuart Hampshire* p.30
The Fate of Erasmian Humanism
   James McConica p.37
From Ramus to Ruddiman:
the *studia humanitatis* in a scientific age
   Anthony Grafton p.62
The Pursuit of Virtue in Scottish University Education:
Dugald Stewart and Scottish moral philosophy
in the Enlightenment
   Nicholas Phillipson p.82
      Comments *by Richard Tuck* p.101
Report of the Discussion
   Anthony Grafton and *Lawrence Stone* p.106

TWO. The Liberal Ideal in a Scientific Age.
The Idea of a University: Newman to Robbins
   F.S.L. Lyons p.113
Liberal Education: an outworn ideal?
   Ian Gregor p.145
      Comments *by Robert D. Anderson* p.160
Technology and the University
   Patrick Nuttgens p.167
Tradition and Innovation
in British Universities c.1860–1960
   Lord Briggs p.186
      Comments *by Robert D. Anderson* p.204
Report of the Discussion *by F.S.L. Lyons* p.209

THREE. British Higher Education and the University System.
Higher Education: the contenders
    Harold Silver p.215
The Leverhulme Programme of Study
into the Future of Higher Education:
Future Prospects
    Gareth Williams p.236
Access to Higher Education in Britain
    Tessa Blackstone p.248
Of the Expense of the Institutions for the Education of Youth
    Gareth Williams p.260
        Comments *by Andrew McPherson* p.285
        Comments *by Sir Kenneth Alexander* p.296
        Comments *by Berrick Saul* p.300
Report of the Discussion *by Peter Scott* p.304

Index p.312

PREFACE

When the University of Edinburgh was established in 1583 Scottish academic life as represented by the three older university foundations of St Andrews, Glasgow and Aberdeen was at a low ebb. Moreover, the new foundation, reflecting as it did the ideas of Reformation Europe in the moral and religious education it provided, was especially attractive, and its student numbers, both Scots and others furth of Scotland, rapidly expanded. The University has maintained a remarkable capacity to respond to the most demanding intellectual and educational challenges of each era, not least in the eighteenth century when its high standing contrasted markedly with the depressing situation at Oxford and Cambridge. So, since its foundation, its professors, scholars and graduates have continued to play a notable role not only in scholarship, but in the life of Edinburgh, of Scotland and of Europe, and today it stands proudly as one of the major institutes of learning in the world. Yet, from its origins, throughout its history it has been very much of the City and a prey to the plans, prejudices, whims and imagination of Edinburgh's citizens.

It seemed to me, therefore, particularly appropriate that the principal academic event to celebrate the University's Quatercentenary year should be a Conference on the University in Society, and I was especially delighted to give the proposal my support. The international dimension of the Conference led to the honour of financial support from the US Embassy, for which all those involved are very grateful.

The proposal, the subsequent Conference and, finally, this volume, which records that event in more permanent form, represent the successful outcome of the ideas put forward by Dr N. T. Phillipson and a group of colleagues. All those interested in the history and role of university education in society are in their debt. Moreover, since the approach was not merely historical but also dealt with the contemporary situation, I believe this volume is worthy of consideration by all those, be they politicians, administrators, academics, parents, or even those potential students, with whom the future of universities lies.

If there are some things in this book for despair there is also

Preface

much for hope and, not least, an immense encouragement to persist in doing all that is in our power to ensure that our university continues, in the words of the late Provost of Trinity College, Dublin, 'to be a liberal place of learning – and to survive'.

JOHN H. BURNETT
Principal and Vice-Chancellor
University of Edinburgh

Professor F. S. L. Lyons FBA

Professor Lyons died tragically after a short illness on 21 September 1983, just as this book was going to press. He accepted our invitation to deliver a major lecture to the conference with alacrity and enthusiasm. He undertook the planning of the seminar that followed his lecture with the imagination, professional skill and good humour of one of the nicest and finest of modern historians. Working with Professor Lyons was one of the pleasures of planning this conference, and his death casts a long, sad shadow over its proceedings.

N.T.P.

INTRODUCTION

NICHOLAS PHILLIPSON

Universities like to celebrate important anniversaries by writing their own histories. Edinburgh University did this in spendid style on the occasion of its three-hundredth anniversary (which it celebrated, curiously, a year late, in 1884) by publishing Sir Alexander Grant's massive *The Story of Edinburgh University*. It is a classic of its kind, an indispensable if sometimes unreliable account of the rise and progress of an 'organism' which was created by great academic administrators and embodied in 'its constitution, its staff and its educational equipment'. To be sure, Grant's copious notes about regents and professors and his exiguous treatment of student life is too anecdotal and unsystematic for modern comfort. Nevertheless, he undoubtedly succeeds in doing what he set out to do, to provide a coherent portrait of a university which was unique and independent, governed by an academic oligarchy which was able to respond rationally and on its own terms to the changing intellectual and educational needs of its time. It is, in fact, a celebration of the ideal of autonomy and independence which lies at the heart of the ideology of the modern university.

A century later this comfortable image seems cracked or hollow. The massive upheavals in higher education of the past generation, and persistent political and financial interference in academic life has whittled away much of the 'independence' that Grant and the Victorians loved to celebrate. But even so, one wonders how much real 'independence' universities have ever enjoyed. Recent research on the universities of early modern Europe – particularly those of England and America – has shown how deeply their fortunes have been shaped, at every point, by political, ecclesiastical and social forces which have been completely beyond their control. What is more such research has shown that once universities are studied from the point of view of these external pressures, they begin to appear as part of an informal system of higher education whose history is best told in terms of the response of individual institutions to the external pressures that have shaped the working of the system as a whole.

Introduction

So, on the occasion of Edinburgh University's four-hundredth anniversary, we decided to discuss the history of the university 'system' at large rather than our own in particular and to think of the external forces that have shaped its history as well as the internal. We also decided to use this perspective to think about changing ideas about the nature and objectives of university education. We decided to range widely in time and geography but to concentrate particularly on Britain and, where possible on the important but under-researched experience of Scotland and Edinburgh. We also wanted to consider the present and to discuss our future from the point of view of the educationalists and politicians who are faced with the problem of planning higher education for the 1980s and 1990s. And we hoped that by tackling higher education in this way we would be able to look at the future from the perspective of the past and think again about the past in the light of the dilemmas of the present. Above all, we wanted to hold a conference that would be worthy of the occasion and would help us to discover how the history of higher education in Scotland and Edinburgh might be written by future historians.

The conference fell into three sessions, each of which was introduced by a public lecture and followed by a seminar discussion of papers devoted to problems arising out of the lecture. The first session dealt with the universities of early modern Europe, the second with British universities in the century before Robbins, the third with the problems of British higher education in the next generation. The lectures, seminar papers and commentaries which follow are the proceedings of the conference and are published here in much the same form in which they were given. Three short reports of the discussions which took place in each session have been added.

Naturally each session took on a character of its own. Nevertheless, the conference as a whole proceeded on two assumptions which are worth underlining here. The first is that from Erasmus' day to our own, the primary function of ordinary university education has *not* been to encourage the pursuit of pure learning, let alone that sceptical, non-dogmatic *mentalité* which Sir Stuart Hampshire reminded us has become the primary educational objective of the most prestigious universities of the western world. Historically, the function of university education has been to provide young men – and

Introduction

later women – with a broadly-based education to equip them with wholesome ideas about religion, morals and citizenship and to give them enough general education to allow them to proceed to further professional education. The second assumption has already been touched on. It is that at every important stage of their history, the universities of England, Scotland and elsewhere, have been moulded by external forces, by changing demands from church and state, professions and industry for young people with particular skills and by parents anxious to launch their offspring on the world successfully. However, in the past universities have been notoriously resistant to change, a point F.S.L.Lyons emphasised by prefacing his lecture with Sir William Hamilton's classic remark of 1853: 'all experience proves that universities, like other corporations, can only be reformed from without'. It was this that led Lawrence Stone to formulate a paradox; the periods in which Oxbridge and Edinburgh had been most efficient and prestigious had been those at which they had been most responsive to external pressure. By contrast, they had sunk into decline when those pressures were at their weakest and when they had been most 'independent' of external control.

The first session, which was devoted to the universities of early modern Europe, dealt with universities as instruments for regulating the behaviour of unruly adolescents and with the pedagogical problems involved in giving them an acceptable education. It became clear that university education needed to be discussed in the context of the history of adolescence – a point reiterated by Robert Anderson in the following session. For, as Professor Stone pointed out, whatever the strictly intellectual functions of a university might be in this, or indeed, any other period, it was clear that a university's success or failure in attracting students and in increasing its reputation depended in the last resort on its ability to convince parents that it was able to control their sons as well as educate them. But what were they to be taught? The seminar which was devoted to the subject demonstrated how durable humanist ideas of what we now call liberal education had been from Erasmus' day to the early nineteenth century and more particularly, how pervasive the influence of Ciceronian ideas of virtue and citizenship had been. Indeed, as Richard Tuck suggested, Cicero seems to have provided the essential framework for the discussion of chang-

Introduction

ing philosophical ideas in unversity classrooms throughout the whole period. It is something which suggests that this era in university history might best be described as its Ciceronian Moment.

The second session of the conference was strikingly different to the first. It was devoted to a close critical discussion of the ever-elusive idea of liberal education which has dominated so much of the discussion about the nature of university education in Britain in the past century. Interestingly, liberal education came over as a singularly defensive ideal. In the previous session, Erasmus and Dugald Stewart had appeared as teachers who were troubled by the notion that students should be encouraged to pursue learning for its own sake without any regard for its consequences for manners, morals, religion and citizenship. And they had been convinced that a broadly based, liberal education, conducted on Ciceronian principles was the best way of warding off this danger. In this session it became clear that the enemy was the sort of intensive specialisation which was associated with the natural and mathematical sciences. Speakers were, on the whole, uneasy about the strand in liberal thought to which Ian Gregor and Robert Anderson referred which held that the pursuit of pure learning would only narrow the mind if it was pursued in the wrong way. But what was particularly interesting about this session, as Professor Lyons points out, was that all the principal speakers had been actively involved in planning the curricula of the new universities of the post-Robbins era and had thus had to face the problem of adapting classic ideas of liberal education to modern needs at a practical level. Much of this session was devoted to their reflections on their own attempts to counteract the effects of over-specialisation by founding inter-disciplinary schools and programmes of study. What experience had taught them was that while it was not particularly difficult to design an inter-disciplinary programme, it was very difficult to keep it alive and to prevent it from being strangled in infancy by classic disciplinary forms of specialisation. In this sense, scholarship itself, 'the invisible college of scholars' as Gareth Williams calls it, has proved to be as formidable a check on university 'independence' in the recent past as the statesmen and ecclesiastics of an earlier age.

The final session of the conference was devoted to the first

Introduction

public discussion of the final report of the Leverhulme Programme of Study into the Future of Higher Education, which is intended to set the agenda for debate about higher education for the next fifteen years. This session did not turn out as expected. It had been planned as a debate between educationalists, politicians and academic administrators but the general election campaign of May–June made that impossible.* Instead, the seminar was devoted to a much more systematic discussion of the report than would have been possible otherwise. And while the discussion was somewhat tentative, Peter Scott thought that it would probably turn out to be a reasonably accurate guide to the response of higher education as a whole.

For a historian with an eye for the continuities and discontinuities in the age-old debate about the nature and purpose of higher education, the seminar had its own interest. In the first place, the Leverhulme report is unique. In the past, debates of this kind have been held at times of expanding demand for higher education and expanding budgets; this took place at a time of contraction. What is more, this is the first occasion in the history of higher education in which it has been suggested that contraction should be planned in the interests of efficiency and equity rather than left to the mercy of market forces. It was a point that had already been unwittingly anticipated by Professor Stone in his remarks about the loss of reputation and efficiency that Oxbridge and Edinburgh had suffered in periods of contraction when the effects of a fall in student demand been left to the market. It was interesting, too, to notice that the authors of the report and Andrew McPherson, a powerful critic, still steadfastly adhered to the classic ideals of a broadly based, liberal education which could provide a wholesome general education and serve as a prelude to more specialised intellectual and vocational training. It led Professor Saul to protest that students liked specialisation and reminded some of us that specialisation has not always been regarded as intellectually or morally debilitating.

But overall, perhaps the most striking historical message of

* The Rt. Hon. Shirley Williams, MP was to have been the principal lecturer in this session. William Waldegrave, MP, then Under-Secretary of State at the Department of Education and Science and government spokesman on higher education, and Phillip Whitehead, MP, his opposition 'shadow', were to have given papers to the seminar.

xiii

Introduction

this session was contained in Harold Silver's opening lecture. As a distinguished teacher in non-university higher education, he demonstrated the limitations of university history which was not set in the context of the history of higher education as a whole and did not take account of the relationship between higher education and education in the final years of school. Dr Silver was able to show how similar in design (if not necessarily in reputation) education in Polytechnics and Colleges of Further Education had become with that of most ordinary universities and how serious the competition for students had become among all sections of higher education. The universities and England and Scotland may have formed the most powerful and prestigious estate in the realm of British higher education but they have never been the only one. It is as such that their history should surely be studied.

What did the conference achieve? In a perfect world we might have devoted more time to pedagogy and to the methods teachers have used to transmit knowledge and square it with the ethical and ideological requirements of a broadly based, liberal education. If more data had been available, we might have paid more attention to students, their social and regional backgrounds and to their subsequent careers. We might have spent more time on the models of university education – particularly Scottish ones – that were exported overseas and particularly to the English-speaking colonies. We might have spent time on case-studies and examined the place of particular universities in particular communities and their relationship to local schools and colleges. But overall, what this short conference did succeed in doing was to map out some of the most prominent contours in the history of higher education which historians will have to hold in sight if they are to make adequate sense of the subject. It will be interesting to see what has happened by the time Edinburgh University celebrates its five-hundredth anniversary in 2083.

ONE

THE EARLY MODERN UNIVERSITY

SOCIAL CONTROL AND INTELLECTUAL EXCELLENCE: OXBRIDGE AND EDINBURGH 1560–1983

LAWRENCE STONE

'Dr. Kettle, the vigilant President of Trinity College, Oxford, said that the great arcanum of government . . . was to keep down juvenile impetuosity.' (Aubrey 1972)

Introduction. The Functions of a University

Presidents, Vice-Chancellors and Principals of major universities usually tell the world that the institutions over which they preside have two functions and only two: first to advance the frontiers of knowledge by the pursuit of original research; and second, to convey a prescribed body of knowledge to undergraduates either in the form of a so-called liberal arts and sciences curriculum for general educational development, or specialised training for a particular profession or occupation. In fact until recently only the liberal arts aspect of this prospectus has ever been a part of the official agenda.

The phrase 'liberal arts' is to us today something of a misnomer, since the world 'liberal' has fundamentally changed its meaning over the centuries. Today, by a liberal education we mean a study in breadth rather than depth, of a wide range of subjects, and a deliberate encouragement of autonomous thought and judgement. An open mind, in theory at least, is the end product of the liberal education of today.

Until very recently, however, the liberal arts and sciences served no such function. On the contrary, their purpose was careful indoctrination in right thinking, based on the study of a very narrow range of materials. For centuries, all knowledge was thought to be embodied in the classical texts, and all wisdom in them and the Bible. Innovation was therefore the last thing a university should be concerned with. At Cambridge in 1824, for example, the object was defined as turning out 'an annual supply of men whose minds are . . . impressed with what we hold to be the soundest principles of policy and religion'. Innovation was especially to be resisted in religion since 'the scheme of Revelation we think is closed' (Rothblatt 1974, 292). All that was required, therefore, was to teach those old and established principles which were beyond the reach of argument. Thus the examination in ethics was dropped since it allowed too much scope for controversy. In my own university, Princeton, in 1854 President MacLean in his inaugural address announced firmly 'we shall not aim at innovation. No chimerical experiments in education have ever had the least countenance here'. In fact, however, President MacLean was wrong, and was merely reflecting a conservative and didactic trend which had set in again in about 1800, after half a century in which Enlightenment ideology had opened a window to allow some fresh air into the stuffy and authoritarian atmosphere of the Renaissance university. In 1760, President Samuel Davies of Princeton had written: 'In the instruction of youth, care is to be taken to cherish a spirit of liberty and free enquiry; and not only to permit, but to encourage the right of private judgment, without presuming to dictate with an air of infallibility, or demanding an implicit assent to the decisions of the preceptor' (Schmidt 1957; Princeton 1978).

Thus over the centuries the self-image of the university has fluctuated wildly between that of an authoritarian dictator of established wisdom in religion, politics, philosophy, morals and all academic topics, to that of an intellectual liberator which has deliberately set out to encourage a spirit of free enquiry. The latter periods have, however, historically been few and fairly short.

Nor has learning always been the prime aim of university education in the past, which is why there were no regular and serious examinations before the late eighteenth century, and only about half the students took degrees. In the late seventeenth century, when John Locke wrote his highly popular and influential book on education, he defined as its first priorities the inculcation of virtue, wisdom, and good manners. 'I put learning last', he said (Locke 1968). I hope I do not shock you when I say that I think Locke was right. These educational ideals are a far cry from the virtual abandonment at Oxbridge today of attempts to inculcate virtue, wisdom or good manners, and the intensive concentration on a single narrowly specialised field of study throughout a student's university career, in preparation for an examination in the very latest research

Social Control and Intellectual Excellence

minutiae on this single topic. In Scotland, something of the older ideal of a broad-based education still prevails, as indeed it does in America, although few faculty today would dare to admit to be attempting to inculcate virtue, wisdom or good manners.

If the patent functions of the university are therefore far from immutable and agreed upon, the latent ones are virtually ignored. A central – perhaps *the* central – one of these has been the difficult task of keeping adolescents out of mischief at their most impossible age, when they are most likely to run wild. These disciplinary problems are happily shifted by the parents to the university faculty and administration, who are supposed to act *in loco parentis*.

There are also other latent functions, often conflicting ones, which I will only touch on. One is to provide a new generation of elite with those skills and values deemed necessary for future leadership roles, and to allow these elite to make influential friends and contacts who will come in very useful in later life. In this respect, great universities are instruments of hierarchy and social stasis. On the other hand, they also serve to open up channels of upward social mobility for bright and ambitious sons of the poor, supported by scholarships; and also a shelter for the germination and fruition of new and possibly subversive ideas. I can think of no revolutionary ideology over the past 400 years, from sixteenth-century Puritanism to twentieth-century Terrorism, which has not begun and taken root in a university.

Another enduring latent function of the university has been to provide the undergraduate with access to a luxuriant and exciting adolescent subculture. Success in sport, sex, social climbing, or love has always counted more than academic success for the bulk of liberal arts students (Rothblatt 1974). The faculty has seen only the surface of these deeper waters, and thus has partly misunderstood the significance of a university experience. Only for the most intelligent, dedicated and academically ambitious of students has class work been the central focus of his life, before the advent in the late nineteenth century of a new over-riding purpose, namely the acquisition of scientific or technological knowledge as a step towards a career.

My theme is an exploration of violent oscillations over time in the most prominent of the many latent functions, namely the enforcement of extremely strict social, moral, religious, and intellectual controls. My argument is first that this function rose to dominate almost all others, both patent and latent, in the two older English Universities in the sixteenth and early seventeenth centuries; that it then collapsed from 1670 to 1770; that it rose again from the ashes in the nineteenth and early twentieth century; and collapsed once more in the late 1960s and 1970s. And second that there is a curious relationship between discipline and intellectual excellence. The problem is first to establish the facts and then deduce the causes. As I proceed, I propose to contrast developments in England with the conditions and evolution at Edinburgh, about which I know only what I can glean from secondary literature, and to draw some conclusions from the differences which emerge.

The Rise of the Oxbridge College Tutorial System 1560–1660

As is now well known, the three most striking social developments in English Universities during the period from 1560 to 1660 were the massive influx of students from middle or upper class background who were paying their own way and not planning on taking a degree; the residential concentration of this expanded undergraduate population within Colleges; and its subjection to close tutorial supervision (Curtis 1959, 36; Stone 1974, I, 34). By 1600, in theory, and perhaps in practice, no student any longer lived unsupervised in lodgings, and none was without a tutor.

The problem that faced the University authorities was how they, who were lower-middle class clergymen, usually in their twenties or thirties, were going to discipline the crowd of arrogant young gentlemen who were flocking in. The answer lies in the development of the Collegiate tutorial system in the Elizabethan period, and to see how it worked we should look at its principle features in its prime, say in about 1600. In theory, and to a considerable extent in practice, the tutorial system involved the subjection of the adolescent sons of wealthy laymen to a set of physical, moral, mental, religious, psychological and financial controls more intrusive than anything which had ever before been attempted in the West.

The system evolved from two sets of interacting causes, the one external, the other internal. Let us start with the more

Social Control and Intellectual Excellence

important of the two, the external forces, and the principles which guided them.

First, of course, there was the overwhelming influence of religious faith in the late sixteenth century, and especially the universally-held doctrine of Original Sin. All men were sinners, and the only hope of avoiding sin was thought to be to remove all occasion for temptation. Above all this meant avoidance of idleness, which was almost universally regarded as the principal cause of sliding down the slippery slope. As Ben Jonson made Touchstone observe in 1605:

> Of sloth comes pleasure, of pleasure comes riot,
> Of riot comes whoring, of whoring comes spending,
> Of spending comes want, of want comes theft,
> Of theft comes hanging.   (Jonson n.d.)

The best hope of avoiding such a declension, especially among sin-prone adolescent males, was thought to be hard academic work under the closest moral and religious supervision. The agent of such a discipline was to be a new breed of teacher, the college tutor of the late sixteenth century. Young college Fellows now suddenly found themselves with an important and exciting new role to play as the absolute masters of a handful of young adolescents. It was a role thrust upon them by the first of the external forces, namely the parents of wealthy elite children aiming at a secular career. The appointment of a tutor was a purely private contract between the parent and an individual Fellow for the supply of certain supervisory and educational services in return for a negotiated fee. Basically the parents wished to transfer to others the responsibilities and anxieties and annoyance of handling adolescents at their most truculent and turbulent age. This question of governance was of critical importance to parents, which explains their insistence upon the twin elements of social control: the college as a living place and the tutor as a disciplinarian. So far as the parents were concerned, a principal – perhaps *the* principal – duty of the tutor was to keep his pupil out of mischief. Thus in the early sixteenth century, a parent asked a college head 'Please find him a severe and grave tutor, who will keep him from excess and stimulate him to good letters' (Pantin 1972; Grosart 1887; Brasenose College *a*). Note that morals come first and learning second.

A father expected four things in return for the fee. First he expected the tutor closely to supervise his pupil's morals, and many of the richest and most influential parents insisted that the pupil actually sleep in the tutor's room so that he was under his eye both day and night. Thus in the late seventeenth century, John North, the son of Lord North, slept in his tutor's room (North 1890). Second, he demanded that the tutor supervise his pupil's religious education. The tutors were responsible for seeing to it that their pupils regularly attended College Chapel twice a day, that they studied the Scriptures, that they absorbed the contents of the sermons they heard, that they imbibed the appropriate doctrines of church government, and that they developed habits of regular private prayer. It was while about to start prayers in his tutor's room at Cambridge that young Simonds D'Ewes and his tutor Holdsworth noticed out of the window the first appearance of the great comet of 1618 – which no doubt put an end to prayers for that evening (Thompson 1900; Trinity College; Clarke 1677; Marsden 1851, 54). Thirdly, a parent expected a tutor to receive and spend every penny of his pupil's money (Edwards 1899, 101; Penton 1688; tutors' accounts for the expenditure of pupils in the archives of Christ's College, Clare College and St Catherine's College, Cambridge, and Brasenose College, Oxford).

Fourth, a parent expected the tutor to supervise the academic education of his pupil by prescribing reading and supervising preparations on an individual basis, quite apart from the lecturing facilities supplied by the College, which were primarily intended for those preparing for a degree. Nearly all the sons of wealthy laity, however, had no intention of taking a degree, and therefore needed personal attention for designing a more general curriculum better suited to their needs (Looney 1981).

An early-seventeenth-century student would therefore spend a good part of every day in his tutor's chamber. When David Baker came up to Oxford in 1590, he 'daily resorted to his tutor's chamber for teaching, and there remained almost all the day's space, save only for mealtimes'. In the 1620s and 1630s, Joseph Mead at Christ's gave daily lectures plus private instruction to his many pupils, and saw them individually every evening to check their progress (Baker 1933; Mede 1664; Curtis 1959, 108).

The second set of external forces were the State and the Church. The State intervened mainly through the Chancellor,

Social Control and Intellectual Excellence

who was always a leading political figure at Court. In 1567 the Cambridge Chancellor, Sir William Cecil, warned the University to tighten up its discipline and to repress 'the lightness and disorder of your youth, as well in apparell as other behaviour'. As a spur to action, he used a new argument, that the flow of endowment income from the rich depended on the good reputation of the University and the Colleges as instruments for the strict control of morals and religion. Here was a new and important incentive behind the drive for discipline, that is the need to attract new endowment funds for scholarships, fellowships and building. What Cecil and the prospective donors wanted to encourage was learning combined with 'godliness, modesty, and the glad embracing of good orders' (Cooper 1842–53, II, 230).

In 1570 at Cambridge and in 1636 in Oxford the State intervened directly in University affairs by issuing new Statutes which drastically modified their medieval constitutions. Power was shifted from the large number of young Regent Masters to a tight little oligarchy of the Vice-Chancellor and the College Heads, all of whom were in practice, if not in law, subject to appointment by the state through letters mandatory.

Nor did the state confine itself to these general constitutional issues, and sometimes its intervention in University affairs took bizarre forms, for example the action in 1542 of the Cambridge Chancellor, Bishop Gardiner. In his desperate efforts to prevent the spread of the new Erasmian pronunciation of Greek, he ordered that any student using it was to be publicly whipped before his fellow students in College. Emphasis on the external appearance of a student took on special significance as political tensions rose in the 1630s, and the new Oxford statutes of 1636, written by the embattled Chancellor, Archbishop Laud, went out of their way to insist that part of a tutor's duties was the supervision of 'the dress, the boots, the wearing of hair, etc.' (Cooper 1842–53, I, 76; Ward 1845).

Religious indoctrination was a matter of particular concern to the State, which realised very well that if the country was to be effectively weaned from its traditional Catholicism, it could only be done by the production of a generation of zealously protestant clergymen, and of gentry patrons willing to provide them with church livings. The State and the Church saw the tutor and the College chapel as the two critical elements in a great missionary endeavour to mould the minds of the leaders of the new generation. The purging of the universities of papists, and the inculcation of the right religious ideas by tutors, were of central concern to the Elizabethan government and church. Judging by the shift in one generation of the English elite and clergy from Catholicism to Protestantism, this moulding process was highly effective. On the other hand, one can also plausibly argue that it was primarily the failure to stamp out Puritan ideas and practices among the tutors and in the chapels of the Colleges that prevented the unchallenged acceptance of the Anglican Church in England.

The University authorities were equally anxious to co-operate with parents, church and state, to enforce discipline among the students, and also to internalise deference to superiors, not least to themselves. They were only too willing to cooperate in repressing vice and disorder. A classic, if rather odd, example of the trend is the Cambridge edict of 1571, which forbade students under the degree of BA to swim in the river, under penalty of whipping or placing in the stocks. The 1580 prohibition on football outside college was more reasonable, since this was a mass sport with few or no rules, which often degenerated into a bloody intercollegiate riot (Cooper 1842–53, II, 277, 382; Mullinger 1873–84, II, 60; Marsden 1851, 94).

The major disciplinary control over the undergraduates, however, was exercised not by the University, but by the Colleges. Values were for the most part successfully internalised by intensive tutorial indoctrination, but when that failed, recourse was had to the birch-rod. Publicity added to the punishment in this shame society, and some colleges had a special time set aside each week for the purpose of a public collective display of the whipping of undergraduates. In Balliol it was in the hall on Saturday nights, and in Caius, Cambridge, it was in the hall at 7 p.m. on Thursday nights (Davis 1900; Venn 1897, III, 180–1).

An alternate shame punishment, which fell slowly into disuse in the late sixteenth century, was placement in stocks. In the 1560s Dr Caius, in his quarrel with the Fellows did not hesitate to place some of them in the stocks in the hall. Yet another shame punishment was public confession. In 1633 a student at Exeter College, Oxford, was 'enjoined first to cut off his hair and then publicly in the hall by a declamation to

Social Control and Intellectual Excellence

confess going without his tutor's leave from College' (Venn 1901; Exeter College).

So far we have only discussed the external forces – parents, State and Church – which encouraged the University and the Colleges to tighten the disciplinary system. The linch-pin of the system was the college tutor, hired on private contract by the parents. But here internal forces came into play, since the College had a direct and urgent interest in seeing that this *ad hoc* system was made obligatory and universal.

There were two reasons for this, the first being financial, the need to secure the prompt payment of college bills. By custom, the college bills for room, board and extras were not paid in advance but at the end of each term. The bursars, who were responsible to the College for all monies due to it, became increasingly alarmed by the mounting size of the terminal credit extended to these rich lay students, and also by the problem of enforcement of unpaid debts. The solution adopted was to make it obligatory for every undergraduate to have a college tutor. Clare and Trinity were the first in the field in Cambridge in 1551–2, Balliol and Brasenose were the first Oxford colleges to follow suit in 1572 and 1576. These tutors were made legally responsible for the payment of their pupils' debts to the College. Instead of dunning the parents, the bursar was now able to deduct the money owed by the pupil from his tutor's college allowance and stipend. It was this which turned a private contract into an obligation enforced by the College (see Mullinger 1873–84, II, 598–9 and *Victoria* 1954).

The second way in which internal college politics became involved in private tutorial contracts with parents was over the allocation of rooms. If the tutor could not get the Master to assign him rooms for his pupils, he would have to reject requests by parents to take their sons under his supervision. The number and quality of pupils a tutor could accept – and therefore his income, status and future prospects – thus depended on the arbitrary decision of the Master about how many college rooms, of what size and comfort, would be placed at his disposal.

The Heads of Colleges inevitably seized this golden opportunity to increase their power, for they could make or break a tutor's career by granting him or depriving him of rooms for his pupils. In the 1610s, the wily Dr John Preston at Queens'

College, Cambridge, assiduously cultivated the President, Dr Davenant, so that 'it was commonly said in College that every time Master Preston plucked off his hat to Dr Davenant, he gained a chamber or study for one of his pupils' (British Library *a*; Fuller 1840; Slingsby 1836).

Between 1560 and 1660 there was thus a near-perfect match between the external desires of patrons, parents, Church and State and the internal willingness of the Heads and Fellows to extend the College tutorial system. All parties, for their own different reasons, had an interest in developing and sustaining the system.

Such was the theory. How effective the system was in practice is a much more difficult question to answer. Given human nature, and the nature of adolescents in particular, there was naturally considerable slippage between the ideal and the actual. Some tutors were more diligent than others, and some College Heads were more careful about the well-being and reputation of their Colleges than others. But some took their duties so seriously that they went to bizarre lengths to ensure diligence and order. President Kettel of Trinity, Oxford, used 'to go up and down the College and peep in at the keyholes to see whether the boys did follow their books or no', and Master Batchcroft of Caius, Cambridge, did the same. It is significant of the character of thought control that when the latter found a student studying a Jesuit mathematical treatise, he ordered him to 'read Protestant mathematical books' (Aubrey 1962).

Even so, the control system was not perfect, the main weakness being that the students could not be forbidden to go into town during the daytime, since they had to go to university lectures and exercises. They were therefore not totally insulated from contaminating influences from outside. On the other hand the students' lack of pocket-money, which was usually securely in the hands of their tutors, and the need to be back in College before the gates shut at 9.00 p.m., severely limited their capacity to lead a life of unbridled dissipation. It is remarkable how relatively few complaints there were about University discipline between about 1580 and 1660. It looks as if the Oxbridge College at that time was as successful in shaping the mind and character and values of the ordinary boy planning a secular career as any institution the Western world had ever seen, or was to see again before the development of the

Social Control and Intellectual Excellence

Victorian Public School. It provided serious academic training; it imprinted lasting religious opinions; and it created behavioural norms which closely conformed to the 'Puritan Ethic' of piety, thrift, hard work and self-discipline. The gentlemen and clergymen exposed to this experience then went out into the world, and in their capacities as MPs, JPs, and preachers attempted the far more difficult task of converting the population as a whole to their ideals. This was an effort whose culminating point was reached in New England in the 1630s to 1660s, and in England in the 1650s.

Moreover it was precisely at this time that the intellectual and cultural Renaissance of England was at its apogee, many of the leaders of which had been trained at Oxford and Cambridge. It was perhaps lucky that Shakespeare was never exposed to an intensive classical education, since this would have ruined his extraordinary capacity to handle the vernacular. But a very high proportion of the other intellectual, cultural and political leaders of England were certainly deeply influenced by their university experience, mostly for the better.

Edinburgh 1583–1660

Meanwhile what was happening at Edinburgh? (The following account is drawn from secondary sources: Grant 1884; Crauford 1808; Horn 1967.) While the predominantly classical curriculum was virtually identical with that at Oxford and Cambridge, the educational structure evolved in a very different manner, for a number of reasons. The first was financial. For the first two hundred years of its existence, the University never had enough money, and could therefore never afford to build itself a residential College. Indeed it did not even have any communal dining facilities until the early nineteenth century or even later. The lack of residential quarters meant that the students were obliged to live with families – often their own – in the town. In a strictly Calvinist city, it was thought to be more natural and more morally secure for adolescents to live 'in the presence of their friends'. Be that as it may, the faculty carried heavy staffs with which to beat the students, so that discipline, as in England, was on the rough side (Horn 1967, 9, 25).

The second difference was that the prescribed religion was Presbyterian, not Anglican. Both faculty and students were expected to take the Covenant, and there was a Divinity School attached to the Arts College to cater for that fifty per cent or so of the students who graduated and went on to become ministers in the Kirk.

The third difference was that the College was run by, and financially supported by, the city corporation, rather than being an independent and autonomous body governed by the faculty under a royal charter. Despite these differences, the College before 1640 seems to have flourished, just as did the well-endowed, constitutionally independent, and wholly residential Colleges of Oxford and Cambridge. It was, however, a College which seems to have catered for the middle and lower middle class, mostly from Edinburgh town itself, rather than for the nobility and gentry of the country. Moreover it showed the same basic educational weakness as did the English Universities, namely that the same tutor – in Edinburgh called regent – taught the same group of students all subjects over the whole four-year cycle, which is hardly the best way to encourage specialised teaching or scholarly research. As in Oxbridge, however, there was no lack of learned Professors in Edinburgh in the first eighty years of its existence.

The Fall of the Oxbridge College Tutorial System 1670–1770

Now let us turn to the second problem – the causes of the collapse of the institution of the Oxbridge College tutorial system. After 1670 the system degenerated into the usual *ancien régime* pattern of sloppy and corrupt enforcement of stereotyped rules which left the individual student free to structure his work and his play, his morals and his religion, very much as he pleased (Stone 1974, 52–6). To explain this decay raises very difficult problems, since there seems to be no specific and chronological, although certainly a vague and general, relationship between changes in the external demands of society, and changes in the internal operation of College discipline. I want to argue that if the causes of the rise were mainly external and social, the causes of the fall were mainly internal and institutional.

The first reason for the decay of the tutorial system is that it fell victim to its own success. In the late sixteenth century, each tutor had charge of no more than about six pupils at a time. This was because the task of tutorial supervision was widely shared and no Fellow was overburdened with too many pupils. By the 1610s, however, the first of the 'great tutors' had made his appearance at Cambridge. Between 1612 and 1622 John Preston was a tutor at Queens', where he took on nearly one-quarter of the freshmen admitted. He was 'the greatest pupil-monger in man's memory', and may have been the first of his kind. But he soon had many competitors (Venn 1897, III, 251–2; Edwards 1899, 97; Morgan 1957; Fletcher 1956–61).

There were several reasons for the emergence of the 'great tutor'. The first was the growing stress by parents upon teaching as well as on moral, religious and financial supervision; this inevitably led to a singling out by parents of the most learned and diligent Fellows. These men became famous throughout elite society as successful teachers, and were therefore besieged by upper class fathers angling to enrol their sons under their tutelage. In the early eighteenth century a third stage was reached. In all Colleges for which records survive, all the students were now allocated to one (or sometimes two) tutors, who were formally appointed to their office by the College Head, who once again increased his power thereby. Statistics from one or two colleges show the effect of these successive stages in reducing tutoring from an occupation of nearly all Fellows to a monopoly of one or two. Thus where fifty-eight Fellows had been tutors at St John's, Cambridge, in 1632–5, only four were tutors in 1762–5, of whom only two held office at any one time (Mayor and Scott 1882–1931).

It is easy enough to establish the facts of this transformation. To explain them is another matter. There were three interlocking developments taking place. First, there was a sharp decline in student enrolments between 1670 and 1730, which reduced the annual freshman intake by about fifty per cent (Stone 1974, 6). Far fewer tutors were therefore needed. Second, there was a growing practice of allowing more and more Fellows to take leaves of absence in order to serve as curate, schoolmaster or private tutor to the son of a nobleman. Fewer Fellows were therefore resident and available as tutors. Third, there was the official concentration of the reduced amount of tutorial work available upon one or two Fellows.

The explanation which I favour is an internal one, that the tight monopoly was the outcome of a power struggle between the College Head and the senior Fellows against the junior

Fellows, in which the first two defeated the second. The junior Fellows were excluded from any opportunity of tutorial work, which was monopolised by two senior Fellows, appointed at the direction of the Head. The Head thus increased his patronage powers, the senior Fellows got very rich, and the junior Fellows were left poor and merely waiting around impatiently for a college living to come their way.

The result was to wreck both discipline and education. The reason for this is that the reduction in the number of tutors was so enormously much greater than the reduction in the number of students that the pupil-tutor ratio rose by a factor of seven or more, from about six pupils per tutor to fifty or more. Personal tuition was no longer possible, so that teaching degenerated into boring public lectures read at dictation speed by the college tutors, geared inevitably to the diligence and ability of the most idle and stupid members of the class. The quality of teaching thus dramatically declined.

Discipline also collapsed at the same time. With fifty pupils per tutor, it was now impossible for the latter to manage every pupil's pocket-money, and he now gave up the attempt, confining himself to paying the college bills, as he was legally obliged to do (Brasenose College *b*; Bodleian Library *a*).

After the mid-1660s, the practice of whipping students ceased in both universities. The reason for this is obscure, but it seems to be part of a late-seventeenth-century movement against the beating of children and youths at home, in school, and at the university (Stone 1977). But this abandonment of whipping meant that the means of controlling the sons of rich and influential parents were now severely limited.

Another important factor in weakening seventeenth-century standards of discipline was the rising age of the freshman, from sixteen-and-a-half to eighteen (Stone 1974, 97–8). Inevitably, the eighteen-month rise in the age of freshmen profoundly altered their relationship with their tutor and their willingness to submit to severe financial and moral controls. They were more adult, and consequently more unmanageable.

As tutors got fewer and busier, students older, scholarship less regarded, society at large more easy-going, and university life more dominated by the pleasure-loving sons of the rich, College discipline became more relaxed in the late seventeenth and eighteenth centuries. No longer were the College gates shut tight at 9.00 p.m. and the keys handed over to the Head, thus immuring both Fellows and students for the night. The Head was now often absent, and the keys were left with the porter who, for a fixed fee, would unlock the gate to admit late comers. The time of early morning chapel was shifted from 5 a.m. or 6 a.m. to the more comfortable hour of 7 a.m., and irregular attendance was now penalised by no more than a fine. Fewer and fewer Fellows bothered to drag themselves out in the early morning to attend, and the students naturally followed suit. Instead of praying with, catechising or instructing their pupils, the Fellows increasingly spent their time after dinner drinking in their own Common Room or Combination Room. Most Colleges set aside such a room sometime between 1660 and 1690 and continued to make it more convenient and elegant in the early eighteenth century. The wealthier students increasingly abandoned the Commons provided in Hall, ordering meals *à la carte*, or else arranging with the College cook for private parties in their rooms. They gambled with cards and dice, drank to excess, and hired horses to take them hunting and shooting.

Most serious of all from the educational point of view was the end of any attempt to maintain regular residential requirements throughout term time. The story can be told from the Battel Books of Oxford and Cambridge colleges which record individual daily residence and tell much the same story. Students were vaguely drifting in and out at all times of the year. Moreover many did not even appear until after Christmas, presumably since they stayed at home to hunt in the Fall. If one looks at individual students, they came and went from week to week as they pleased, making any coherent course of study quite impossible. The tutors' lectures were now utterly tedious, as everyone admitted: in 1772 Gilbert Wakefield described them as 'odious beyond description' (Wakefield 1804). This being the case, neglect of them was understandable, and perhaps not very important except as statistical proof of the bankruptcy of education in most (not all) colleges in Oxford and Cambridge between 1700 and 1770.

We may thus conclude that the Collegiate tutorial system was begun in the mid-sixteenth century in response to external demand by parents, Church and State for careful moral and religious supervision and personal academic tuition; and that it decayed primarily as a result of internal factors peculiar to the power structure and the economic organisation of the Colleges themselves.

This decay coincided with and was closely related to a major decline in the intellectual excellence of Oxford and Cambridge. Despite a few men of outstanding talent, like the classicist Bentley at Cambridge or the lawyer Blackstone at Oxford, the period 1680 to 1780 was in general one of apathy and torpor. It is no coincidence that Newton was the end of the line, and thereafter the lead in science shifted to France. Nor is it a coincidence that the catastrophic fall in student enrolment by fifty per cent, and the concurrent rise of private academies instead, was accompanied by a flood of complaints by parents that the Oxbridge Colleges were now places of uncontrolled debauchery, where their sons ran grave risks of acquiring bad moral habits that would permanently affect their lives (Stone 1974, 52–3).

The Rise of Edinburgh 1660–1780

An illuminating comparison is provided by the remarkably different path followed during these years by the University of Edinburgh. At first, in the late seventeenth century, Edinburgh seemed to be proceeding on the same downward slide as Oxbridge. By the 1690s discipline had declined. The regents lay in bed half the day, and drank or brawled among themselves, while the students rioted in the town, disrupted classes, and haunted the taverns and brothels in the vicinity. They ceased to speak Latin among themselves in college, and reverted to English or Scots, and they ceased to wear their red gowns in the street. The regents so abused their privilege of beating the students with their staffs that the practice had to be abolished.

Thirty years later Edinburgh was one of the leading universities in Europe, far superior to Oxbridge, and comparable with or superior to the very best universities of the Continent. English and American students poured in, new chairs were founded and filled, distinguished schools of law and medicine were set up. Some scholars at Oxford might still be superior in classics, and some at Cambridge in mathematics, but the general quality and range of the education offered and the sense of intellectual excitement provided, were both infinitely higher at Edinburgh. So successful was Edinburgh that though

Social Control and Intellectual Excellence

a very much smaller institution, it educated nearly half as many men as Oxford or Cambridge who were distinguished enough to earn a place in the *Dictionary of National Biography*. In 1789 Thomas Jefferson declared that for science 'no place in the world can pretend to a competition with Edinburgh'. Between 1726 and 1785 Edinburgh was indeed producing far more eminent scientists than either Oxford or Cambridge – and this despite the ingrained eighteenth-century prejudice of the English against the Scots, and the much smaller size of the student body (Horn 1967, 64; Hans 1951. The figures are thirty-eight for Oxford, forty-eight for Cambridge and sixty-six for Edinburgh).

How was this miracle achieved? The answer seems to be that in 1708 the Edinburgh City Council, which ruled the College, took charge and restructured it on a Dutch model, in a manner radically different from that of Oxbridge. Where the English colleges shrank their teaching faculty down to two overworked and non-specialised tutors, Edinburgh abolished the regent system of indiscriminate Jack-of-all-Trades teachers, and began appointing professors for each discipline and speciality. Many new chairs were created to expand the offerings, and the curriculum was modernised to include the latest scientific, philosophical and medical advances. The curriculum was freed from its degree-oriented straightjacket, and the students were left free to attend what courses they wished, in what order they wished, in a kind of intellectual smörgåsbord, known in America today as the elective system. Since only a minority of students graduated, and so were tied to preparation for the final examination, the rest were liberated to study how and what they pleased. Finally the City Fathers, who ran the College, deliberately sought to fill the chairs with men who possessed the highest qualifications of scholarship, moral rectitude and teaching ability. They paid them small salaries, but allowed them to charge per capita fees for every pupil who attended their classes, which was a remarkable stimulus for raising the quality of the lectures. These fees were £3.3.0 per student per course, so a lecturer who could attract 300 students, as some did, could earn as much as £1000 a year, which made him a rich man. It is no coincidence that moral philosophy at Edinburgh only took off in the mid-eighteenth century, when the professor was at last allowed to charge per capita fees. As a result, not merely did many of the professors enjoy international reputations as scholars, but they also won the admiration and respect of their students. The Edinburgh professor was being described as 'an example of civility and good manners, as of morality and virtue . . . though all of them are men of letters and skilled in the sciences they profess', at much the same time when the Oxbridge don was being characterised as 'weak, obstinate, conceited, bigoted, unfriendly to man, ungrateful to God, melancholic, fretful, timid, cruel' (Horn 1967, 60, 66; Rothblatt 1974, 262). It was at Edinburgh and Glasgow that there was developed the Scottish Philosophy which crossed the Atlantic to my own university, Princeton, in the person of John Witherspoon, with enormous effect on the whole character of American higher education, as well as stimulating that salutary blow for democratic liberty, the American Revolution.

As for the students, they flocked to the lectures, put up with the inconveniences of the squalid physical side of the College and the total lack of residential housing, apparently avoided most of the temptations which, as we know too well from Boswell's *Journal,* were available at almost every street corner, and came away with a respect for the institution and for the broad range of learning that they had picked up. It helped that they were mostly middle-class boys, and that the idle and raffish sons of English aristocrats and gentry who dominated Oxbridge tended to stay away. As a place to obtain a free-floating, slightly chaotic, but intoxicatingly exciting liberal education, not deep but broad, there was perhaps nowhere in the world better than the College of Edinburgh in the last half of the eighteenth century. In its prime it was said that 'it is not easy to conceive a university where industry was more general, where reading was more fashionable, where indolence and ignorance were more disreputable. Every mind was in a state of fermentation' (Horn 1967, 94; the author was Sir James Macintosh). A better description of a really distinguished university could hardly be penned.

When he visited Scotland in 1810, the Americanised Frenchman Louis Simond noted the two characteristic features of that College, the payment of the professors by results, and the lack of any kind of social control over the students. 'The professors,' he said, 'are soldiers of fortune who live by their sword – that is to say by their talents and reputation. They generally depend

Social Control and Intellectual Excellence

for their income on the number of students who attend their lectures.' Since the fee was £3.6.0 per course, and attendance rates varied between 30 and 400 students, a professor could be either a pauper or a very rich man. As for the students they 'do not appear to me to be subject to much, if any, collegial discipline. They board out, wear no particular dress, and make what use they please of their time. I understand, however, they are generally studious and I have certainly observed much zeal and emulation among them' (Simond 1815).

By 1810, however, things were beginning to go wrong. For one thing, there at last started to be some competition from Oxford and Cambridge, and the English students began drifting away. But more important, it seems, were causes internal to the institution, just as had happened to Oxford and Cambridge in the late seventeenth century. The medical school was in decline by 1800, and a series of poor appointments made things worse. Thus the anatomy chair became a hereditary place for the Monro family, grandfather, father and son, ending up with the last of the Monros reading his lectures from his grandfather's notes, which were by then some eighty years old. (In about 1820 he is said to have begun a lecture with his grandfather's words: 'When I was a student at Leyden in 1719 . . .' (Horn 1967, 108).) Infighting began between professors in competition for fees from students attending their courses. New chairs were blocked by professors fearful of inroads into their attendance and therefore their income. Next came the abandonment of the elective system and a return to the rigid curriculum of the sixteenth and seventeenth centuries, which was certainly in accordance with the trend of the time, but destroyed that flexible system of open choice which had formerly been so attractive. Finally the faculties' energies were diverted into a ferocious and long drawn-out battle with the City Council over the issues of power and independence.

It must be admitted that there is a lot which is obscure to me about this decline of the College of Edinburgh so soon after its finest hour, but it certainly looks as if the causes were internal to the institution rather than pressures from outside. The cause of the earlier revival, however, is clear enough. Unlike the Oxbridge Colleges, Edinburgh was constitutionally ruled by an external authority, the City Council, which could and did intervene vigorously in 1708 to restructure the whole system of education. This was something which could only be done at Oxbridge by a Parliamentary Commission and Act of Parliament, that is by a major political effort, almost a revolution, which only became possible 150 years later, in the mid- and late-Victorian period. The story of the subsequent revival of Edinburgh to reach its present international eminence is beyond both my knowledge and the scope of this study. I do not mention it further, merely out of ignorance.

The Reform of Oxbridge 1770–1960

From about 1770 onwards Oxford and Cambridge began slowly to put part of their house in order, the first priority being a restoration of discipline.

There were several causes for such a restoration. First and foremost was a religious revival which affected all classes except perhaps the rough and disreputable poor, who had no hope of going to college anyway. First Methodism, then Evangelical piety, spread rapidly through the middle and upper classes, and the dark but realistic concept of Original Sin returned. The only hope for salvation was once more thought to be the imposition of strict control, and soon after 1770 some university clergymen-dons were beginning to tighten up the reins of discipline once more. By the 1790s, this attitude was reinforced by not unfounded fears that if the elite did not put their house in order and show an example to their inferiors of piety and morality, the ideas of Tom Paine and the French Revolution might sweep the country. The Dons were now under heavy pressure to tighten up college discipline. Since fines were ineffective in penalising the rich, and flogging was not allowed, impositions, that is the writing out of hundreds of lines of Latin or Greek verse or prose, were substituted as a punishment. Rustication for a term or year was revived for more serious offences, and expulsion for the most serious of all.

By 1770 Brasenose was once more demanding that all students be in college by midnight, and the gates were closed at 9.00. After 1790 at Corpus, riot and drunkenness were severely punished, even if the accused were Gentlemen Commoners. In every college a stream of regulations were issued. Compulsory early morning chapel was reinstated as an obligation on all; dress regulations were tightened up – pantaloons and trousers

Social Control and Intellectual Excellence

being forbidden in hall or chapel at Trinity and St John's, Cambridge. Rustication was imposed on any student found driving gigs and tandems, and blowing horns, firing guns or betting on horse races. After 1825 academic dress was once more to be worn at all times, on pain of severe punishment (Brasenose College *c*; Cambridge University Library *a*, *b*; Bodleian Library *b*; Rothblatt 1974, 270).

So great was the stress now placed on discipline and obedience that the faculty were fearful of supporting even the most worthy cause proposed by undergraduates. In 1811 the clerical Vice-Chancellor of Cambridge was approach by some undergraduates with a request for permission to start a Bible Society. Despite his sympathies, he rejected the request since he was 'fully aware of the danger of encouraging, or of being thought to encourage, insubordination, by appearing as a leader in any plan which originated with undergraduates' (Rothblatt 1974, 267).

Slowly, little by little, drunkenness is said to have declined, and earnest efforts – none too effectual, it seems – were made to clear the evening streets of prostitutes. Organised games, especially rowing, were instituted and encouraged in order to divert youthful energies into other channels. In 1818, one enthusiast at Cambridge suggested removing 'the disgraceful and licentious pictures exhibited in the FitzWilliam Museum', in an effort to deprive the students of the visual stimulus of 'naked women beautifully painted'. Others believed that while they were about it, it would be wise also to delete Ovid and Anacreon from the syllabus (Rothblatt 1974, 270–1; Engel 1979; Maberley 1818; Lawson 1818).

There remained, however, the critical problem of how to deal with the idle, ill-disciplined, extravagant and debauched Gentlemen Commoners and Fellow Commoners, whose numbers were actually increasing up to 1800. They regarded themselves as above the law, and indeed had been allowed to behave as if they were. But the records of several colleges make it clear that this special status for the rich, with its gold-embroidered gown, its special privileges, both social and academic, and its high fees, appeared more and more like the relic of a more easy-going period. First, the privileges were reduced in many colleges, beginning in the 1770s, and then the status was abolished altogether in college after college between 1810 and

1850, not because of egalitarian or meritocratic objections to the flaunting of social privilege by the rich, but because of the threat to tightened college discipline by the example set by these uncontrollable young men. (These observations are taken from the records of many colleges in Oxford and Cambridge.) The conflict of values between the new and the old Oxbridge created by the survival of the Gentleman Commoner is set out very clearly in Thomas Hughes's novel, *Tom Brown at Oxford*.

By 1810 these new attitudes, and the major changes to which they gave rise, had transformed the quality of Oxbridge life, and regular residence during term-time was once more the rule, as it had been in the 1660s. The Battel Books of Brasenose and Balliol show that undergraduates came up punctually at the beginning of term, and stayed to the end, making it possible once more to plan a coherent course of study, something which had simply not been feasible so long as students drifted in and out of residence at will. This in turn was both cause and effect of the most important innovation of all, the imposition upon all students of examinations of a serious nature to replace the old medieval tests which had long since become entirely ritualised and symbolic. It is difficult today, in our examination-ridden society, to appreciate the significance and novelty of this move. When serious examinations for all were first introduced into Yale in 1785, the students rioted in protest for four days, and broke the doors and windows of the rooms of the faculty. But the faculty won, as usual.

Serious honours examinations began at Cambridge in the 1770s and spread to Oxford by 1800. But these were only taken by a minority, and more important was the introduction in College after College in the early nineteenth century of terminal examinations for all, called 'collections'. The purpose of these innovations was evidently discipline rather than a stimulus to learning or as a step towards a modern meritocracy, since success in these exams did not lead anywhere, except possibly to election as a College Fellow. Their purpose was to keep the students from idleness, inspired by the spur of competition and the threat of humiliation.

But if discipline was effectively reformed, and idleness suppressed by the institution of constant examinations by Colleges and the University, the method of teaching was left entirely

Social Control and Intellectual Excellence

unaltered. The old system of teaching by one or two tutors per College remained entirely unchanged, despite the doubling in the number of students enrolled and the demand for more specialised tuition to prepare for the new exams. The encrusted vested interests of the senior Dons and the Heads were just too great to be overcome by any pressure for reform from within. Thus the college discipline could be radically improved, but the college teaching could not be changed at all.

In order to fill the vacuum there developed a new, unofficial and extra-collegiate educational body – the private tutors or 'coaches' hired by the parents but now wholly outside the College system. These private coaches were hired hacks, working long, dreary hours at low pay, coaching their pupils to pass their examinations – doing in fact what the increasingly wealthy college tutors were paid to do but did not (Engel 1983, 4, 18, 39-41).

Between 1770 and 1850 the Oxbridge Colleges thus fully adapted to new *moral* and *social* needs by strengthening discipline, but allowed the new *academic* needs created by the disciplinary device of examinations to be filled by a parallel unofficial educational system of the private coach. It was the continuing failure of the Colleges to remodel their tutorial system to provide the necessary academic training for the new honours examination which exposed them to increasing and well-justified criticism. Oxbridge now had life-tenure professors who did not research, life-tenure lecturers who did not lecture, and temporary tutors who did not give tutorials. These were anachronistic hangovers of the *ancien régime* in a modernising society. This situation eventually led to forcible Parliamentary intervention in the middle of the nineteenth century. The result was the creation of a body of professional teachers and moral supervisors – the College Fellows and Tutors of the late nineteenth and early twentieth centuries, and also the creation of a minority of professional researchers advancing the frontiers of knowledge, namely the Professors. It was these latter, fashioned on the German model, who were primarily responsible for the restoration of a reputation of intellectual excellence to Oxford and Cambridge. By 1880 Oxbridge once more enjoyed both student discipline and academic distinction.

Since these major reforms imposed by Parliament through

two Royal Commissions in the 1850s and 1870s, the two older universities have evolved in unexpected ways. The College Tutorial Fellowship, instead of being the first stage in a natural progression to a University Readership, and perhaps a Professorship, has become a permanent and increasingly burdensome life-time occupation. The reason for this is that the money intended for the creation of the new Readerships and Chairs was never forthcoming, because of the great depression of agricultural rents that lasted for nearly a century, from 1873 to the 1950s. Oxbridge never had the money to create a regular ladder of professional advancement (Engel 1983, ch.v).

In the late nineteenth and early twentieth centuries, discipline tightened still further, as proctors prowled the streets, deans lurked in the dark to catch unlucky revellers climbing into college, and as new and extraordinary precautions were taken to limit the mingling of the sexes when women's colleges were established. For example, at one woman's college at Oxford in the early years of this century, if an undergraduate wished to invite a young man to tea in her room, she had first to give his name to the college authorities to check that he was not on their black-list, and then to drag her bed out of the room and stack it in the corridor during his visit. Male students could become hopelessly inebriated inside their Colleges, but were subject to serious punishment if caught drinking a glass of beer in a pub. So long as the pass-degree existed, however, there were always a number of rich young men who could lead a life of idleness and frivolity, secure in the knowledge that their inherited position would secure them a comfortable place in life, regardless of their academic qualifications, or lack of them. It was the virtual disappearance of the pass degree immediately after World War II which led to the final disappearance of these amiable but dissipated young wastrels. The Universities became more serious, but much duller, by the forcible removal of people like Brideshead and his friends.

By now, moreover, legal changes enforced by statute law were undermining many of the ancient symbols and rituals of that moral and religious training which had once loomed so large in the conceptualisation of the true function of a university education. Compulsory chapel, for example, became difficult to maintain in the face of the abolition of all religious tests, and the admission of Dissenters, Catholics and Jews. Only in

Social Control and Intellectual Excellence

America did compulsory chapel survive here and there into the 1960s, as at Princeton. Another survival from pre-modern times, the honour system of supervising examinations and preventing cheating still exists in a number of American universities and colleges. But its ethical requirements, involving putting the denunciation of a fellow student detected in cheating above loyalty to one's peer group, no longer conform to the moral standards of modern youth. The system is evidently failing.

The Decline of Discipline

The final twist to the story has occurred in the last two decades. The strictly educational function of this new professional group of College Tutors has endured unchanged, and examinations are now the principal mode of social control of the student body. But the Tutors' disciplinary, moral and religious functions, their responsibility for acting in loco parentis – as moral tutors – have in the last twenty years been largely abandoned. This has occurred partly under the influence of the values of an agnostic, hedonistic and individualistic society, partly under severe pressure from the students themselves. Partly also it has occurred for internal reasons. The dons are now nearly all married, and it has become too much trouble for married men living out of college to enforce such regulations. They would rather go home, play with their children, and watch television. And so the ideal of the Oxbridge College and tutorial system as a 'total institution' for religious and moral control – although not as an excellent, but not ideal, educational system for preparation for an examination – has today virtually disappeared for the second time, even more completely than it did by the mid-eighteenth century. College gates are kept open, men and women live unsupervised side by side in the same colleges, and students are free to enter the pubs of the city. Provided they behave discreetly, no one bothers any more about how they conduct their private lives. If they get into trouble, they resort to the psychiatric counselling services of the local hospital rather than to the moral tutor – the result of the change being a significant decline in the suicide rate.

Thus the wheel of social control has spun full circle twice since the mid-sixteenth century, but the causes and consequences of the spin have varied widely over time.

Conclusion

Several general conclusions may be drawn from this complex story:

1) The ostensible functions of a university often conceal equally or more important latent ones, the most critical of which is keeping adolescents out of trouble.

2) There is no grand social scientific theory that can be made to apply to changes in social control by institutions over time and space; thus, neither a purely externalist model, based on response to the changing values and needs of a society, nor a purely internalist model, based on changing fortunes in the struggle for power and money of the members of an institution, will suffice to explain the complex reality. Sometimes one and sometimes the other has predominated.

3) The *creation* and *development* of an institution for social and educational control tends to be mainly the result of *external* forces: parents, Church and State in late-sixteenth-century Oxbridge; Parliament in late-nineteenth-century Oxbridge; and the City Council in mid-sixteenth- and early-eighteenth-century Edinburgh. The functional decay of that institution tends to be mainly the result of *internal* pressures and contradictions, as in late-sixteenth-century Oxbridge and late-eighteenth-century Edinburgh.

4) The case of Oxbridge, but not that of Edinburgh, suggests that there is a clear correlation between student discipline and intellectual excellence, the former being a necessary prerequisite of the latter. In the past, this discipline was imposed by the tutorial system and the use of physical punishment. Today, the honours examination system works even better, both as a disciplinary instrument and as a spur and goad to intellectual distinction. Its weakness is that, as operated in England, it suppresses that freedom of intellectual choice that was one of the glories of Edinburgh in the eighteenth century.

The contradictory history of both Oxbridge and Edinburgh from the sixteenth to the twentieth century thus not only provides two case studies in the rise and fall and rise again of institutions, but also offers a paradigm for examining the forces that first create and then erode such institutions, and studying the interacting roles of discipline, education and intellectual excellence.

REFERENCES

Aubrey, J. (1962) *Brief Lives* (ed. O. L. Dick), pp.183, LXXIX. Ann Arbor.
— (1972) *Aubrey on Education* (ed. J. E. Stephens), p.69. London.
Baker, A. (1933) *Memorials of Father Augustine Baker, O.S.B., Catholic Record Society* 33, p.40.
Bodleian Library (a) Locke MSS, F.11.
— (b) Gough, Cambridge 99, 67.
Brasenose College (a) Leigh Letters Transcripts, p.11.
— (b) MSS B.2.a.71.
— (c) MSS A1/6.
British Library, Harleian MSS 389f.427; 390ff.203, 349, 225.
Cambridge University Library (a) Catalogue of Cambridge University Edicts.
— (b) Cam C.500.
Clarke, S. (1677) *A General Martyrologie . . .*, sub Herbert Palmer and Stephen Goffe.
Cooper, C. H. (1842-53) *Annals of Cambridge*. Cambridge.
Crauford, T. (1808) *History of the University of Edinburgh 1580-1646*. Edinburgh.
Curtis, M. (1959) *Oxford and Cambridge in Transition 1558-1642*. Oxford.
Davis, H. W. C. (1900) *Balliol College*, p.58. London.
Edwards, G. M. (1899) *Sydney Sussex College*. London.
Engel, A. (1979) 'Immoral Intentions': the University of Oxford and the Problem of Prostitution 1827-1914. *Victorian Studies*, Autumn.
— (1983) *From Clergyman to Don*. Oxford.
Exeter College MSS, Bursar's Day Book 1613-40.
Fletcher, H. F. (1956-61) *The Intellectual Development of John Milton*, II, pp.38, 44-5, 52. Urbana.
Fuller, T. (1840) *History of the Worthies of England* (ed. T. A. Nuttall), p.517. London.
Grant, Sir A. (1884) *The Story of Edinburgh University*, I. London.
Grosart, A. B. (1887) *Lismore Papers*, London, 2nd Series, I, p.252.
Hans, N. (1951) *New Trends in Education in the Eighteenth Century*, pp.18, 32. London.
Horn, D. B. (1967) *A Short History of the University of Edinburgh 1556-1889*. Edinburgh.
Jonson, B. *Eastward Ho*, IV, iii.
Lawson, M. (1818) *Strictures of F. H. Maberley's Account of the Melancholy and Awful End of Lawrence Dundas*, p.30. London.
Locke, J. (1968) *The Educational Writings of John Locke* (ed. J. Axtell), pp.200, 244-53. Cambridge.
Looney, J. (1981) Undergraduate Education at Early Stuart Cambridge. *History of Education* 10.
Maberley, F. H. (1818) *The Melancholy and Awful Death of Lawrence Dundas*, p.27. London.
Marsden, J. H. (ed.) (1851) *College Life in the Time of James I*. London.

Mayor, J. E. B. and Scott, R. F. (1882-1931) *Admissions to the College of St John the Evangelist.* Cambridge.

Mede, J. (1664) *Works*, I, p.vii. London.

Morgan, I. (1957) *Prince Charles's Puritan Chaplain*, pp.28-33. London.

Mullinger, J. B. (1873-84) *The University of Cambridge.* Cambridge.

North, R. (1890) *Lives of the Norths*, III, pp.285-6. London.

Pantin, W. A. (1972) *Oxford Life in Oxford Archives*, p.6. Oxford.

Penton, S. (1688) *The Guardian's Instruction*, pp.57-67. London.

Princeton (1978) *Princeton University Chronicle* XL, p.11.

Rothblatt, S. (1974) The Student Sub-culture and the Examination System in early 19th Century Oxbridge, in *The University in Society* (ed. L. Stone). Princeton.

Schmidt, G. P. (1957) *The Liberal Arts College*, p.67. New Brunswick.

Simond, L. (1815) *Journal of a Tour and Residence in Great Britain during the Years 1810 and 1811*, I, p.371. New York.

Slingsby, Sir H. (1836) *Diary of Sir Henry Slingsby* (ed. D. Parsons), pp.302-3, 317. London.

Stone, L. (1974) The Size and Composition of the Oxford Student Body 1580-1909, in *The University in Society* (ed. L. Stone). Princeton.

— (1977) *The Family, Sex and Marriage in England 1500-1800*, pp.439-44. New York.

Thompson, H. L. (1900) *Christ Church*, pp.74-7. London.

Trinity College MSS 10A.33, 'Rules of Dr. James Dupont of Trinity College, Cambridge'.

Venn, J. (1897) *Biographical History of Gonville and Caius College 1349-1847*. Cambridge.

— (1901) *Caius College*, p.56. London.

Victoria County History of Oxfordshire (1954) III, pp.83, 109-10, 209, 328. London.

Wakefield, G. (1804) *Memoirs of the Life of Gilbert Wakefield*, I, pp.82, 87. London.

Ward, G. R. M. (1845) *Oxford University Statutes*, I, pp.155-67. London.

COMMENTS BY SIR STUART HAMPSHIRE

I'm not a historian and I haven't been once since 1933 – I'm a philosopher and so will develop a philosophical theme which I hope is closely connected to what Professor Lawrence Stone said in his paper. You will recall that he distinguished phases in the history of the two ancient English universities and Edinburgh, and developed a theme about the relation between discipline and learning, pointing out that in the earlier phase which he dealt with, the seventeenth century, discipline was more stressed than was learning. I want both now and in subsequent discussion to raise some doubt about that distinction or the manner in which it was drawn. I shall be attending, as he was not, to the question of the content of university teaching, because, being a philosopher, it is easier for me to talk about content than about institutional change. I shall anchor this talk about content to the City of Edinburgh by speaking about Hume, partly because I enjoy speaking about Hume and partly because I think that he is relevant to our discussion.

There is just one critical note that I have to sound about Professor Stone's lecture, that he spoke of abandonment at Oxbridge today of attempts to inculcate virtue, wisdom and good manners. I'm a little uneasy in the defence of the inculcation of good manners as being a prominent feature of Oxford education, but I would want to defend the inculcation of virtue and wisdom, even though I have to put some restraints on those two very disputable notions. I shall argue that our notions of virtue and wisdom have changed (and so indeed has our idea of good manners in the wider sense) but that we still aim to inculcate them. Perhaps we ought to note at the very beginning that what we are talking about is not the university or universities as such, but universities within a particular nation and within a particular national context and that what we would have to say – as no-one knows better than Professor Stone – would be wholly different if we were speaking, for example, of the history of the universities of the United States or of France. We shouldn't deceive ourselves that we are speaking, at any rate so far, of universities in general. It is plain that our universities are not aimed at fulfilling the same function, and haven't been at any time aimed at fulfilling the same function, as is fulfilled by universities in the United States, where a larger proportion of the age group goes to university and where the universities perform a socialisation function of a more general character. We are speaking of the universities within Britain and, specifically, so far, of the older universities. On the other hand, since the late eighteenth century and even more within the last fifty years, the faculties in universities have not only preserved but further developed an international character. I feel sure that we are used to corresponding with, and probably visiting, scholars and research workers in other countries right across the English-speaking world at least. Philosophy, history, literary studies

Sir Stuart Hampshire

and *a fortiori* the natural sciences are in fact studied internationally at the level of research, and since the late eighteenth century humanistic studies, under the influence in part of the natural sciences, have acquired also this ecumenical character – necessarily acquired, as the natural sciences necessarily have, this character. So there is a tension between the national role of universities and the international character of their subject matter.

Professor Stone has traced the change from the seventeenth to the nineteenth and twentieth centuries in the requirements imposed on universities: first, the improvement and control of the privileged young and, only later, a serious academic programme on what he at one point called a more-or-less meritocratic basis. The late nineteenth century in Oxbridge saw the imposition by government action of programmes of serious study adding to the universities' function not so much a discipline as serious education in specific subject matters, and he alluded – and we will hear more about it later – to the German influence, incorporated perhaps as much in Mark Pattison as anybody, the influence of the authoritarian professor – intellectually authoritarian – and a similar process took place, Professor Stone says, in Edinburgh from the 1770s onwards. I would like to stress the universities' intellectual as opposed to their social disciplining aspects and I would argue that at any time in the history of Britain, intellectual skills and habits needed for success in later life, and a fund of knowledge conceived as necessary and advantageous equipment for later life, have always been at the centre of the university's interest. What has changed is what kind of knowledge is thought relevant and thought desirable, what kind of intellectual skill and intellectual habit. We pass from a position in which certain dogmatic beliefs or systems of thought – I use the word dogmatic in a more or less neutral sense, if that is possible – were thought sufficient for educated persons to be able to sustain their later social roles to a position in which, from roughly the eighteenth century onwards, more was required from an educated person, because more was known and because the systematic pursuit of the natural sciences changed the position. I would claim that the position is exactly the same now, that is, that undergraduates expect to be given, and the universities expect to supply, those intellectual habits and skills which are needed for success in the higher kinds of professional employment and elsewhere in later life; this utilitarian view – so to call it – of universities and their education is one that is hard to challenge with any plausibility, so it seems to me. It is the only realistic view. We have here the main theme drawn from Professor Stone's paper, where he picks out a golden age in Edinburgh – the age of Sydney Smith and Cockburn and Jeffrey – where a genuinely educated upper middle class of lawyers, higher journalists, reform politicians and so forth – a professional upper middle class – for the first time aimed at a high literacy and set up, ahead of any reform of Cambridge and Oxford, an intellectual society which was a long way from the aristocratic society portrayed in Greville or indeed by Sydney Smith, who moved between the two.

There is, I believe, and here I am speaking in praise, in contrast with Professor Stone, a contemporary equivalent to the teaching of wisdom or the inculcation of morals. What has changed is the conception of morals and indeed the conception of wisdom and not the aim of inculcating them. It is true that the inculcation of morals or inculcation of wisdom is on the whole indirect. They are nonetheless real for that. They are indirect in the sense that the inculcation is not done under that heading. There are certain things which it is generally believed the educated person or the educated citizen needs to understand for his own good and for the good of the institutions of the society in which he lives. For example, it believed that he ought to understand what scientific method is and how to reason on empirical questions and what are matters of probability and what are matters for decisive verification. It is thought that he should have some knowledge of the history of the species and perhaps of his own country and its literature; and with these goals a particular, and no doubt transient, ideal of the issues that are open to rational argument and the issues that are not, and with that an accompanying ethic – so to call it – or accompanying norm of toleration of variety and an inbuilt sense of relative values; these contrast, of course, with the conception of wisdom and virtue which is best inculcated, when already well known, by physical means as was described by Professor Stone. It is characteristic of this no doubt transient, certainly recent and not universal personal ethic of intellectual transactions and behaviour that the word *dogma* is used as a term of abuse – perhaps it should not be but it is – and this goes with the belief that intellectual privacy – intellectual and imaginative privacy – even solitude – is a feature of liberty; privacy in the sense that people should be left to form their moral convictions idiosyncratically and by themselves, though equipped with the means to make comparisons and to recognise varieties. These are intellectual manners or morals which have their virtues and shortcomings – and this is where I come to Hume.

They have their background, of course, in the enlightenment of the late eighteenth century and this projected from France into England an image of science and of reason which made reason identical with the exercise of thought in the natural sciences, pure and applied. There were of course thinkers who could properly be called enlightenment thinkers, conspicuously Kant, who reserved morality and aesthetics from the all-embracing sphere of science. Still, what we called the enlightenment, which came to its full strength with utilitarian thought in England, supposes that reason and science would be all conquering and would enable us to found law and morality on a proper scientific basis. We would develop a social science, and in conjunction with that social science a utilitarian morality which would permit and guide social engineering under due restraint. So we should finally have a political and moral thought simplified, secularised, modernised, scientific. Hume belonged to the enlightenment, but he did not believe its claim. This idea of reason is precisely what he did not accept and he remains the most powerful critic of this enlightenment hope. He was indeed a utilitarian. He spoke of the welfare of mankind, but he was a subtle utilitarian for he was also a historian, indeed, a prime source of historical consciousness. I need not go into the development of historical consciousness – but I do need to develop Hume's notion of custom to force him a little along a path which he opened up – a path that leads as much to Burke as to Bentham and Sidgwick. Particularly in the essay on *The Idea of a Perfect Commonwealth* he assumes that it is true that there are species-side sentiments, particularly the sentiment of sympathy, which grounds our concern universally and is part of the constitution of human nature, and also a sense of fairness which may or may not be reducible to that sentiment. That is indeed a sentiment which men share, but there is something else that is built into the human constitution, namely, customary sentiments which are only to be explained historically because they are, as is language, essentially diverse, scattered and distinctive. These two aspects of morality contrast with each other and move in opposite directions. There are sentiments common to the species which the wisdom of nature has implanted in us for our good, which really are biologically part of our nature. But the other thing that is biologically part of our nature is precisely the opposite, namely, that we are governed by custom (a second nature), and morality is under-determined by merely utilitarian considerations. Morality has two layers, two layers of moral feeling, two kinds of sympathy and repugnance or two sources of them. So, says Hume, the best reason to allege in support, if somebody says do we have a right to walk across a field, is that people always have walked across that particular field in that particular direction. This is a concluding or terminating reason just as much as is the reason that it is for the ultimate benefit of mankind that people should walk there.

This undermines the project of the enlightenment, and undermines it particularly from the point of view of the university syllabus, if there are indeed two aspects of the way in which the human mind works, the universal and the local, the customary, the diverse, that people speak languages not in order to communicate with all mankind, but precisely not to communicate with all mankind, that is, to divide themselves up into chunks and separate bits; if this is so, then social science will turn out to be insufficient for the study of human nature and insufficient ground for politics and morality. When it comes to the point, Comte and Spencer and, more cautiously, Mill were deceived in their ambitions for complete absorption of the study of languages and history, of means of expression and custom, into an all-embracing social science. This will not happen. Social science turns out to be history with a particular slant and the study of languages and the study of institutions in the manner of a social anthropologist.

To conclude and not take too much time: along these paths a decent scepticism is engendered. The scepticism may not last, since after all some of us, including I think Professor Stone, will recall that just after the war, certainly in the United States in the 1950s and 1960s there were all sorts of wild ambitions

Sir Stuart Hampshire

for the future of social science, and as I'm sure everybody in Britain knows, it was very hard to persuade the Government nine months ago not to withdraw all public support from the Social Science Research Council. It shows these opinions and speculations go up and down rather rapdly. But at least I think a decent human scepticism about the prospects of social science and the social engineering based on it has been accepted, the necessity of preserving the study of languages alongside the preservation of scientific method (all that was set back by the unfortunate phrase 'two cultures'), these necessities have been recognised and the philosophical father is certainly David Hume who combined the utilitarian and the historical approach to morality and politics. That is my slightly oblique defence against Professor Stone's suggestion that we have abandoned inculcating virtue or wisdom. Wisdom is really another name for scepticism, for the habit of doubting. And virtue, what is that another name for? No, I am not going to say what; but at least recognition of diversity is one aspect of it, and recognition of reason is another.

THE FATE OF
ERASMIAN HUMANISM

JAMES McCONICA

The eminence of Erasmus needs no explanation in this age; a respected authority has recently called him 'the greatest man we come across in the history of education' (Bolgar 1954, 336). For Erasmus, as for others of his humanist colleagues, the renewal of education was the indispensable propaedeutic to the renewal of religion and society at large. His treatises, although they were not alone, were the principal channel through which the doctrines of the Italian theorists and the authorities of late antiquity reached northern Europe, and it is scarcely an exaggeration to say that every educated man and woman in Europe by the mid-sixteenth century would have read at least some works by him, and have learned most of their Latin from his textbooks. All of this is well known. It is natural therefore to inquire into the influence on the sixteenth-century university of that humanism associated with his name, not of humanism of the Ciceronian variety, but the humanism committed to the revival of Latin as a vibrant, living language, and with it to the revival of both classical and Christian antiquity with a particular 'civic' aim in view. Of that I shall say something more in a moment.

Erasmus was almost entirely concerned with education in schools; universities played an ambiguous and often antagonistic role in his own career. Preeminently the don in his attitudes and achievement, he was almost the archetype of the university man who remains all his life an outsider in the world of the university. He took refuge, as we know, in the protection and patronage of friends; he never held what might be considered a major university post. His real intellectual home was the domestic circle, the *societas litteraria*, or the publishing house. And yet he moved constantly on the fringes of the university world, in touch with its denizens, even occasionally – as at Cambridge and Louvain – living and teaching within universities in what seems to have been a state of more or less constant apprehension. His experience of the college of Montaigu at Paris, where he was launched upon his mature career, seems in retrospect to have foreshadowed all of this. He used the college, about which he complained with such bitter eloquence, as a place to find pupils, and as a base from which to enter the literary circles in Paris through the influence of its head, Robert Gaguin. There, in order to fill out two of the printer's pages of Gaguin's history of the French, Erasmus composed an elegant and flattering epistle, his first printed work. Did the muses pause in their celebrations? Thenceforth he was unstoppable. Erasmus's discovery of the allure of print was a turning point in the history of letters, of religion, of education, and indeed, of universities. In what follows I will attempt to sketch the influence of the new ideals especially on the teaching of arts in most of northern Europe, but for the sake of some economy I will concentrate on those universities with which Erasmus had direct contact – Paris, Oxford, Cambridge and Louvain – and conclude by looking, however inadequately, at the Scottish universities to which Erasmus occasionally referred, and whose subsequent history is integral to our story. There was something mildly prophetic in the fact that, once 'blooded with the printers', Erasmus published his first book, a collection of poems, and dedicated it to a Scottish Parisian friend, Hector Boece of Dundee, the future principal of King's College, Aberdeen, and the historian of Scotland (Allen 1914, 103).

What then was his educational doctrine? It is contained in a few early works: the *Antibarbari*, the *De ratione studii*, the *De pueris instituendis*, and in the less well known *De pronunciatione*. It is fleshed out in the ancillary treatises, *De copia*, *Parabolae*, *De conscribendis epistolis*, as well as in the great *Adagia* and the notorious and irresistible *Colloquia*. In all of these and in other works where he turned to the question, he taught the same thing: 'Everything in the pagan world that was valiantly done, brilliantly said, ingeniously thought, diligently transmitted, had been prepared by Christ for his society. He it was who supplied the intellect, who added the zest for inquiry, and it was through him alone that they found what they sought. Their age produced this harvest of creative work, not so much for them as for us' (*Antibarbari*, CWE 1978a, 60). This is the charter of Christian humanism, of course, and the view it expresses was far from original with Erasmus. As he freely acknowledged, his educational theory was an amalgam drawn from the authorities of antiquity: Cicero, Quintilian and Plut-

The Fate of Erasmian Humanism

arch preeminently among the pagans, and the *De doctrina Christiana* of St Augustine above all among the Christian authorities. From these he absorbed the view that education was for the good of the commonweal, and for the Christian commonweal at that. At root the ideal was rhetorical, envisaging the formation of youth with all the learning needed to deepen their understanding of society, to make them familiar with its history, and then to turn them into effective agents of moral good, equipped to move others to pursue the ends needed for the benefit of all. If it was the ideal of the Ciceronian *doctus orator*, it was also an ideal that could be applied to the preacher, or to the layman, as in the case of Thomas More. And in the providential plan, as he maintained, the elements of this education were all in place when Christ appeared with the final revelation of God's purpose. 'So while Christ, the greatest and best of disposers, allocated to his own century in a special way the recognition of the highest good, he gave the centuries immediately preceding a privilege of their own: they were to reach the thing nearest to the highest good, that is, the summit of learning' (*ibid.* 61).

Learning devoted to the improvement of Christian society was not learning devoted primarily to speculative ends, so little was heard from Erasmus about philosophy. The exception was philosophy turned to the refinement of theological doctrine, which attracted his most lethal invective. If the pursuit of divine wisdom – the *philosophia Christi* – was the highest calling of all, it was because the persuasive presentation of its findings, in preaching, in devotion, and in lives well led according to the teachings of Christ, was the remedy best calculated to rescue Christendom from the morass of superstition, folly, violence and war into which it had fallen. The use of Christian learning for purely speculative ends was to Erasmus a double crime: it was achieved by subjecting the supreme wisdom of the Christian scriptures to the categories of pagan Aristotle, and it led to contention and confusion where there should be harmony and light. In any case, the theologians of the schools were illiterate in the texts of the true learning – the *bonae litterae*. 'They get by heart a few rules from Alexander Gallus (Alexander de Villa Dei), and strike up an acquaintance with a little idiotic formal logic, and then get hold of ten propositions out of Aristotle, and even those they do not under-

39

stand; after that they learn the same number of *quaestiones* from Scotus or Occam, intending to resort for anything else to the *Catholicon*, the *Mammotrectus*, and similar wordbooks, as though they were a sort of horn of plenty. Whereupon it is astonishing the airs they give themselves, for nothing is so arrogant as ignorance' (*CWE* 1976, 121–2). The textbooks Erasmus denounced to Maarten van Dorp in this defence of the *Praise of Folly* were among the favourite symbolic targets of his warfare against the learning of the Schools: a Latin grammar and dictionary composed in the late thirteenth century by a Genoese Dominican and widely used throughout the later Middle Ages, and a glossary to the Vulgate and other writings like the *Legenda sanctorum* from about the same time. These medieval compilations, dissociated from the authentic understanding of antiquity as he saw it, were to Erasmus the chief pollutants in the lifestream of good learning. 'These are the men', he went on, 'who condemn St Jerome as a schoolmaster, because he is over their heads; who poke fun at Greek and Hebrew and even Latin, . . . These are the men who conspire with such zeal against the humanities. Their aim is to count for something in the councils of the theologians, and they fear that if there is a renaissance of the humanities, and if the world sees the error of its ways, it may become clear that they know nothing, although in the old days they were commonly supposed to know everything' (*ibid.* 122).

It is a representative passage, a scathing and partial statement of the case. There was indeed something at stake. The education thought appropriate by Erasmus for the study of scripture required mastery of texts of pagan antiquity that could illuminate both the historical setting of the sacred texts and the common understanding of the languages in which they were written. This was the ancient art of the grammarian, brought to bear upon the sources of Christianity. Erasmus was equally committed to the continuous tradition of exegesis by the best and most learned of the Church's teachers, from Jerome and Origen to the *glossa ordinaria* and Thomas Aquinas. Always fearful of the pretension of the papal monarchy and sceptical of its claim to divine authority (though not of its practical necessity) he found his rule of faith in the *consensus fidelium* and – illuminated by the light of this true erudition and the radiance of the Holy Spirit in the mind of the prayerful

The Fate of Erasmian Humanism

scholar – the sacred page itself (McConica 1969).

The educational programme of Erasmus thus inevitably emphasised the early learning years rather than those of the university, except in the matter of theology. To him as to the other humanist reformers, it was vital that the ancient curriculum be restored, following more or less exactly the first books of Quintilian's *Institutio oratoria*. He even adapted the formal principles of ancient oratory both to the art of preaching and to the art of letter-writing – in this he was perfectly medieval. The most crucial single change was the replacement of medieval grammars with those of humanist grammarians, and the corresponding displacement of logic and dialectic by the early study of grammar and rhetoric; in the latter were found, of course, poetry and history as well as the art of persuasive speech. It was to be an education in virtue as well as knowledge, and the conduct of the child was to be as much a part of discipline as the languages it would learn. In the title of his *De pueris statim ac liberaliter instituendis* every word was made to count. The education of the child should begin without delay, and the design should be 'liberal' – that is, on the lines of the *bonae litterae*. Latin and Greek must begin it: first speaking, then reading and writing. The child was to be drilled in grammar in the strict sense – syntax and the parts of speech – then encouraged to acquire the formidable command and ease of manner in which Erasmus himself was preeminent by the constant practice of rhetorical variation, by the assiduous study of terms, especially the vivid vocabulary of everyday objects and events, and by immersion in the best stylists of the ancient world. Aphorisms, those memorable bearers of distilled wisdom, would instruct in ethics, as would proverbs and the sayings of ancient men – *parabolae* and *adagia*. Any natural bent to the artistic, or to the study of nature, or mathematics, or geography, should be encouraged. It was of prime importance that study should be attractive, combining instruction with enjoyment: what he disparaged was the abstract, the formal, the purely logical. The implicit aim was an international society of men – and of women – clerical and lay, who were steeped in a common cultural discipline derived from the ancient world, divorced from the arid, exclusive, dialectical technicalities of the Schools, and bound together essentially by Latin eloquence, although Greek too was to play its part: hence the *De pronunciatione*. It was an alternative culture of formidable pretensions, well aware of the threat it posed to the established intellectual disciplines, as it was aware equally of being excluded from the citadels in which those disciplines held sway. Chief among these were the universities; they would be subverted at the source of their recruitment, in the schools.

In the course of his lifetime this humanist curriculum made remarkable gains. In the *De conscribendis epistolis*, which appeared first in an authorised version in 1542, Erasmus wrote, 'We see how much progress has been made in a few years. Where do we hear the name of Michael Modista now in the schools? Where do we find quoted the glosses of James, the *Catholicon, Brachiloquus*, or *Mammetrectus*, which the libraries of the monks once guarded like a rare treasure written in letters of gold?' (On all the foregoing, see J.K. Sowards' introduction to CWE 1984). The greatest alteration without doubt occurred in the schools, where Melanchthon's doctrines, the Jesuit *ratio studiorum*, and the local enterprise of thousands of schoolmasters and city officials throughout Europe completely transformed the education of the young. No revolution at that level could be without its impact on the universities.

Nor was the distinction between school and university absolute. The first year or so of university training was commonly given over to the more mature topics of schooling, in the arts of rhetoric and dialectic. It was here that the demands of the new humanist curriculum were felt most strongly at the higher level – in the preliminary studies of the *trivium*. The effects were inevitably profound. Terence Heath (1971) has shown how, in the specific cases of Freiburg im Breisgau, Ingolstadt and Tübingen, the introduction of humanistic grammars foreshadowed the end of traditional logic in the faculties of arts. The late medieval grammars of Donatus and Alexander, both of them targets of Erasmian invective, were indispensable for the further study of late medieval logic with its considerable sophistications, and the problems of universals, of signification and of speculative grammar were virtually abandoned in the sixteenth century (Thomas 1964). In the words of Heath, 'The very unity of studies that the scholastics had achieved meant that the humanist assault on grammar was an assault on dialectical studies' (*ibid.* 60). Indeed, we find that throughout northern Europe the arts faculties shifted away from the specu-

The Fate of Erasmian Humanism

lative, dialectical disciplines towards the oral and rhetorical conception of language; logic everywhere survived, but it was the logic of the assembly and debating hall, rather than the logic of the philosopher of language. A new exercise also appeared alongside the traditional lecture and disputation, and that was the rhetorical declamation, the ancestor of the tutorial essay (Costello 1958, 31–4). And as manuscript survivals tell us, the habit of gathering potentially useful rhetorical material in notebooks of commonplaces, so strongly urged by Erasmus, was universally adopted by undergraduates and graduates alike.

Humanism – or the humanists – made an impact on the universities of northern Europe according to local circumstance, and it is instructive initially to consider some of the varieties of change they provoked. Responses in the German universities have recently been set forth by John Fletcher (1981), and they serve to illustrate the general pattern. At Wittenberg in 1508, only four years after the first statutes were promulgated for the Faculty of Arts, a revision of the arts programme provided three hours of humanistic lectures daily; by 1518 Greek and Hebrew lectures were established. The next year it was proposed to end lectures in the Thomist *via* and set up a lectureship on Ovid. Declamations were introduced by Melanchthon in 1523; in 1545 a further reform named ten lectureships, including two in Latin rhetoric, one in grammar, one in Greek and another in Hebrew. By the end of the century there were lectures as well in physics, ethics, mathematics and history. The study of logic had been relegated from its once dominant position as the gateway to the arts course to one simply among a number of special subjects (Fletcher 1981, 4–5). By 1540 Ingolstadt and Tübingen had likewise given much prominence to the rhetorical exercise of declamations, and by the end of the sixteenth century, the ancient division of arts studies into the seven liberal arts and three philosophies had been widely deserted in Germany (*ibid*. 8–9). In general the German universities, small and competitive, dominated by the local prince and a small council of paid lecturers, seem to have responded with much more alacrity to the new intellectual influences than did their French or English counterparts (*ibid*. 15f.). But in broad outline their story may be taken as fairly typical of the continental arts faculties by the end of the sixteenth century. There was another form of intervention, however, which might be thought to be more precisely Erasmian, since Erasmus himself had a large part to play in it: the establishment of a humanistic foundation outside the ordinary centres of study and faculty government. This is what occurred at both Louvain and Paris, the former university rather setting the pattern for the latter.

Louvain had an honourable tradition in the humane studies more or less from the time of its foundation (IJsewijn 1975; de Vocht 1951). By the late fifteenth century Greek was taught informally; the standards in classical Latin were as high as any in northern Europe. Erasmus arrived in July 1517 for an initial stay of ten months after a year of intermittent travel and attendance at courts in London, Antwerp, Brussels and elsewhere in the Low Countries. He was made a member of the theological faculty without any academic duties, and lived in reasonable comfort in the College of the Lily. It was during this time, while he was working on a complete revision of his edition of the New Testament, that he became involved in the foundation of the Collegium Trilingue.

The College of the Three Languages at Louvain was the creation of Jérôme de Busleyden, provost of Aire and a councillor to Prince Charles, the future Emperor Charles v. On 27 August 1517 he died at Bordeaux of pleurisy while returning from a diplomatic mission in Spain. In his will he left a considerable legacy to provide at Louvain for public instruction in the three biblical languages, Latin, Greek and Hebrew. In this purpose he was much influenced by Erasmus who, as one of the executors of the will, devoted his energies to securing an immediate start (de Vocht 1951, 240f.). A Hebrew professor was appointed almost at once; appointments in Latin and Greek took a little longer. But the university's Faculty of Arts complained almost at the outset that such a foundation, provided with a small number of bursaries for its students, would threaten its control of teaching (de Vocht 1951, 283f.). By the autumn of 1518 there was a complete breakdown in negotiations with the faculty, and lectures began that September in a property – the former fish market – which was not controlled by the university. In the course of the next year, the issue was further clouded by the complaints of the Faculty of Theology, alarmed in any case by the appearance on the scene of Martin

The Fate of Erasmian Humanism

Luther's first publications. Erasmus took a cautious attitude to the German theologian, but was exasperated by the attacks of the theological faculty, which seemed likely to threaten further the existence of the College of Three Languages. In May 1519 he wrote to Luther in complimentary and sympathetic terms, quietly urging the other man to a moderate and irenical course of action, but making full play of the attitude of the Louvain theologians: 'In the whole business their weapons are clamour, audacity, subterfuge, misinterpretation, innuendo; if I had not seen it with my own eyes . . . I would never have believed theologians could be such maniacs. One would think it was some disastrous infection. And yet this poisonous virus, starting in a small circle, spread to a larger number, so that a great part of this university was carried away by the spreading contagion of this epidemic paranoia' (*CWE* 1982, 391–2).

The passage is worth quoting both to indicate his settled attitude towards a theological faculty with traditional training, and the inherent difficulty in keeping the changes desired in the arts curriculum separate from the interests of the theologians. Since the three languages were chosen precisely because they informed the study of scripture in a properly humanistic way, a conflict of interest was only too easy to predict, and would characterise the fate of the reform of studies through the century from this point onwards. In the end, and after a further period of controversy and negotiation which at one point reached the council of Brabant, Busleyden's foundation received its final sanction on 12 March 1520. It remained, however, simply an adjunct to the Faculty of Arts with no direct influence over curriculum or policy. There survived no roll of students, there were no fees, and it gave no degrees. Within the University of Louvain it attracted distinguished scholars and pupils alike, but as a measure of university 're-form' it must be judged at best a partial success.

Much the same might be said of parallel developments in France, where ever since 1517, Guillaume Budé, the premier Grecian of the northern European scene, had been attempting to persuade the King, Francis I, to the establishment of a trilingual foundation in Paris (Lefranc 1893, 40f.). In 1517, Erasmus himself was sounded out as part of a plan to create a 'nursery bed of scholars' (*CWE* 1977, 205), but he was properly cautious, and in the event, the Italian wars proved a prolonged

James McConica

diversion for the King. Finally in 1531 the *lecteurs royaux* were established, the ancestors of the College of France as it came to be, against the strong resistance of the Sorbonne. There were three professors in Hebrew, two in Greek, and one in mathematics, lecturing in various colleges and extraneous to the Faculty of Arts (Lefranc *op. cit.* 120f.). In the meantime, the new pedagogy was nevertheless taking hold in the colleges of the university. At the College of Montaigu of Jean Standonck the division of instruction by classes and following a progressive order of difficulty was slowly developing, taken over from the Brethren of the Common Life, and by the years 1530–40 became general among the colleges of Paris (Codina Mir 1968; Elie 1950–1; Renaudet 1916). It was the masters in the colleges who for the most part introduced humanism (*op. cit.*; Reulos 1953), where the traditional exercises of disputation were modified in their effect by the introduction of new authorities and new exercises: public declamations, plays on moral and historical themes, and the replacement of the old grammars with those of the new humanism. In 1542 the statutes of the Faculty of Arts effectively acknowledged the abandonment of the medieval lecture halls in the Rue de Fouarre by decreeing that public lectures could not be given in colleges that were not well known (*in collegiis non famatis*), i.e. where the exercises and disputations of the artists were not held – *in quibus non fiunt actus et disputationes Artium* (Du Boulay 1673, 379; on the above cf. Chartier, Compère and Julia 1976, 148–51). The tragic loss of the records of the University of Paris makes it difficult to estimate the exact nature of the developments in the later decades, but one of the most important beneficiaries of the variety of teaching and scholarly ferment at Paris in the early 1560s was the young Alexander Melville, with momentous consequences later for Scotland.

From what has been said it is perfectly clear that the universities of northern Europe, like the aristocracy itself, and with whatever reservations and reluctance, effectively accepted the humanist notion of the conduct of general education by the latter half of the sixteenth century. In part this came about as a response to a wider acceptance of the humanist argument for a classical curriculum from the members of the universities' constituencies; in part (and this influence was frequently much the same) from the demands of state intervention. It is

The Fate of Erasmian Humanism

time to look more closely at the actual results of this 'reform', but before we do, we should pause to consider again the aims of our principal humanist spokesman. The accepted view of the humanist achievement in the schoolroom has been seriously questioned in the case of Guarino, and the issue raised, whether in most cases the classroom culture really did achieve the ends of civic humanism, or whether 'the general approval expressed for Guarino's kind of humanist instruction on the part of the Italian establishment has more to do with its appropriateness as a commodity than with its intrinsic intellectual merits' (Grafton and Jardine 1982, 76–7). The question is important in itself and it also serves to illuminate a significant ambiguity in the educational objectives of our chief advocate, Erasmus.

As we have already seen, the educational programme of Erasmus was intended primarily for schoolboys, and its basic methodology and philosophy was drawn from the classic theorists and teachers of late antiquity, especially from Quintilian and Cicero. In this it was exactly like the teaching of Guarino, whom Erasmus held in high esteem, and not only for personal reasons – in his *Compendium vitae* he recalled that his father, when studying as a scribe of Greek in Rome, had heard Guarino lecture (*CWE* 1977, 404). However, there was an element pervading the educational philosophy of Erasmus and indeed, of the other northern humanists, which distinguished it markedly from that of their Italian predecessors, and that was its intimate connection with Christianity. As IJsewijn (*op. cit.*) pointed out in his study of the coming of humanism to the Low Countries, the northerners were moved less by the legacy of Latin civilisation as such than by the ideals of Christian piety: the *transitus humanismi ad christianismum*. And as we have seen, even Erasmus, steeped in classical culture as he was, commended the learning of classical civilisation as part of the mysterious *preparatio evangelica* of the pagan world for the reception of the revelation prepared among the Jews. This conviction pervades even the most purely pedagogical of his writings, famously in the case of the *Colloquies* (which were largely converted over the years into a collection of satirical and evangelical *causeries* directed against superstition and religious abuses), but also with less well-known works. Thus in the *De copia*, where he is discussing the eleventh method of enriching style by the accumulation of proofs and arguments,

we find him pointing out,
> Whenever we are endeavouring to turn men towards piety or from wickedness, we shall find very useful anecdotes drawn from the Old or the New Testament, that is from the Gospels. The hidden meaning of these can be variously handled; it can be explained in terms of human life, or of the body of the church joined and connected to Christ the head, or of the fellowship of heaven, or of those early days when the faith was new-born, or of our own times. However, I shall deal at greater length and in more detail with this subject in a short work I have in hand on scriptural allegories... (*CWE* 1978b, 635)

If there was a single aim to all of his educational doctrine, therefore, it would seem to have been to make possible the informed conduct of a Christian life, lay or clerical, by individuals having a command of both Greek and Latin who were familiar with the legacy of classical antiquity and with the New Testament. These men and women would have not only the tongues but a mastery of language in its rich resources for the greatest facility of expression, either in speech or in writing. They would be accomplished in the arts of persuasion, of deft variety, of the apt allusion, with minds (and notebooks) well stored with 'everything worth learning'. They would be expert in moral philosophy rather than logic, history rather than metaphysics. Their culture would be directed to their fellows (and especially to those with a like education), and its implicit aim would be the renewal of devotion to Christian ideals in a world troubled by wars, private greed and public contention, for which the Church had, alas, too frequently to share the responsibility. It was not a popular ideal but that did not matter; he was concerned to reform the elite, for the common benefit of all.

Within this general aim, a second was evident which was reserved for his own peers, and that was the scholarly restoration and publication of the sources of antiquity, especially of Christian antiquity. Since much is made of his zeal to edit scripture and the fathers of the church, it should be pointed out how greatly he admired Budé's *De asse*, and that he praised LeFèvre's translation of Aristotle. Nevertheless the first and chief matter was, of course, the restoration of the sources of the Christian tradition, *ad fontes*, as the others just mentioned

The Fate of Erasmian Humanism

would have been quick to agree. Just how far he expected the average Christian to go in mastery of those sources is never clear; he himself wrote volumes of devotional works, pastoral advice, his commentaries on the Psalms, and his famous Paraphrases on the New Testament all as a popular application of his expert knowledge.

Of these two aims, it is clear that only the second had direct importance in the universities, and it is luminously clear in all his writings that to Erasmus, universities meant theologians and the study of scripture. It is possible, therefore, to draw out of Erasmus' highly influential writings a double aim in education: on the one hand, to create a cultivated minority of classically-educated Christians informed by evangelical zeal, on the other, to inspire a yet smaller minority of scholar-editors who would turn their backs on the scholastic formation of their predecessors in order to purify and disseminate the sources of Christian faith. Let us see what the impact of Erasmian methods on the late medieval university might mean in practice.

Corpus Christi College, Oxford, was the landmark foundation for the Tudor universities. Its founder, Richard Fox, a patron of Erasmus, was as familiar with the writings of the humanist circles as he was with affairs of state and episcopal administration, and his college statutes (1517), which were the model for St John's, the corresponding foundation at Cambridge, went far to implant their programme. The college records enable us to follow its application to undergraduates.

Undergraduates admitted to Corpus were expected to have acquired some genuine proficiency in Latin, and to be sufficiently well-educated to be able to compose verse and dictate letters *extempore*. We may suppose that they would at least have had a good grounding in humanistic grammar and some composition; the college readers in Greek and Humanity took part in the examination of candidates in chapel, *viva voce*, in Latin and plainsong. Once admitted, they came under the authority of one of two fellows chosen by the president and dean of arts to serve for a year, and were set to work on the traditional introduction to the medieval schools – exercises in sophistry, or elementary logic from the *Peri Hermeneias*, *Prior analytics* or *Topics* of Aristotle, or from the first three books of the *Topics* of Boethius. They performed 'variations' after supper, 'sophisms' before noon, and all who had studied sophistry and logic for six months were also bound to attend the exercises 'in Parviso', which were elementary dialectical disputations. This is clearly a far cry from the *De ratione studii*. To be sure, from the time of Fox's revision of his statutes in 1528, these freshmen were taught their Porphyry and Aristotle first in Latin, then in Greek. Until mid-century it was common for an undergraduate to do two or three years of Greek with his tutor; later on the normal limit was three terms. Moreover, like all the members of the college below the degree of BTh, they were bound to attend the public lectures by the college readers in Greek and Humanity or Latin. According to Fox's Statutes, this meant a daily lecture on the authors of Latin eloquence, the historians Sallust, Valerius Maximus and Suetonius, and Pliny for natural history at eight a.m., and another at ten a.m. on Greek grammar, the poets and rhetoricians. During holidays the undergraduates were to use their time in rhetorical exercises, composing verses and epistles according to the rule of eloquence, and their compositions were to be shown to the reader in Humanity for correction. After three years or at most four in sophistry and logic, every undergraduate was to become a BA with the approval of the college, and again in 1528, a clause was added to the statutes requiring him to expound a book of some Latin poet, orator or historian on which he might have heard lectures.

This account will give a sufficient impression of the curious blend of humanism and traditionalism that grew up in the Tudor curriculum, and similar arrangements are not difficult to find in the other universities. The mixture was continued at Corpus after the BA, when the chief scholastic exercise of the college was disputation; yet natural and moral philosophy were added to the candidate's training with metaphysics, and every BA had to lecture on Greek logic or philosophy in order to proceed to the master's degree. Unfortunately we cannot come much closer to the classroom than this, except to say that the grammars and texts used in Latin and Greek were the well-known staples of the new humanism (McConica 1965; Jardine 1974).

In another place, I have already indicated the kind of theological culture that emerged, especially in Oxford, in the case of John Rainolds (McConica 1979). Rainolds was the most eminent divine produced in Elizabethan Corpus, probably in

The Fate of Erasmian Humanism

the whole of the university, and he showed both the dialectical discipline and assimilativeness, or eclecticism, that can be thought of as a natural result of the kind of intellectual formation I have just described. What he and his peers lacked was an organisational method; but he was widely and genuinely learned in the sources and commentators of the Christian tradition, from patristic times to his own, and he perfectly embodied the Erasmian zeal to improve the Christian commonweal, most notably in his advocacy of the Authorised Version.

A contemporary in part of Rainolds at Corpus left an unusually rich archive of letters, poems, and other exercises that validate another aspect of the humanist invasion of the old curriculum. Simon Tripp was admitted to Corpus from Devon on 24 April 1559 at the age of fifteen years. Four years later he was admitted a scholar, and five years after that, as a junior fellow, he was made college lecturer in logic. In the same year he became reader in humanity in succession to John Rainolds, the future president. He was a central figure in the row that broke out early in the presidency of the Marian exile, William Cole (1568–98), and his appeals at that time to Jewel and the college Visitor, Bishop Robert Horne, may have been important enough to help preserve the archive of his letters. More interesting to us are the many letters to his pupils and friends. The college historian, Thomas Fowler, DD, declared they did no credit to Tripp's character. Several of Tripp's communications with a pupil Fowler found to be 'nothing short of love letters, alluding to his personal appearance and indulging in gross flattery of his social and mental gifts. They are certainly not such letters,' he went on, 'as would be written by any man of self-respect or of a healthy mind to a boy . . .' (Fowler 1893, 136).

I am bold enough to say that I think Dr Fowler was quite wrong. The letters are couched in the conventional phrases of familiar humanist correspondence and stand in a well-known tradition of rhetoric about friendship. If to the modern ear they sound sentimental, an impression inevitably heightened by translation from the Latin, they would certainly have been recognised at the time as, in their way, highly conventional. He wrote to an ex-pupil William West (otherwise unknown) in London: 'If you love me, most charming William, and if you wish to be loved by me, love virtue, cherish God, fear your parents. And watch carefully whom you take as companions. Above all, avoid all whom you know to be prone to lasciviousness, luxury, licentiousness or any other notable vice of the sort ... That dictum of your father, a very wise man, is wise ..."In the company of a saint, you will be a saint; in the company of a corrupt man you will be corrupted". This is my advice to you – choose as familiars and friends those who excel others in virtue, learning, and piety'. There are simply the rhetorical commonplaces of moral advice to the young; scarcely the blandishments of a seducer. A little further along, urging the young West to work hard at his studies, an exhortation to civil accomplishment is entirely predictable: 'If you are good, pious and learned in the laws of your country, you will pursue honour and glory and all the fullest benefits of the state'. His parents will rejoice. 'As for what I shall do, I shall boast among my friends that I was once his tutor, I taught him Greek and Latin letters...'

References to Tripp's Greek instruction occur in other of the letters, which in general entirely conform to the style and conventions of humanistic epistolary rhetoric. The letter to Jewel is embellished with Virgilian quotations; elsewhere there are citations of Aristophanes, Xenophon and Demosthenes, along with the more predictable Latin authorities. One part of the collection preserves a particularly interesting passage in which he urges a friend, George More (MA January 1574) to go forward into the metaphorical battle-line of his Lenten disputation, having on the right the sword of dialectic, which fells many with many words, and on the left the shield of rhetoric, which wards off the charges of the enemy. In the van is the Greek tongue, at the rear is Latin; moral philosophy is at the head of all. The arts curriculum of Elizabethan Oxford is epitomised.

These letters seem to bring us nearer to the actuality of the domestic teaching at Corpus, and suggest that the statutory requirements were not purely a formality. On the other hand, it is impossible not to wonder just how much of substance was taken by the ordinary pupil from such a disparate range of texts, delivered in such concentration. It is noticeable that much was made throughout the university career of disputation, both as a teaching instrument and as a method of examination, and that there is no evidence from any of the wit-

The Fate of Erasmian Humanism

nesses that retention of this medieval exercise was widely resented – quite the contrary. It is tempting to think, but difficult to demonstrate, that the actual teaching of this mass of material was chiefly shaped by the needs of disputation, which would have provided both an organising principle and a method of selection for the undergraduate trying to make his way through such a demanding course of study. The 'professionals', like Tripp, who stayed in the university for many years, might indeed acquire the range of erudition that emerged in the writings of a Case, or a Rainolds, or a Hooker. The ordinary pupil was perhaps another matter. Tripp's correspondent, who to judge from the letters was much better than the average student, seems to have left the classical training at Corpus behind him rather quickly. At least, that is one construction to place on a letter, subsequent to the one just quoted, in which Tripp complains that for two years West has not written. So excellent a brain, he feels, cannot have grown dull. Is West so busy with his law that he has time only to keep in touch with family and friends? Or is it that London gentlemen do not write in Latin, and he fears his old tutor will not like letters in English?

Just when the Elizabethan universities were emerging from the successive upheavals of Tudor religious politics, the Scottish universities received their refoundation as renaissance academies, and the history of those events forms a natural conclusion to our survey. In one way these 'new foundations' help to confirm the universality of the mixture of Erasmian humanism and traditional scholastic culture we have already noticed, in another, they show a new awareness of its limitations.

All scholars up to this time seem to agree that the revival of the Scottish universities after the Reformation can be fairly summed up in the work of Andrew Melville; he is one of those rare figures whose talents and personal genius seem to have been so perfectly suited to the moment when he walked onto the stage of history that it is literally impossible to abstract public events from his personality. I leave it to those better qualified than I to explain the growth of university foundations in fifteenth-century Scotland, in a country with perhaps half-a-million souls and very limited resources; the remarkable concern of the Book of Discipline in 1560 for the future welfare of the universities suggests – even apart from the need for a godly ministry – that this spirit had in no way altered. Melville's career first at Glasgow and then at St Andrews, and the subsequent influence of his ideas on Marischal College at Aberdeen and on the early history of Edinburgh's 'town college' were evidently decisive.

The story of Melville's initial enterprise on his return to Scotland from Geneva in 1574 has been well told by the distinguished historian of Glasgow University, to whom I am largely indebted for what follows (Durkan 1977). What I find most impressive in my own inquiry is the suggestion that despite his experience in Geneva and tuition by Théodore de Bèze, Melville is best understood as a product of the cultural environment of Paris in the 1560s, an experience which he shared with a considerable community of Scottish exiles, most of them Catholic (Durkan 1977, 266–7). Melville seems to have attended the lectures at the Collège de France, since acquisition of the biblical tongues was probably his chief aim. He was taught by Ramus and Ramus' opponent, Turnèbe, and attended lectures in mathematics, medicine, and law. His interest in Hebrew also took him to hear Scaliger. It is the variety of this experience, centred in the Three Tongues but including also the most up-to-date teaching in the higher faculties, that suggests both the range of Melville's intellectual ambition and the importance of Paris to him as a preparation for his later career in Scotland.

Perhaps the earliest indication of Melville's notion of a proper undergraduate education comes from the 'crash course' he invented for his diarist nephew, James Melville, during the summer of 1574. This began with the Erasmian paraphrases on the Psalms composed by George Buchanan, an apt vehicle for the teaching both of Latin and of religion. Although these have been seen as almost purely rhetorical exercises, the leading authority on the humanist has written of Buchanan, 'his motives were by no means purely literary: he was using contemporary scholarship to make the understanding of the psalms more precise. He did not always eschew the Vulgate ... but it is not unreasonable to see in Buchanan's psalm paraphrases an attempt to make the results of Biblical scholarship more widely known' (McFarlane 1972, 62). From this the younger Melville progressed to works by Virgil, Horace, Terence, Caesar, Sallust

The Fate of Erasmian Humanism

and to Cicero's Catiline Orations; to history according to Bodin's 'method', to Greek grammar, the New Testament and finally, the elements of Hebrew grammar (Durkan 1977, 275). All of this would seem to be the *De pueris instituendis* adapted to the needs and scriptural interests of a mature young man.

Less obviously Erasmian, however, was Melville's interest in Ramism, which according to Durkan he first introduced to Scottish university circles on an official basis (*ibid.* 279). Its appearance there would seem to have coincided with its introduction to Cambridge, where from all the present evidence, its 'reception' seems unquestionably to have been much more general than ever it was at Oxford. This appearance reveals a fundamental weakness of the Erasmian 'reform': its scepticism about – if not indeed, repugnance toward – all systematic methodology apart from that which a later age would call philological. By the mid-sixteenth century, the educational aim *ad perfectum eloquentiam informare* was one upon which all could agree. There were those, however, like Sturmius, Latomus and Ramus, who followed the lead of Rodolphus Agricola in preferring a new relationship between rhetoric and dialectic, one in which the rules of discourse should yield up the foundation of a new process of reasoning and persuasion. Others, like Erasmus and Vives, preferred to divorce rhetoric and logic entirely (cf. Chartier, Compère and Julia *op. cit.* 154–5). As an approach to the 'renewal' of an ancient text the latter method could scarcely be faulted. It could be adapted to the needs of a university curriculum only by altering the attitude to the traditional texts beginning with a return to the original languages and early commentators, and this of course occurred; indeed, it formed the basis for the great renewal of studies in all the disciplines dominated by Aristotle, as well as in the higher faculties of law and medicine; its implications for theology are well known. As new texts appeared, however, and as the zeal for commentary spread, this strictly 'Erasmian' method could become and was overloaded, until the interest in citation, allusion and reference loomed larger than the text itself. It was this crisis that provoked the concern about the reform of methodology in which Ramus was the single most important pioneer, and that concern seems to be particularly clear in the new designs for Scotland's universities.

The further question as to whether Melville can be considered a 'Ramist' and in what sense I leave to the experts. It is noticeable that he did not entirely shun the works of Aristotle, including his logic and ethics, which matches his teaching squarely with that of John Rainolds in Oxford (Durkan 1977, 281; McConica 1979). His concern to abolish the medieval 'regenting' and establish readerships so that 'young men who ascend step by step may find their preceptor worthy of their studies and gifts' is an adoption of standard European practice throughout the universities influenced by the new curriculum (Durkan citing the charter of James VI for the New Erection 1577, 262). The division of responsibilities between the three regents in arts in Glasgow's *nova erectio* shows the same reluctance to break entirely with the medieval curriculum that we have remarked elsewhere: the first reader was to instruct in rhetoric and Greek; the second, who was responsible for moral philosophy from such as Cicero, Plato and Aristotle, was also to teach dialectic and logic, arithmetic and geometry. The third reader, whose duties included another part of the old quadrivium, astronomy, taught it in the new setting of geography and chronology, no doubt from a work like Glareanus's *De Geographia*. As Durkan has pointed out, this curriculum actually represented a return to earlier practise from that of the town's foundation in 1573, where the emphasis had been entirely on philosophy (*ibid.* 285; cf. 249).

Melville's reform of Glasgow was repeated with his removal to St Mary's College at St Andrews in 1580, and showed also at Aberdeen, especially in the foundation of Marischal College. In each instance, the introduction of Ramus was a mark of the new curriculum (Durkan 1977, 290–1; Henderson 1947, 11f.; Cant 1970, 48f.). Everywhere, too, there was the new emphasis on grammar and rhetoric, on languages (especially Greek and Hebrew), and on the use of original texts, and everywhere the moral and religious purpose of the curriculum infused the whole. It was only at Glasgow, however, that 'regenting' was successfully supplanted by the establishment of chairs.

The 'tounis college' which opened in Edinburgh on 14 October 1583 was seemingly in no way an exception to the general victory of Melville's programme. Although the university's historian pointed to Geneva as a precedent for the constitutional position of the new academy (Grant 1884, 126–7) there is no doubt that the courses of studies and general academic structure was of entirely native growth. The fact that the first detailed account of the curriculum can be dated to the decade between 1619 and 1628 (Morgan and Hannay 1937, 56) may confirm this, since we find that by the time the college was in full operation, its teaching and examination system were completely in harmony with that prevailing in the older Scottish universities of reformed curriculum. The surviving records of the town council for the period never touch on such matters, and it seems clear that the academic programme was the work of its first Principal, Robert Rollock, who was bound to govern 'according the lawes, statutes and fundation', and to conduct himself as 'ony uther principall or first maister of ony colledge within the universities of this realme' (Morgan and Hannay, 55 and note 2). At St Andrews, Rollock had been in contact with Melville, and the second master retained, Duncan Nairn, had been a pupil of Melville's at Glasgow.

The *Disciplina academiae Edinburgenae* (Morgan and Hannay, 60f.) shows a first year spent in the classic exercises of translation from and into the Latin of such models as Cicero, with introductory Greek from the grammar of Cleonardus, and including some of the New Testament. In the second year, after further work on Greek, the pupils were turned to the study of rhetoric from the works of Ramus, or rather of his disciple, Talon. Nevertheless, they were also to become familiar with the *Isagoge* of Porphyry, that well-tried propaedeutic to Aristotle so familiar in the medieval university, and with the logical books of Aristotle, including the *Categories*, *Prior Analytics* and *Topics*. Towards the end of the year the students would also be introduced to arithmetic. In the third (Bachelor) year they began Hebrew grammar, were introduced to analysis in dialectic and rhetoric (*in analysis dialectica et rhetorica*), read through the *Ethics* and *Posterior Analytics*, and at the conclusion of the year were introduced to the study of the anatomy of the human body – a provision exclusive to Edinburgh. The fourth and final (Master) year would seem to have been the most nearly medieval: the *De coelo*, the *De sphaera* of John of Sacrobosco, dialectic and cosmography and frequent disputations seem to have filled the year. As in the other colleges, the teaching of theology, which crowned the achievement of the arts curriculum, was reserved to the Principal, again, an expression of the ideas of Melville (Grant, 156).

'What I need is ready money. For various and definite reasons I have not given Dorp your letter. He and I are getting on pretty well, and the course of things demands that I should have some universities on my side.' So wrote Erasmus to Richard Pace in the early spring of 1518 (*CWE* 1979, 333). It is no more than a fragment of an overheard conversation, yet in its way it forms an epitome of the part played by universities in the life – and thought – of Erasmus. It is fair to say that, in the end, he made a greater mark on them than they left on him. But that is only one side of a more complicated story, and by the end of the sixteenth century, the first part of it – the part in which the name of Erasmus is most important – was played out. The age of Erasmian humanism as such was a season which could be spanned almost by two consecutive lifetimes. It was formed by the dawn of print, coinciding with the revival of the educational ideals of antiquity, and allowing extension of the familiarities of its highly personal world to an international community of those with the correct education; the vast correspondence of the most proficient sustained this elegant and fragile society. Its most enduring achievement was the recovery of the ancient tongues and the restoration and propagation of learned texts; it has never since been possible to approach the sources of the Christian faith without the instruments of erudition prescribed by Erasmus and his followers. In the north its ideals were so intimately intermingled with those of religion that it is impossible to detach the Italian contribution of civic humanism in estimating its impact, yet, as Anthony Grafton shows in the next paper, humanistic method brought many benefits in other spheres of practical concern well into the succeeding century. Its liberal pedagogical methods too survived, to be adapted to the teaching of those new vernaculars made classical in their turn by authors imbued with the Latinity of Erasmus.

In the universities it can be said that Erasmus's personal concern with the sources of Christianity was achieved and indeed, triumphant. So in a degree was his hope that the gateway to sacred letters could be constructed of the literary monuments of classical civilisation. He was not followed however in his indifference to the dialectical content of the old curriculum, and in the universities the need to debate and organise knowledge finally prevailed in the search for a new methodology, and in the birth of a new scholasticism. The grammatical and rhetorical foundations of his training could not forever assimilate the multiplication of texts and topics, and the popularity of notebooks, Ramistic short-cuts and printed *compendia* was one result. Another was the 'short course' in Latin letters, with possibly a smattering of Greek, that was pursued by so many who used the Erasmian side of the curriculum to supplement their schooling before going on to secular careers, or back to their estates. A third possibility was the kind of university culture that in England showed itself in the splenetic world of the university wits, and that was so tellingly satirised by writers like Jonson. None would have been more ready to laugh at it than Erasmus.

More serious was the collapse of religious consensus. With the rise of philosophic scepticism, the anti-theoretical, anti-deductive bias of Erasmianism was swept aside, so that its lasting influence in the academy was channelled into philology. Nonetheless, the notion of a liberal education founded on classical letters – *bonae litterae* – would endure in the schools and faculties of arts up to the First World War and beyond as the common culture of the intelligentsia and the propertied classes – at least in theory. It was as vulnerable as the curriculum it displaced to death-dealing pedantry, but it bestowed on its adherents the credentials of a cosmopolitan and patrician legacy that, for better and for worse, dominated Europe up to recent times. It also remains the classic instance of the degree to which the curriculum of universities can be subverted at the level of the schools.

REFERENCES

Allen, P. S. (1914) *The Age of Erasmus*. Oxford.
Bolgar, R. R. (1954) *The classical heritage and its beneficiaries*. Cambridge.
Cant, R. G. (1970) *The university of St Andrews*, new and revised edition. Edinburgh/London.
Chartier, R. and Compère, M. M. and Julia, D. (1976) *L'éducation en France du XVIe au XVIIIe siècle*. Paris.
Codina Mir, G. (1968) *Aux sources de la pédagogie des Jesuites: le 'modus parisiensis'*. Rome.
Costello, W. T. (1958) *The scholastic curriculum at early seventeenth century Cambridge*. Cambridge, Massachusetts.
CWE (1976) *Collected works of Erasmus volume 3: the correspondence of Erasmus letters 198 to 445, 1514 to 1516* (trans. R. A. B. Mynors and D. F. S. Thomson, annot. James K. McConica). Toronto.

— (1977) *Collected works of Erasmus volume 4: the correspondence of Erasmus letters 446 to 593, 1516 to 1517* (trans. R. A. B. Mynors and D. F. S. Thomson, annot. James K. McConica). Toronto.

— (1978a) *Collected works of Erasmus volume 23: literary and educational writings, Antibarbari/Parabolae* (ed. Craig R. Thompson). Toronto.

— (1978b) *Collected works of Erasmus volume 24: literary and educational writings, De copia/De ratione studii* (ed. Craig R. Thompson). Toronto.

— (1979) *Collected works of Erasmus volume 5: the correspondence of Erasmus letters 594 to 841, 1517 to 1518* (trans. R. A. B. Mynors and D. F. S. Thomson, annot. Peter G. Bietenholz). Toronto.

— (1982) *Collected works of Erasmus volume 6: the correspondence of Erasmus letters 842 to 992, 1518 to 1519* (trans. R. A. B. Mynors and D. F. S. Thomson, annot. Peter G. Bietenholz). Toronto.

— (1984) *Collected works of Erasmus volume 25: literary and educational writings* (ed. J. Kelley Sowards). Toronto.

Durkan, J. and Kirk, J. (1977) *The university of Glasgow 1451-1577.* Glasgow.

de Vocht, H. (1951) *History of the foundation and the rise of the collegium trilingue Lovaniense 1517-1550*, vol.1. Louvain.

Du Boulay, C. E. (1673) *Historia universitatis Parisiensis*, vol.6. Paris.

Elie, H. (1950-1) Quelques maitres de l'université de Paris vers l'an 1500. *Archives d'histoire doctrinale et littéraire du moyen age* 18, 193-243.

Fletcher, J. M. (1981) Change and resistance to change: a consideration of the development of English and German universities during the sixteenth century. *History of Universities* 1, 1-36.

Fowler, T. (1893) *The history of Corpus Christi College.* Oxford.

Grafton, A. T. and Jardine, L. (1982) Humanism and the school of Guarino: a problem of evaluation. *Past and Present* 96, 51-80.

Grant, Sir Alexander (1884) *The story of the university of Edinburgh*, vol.1. London.

Heath, T. G. (1971) Logical grammar, grammatical logic, and humanism in three German universities. *Studies in the Renaissance* 18, 9-64.

Henderson, G. D. (1947) *The founding of Marischal college Aberdeen.* Aberdeen.

IJsewijn, J. (1975) The coming of humanism to the Low Countries, in *Itinerarium Italicum* (eds H. A. Oberman and T. A. Brady), 193-301. Leiden.

Jardine, L. (1974) The place of dialectic teaching in sixteenth-century Cambridge. *Studies in the Renaissance* 21, 31-62.

Lefranc, A. (1893) *Histoire du collège de France.* Paris.

McConica, J. K. (1965) *English humanists and reformation politics.* Oxford.

— (1969) Erasmus and the grammar of consent, in *Scrinium Erasmus* (ed. J. J. Copens), vol.2, 77-99. Leiden.

McConica, J. K. (1979) Humanism and Aristotle in Tudor Oxford. *English Historical Review* 94, 291-317.

McFarlane, I. D. (1972) Notes on the composition and reception of George Buchanan's Psalm paraphrases, in *Renaissance Studies* (eds I. D. McFarlane, A. H. Ashe and D. D. R. Owen), 21-62. Edinburgh/London.

Morgan, A. and Hannay, R. B. (1937) *University of Edinburgh charters, statutes and acts of the town council and the senatus 1583-1858.* Edinburgh/London.

Thomas, I. (1964) Medieval aftermath: Oxford logic and logicians of the seventeenth century, in *Oxford Studies presented to Daniel Callus* (ed. R. W. Southern), 297-311. Oxford.

Renaudet, A. (1916) *Préréforme et humanism à Paris pendant les premières guerres d'Italie 1494-1517.* Paris.

Reulos, M. (1953) L'université et les collèges. *Bulletin d'association Guillaume Budé* 3 ser., no.2, 33-42.

FROM RAMUS TO RUDDIMAN: THE *STUDIA HUMANITATIS* IN A SCIENTIFIC AGE

ANTHONY GRAFTON

When Dr Johnson looked over the Latin thesis that James Boswell had submitted to the Edinburgh Faculty of Advocates, he remarked, sadly, 'Ruddiman is dead'. For Thomas Ruddiman, grammarian, printer, and the Faculty's librarian, had in his lifetime edited theses before they were presented to the Faculty – and thus preserved their authors from the gross errors in Latinity with which Boswell's work shocked Johnson. As Douglas Duncan showed almost twenty years ago, Johnson's comment was less a crack at one young Scot's ignorance than an epitaph for an old Scottish culture. As a teacher and writer, Ruddiman had defended throughout his life the belief that what was worth saying should be said in good Latin. As a publisher he had tried to show that the true classics of Scottish literature were the Latin writings of sixteenth-century humanists like George Buchanan. And as a librarian he had tried to keep Edinburgh an up-to-date capital, not so much of Scotland as of one province of a pan-European, Latin-speaking Republic of Letters. But by the early eighteenth century this enterprise seemed to many not merely conservative but hopelessly reactionary. Locke had already overthrown the assumptions on which the traditional curriculum rested; Hume was waiting in the wings (he succeeded Ruddiman as the Faculty's librarian). The old Scottish Latin culture inevitably made way for the brave new English-speaking culture of Enlightenment; and none of Ruddiman's polemics could have saved it (Duncan 1965).

Ruddiman's death was no isolated event, but one act among many in the long tragedy by which the rhetoric and scholarship of Renaissance humanism lost their hold on European culture. Like an Irving playing Lear, Renaissance learning managed to stagger on far longer than its critics imagined that it could, despite its deep age wrinkles, rattling breath, and howls of rage at its betrayal by the other players on the stage. Modern historians – a literal-minded race – have taken the humanists at

From Ramus to Ruddiman

their word and appearance, writing them out of the script at the early date when they first showed a lack of confidence in their powers and a willingness to retire from centre stage. Such views of early modern European culture are not so well-founded as they seem.

To be sure, it is not hard to see why historians in the French and English-speaking worlds have underestimated the longevity of humanism. Hindsight seems to expose the humanists as the party of reaction, at least after 1600. They ignored the historical insight of Bodin and Bacon, who realised that gunpowder, the compass and the printing press had changed the face of the world, creating a new society that need not draw its wisdom from old books. They ignored the discoveries of Galileo and Descartes, who showed that new knowledge was to be found by profound study of nature or intense meditation on first principles, not by reading, which served only to add to one's confusion. They ignored the merchants who were extending Europe's power throughout the world, the writers who were surpassing the depth and complexity of classical literatures in the modern vernaculars, the artists and artisans who were building democratic cultures outside the stultifying belljars of the universities and academies. They even failed to see that the borders and language of the mental territory they inhabited were being transformed by what was going on outside it — that the Latin-speaking *Respublica litterarum* of Lipsius and Scaliger had become the French-speaking *République des lettres* of LeClerc and Bayle, with its critical attitude towards the old religions and its adulation of the new science. These views still inspire much research into the 'modern' side of early modern European culture (Hill 1965; Webster 1976; Alpers 1983).

These prejudices are reinforced by the requirements of pedagogy. Teachers who must move rapidly from Renaissance to Reformation to Scientific Revolution, showing that each naturally superseded what went before, have incorporated the standard account in textbooks and lectures. After all, it fits the prejudices of a modern, Latin-less society, endows the manifestos of Bacon and Descartes with the dramatic qualities needed to keep them interesting, and gives early modern intellectual history a logical, attractive shape. One sees the backward-looking humanists swept off the stage by newer men with newer brooms, and who can regret the change? Not only writers of American handbooks of Western Civilisation subscribe to these simple verities. Enlivened with Gallic salt, they supply the central argument of Robert Mandrou's *From Humanism to Science* (Mandrou 1979). Expressed with characteristic gravity and eloquence, they inspire the moving finale of Robert Bolgar's *The Classical Heritage and its Beneficiaries* (Bolgar 1954). True, historians of early modern education have not completely ignored the continued existence of humanist teaching and scholarship. They admit that the educational programmes of the later sixteenth century – those of Sturm and Ramus on the Protestant side, of the Jesuit *Rationes Studiorum* on the Catholic side – modernised to some extent the humanist curriculum. To be sure, it remained embalmed in spoken Latin. But it now included at least a pinch of mathematics along with its intolerable deal of grammar. It incorporated a limited but significant training in logic, since pupils were encouraged to dispute as well as to hear lectures, and to find in classical texts coherent arguments as well as vivid phrases. It even offered limited training in such practical skills as poise, posture, dancing, and fencing. This renovated humanism became standard equipment for the aristocracy and gentry. A form of it was offered by universities, colleges, and illustrious academies throughout Europe to well-born students who wanted practical skills rather than paper credentials (Dainville 1978; Grafton 1981b). But even the new encyclopedic humanism was not modern enough. It survived, entrenched in curricula, embodied in textbooks, reinforced by statutes, and supported by monarchs and pedagogues with a vested interest in the status quo. But it was still too traditional in content, too conservative in orientation, and too laborious in method to serve a rapidly changing society that wanted modern forms of knowledge. The new scientific societies, Gresham College, Comenius's progressive short cuts to attaining knowledge and developing the character – these met the needs of the new Europe far more fully than the arteriosclerotic dons who made Milton and Newton waste their time learning history and rhetoric. So we read in standard works.

The Creation of a New Scholarship

As it happens, the standard account that I have summarised does not fit the decades just before and after 1600. In fact that period saw a concerted effort take shape to modernise humanist scholarship and teaching. To start with a vignette: No one did more to infuse the drying bones of humanism with new life than Justus Lipsius (1547–1606). A liar, a plagiarist, and a heretic, a man who switched religious allegiances with so much abandon that he was stigmatised in print as *Lipsius Proteus*, he followed a line of scholarship as plausible and consistent as his religious views were vague and opportunistic (Oestreich 1982; Schrijvers 1981). As a professor in the new Protestant university of Leiden and the older Catholic one of Louvain, Lipsius built from classical ingredients exactly the equipment his aristocratic students needed to survive in an age of religious war. In the philosophy of the Stoics Lipsius found a simple guide to life, one that would enable the young aristocrat to put off fear and anger, to master his passions and then to discipline himself and his soldiers. In the detailed study of Roman antiquities Lipsius found a perfect guide to the most pressing problems of state-building and army-formation. Above all, in the detailed accounts of Roman military organisation and technology given by Polybius and others Lipsius found not old but new knowledge – a full set of instructions for building a shatteringly effective military machine. 'I hold this one thing as certain: if ancient arms and the ancient order and line of battle are combined with our new arms, old and new world alike will soon come under one man's sway' (Lipsius 1630, 361).

Like any humanist, Lipsius idolised the ancients: 'qui gloriam aut imperium vult, flectendum ad antiqua'. He could not find enough good to say about the Roman soldiers' spartan habit of living off bread and water in the field, their unpretentious willingness to dig their own ditches and pitch their own camps, their calm acceptance of a strict code of military law enforced by condign punishment. He refused to see the Ottoman Janizaries, perhaps the most feared soldiers of his own time, as anything like the Romans' equal. He made his *De militia Romana* the first panel of a triptych of works meant to portray ancient warfare in its full, concrete reality (the others treated war machines and triumphs after victory). And he sought out with zeal the minutest details of Roman armaments, terminology, and customs.

For all his scholarly diligence, however, Lipsius was no proponent of *philologia gratia philologiae*. He explicitly compared modern sloth with ancient diligence in fortifying camps and disciplining soldiers. He made specific recommendations about tactics on the basis of his historical research (five years before the *De militia* came out, Lipsius advised the Estates General of the Netherlands to make their soldiers dig ditches, rather than hire workmen, and thus encourage pride and laziness (Oestreich 1982)). And he by no means argued that the revival of ancient tactics should be a matter of simple, slavish imitation:

> As to pikes, this is my view. The Romans did not need them, we have found and will find them quite useful, even if we revive some of the Roman armaments. (Lipsius 1630, 360)

Lipsius equipped his work, moreover, with all the aids his own rhetorical skills and a great printer's art could supply: vivid dialogues to keep the exposition lively, tabular summaries to make it clear, elaborate illustrations to make the physical forms of ancient weapons and formations vivid and plain. Even those who disagreed with specific points were fascinated by the new field of study that the work opened up. On his deathbed Lipsius's great rival Joseph Scaliger was still trying to show, by drawings of his own, that Lipsius had been in error about the shape of the Roman *pilum* (Robinson 1927).

Lipsius, in short, developed a brand of humanist scholarship that was in all respects up-to-date; it laid the philosophical and technical foundations for the seventeenth-century professional army with its aristocratic experts on drill and fortification. And it was taken up with interest by both Lipsius's wellborn students and his professional colleagues. Maurice of Nassau and his many relatives found Lipsius to be that rarity, a scholar with nothing of the pedant about him, able to pronounce on practical affairs as well as variant readings (Lipsius 1630, 355). William Louis of Nassau advised that his brothers go to Leiden to study with Lipsius, since he was considered 'nicht allein ein gelehrter *philosophus*, sondern auch ein weiser *politicus*' (Groen van Prinsterer 1857, 131). And John of

Nassau-Siegen, the founder of the great military school at Siegen, carefully analysed Lipsius' *De militia* in his *Kriegsbuch* and eagerly recommended as the basis of military reform the very blending of classical and modern arms and methods that Lipsius had called for. Sometimes, indeed, Lipsius proved more practical in his attitude towards the ancient past than his statesmen pupils. It was the brilliant general Maurice of Nassau who tried to prove the superiority of Roman to modern warfare by equipping two small groups, one with Roman swords and the other with modern pikes, and pitting them against each other (the pikemen, who were fewer, eventually won). It was the humanist Lipsius who had to explain to Maurice that the real superiority of the Roman armies had lain not in the details of their armament but in their ability to coordinate the activities of a large number of small units during battle (Hahlweg 1973).

Even Lipsius' colleagues admitted the success of his programme. Joseph Scaliger made fun in the 1580s of the notion that classical studies could help modern rulers: 'If M. the Prince of Orange has no counsellors but those who stick always to Livy and Spartianus, the Duke of Parma will soon shave his beard' (Grafton 1979). Even in his last years as a Leiden Professor he ridiculed Lipsius as a pedant who had failed ludicrously to teach practical politics. Yet Scaliger too yielded, as we have seen, to the fascination of ancient military technique. More surprisingly, he too yielded to the temptation to show that his scholarship could help the military elite, and produced for Plantin a trimmed-down edition of Caesar, devoid of commentary and designed to impart military wisdom to well-born youth without the distracting accompaniment of variant readings.

Lipsius did not confine his interest in practical subjects to war. Drawing above all on Tacitus, he and others founded a new discipline of 'politics'. Its practitioners lectured from modern handbooks and ancient histories on 'states and their forms, rituals, laws, institutions and customs' – as Daniel Heinsius put it before he began his lectures on the field at Leiden, which he prefaced with a course on the political content of a startlingly original choice of ancient text: Seneca's *Apocolocyntosis*, a book 'both comic and written with complete freedom by a great expert in the civic discipline, against the ruler of the world, and about the Roman People in its most corrupt and wretched state' (Heinsius 1627, 240). They offered their pupils instruction in all the *arcana imperii* they could distill from the grim pages of Tacitus and the philosophical ones of Aristotle. Those who trace the power of the early modern state to its ability to stage spectacular rituals and manipulate powerful symbols might do well to consult Clapmarius's textbook. Symbols were for Clapmarius the consolation of those excluded from power, since 'those who hold the power itself hardly care about those things that are merely shadows of real power, meant for display; while those who lack the real thing would rather seem to have it than both not have it and not seem to do so' (Clapmarius 1644, 272). Thus even after the Roman republic was converted to an empire, its wise rulers left in existence some 'images of liberty' like the Senate; thus the wise Henry IV allowed his rival Rudolph a royal funeral, since such a ceremony was merely a *simulacrum regium* that could satisfy the dead man's supporters without conceding them any power — and remarked to a critic 'I wish all my enemies could have so splendid a burial'. Clapmarius outdid Machiavelli in pragmatism; for where Machiavelli had demanded that all vestiges of old institutions be frankly swept away by the prince who wished to hold a new state, Clapmarius showed how to exploit old forms and ceremonies to project a deliberately deceptive image: *aliud simulatur, aliud agitur* was his recipe for success. Lipsius and the other 'politici', in short, planned the early modern state as well as the early modern army. Humanism could provide the underpinnings for absolute kingship, manipulation of public opinion and relentless 'police', or social discipline, as well as for the Ciceronian republicanism more commonly associated with it. To have demonstrated this is the great merit of Gerhard Oestreich (1982).

The humanists of the late sixteenth and early seventeenth centuries were not this successful in their dealings with every segment of the curriculum or every set of university authorities. The new political history made less headway in Jacobean and Caroline Oxford and Cambridge than in contemporary Leiden and Louvain. And the vast expansion of facts, theories and skills that a learned man had to master in order to produce the new, technical humanist scholarship posed drastic problems of organisation and compression. All too many humanists degenerated into charlatans selling short-cuts to knowledge, claiming that they 'could teach Latin in eight months, Greek in twenty days, astronomy in eight or ten days, philosophy and music in a month or less' – as the grammarian Sanctius boasted (Aarsleff 1982, 106). Anyone who reads the encyclopedias and textbooks produced by men like G.J. Vossius has to marvel at the contrast between their elaborately systematic accounts of the structures of the scholarly disciplines and their empty, vague accounts of content and methods. But on the whole the humanist curriculum was reformed between 1570 and 1630. Traditional in its aim of training the minds and forming the characters of public men, traditional in its faith that philosophy was best taught through well-chosen historical examples, the new humanism was entirely up to date in its choice of spheres of ancient life that deserved close study and in its ruthlessly pragmatic methods of analysis. In the hands of one of the few atheists among the French *libertins érudits*, in fact, it could even provide the building blocks for a history of religion designed to show that God had never existed, and that all religions had been devised by priests and rulers intent on imposing social discipline (Gregory 1979). There was a New Scholarship as well as a New Philosophy.

Humanists did not confine themselves to philology alone. From Petrarch on, they had singled out moral philosophy as a crucial study for the future citizen or governor and as a fruitful field for the application of their standard method, the close reading of such canonical texts as Cicero *De officiis*. In the seventeenth century this discipline too was renewed. From Grotius to Pufendorf, from More to Thomasius, moral philosophers tried to develop a system of ethical precepts economical in size, universal in validity, and irenical in intent: a code that all good men must follow, whatever their nation or sect. This minimal morality, they held, would do more than anything else to rid Europe of religious war and persecution, since it would instill respect for the convictions of all reasonable and pious men. Though in fact the new moral philosophy brought about no great changes in European society as a whole, it did bring forth such attractive, undogmatic textbooks as More's *Enchiridium Ethicum*, and some equally attractive new readings of the ancient works that continued to form the foundation of the discipline. Seventeenth-century students of moral philosophy learned anew that unaided human effort could produce good actions even if it could not win salvation, that man's emotional experience provided a better test than any strict scholastic system could of the rightness of his actions. It was in the universities that these central tenets of humanist moral thought were preserved, revitalised, and incorporated in part into the moral philosophy of the Enlightenment. To that extent the formal teaching of moral principles managed to keep up with the moral needs of a larger society (Cassirer 1932; Fiering 1981).

Humanism, then, shored itself up against the first tremors of change; but could it withstand the full earthquake of the seventeenth-century Revolution? By 1700, after all, the visions of Bacon and Descartes had been surpassed by the reality of the Mechanical Philosophy. Ancient science was outmoded in every field from anatomy to astronomy. Ancient literature was finding rivals in every genre from epic to lyric. Even ancient military technique had lost its appeal for the military expert now in search of mathematically rigorous rules of ballistics. True, the new science continued to draw elements from humanism. The humanists enabled the scientists to build their corpuscular theories of matter by supplying a connected account of Epicurean physics. They encouraged the scientists to study the powers of the human mind historically. When Leibniz proclaimed the need for a 'historia literaria' or cultural history of man, as a way of determining the powers of the human mind and the conditions that fostered their growth most effectively, he was reframing a central enterprise of late sixteenth- and early seventeenth-century humanists like la Popelinière and Barclay (Hassinger 1978). The humanists even won scientists to attack some of their favourite fields of study – like etymology, which captivated Leibniz, and chronology, which obsessed Newton (Aarsleff 1982, 84–100; Manuel 1963). But to show that scientists could be in some respects traditional scholars is not to show that scholarship could be once again brought up to date.

In fact, some professors of the studia humanitatis did manage to modernise the tone and method, if not the content, of their studies. Richard Bentley showed that textual criticism was as good a field as any for the sharp and searing tool of reason,

From Ramus to Ruddiman

which burnt and cut away the vestiges of medieval superstition and error represented by textual corruptions (Gossman 1968). And if Bentley was a bit of an isolated figure in his own country, ridiculed by the wits, unable to find disciples, hated for his habit of treating the fellows of his college as if they were so many defective MSS, some of the Europeans with whom he corresponded in grave Latin applied a similar approach in more attractive ways. Jacob Perizonius (1651–1715), for example, met the attacks of philosophical sceptics by honing the edge of historical and critical method. He devised sensible criteria for judging the *fides*, or credibility, of different witnesses and sorts of evidence. This line of attack enabled him, for example, to try to put an end to the long-running controversy about the great age of the ancient kingdoms of the Near East, a dispute that had done much to bring the discipline of chronology into discredit. Perizonius argued that the lists of names and dynasties that Joseph Scaliger had found in Byzantine chroniclers were so corrupt that in the absence of further evidence one could not hope to distill the truth from them – and one certainly need not worry about the embarassing fact that the kingdom of Egypt seemed to have its beginning before the universe was created (Grafton 1975). Yet his criticism was not entirely destructive. He showed that the Romans had not lost all records of their early past when the Gauls sacked and burned their city. Legal sources and traditional songs might have preserved the central narrative of Rome's origins, which thus deserved faith even if its embroidery of myths did not. And he incorporated these new methods in the dissertations that his students had to defend in public (Erasmus 1962).

Perizonius tried to widen the base of humanist scholarship as well as to sharpen its edge. His lectures on universal history lived up to that much abused title. Like the pioneer Georg Hornius who preceded him at Leiden, Perizonius tried to break out of the archaic straight-waistcoat of the Four Monarchies and similar inherited schemes. He included the Far East and the Americas in his narrative, religion, culture and science in his analysis. His lectures on Greek literature aimed less at the traditional explication of texts than at the more modern task of sketching the institutional and social history of Greece:

> In my public lectures (he announced) ... I will explain not the language ... but the histories, the origins of nations,

> the forms of states ... For I think this is useful to everyone, and to jurisconsults and students of politics, even if they know no Greek. (Meijer 1971)

And if Perizonius was unusually original, he was hardly unique. Recent scholarship has revealed similar practices at less glamorous centres of late-seventeenth-century learning like Marburg and Wittenberg (Wirth 1977; Grafton forthcoming). And Vico's *New Science*, that most precocious and notorious of all efforts to show that philology could be made as philosophical as geometry, clearly belongs to the same general movement (and is also the work of a university professor solidly attached to the humanist tradition) (Cantelli 1971). Even when the classics were outmoded as sources of practical knowledge, then, the method by which they were studied could be made attractive. Such tactics enabled humanist scholarship to survive the full challenge of the *philosophes*, with their scorn for mere antiquarianism and the faculty of memory. In England and France, to be sure, the methods of Perizonius and Bentley were applied in the vernacular rather than in Latin, by members of learned societies not by university teachers, to medieval rather than to classical subjects (Gossman 1968). But in Holland and Germany the universities remained the seats of innovative scholarship. Tiberius Hemsterhusius, a teacher so vital he could fire his students with enthusiasm for the analysis of Byzantine commentaries on the ancient poets, trained his followers in a method of linguistic analysis as clear, distinct, and opposed to tradition as any *philosophe* could have desired:

> Lead by the thread, so to speak, of analogy, he searched out the simplest forms of words and the original meanings born with them, recalled to reasonable order all their forms and inflections, derived from the primary senses [of each word] the secondary and consequent ones, and revealed both their relations and their migrations. He expelled the false anomalies with which the grammarians had thrown everything into confusion and dispelled the shadows that had clung about the Greek language for so many centuries. Thus that language, incomparably rich in words and forms, was made as easy to learn as any other. (Ruhnken 1768, 307)

Thus humanism added its mite of contribution to the linguistic discoveries of Condillac and Humboldt.

Even the great eighteenth-century flowering of historical thought and teaching grew from seeds the humanists had planted. Turretini, Chladenius, Ernesti and Semler showed that one way to defend the search for knowledge in sacred and classical texts was to show that interpretation could be given fixed rules and clear criteria of truth and falsehood. The discipline that they created, hermeneutics, sought to find meaning in books not by forcing them to yield a predetermined set of dogmas but by setting them back into their original contexts and rediscovering the message they had held for their original audience. And it derived from no less a humanist – as Semler proudly stated – than Erasmus, from whose notes and textbooks the eighteenth-century scholars learned their methods (Hornig 1961, Merk 1980). Heyne and Wolf showed that one way to defend the study of the classics as the proper education for modern civil servants was to turn that education into a coherent effort to understand the ancient world as it had really been, in all its colourful detail and with all its alien assumptions and beliefs. The discipline that they created, *Altertumswissenschaft*, did not abandon the old humanist effort at encyclopedic knowledge but transformed it. The educated man now had to know not every discipline in the world but every discipline that could inform him about the ancient world; his reward was not erudition without form but cultivated mental and emotional faculties. In this revivified form the *studia humanitatis* lived on into the nineteenth century (Grafton 1981a).

Modern students of early modern education and culture, in short, have applied too sharply Darwinian terms of analysis to the competing educational traditions of the seventeenth and eighteenth centuries. True, humanism faced aggressive competitors, some with more up-to-date systems for self-defence. But strong competition and harsh criticism were less poisonous than tonic. The humanist enterprise never ceased, so far as its hard core of technical methods was concerned, to adapt to new requirements.

The Preservation of an old Rhetoric

If the core remained intact, what of its stiff husk of Latin? Surely that above all was sterile, useless, out of date. By 1600, we are inclined to think, the vernacular languages had reached maturity. They could express anything from a shade of emotion to a logical distinction as fully, clearly, and powerfully as the classical languages which had served as models for their enrichment. Why then treat eloquence in Latin as the mark of a learned man? It seems almost self-evident that the detailed study of ancient languages had become by 1600 a mere fossil of the time when the vernaculars had not fully developed their lexicon and syntax. And it seems difficult not to sympathise with those seventeenth-century intellectuals, like John Webster, who denounced the humanists for locking their secrets away from ordinary people in a learned language, or with those seventeenth-century educators, like Rudbeck and Comenius, who tried to develop easy means for mastering Latin and thus to do away with the heavily grammatical and rhetorical emphasis of the school and university curriculum. Why not teach languages several at a time through visual aids, as Comenius tried in his *Orbis pictus*? Why not found a city where only Latin would be spoken, so that students could settle there and become fluent within months, as Rudbeck proposed (Källquist 1936)? Surely anything was better than such curricula as that of the Altdorf academy – which culminated, deep into the seventeenth century, by enabling the student to expound in stylised Latin, to an audience of parents paralysed with boredom, the equally stylised emblematic medals that were struck for the academy's graduation ceremonies (Stopp 1974). Latin might still retain its utility as an instrument of communication, but surely not its attractiveness as an object of lifelong study.

Viewed from hindsight, the Latin rhetoric of the seventeenth and eighteenth centuries looks a mere heap of dead bones. But if we choose a less anachronistic vantage point we can see that there was much life in the old fossils yet. Consider, first of all, the point of view of a noted practitioner of the art – Conrad Samuel Schurzfleisch (1641–1708), the chief adornment of the university of Wittenberg for the last three decades of the seventeenth century and the first one of the eighteenth. For a German professor of the time, he was a remarkably cosmopolitan figure. He lived in the Arcadia of all humanists, Italy, where he studied ancient ruins and was given a cool drink by the Medici Grand Duke of Tuscany. He travelled in Holland and England.

He appreciated Leibniz's subtle discoveries 'in that recondite art of counting called Algebra' as well as Bochart's fabulously learned treatments of the migrations of ancient nations. And he kept up his contact with intellectual life outside his *Kleinstadt* by buying books and book catalogues with unwearied avidity and by corresponding in Latin with almost anyone who could be troubled to reply.

For all Schurzfleisch's breadth of experience and reading, he remained a rhetorician of the old school. What he loved above all else was to whip up a froth of metaphors and exempla quite devoid of any direct contact with reality. 'Frisia', he exhorted a young woman whose Latin prose he admired:

> you have joined the ranks of the Heroides; if only Barth and Reinesius survived they would marvel at your merits. You have imitated the imperial virago Alexia Comnena. You have equalled Hroswitha, once the famous ornament of Saxony. There was nothing left for you, save to transfer those incomparable virtues to the wedding bed, and spread them among your children and grandchildren...

And what he loved to pass on to his students were the very formal skills that so enhanced his encomium to *Kinder, Küche* and *Kirche*. Like any good sixteenth-century intellectual Schurzfleisch saw the Greek and Latin languages as the foundations of all other forms of learning and the only defence against barbarism. Like any earlier humanist, Schurzfleisch gave his students long lists of linguistic do's and don'ts, warning them gravely that the study of lexica alone would not win them the linguistic prowess they needed:

> They who think that eloquence can be learnt from Nizolius and other lexica are foolish, for not everything in lexica is Latin. For lexica refer sometimes to writers of inferior periods. Thus *actum est tecum* is a barbarous expression; *actum est de te* is how a Latin would say it. You won't learn this from Nizolius, but from the instruction of a teacher well acquainted with the genius of the Latin language. (Schurzfleisch 1741, 209)

Like any earlier humanist, too, Schurzfleisch judged other scholars as much by their style as their ideas. Selden, he said, would have been entirely superior to Grotius had he not written so poorly and quoted more Hebrew than was reasonable. Schurzfleisch knew but rejected without feelings of insecurity the attacks that philosophers and scientists had made upon his classical citadel. He had read Descartes' *Discourse on Method*; what he took away from it was not the view that Cartesian mathematics were more modern and powerful than Ciceronian rhetoric but the sense that Descartes must have had some difficulty finding his vocation, since it had only been after he failed as a rhetorician that he achieved success as a physicist.

Schurzfleisch's humanism was both strictly pragmatic and highly traditional. Writing for him was the elegant execution of a set-piece. The product must fit its author, audience, and occasion, and follow the rules traditional in its genre. Some barbarisms were not allowed in elegant writing but 'could be tolerated in philosophy and theology'; Greek quotations were allowable in letters to fellow scholars but not in addresses to public officials (Schurzfleisch recalled with gratitude how his teachers at Giessen had won him preferment by cutting the excess Greek from his dissertation). Above all a piece of writing should exemplify the true principles of imitation. The central elements should be borrowed from a good ancient author but rearranged in some new way:

> I once . . . imitated Pericles, addressing the Athenians in Thucydides, adapting it to be appropriate to a prince; then all flowed so naturally that it was amazing. And that is how the Greeks are useful. Had I kept all the words I would have been what Horace calls a *servile pecus*. Imitation should resemble theft. If someone stole a cloak and had it made into a tunic or some other garment, no one would know it had been a cloak before. (Schurzfleisch 1741, 214)

Exactly the same instructions had battered the ears of the humanists' students for two hundred years and more.

Yet if Schurzfleisch seems old-fashioned for an older contemporary of Bayle, Vico, and Leclerc, he was no figure of fun. His students mourned his death in elaborate verses and printed his bibliographical lectures in elaborate editions. And there was every reason for his views to seem plausible. The Germany of his youth had considered Latin far preferable to German. Gryphius's biographers in the 1660s praised the gruelling six-hour vernacular tragedies that had made him Germany's answer to Corneille, but they waxed ecstatic over the fact that he had written notes on Rosinus's Corpus of Roman antiquities and delivered Latin lectures at Leiden. Schurzfleisch too had found Latin his entrée to the great world outside North Germany. And in fact, in the early years of his professoriate Latin literary culture seemed as vital a part of cultural life as it ever had. In Turin Emanuele Tesauro had just created an entire new genre of semi-poetic Latin writing – the mock-inscription in Tacitean Latin, which provided such an ideal medium for political comment and lampoon that it spread rapidly north of the Alps. Though Jesuits were more prolific and deft at the new epigraphy than their rivals, it was Christian Weise, a professor at Protestant Jena, who codified the rules of the 'new political poetry' (Sparrow 1969). At the same time in Scotland Archibald Pitcairne was proving that Latin verse could express Jacobite political views and praise modern science as well as it could celebrate country life (Duncan 1965). And Casimir Sarbiewski, the Sarmatian Ovid, continued to be one of Europe's best-sellers, his Latin poems reprinted every year. In short, Latin lived. Eloquence still found rewards and enjoyed a substantial public – especially in those areas of old-regime Europe that would seem most in need of reform to the philosophes, where Latin learning remained a formidably effective device for keeping good jobs in the hands of an entrenched order, and in those that lacked fully developed vernaculars and rejected the alternative of French.

Even at the epicentres of change some intellectuals loved the old curriculum. Ismaël Boulliau was as up-to-date in his scholarly pursuits as anyone in mid-seventeenth-century Europe. A mathematician and astronomer in his own right, he travelled from Paris to Poland to meet Hevelius 'so that I may discuss matters Astronomical with him, and see his splendid and exquisitely designed Astronomical instruments' (Burman 1727, v, 602). He reported to his friend Nicolaas Heinsius on the new literary and scientific societies that formed in Paris in the 1650s, notably the 'Neo-Pythagorean' Academy of Montmor. Yet he mourned his contemporaries' defection from the study of the classics: 'Aevum illud doctorum virorum abiit, succeditque peior aetas'. And he congratulated Heinsius on winning preferment in Holland by his 'eloquence, and his elegance in writing Latin letters' (Burman 1727, v, 596–7). The Dutch government, said Boulliau, was to be congratulated on employing one who could cow their enemies and mollify

Anthony Grafton

their friends with his deft and powerful Latin.

In fact, the seventeenth and eighteenth centuries witnessed two parallel and protracted efforts to preserve the modern Latin tradition. Gruter in Heidelberg, Huet in Paris, Magliabecchi in Florence, Burman in Leiden were among the protagonists. On the one hand they collected the results of humanist scholarship in the variorum editions that were a specialty of the age, in the hideous small volumes of Gruter's *Lampas* and the stately big ones of the *Thesauruses* of Greek and Roman antiquities. On the other hand they collected the products of humanist eloquence in their editions of Latin letters, poems, and histories, offering to a European public – here was false advertising *avant la lettre* – the 'Delights of the Italian Poets' and the 'Pleasures of the Learned'. They drew up the first bibliographical maps and guide-books to help later explorers of this vast country: Fabricius's *Bibliothecae*, Morhof's *Polyhistor*, Jöcher's *Gelehrten-Lexikon*, all as indispensable now as when they were published. These enterprises brought academicians, professors, and amateurs together in a common effort. In so far as he contributed to both of them with his editions of Buchanan and Wilson, Ruddiman emerges again as a figure of European meaning (Duncan 1965).

Admittedly, even where an entrenched social system supported it, Latin had lost much of its vitality by the mid-eighteenth century. In Germany and Holland the vernaculars were taking over the book markets and the humanists themselves were beginning to make fun of their efforts at eloquence. Yet the tradition never quite vanished. F. A. Wolf's great *Prolegomena ad Homerum* of 1795, that manifesto of modern historical scholarship, won a readership as much for its masterly Latin style as for its technical content (Grafton 1981a). As late as 1805, indeed, the great Leiden scholar Daniel Wyttenbach recalled how he had met his great friend Bosch more than thirty years before, on arriving in Amsterdam to take up a teaching post. He had conveyed to Bosch Valckenaer's compliments on the latter's Latin prose and verse. The conversation continued:

> 'But you (asked Bosch) do you also write verse?' 'Not yet,' I answered. 'Why not yet?' 'Because I haven't learnt enough other things yet.' 'What other things do you mean?' 'Both the writing of prose,' I answered, 'and many

other literary skills.' 'And yet,' you said, 'it is a fine thing to make verses.' (Wyttenbach 1821, II, 47–8)

Wyttenbach listened with pleasure as his friend demolished the pretensions of those impudent literary critics who created aesthetic systems even though they neither knew Latin nor wrote verses. In this meeting of two young strangers from divergent origins (Wyttenbach was Swiss, Bosch Dutch), sending up their clouds of Latin as American Indians are said to have sent up smoke signals – to show they shared an artificial, international language – we see how long there was some vestige of a pan-European, Latin-speaking republic of letters – and some life in the humanist tradition.

In Place of a Conclusion

This rapid survey of a large terrain will have done its work if it has suggested that in our present state of knowledge there are far more areas of darkness than of light. We can give no firm chronology of the metamorphoses of humanist scholarship or the later adaptations of humanist rhetoric; we can draw no neat maps to mark off the areas where the humanist enterprise persisted from those where it was changed beyond recognition or beaten into insignificance. Yet one suggestion may be in order. One can learn much about the fundamental concerns of society from the quick fixes and nostrums with which it tries to solve its most pressing problems. The American obsession with education of the 1960s was reflected as in a mirror by the rise of 'speed-reading'; the American obsession with self-improvement in the 1970s is embodied in the grim spread of the health club and the squash court. The quick fixes of seventeenth-century educationalists show a desperate concern with erudition and eloquence even when they urged that these should be eliminated from the universities. That alone would be enough to show that such segments of a traditional literary curriculum still mattered in a scientific age.

Acknowledgment

My thanks to P.R.Dear, A.C.Dionisotti, and R.Tuck, whose comments on an earlier draft resulted in material improvements. Errors that remain are mine.

REFERENCES

Aarsleff, H. (1982) *From Locke to Saussure*. Minneapolis.
Alpers, S. (1983) *The Art of Describing*. Chicago.
Bolgar, R. (1954) *The Classical Heritage and its Beneficiaries*. Cambridge.
Burman, P. (1727) *Sylloge epistolarum*. Leiden.
Cantelli, G. (1971) *Vico e Bayle. Premesse per un confronto*. Naples.
Cassirer, E. (1932) *Die Platonische Renaissance in England und die Schule von Cambridge*. Leipzig.
Clapmarius, A. (1644) *De arcanis rerum publicarum*. Amsterdam.
Dainville, F. de (1978) *L'éducation des jésuites (XVIe-XVIIIe siècles)*. Paris.
Duncan, D. (1965) *Thomas Ruddiman*. Edinburgh.
Erasmus, H. J. (1962) *The Origins of Rome in Historiography from Petrarch to Perizonius*. Assen.
Fiering, N. (1981) *Moral Philosophy at Seventeenth-Century Harvard. A Discipline in Transition*. Chapel Hill.
Gossman, L. (1968) *Medievalism and the Ideologies of the Enlightenment*. Baltimore.
Grafton, A. (1975) Joseph Scaliger and Historical Chronology. *History and Theory* 14.
— (1979) Rhetoric, Philology and Egyptomania in the 1570s. *Jl. Warb. Court. Insts.* 42.
— (1981a) Prolegomena to Friedrich August Wolf. *Jl. Warb. Court. Insts.* 44.
— (1981b) Teacher, Text and Pupil in the Renaissance Class-Room. *History of Universities* 1.
— (forthcoming) Polyhistor into Philologe. *History of Universities* 3.
Gregory, T. (1979) *Theophrastus redivivus. Erudizione e ateismo nel Seicento*. Naples.
Groen van Prinsterer, G. (1857) *Archives ou correspondance inédite de la maison d'Orange-Nassau*, Ser. II, 1. Utrecht.
Hahlweg, W. (1973) *Die Heeresreform der Oranier*. Wiesbaden.
Hassinger, E. (1978) *Empirisch-rationaler Historismus*. Bern.
Heinsius, D. (1627) *Orationum editio nova*. Leiden.
Hill, C. (1965) *Intellectual Origins of the English Revolution*. Oxford.
Hornig, H. (1961) *Die Anfänge der historisch-kritischen Theologie*. Göttingen.
Källquist, G. (1936) Jacob Rudbeckius' latinstad, in *Lychnos*.
Lipsius, J. (1630) *De militia Romana libri quinque, Commentarius ad Polybium*. Antwerp.
Mandrou, R. (1979) *From Humanism to Science*. Hassocks.
Manuel, F. (1963) *Isaac Newton, Historian*. Cambridge, Mass.
Meijer, Th. (1971) *Kritiek als herwaardering. Het levenswerk van Jacobus Perizonius*. Leiden.
Merk, O. (1980) Anfänge neutestamentlicher Wissenschaft im 18. Jahrhundert, in *Historische Kritik in der Theologie. Beiträge zu ihrer Geschichte*. Göttingen.

Oestreich, G. (1982) *Neostoicism and the Early Modern State.* Cambridge.

Robinson, G. (1927) *Autobiography of Joseph Scaliger.* Cambridge, Mass.

Ruhnken, D. (1768) *Elogium Tiberii Hemsterhusii*, in *Eloquentiae Latinae exempla.* Leipzig 1832.

Schrijvers, P. (1981) Justus Lipsius. Grandeur en misère van het pragmatisme, in *Rijksuniversiteit te Leiden, Voordrachten, Faculteitendag 1980.* Leiden.

Schurzfleisch, C. S. (1697) *Orationes.* Wittenberg.

— (1729) *Epistolae selectiores.* Wittenberg.

— (1735-8) *Notitia scriptorum librorumque varii argumenti.* Wittenberg.

— (1741) *Schurzfleischiana.* Wittenberg.

Sparrow, J. (1969) *Visible Words.* Cambridge.

Stopp, F. (1974) *The Emblems of the Altdorf Academy.* London.

Webster, C. (1976) *The Great Instauration.* London.

Wirth, G. (1977) *Die Entwicklung der Alten Geschichte an der Philipps-Universität Marburg.* Marburg.

Wyttenbach, D. (1821) *Opuscula.* Leiden/Amsterdam.

THE PURSUIT OF VIRTUE
IN SCOTTISH UNIVERSITY EDUCATION:
DUGALD STEWART AND
SCOTTISH MORAL PHILOSOPHY
IN THE ENLIGHTENMENT

NICHOLAS PHILLIPSON

One of the most important themes in the history of the Scottish enlightenment is the success of Scottish university education in penetrating the academic culture of the west in the eighteenth and early nineteenth centuries. The Scots first made their academic mark overseas in colonial America where they and Scots-Irish teachers showed remarkable skill in exploiting a lively educational market in the presbyterian colonies. Some set up little schools and academies to teach the classics and a smattering of philosophy to boys preparing for university or the professions. Others were university teachers who introduced Scottish texts and methods into their colleges sometimes with spectacular results. Thus John Witherspoon, a minister from Paisley and President of Princeton from 1768-94 reorganised its curriculum on Scottish lines and turned what had been little more than a seminary into a college designed to service the secular as well as the spiritual needs of a strict presbyterian community. The College of Philadelphia was transformed in the same way by two Scottish teachers, Francis Alison and William Smith, powerfully egged on by Scotophiles like Benjamin Rush. As at Princeton, the philosophy curriculum was redesigned in the 1750s and 1760s and a medical school, modelled on that of Edinburgh was added in 1765. In fact Rush's scotophilia knew no bounds. He looked forward to the day when Pennsylvania would be organised culturally like Scotland. It would have four regional universities, the College of Philadelphia servicing the needs of 'the Edinburgh of America' (Sloane 1971).

All of this presupposed an American taste for Scottish textbooks – philosophy textbooks in particular – and it is on these that Scotland's importance in the history of academic culture depends. Scottish textbooks began to penetrate the American academic market in the middle of the eighteenth century.

The Pursuit of Virtue in Scottish University Education
Francis Hutcheson's *Short Introduction to Moral Philosophy*, which first appeared in English in 1747, Adam Ferguson's *Institutes of Moral Philosophy* (1769) and, above all, William Duncan's extraordinarily popular and durable *Elements of Logic* (1748) ('Design'd particularly for young Gentlemen at the University and to prepare the way to the Study of Philosophy and the Mathematicks') represent the principal texts in the first wave of this Scottish pedagogical invasion. By the 1790s a second, more formidable generation of philosophy texts had begun to flood the American academic market (Martin 1961; Howe 1970; Hook 1975). This consisted of the works of the Scottish Common Sense philosophers, Thomas Reid, Dugald Stewart and lesser figures like James Beattie and George Campbell. By the 1820s Reid and Stewart had been extensively republished in places like Philadelphia, Boston, New York and Charleston. Indeed by 1824, Stewart's *Outlines of Moral Philosophy* was in its eighth American edition and had already sold over 7,500 copies. By then American moral philosophy was more or less synonymous with that of Scotland. Paley, the Scots' nearest rival had been swept aside and Reid and Stewart ruled supreme in the class room. Francis Bowen of Harvard spelt out the virtues of Common Sense philosophy in his preface to Stewart's *Elements of the Philosophy of the Human Mind* (1864):

> The doctrine which [Stewart] inculcates are those of vigorous common sense and sound morality, never defaced by love of paradox and never compromising the interests of truth by straining after novelty, or by unseasonable attempts to appear ingenious or profound. The principles of social order and good government, and the great interests of virtue and religion were never more impressively taught, or eloquently defended, than by this professor of Scotch metaphysics.

By then, however, Common Sense philosophy had begun to reach the continent. Reid and Stewart were being studied in France, Switzerland, parts of Germany, Italy and in Oxford, Cambridge and after 1826 in the new University College of London. But its true continental home was restoration France. It was apparently first used by P.-P. Royer-Collard, professor of the history of philosophy in the Sorbonne from 1811–14, as a way of attacking the scepticism and materialism of Condillac.

The key texts were translated by Théodore Jouffroy in the 1830s and the whole system introduced into the French educational system by that formidable educational engineer, Victor Cousin, who became the formative influence on French education after the July revolution of 1830. By 1833 Cousin was able to claim 'Il n'y a presque pas un collège royal en France où en n'enseigne Reid et Stewart' (Barthèlmy-Saint Hilaire 1895, iii, 232) and he commended their philosophy for much the same reason as the *North American Review*:

> Une philosophie libèrale, l'amour de la vertu, un bon sens inexorable, la vraie méthode philosophique, tels sont les caractères généraux de l'école écossaise; c'est a ces titres que nous la présentons avec confiance à la jeunesse de notre pays. (Cousin 1857, 23)

It is clear that Common Sense philosophy had become the official academic philosophy of France as well as of Britain and America. But what was it? What were its roots in the academic culture of enlightened Scotland? What was its relationship to the sceptical and more 'sociological' philosophy of David Hume, Adam Smith and their circle? How are we to account for its astounding success in penetrating the universities of the west at a time when the idea of a university education was beginning to emerge from the doldrums in which it had lain in Europe for so much of the eighteenth century?

The simple answer to the first question is that Common Sense philosophy (at least in the form in which it was to be known abroad) was the work of Thomas Reid and that all its essential elements are embodied in his first book the *Inquiry into the Human Mind on the Principles of Common Sense* (1764). But for a student of academic culture, this only raises more questions. For none of Reid's published work was designed for the classroom and there is nothing in it to suggest that he had any interest in pedagogical problems at all. His books are unsystematic, exploratory, highly personal in character, designed to set out the principles upon which a Baconian investigation of the contents of the mind should proceed and to apply them to various questions about the principles of knowledge, taste and morality. As we shall see the *Inquiry* was warmly welcomed by university teachers as an important contribution to the contemporary battle against scepticism and materialism. But it is a striking and significant fact that

The Pursuit of Virtue in Scottish University Education
Common Sense philosophy did not take off as a pedagogical system of world-wide significance until the 1790s. For Reid's difficult and elusive philosophy needed to be backed up by authoritative and comprehensive textbooks before it could take a firm hold on philosophy curricula in the universities. That it did so is due to the fact that Reid's favourite pupil, Dugald Stewart, professor of Moral Philosophy at Edinburgh from 1785–1810 was a pedagogue of genius who became the most influential philosophy teacher in the West outside Germany. His first texts, notably his *Elements of the Philosophy of the Human Mind* (1792) and his *Outlines of Moral Philosophy* (1793) turned Common Sense philosophy into a pedagogically viable system. As we shall see, this was not just a matter of simplifying and generalising a particularly difficult metaphysical system. It was a matter of drawing out the implications of Reid's teaching for the teaching of practical morality. And for an Edinburgh academic grandee like Stewart that meant presenting it as his own contribution to the development of a distinctively Scottish programme for teaching the principles of practical morality to young students who were destined for careers in public life. This pedagogical exercise was Edinburgh's distinctive contribution to the shaping of Common Sense philosophy. And it was of integral importance in turning it into the most successful and admired pedagogical system available in the universities of the western world at the turn of the eighteenth and nineteenth centuries.

To understand Stewart's achievement it is necessary to start with Reid (Stewart xc; Veitch 1857; Fraser 1898). Reid spent most of his life as a university professor, first as regent at King's College Aberdeen from 1751 to 1764, later as Adam Smith's successor in the Glasgow Moral Philosophy chair from 1764 to 1780. He was no recluse but he kept his distance from the formidable intellectual world of enlightened Edinburgh. He was not particularly interested in the cut and thrust of Scottish intellectual life. He was not particularly responsive to the political, ecclesiastical and patriotic concerns of the Edinburgh and Glasgow literati. He was not very widely read philosophically and did not even bother to keep up a philosophical correspondence. As Stewart put it, with pointed metropolitan delicacy, his life was spent 'in the obscurity of a learned retreat, remote from the pursuits of ambition and with little solicitude about literary fame' (Stewart xc, 245). He was, in other words, a private, rather unwordly man.

At one level, the *Inquiry* can be read as a discussion of modern scepticism, and of Hume's in particular. It begins with a quasi-Cartesian account of the uncertainties of modern philosophy and of the anxieties it caused him. He was dismayed to find that philosophers were unable to provide decisive proofs of the existence of a material world, personal identity and God. He decided that all modern scepticism stemmed from a single source, an erroneous theory of ideas. This held that our knowledge of things is not derived from things themselves but from ideas of things. What worried him was Hume's apparently conclusive demonstration that there was no way of knowing whether those ideas were exact representations of things or not and the alarming implications this had for an understanding of the world and our place within it. Hume seemed to have shown that the world was only a mental construct, shaped by sensations and fantasies over which we had no real control. Reid thought this was silly and dangerous. It was silly, as Hume himself had admitted, because it was a theory which was contradicted by ordinary human experience. This led Reid to exclaim:

> Poor untaught mortals believe undoubtedly, that there is a sun, moon, and stars; an earth, which we inhabit; country, friends, and relations, which we enjoy; land, house, and moveables, which we possess. But philosophers, pitying the credulity of the vulgar, resolve to have no faith but what is founded upon reason. They apply to philosophy to furnish them with reasons for the belief of those things which all mankind have believed without being able to give any reason for it. (Reid 1764, 19)

It was silly because this sort of scepticism was simply a philosopher's invention, a product of an absurd and arrogant belief that reason could penetrate every secret of the mental universe God had created. But it was also dangerous because it discouraged belief in religion and in the rules of morality which ordinary men find real and compelling. In other words, this overintellectualised scepticism would encourge the worst sort of epicureanism and immorality and Reid could only hope that the candid thinker would conclude 'I despise Philosophy, and renounce its guidance; let my soul dwell with Common Sense'

The Pursuit of Virtue in Scottish University Education (Reid 1764, 20).

What, then, was Common Sense and how could its true nature be discovered (Davie 1953; Grave 1961; Howe 1970)? Common Sense was not, Reid insisted, the same as vulgar prejudice. It was a capacity to recognise truths which can only be grasped intuitively and to learn how exactly they differ from opinions and prejudices which are acquired in the course of ordinary life. The nature of these truths could be discovered by a process of painstaking and systematic introspection. This would eventually teach us which of our beliefs about the world *had* to be true if the mind was to perform its primary function of making sense of the world and allowing us to live virtuously within it. Thus Reid believed that the truth of these beliefs would be evident from their clarity and from their self-evident necessity to the efficient working of the mind. More precisely, he believed that a proper examination of the mind would show the necessary truth of beliefs in the existence of the material world, personal identity and a world of conscious and morally competent beings. Above all, it would serve to confirm Bishop Butler's celebrated proof of the necessary existence of the beneficent deity who guaranteed the harmony on which this ordered world depended. As Reid's epigraph from Job put it,

> The inspiration of the Almighty giveth them understanding.

To be sure, this list of fundamental truths which could be established by Common Sense was fairly short. Nevertheless Reid was sure that an intensive and painstaking investigation of the mind would demonstrate the existence of others. But it would take time to discover them.

> Perhaps it is possible, by caution and humility, to avoid error and delusion. The labyrinth may be too intricate, and its thread too fine, to be traced through all its windings; but if we stop where we can trace it no farther, and secure the ground we have gained, there is no harm done; a quicker eye may trace it farther. (Reid 1764, 12–13)

This attack on scepticism, in the name of a cautious craftsmanlike approach to the study of the mind attracted much interest in Edinburgh. The elderly John Stevenson, an influential and shadowy philosophy professor, seems to have introduced his best students like Stewart to Reid's philosophy as soon as it appeared. Adam Ferguson, Stewart's influential predecessor in the moral philosophy chair made idiosyncratic use of it in his own lectures on moral philosophy (Veitch 1857). At Princeton, John Witherspoon used Reid as a means of attacking the fashionable metaphysics of Bishop Berkeley. At Aberdeen, Reid's own pupil James Beattie, a tormented and iconoclastic critic of Hume developed an erratic and astonishingly popular Reidian attack on his enemy in the belief that Reid would be of no value to the world unless he was popularised (Phillipson 1978). Stewart disliked 'the asperity of invective' which Beattie had introduced into philosophical argument and believed that it had 'not a little diminished the utility of his book to that very class of his readers whose instruction (it may be reasonably presumed) he had chiefly in view' (Fettercairn MSS) and it is to his own solution to the problem of presenting Reid's philosophy to students that we must now turn.

Dugald Stewart was first and foremost a pedagogue; that is to say, there was never any point in his career before his retirement in 1810 at which philosophy was or could have been an activity separate from university teaching (Veitch 1857). He was born into the academic purple in 1753; his father was the professor of mathematics at Edinburgh. He entered Edinburgh University in 1765 and heard Ferguson's lectures. Later he went to Glasgow to study with Reid. By age of twenty-five he was assisting his father and Ferguson in the mathematics and moral philosophy classes. In 1785, at the age of thirty-two, he became Ferguson's successor as professor of Moral Philosophy. He had no original philosophy to his name apart from an unpublished essay on dreaming. The next twenty-five years his life was devoted to the gruelling business of teaching the moral philosophy curriculum. On top of that he often stood in for colleagues in other subjects, teaching natural philosophy, mathematics, rhetoric and belles lettres and, famously in 1800–02, a course of lectures on political economy. All of this made him the most celebrated philosophy teacher in the western world. His classes were large and his pupils illustrious; indeed his classroom was the nursery for British whiggery for the next generation. His lectures were classic rhetorical performances, designed to encourage students to pursue truth in order 'to cherish by reflective studies, a noble life in man, humble, reverent and hopeful and [to] raise liberal self-culture on the basis of true self-knowledge' (Veitch 1857, xxxv). More

The Pursuit of Virtue in Scottish University Education
particularly, he hoped that they would enlighten 'those who are destined for the functions of government, and . . . public opinion in respect of their conduct' (Stewart VIII, 17). James Mill said that he had heard Pitt and Fox at their best 'but I have never heard anything so eloquent as some of the lectures of Professor Stewart' (Chitnis 1968, 41). Henry Cockburn, in a classic character sketch, spoke of him as 'one of the greatest of didactic orators'.

> Flourishing in an age which requires all the dignity of morals to counteract the tendencies of physical pursuits and political convulsion, he has exalted the character of his country and his generation. No intelligent pupil of his ever ceased to respect philosophy, or was ever false to his principles, without feeling the crime aggravated by the recollection of the morality that Stewart had taught him.
> (Cockburn 1974, 24)

But for those who had to judge Stewart from the printed word, his reputation rested on his first books, *The Elements of Philosophy of the Human Mind* (1792), the *Outlines of Moral Philosophy* (1793) and his *Biographical Account of the Life and Writings of Adam Smith, LL.D.* (1793) which contained all his published remarks about political economy. He promised to publish a complete account of the principles of moral philosophy, politics and legislation but the project was never completed. The *Essays on the Active Powers* only appeared in 1818 and met with a lukewarm reception. The works on politics and legislation never appeared at all. Stewart's grand design had run into the sand. But it is Stewart's success as a pedagogue, not his failure that concerns us here. The key to it lay in his skill in linking the discussion of metaphysics to the all-important task of teaching students the principles of practical morality.

For Stewart, being a practical moralist meant being a Ciceronian. It went without saying that:

> In illustrating the doctrines of practical morality . . . the ancients seem to have availed themselves of every light furnished to human reason, and indeed these writers, who, in later times have treated the subject with the greatest success are those of have followed most closely in the footsteps of the Greek or Roman philosophers.
> (Stewart xa, 16)

The problem was to discuss these illustrations according to the principles of human nature. That meant dealing with the metaphysical principles which explained the origins of ideas of morality, justice and virtue and those which explained the organisation of the human world. As Adam Ferguson put it,

> The laws of Morality relatively to men refer either to his Mind or to his External condition. And moral Philosophy consists of two Parts.
> The first relates to the mind and happiness of Man.
> The second relates to his external condition and Conduct, or to the relations and duties of man in civil life.
> (Ferguson 1766, 29)

Thus the study of metaphysics and what came to be known as the adventitious states were not ends in themselves but means of showing students how to cultivate their personalities and acquire 'all the intellectual and moral improvement of which their nature is possible' (Stewart II, 64). To the sour presbyterian divine who had once claimed that metaphysics was the 'dishclout of theology' Stewart might have replied that, on the contrary, it was the dishclout of practical morality.

Now in adopting this programme for teaching moral philosophy, Stewart was simply aligning himself with the mainstream of the academic Scottish moral philosophy of the Scottish enlightenment. Since the restoration of presbyterianism in 1690 the central problem which had faced the Scottish universities had been to devise an intellectually respectable form of education which would ensure that the churches and schools were provided with clergy and teachers who had a decent general education and held a consensual rather than an adversarial view of the relationship between the church and secular society. On top of that there was the additional problem of providing an acceptable form of polite education for young men of rank, property and position and for young men destined for the legal and medical professions who had hitherto been forced to resort to the Dutch universities or to private tutors in Edinburgh in order to get it (Phillipson 1974). The reorganisation of Edinburgh and Glasgow universities at the turn of the seventeenth and eighteenth centuries was a complicated and protracted exercise whose details do not need to detain us here (Phillipson 1974; Horn 1967; Mackie 1954). It involved introducing law and medicine into the curricula and making philosophy the essential preparation for further

The Pursuit of Virtue in Scottish University Education
professional education. Thus, for those who proposed to graduate or who wanted a general education, moral philosophy was enthroned at Glasgow and Edinburgh as the 'Queen of the Sciences'.

That was the theory. In practice, however, things worked rather differently. For while moral philosophy quickly became the pivot of the Glasgow philosophy curriculum in the early eighteenth century, it remained an undernourished subject in Edinburgh until 1764. The reason was partly financial. When the chair was founded in 1708, the statutes required the professor to live off his salary and did not allow him to collect class fees from his students as was the custom in other professions. But the original salary was quickly eroded by inflation, was never increased and was, by the middle of the century, exiguous. Thus the chair held few attractions for ambitious moral philosophers and soon became a haven for sinecurists and dullards. It is no coincidence that it did not become an important source of innovative moral philosophy teaching until 1764, when the professor was at last allowed to levy class fees on his students (Sher 1980). Until that time, Glasgow was to be the laboratory for the new academic moral philosophy of the Scottish enlightenment.

It is the intellectual implication of this story that concerns us here. At one level, the problem of devising a suitable moral philosophy curriculum was simple enough. It was to introduce Pufendorf's *De Officio Hominis et Civis* into the universities. This was the most famous textbook of moral philosophy in the western world, teaching the Ciceronian offices according to the principles of the natural jurisprudence of Grotius and Pufendorf. But it was a problematic text for presbyterians. For one thing, Grotius' own philosophy was arminian and thus heretical. For another, Pufendorf's attempt to overcome this problem had forced him to sail too close to Hobbesian winds for Christian comfort. Gersholm Carmichael, who taught moral philosophy as regent and professor from 1694 to 1729 and his successor Francis Hutcheson (1729–46) both wrestled with this problem. Carmichael wrote an edition of Pufendorf's compend, heavily loaded with critical commentary (Moore and Silverthorne 1980); Hutcheson composed an alternative text of his own which involved demolishing the intellectual foundations on which the natural jurisprudence of Grotius and Pufendorf rested and putting a new one in its place. Grotius and Pufendorf had explained the origins of our ideas of morality and justice in terms of our rational appreciation of God's instructions to us. Hutcheson, however, thought that moral behaviour could not be satisfactorily explained in such intellectualised terms and instead proposed to account for them in terms of the operations of a moral sense which functioned independently of the intellect or considerations of self-interest (Forbes 1975 and 1978).

Stewart, who was a close and perceptive historian of philosophy, thought that the results of this heroic Glaswegian experiment had been disastrous as far as the history of morals was concerned for it had opened the door to the devastating scepticism of Hume and the equally disturbing materialism of Adam Smith (Stewart xa, 6–17). For Hume had shown how the rationalist and sentimental ethics of Grotius, Pufendorf and Hutcheson could be collapsed into a theory of belief which stressed the importance of the sensations and the imagination in furnishing us with ideas. This had allowed him to discuss morality in terms of utility and virtue in terms of man's natural sociability. For in Hume's theory, to be virtuous seemed to mean little more than to be able to cultivate a capacity for critical detachment and to think sceptically about any truths we might suppose our beliefs contained. But there was worse to come. Adam Smith had succeeded to the Glasgow chair in 1752 and had devoted his moral philosophy lectures to an account of the principles of morality and natural justice which was based on a meticulous examination of the process of social interaction. This had shown how all our ideas of morality and justice are formed in the course of ordinary life in pursuit of two great social goals, social approval and self-respect. For a moralist like Stewart this was to explain our respect for the principles of morality and justice in terms of our respect for propriety. What was worse, Smith had extended his discussion to an account of the principles of virtue and had demonstrated that that, too, was simply a form of propriety (Phillipson 1983).

By 1763, when Smith retired from the Glasgow chair, Scottish academic philosophy had run into difficulties on ethical grounds. Rationalist and sentimental attempts to discuss the Ciceronian offices had exploded in a mass of relativism. It had

The Pursuit of Virtue in Scottish University Education
become possible for students to believe that morality was simply an extension of the study of the social history of man and that virtue was simply a code word for adaptability to the values of an increasingly materialist world. Stewart's first teacher, Adam Ferguson, was the first professor of moral philosophy at Edinburgh to be able to make a decent living out of his chair. He decided to build up a curriculum which would rebut Smith's materialist Glaswegian ethics and demonstrate on classical republican principles, that virtue was more than a species of propriety and that its roots lay in the constitution of the mind rather than in the organisation of society (Veitch 1857). In the *Institutes of Moral Philosophy* he set out to show that men were animated by a restless search for perfection which was powerful enough to transcend ordinary considerations of utility and propriety. This love of perfection was released in society and shaped by social experience in the form of competitive relations with others and with oneself. It was, Ferguson thought, in this search for perfection that men learned to love virtue. Moreover, by exercising it, men sometimes made discoveries which enriched civilisation and forwarded its progress. As we shall see, Stewart was greatly attracted by Ferguson's discussion of perfection but he distrusted his classical republican emphasis on the importance of social interaction in shaping our ideas of virtue. If man's natural love of perfection was a useful concept for the practical moralist, it was so because it could be shown to be part of the original constitution of the mind, operating according to principles which had nothing to do with social experience. The trouble was that Ferguson had failed to give an adequate account of the metaphysical principles which governed its operations. What Stewart wanted was a moral theory which would show that the love of perfection and the principles of virtue that arose from it could be explained in terms of the operation of the mind and not in terms of the operation of society. It was this that he got from Reid.

What Stewart most admired in Reid was his method. He had shown how 'to record and classify the phenomena of the human mind present to those who reflect carefully on the subjects of their consciousness' (Stewart xc, 258). He had insisted on the importance of cautious, careful observation to a successful Baconian examination of the mind. He had pointed out the connections between overintellectualisation, excessive faith in the powers of the intellect and the tendency to create sceptical and materialist accounts of human nature. And in so doing, he had cleared away the 'rubbish' of all previous inquiries into the mind (*ibid.* 259). Nevertheless, Reid's philosophy was still open to criticism on several grounds. He had not done enough to show that this was a philosophy for the intelligent, not the vulgar and that it was more than a device for legitimising deeply seated, vulgar prejudice as Priestley and others had supposed (Sell 1979). His treatment of the all-important question of methodology had been surprisingly cursory and he had been too self-indulgent in pursuing metaphysical niceties which were of little interest to practical moralists and students preparing for public life. Above all, Reid had paid far too little attention to the all-important question of 'tracing the numerous relations by which this philosophy is connected with the practical business of life' (Stewart xc, 273). In fact, Stewart concluded, Reid had only laid the foundations of a new system of moral philosophy. It was up to him to erect the 'superstructure' (Stewart II, 56).

This needed a bolder hand than Reid's and Stewart showed little of the philosophical circumspection he commended in Reid and urged on his pupils. What worried him was the prospect of precocious students devoting too much time to one or two of the faculties of the mind to the exclusion of the rest; this would encourage exactly the sort of overgeneralisation which had encouraged the spread of modern scepticism and materialism. Thus it was essential to show that the mind was a complex system of interlocking parts none of which should be considered in isolation from the others. Stewart's own analysis of the constitution of the mind was firm and confident. The powers of perception, attention, conception, abstraction, memory, imagination and the association of ideas were discussed with notable clarity and economy. They were illustrated by the wealth of happily chosen examples for which he was famous and by reference to the treatment of the subject in question by other philosophers, sceptics and materialists in particular. In general Stewart was at pains to stress that the mind could be inspected, documented and manipulated by those who knew how it worked.

Take, for example, his discussion of the all-important ques-

The Pursuit of Virtue in Scottish University Education
tion of the association of ideas (Stewart II, ch.v). Stewart gave Hume credit for his innovative discussion of the process by which a succession of ideas pass through the mind but he was not happy with it. For one thing, Hume had oversimplified, reducing the principles which governed the process to three; resemblance, contiguity in time and place and cause and effect. This, he thought, had simply resulted in the sort of reductionism that had done so much to encourage the spread of scepticism. For another, Hume did not seem to think that the will played much part in controlling the association of ideas and in regulating our mental habits. Stewart disagreed. He pointed out that the musician who was able to make difficult manual operations second nature by hard practice, used his will to regulate the association of ideas (*ibid.* 257–8). He concluded 'A correct analysis of the association of ideas would show the error of assuming that the will possesses no influence over it' (*ibid.* 267).

Stewart was most anxious to show how the will controlled the various operations of the mind. Indeed, there is a case for saying that he wanted to *define* the faculties of the mind in terms of processes which could be controlled by the will. Nowhere is this more evident and important than in his discussion of imagination which differed sharply from Reid's. Reid had a singularly unworldly view of the imagination and its place in our mental equipment. He thought that our ability to imagine something was quite different from our disposition to believe in it. Thus, it was perfectly possible to imagine Glasgow Cathedral standing on its spire. But that did not mean that we believed in the possibility for a moment (Grave 1960, 31–2). Stewart, however, had a much livelier sense of the power of the imagination to shape our beliefs. It was undoubtedly true that there was a formal difference between *conceiving* an object we remember which is not before us and *imagining* something we've never seen before. But in real life the distinction was much more obscure. Conceptions were instantly overladen by the imagination and 'are frequently so blended, that it is difficult to say which of the two same particular operations of the mind, conception or imagination, are to be referred' (Stewart II, 149). For Stewart had a much sharper sense than Reid of the power of the imagination to furnish the mind with the sort of prejudices, fantasies and errors which a correct moral education ought to be able to bring under control. What is more, he knew that Hume and Smith had given the imagination a pivotal role in explaining the origin of beliefs and the process of social interaction. If modern scepticism was founded on an erroneous theory of ideas, that theory depended on a theory of the imagination. Thus a new theory of the imagination was essential if Stewart was ever to construct an alternative, non-sceptical moral theory to define 'the general rules of a wise and virtuous conduct in life' (*ibid.* 11).

For Stewart, the only sort of imagination that really mattered to the moralist was 'Poetic' or 'Creative' imagination.

> It is not the gift of nature, but the result of acquired habits aided by favourable circumstances. It is not an original endowment of the mind, but an accomplishment formed by experience and situation; and which in its different gradations, fills up all the interval between the first efforts of untutored genius, and the sublime creations of Raphael or of Milton. (*ibid.* 437)

This was quite different from the sort of imagination that activated the fantasies and the instinctive mental processes which played so important a part in Hume's and Smith's accounts of the acquisition of moral sentiments. Nevertheless, 'poetic imagination' was destined to play as important a part in Stewart's moral philosophy as 'imagination' had done in theirs. It was 'the great spring of human activity and provided men with images of heroism and patriotism and with ideals of benevolence and virtue. It was, in short, the life-blood of human progress. 'Destroy this faculty and the condition of men will become as stationary as that of the brutes' (*ibid.*). Thus poetic imagination was the Fergusonian quantity in Stewart's philosophy. It was the capacity men possessed to formulate goals to maximise their own happiness and that of a society at large. For Stewart 'cultivation of the mind' meant careful introspection, careful weeding out of prejudice and fantasy, assiduous questing for an understanding of those fundamental beliefs of human nature that were essential to human happiness. Cultivation of the mind would release the imagination from its dependence on fantasy, and harness it to the cause of virtue. The restless love of perfection, which had animated Ferguson's philosophy was to be tamed by Stewart's formidable mental exercises and turned into a source of highly-directed social and political energy.

In these early writings Stewart had tried to set the Scottish Ciceronian tradition to rights. In their search for ways of teaching the students the Ciceronian offices, previous Scottish moral philosophers had blundered into ever deeper and murkier waters. In their attempts to account for the origins of our ideas of morality and justice they had pursued a course which had lead inexorably from rationalism to sentimentalism to scepticism and materialism. In the process they had found themselves teaching students that the will was far weaker, far less capable of helping them to shape their beliefs and their personalities than they had supposed. The sceptics and materialists had annexed the study of morality to the study of society. They had turned the study of virtue into a study of human adaptability. Now, with the promising discoveries of Reid and Ferguson to draw on, Stewart could present himself as a teacher who had laid the metaphysical foundations on which any student, anxious to understand his duties could rely. He could show that the capacity for virtue was a mental attribute which could be shaped by the will provided the exact nature of the faculties on which it depended were understood. Classical republicans like Adam Ferguson had thought that man's capacity for virtue would be released by participating in public life and defending the liberties which were enshrined in the constitution of their country. Stewart had replied that the capacity for virtue was released by cultivating the constitution of the mind and by defending the freedom of the will.

Stewart had intended to continue his work by discussing the organisation of political society and the duties of citizens and legislators. Indeed he proposed to do what Adam Smith had once hoped to do himself, 'to ascertain the philosophical principles of jurisprudence; or (as Mr. Smith expresses it) to ascertain "the general principles which ought to run through the foundation of the laws of all nations"' (Stewart xa, 55). But he only managed to sketch out the problems involved in such a work in his published works. He agreed with Hume and Smith that a science of politics must be founded on the principles of human nature, that it must be directed to discovering what legislators could learn from the past (*ibid.* 53). He agreed that the object of such an enquiry should be to discover 'those universal principles of justice and expediency which ought under every form of government to regulate the social order' (*ibid.* 54) and that those principles of justice should aim at disposing national resources so as to secure the happiness of the people. In general, he thought, it was possible to conclude that 'whenever a government has existed for ages and men have enjoyed tranquillity under it, it is a proof that its principles are not essentially at variance with each other' (Stewart II, 223). Moreover, in a world in which men's needs were constantly changing 'the perfection of political wisdom does not consist in indiscriminate zeal against reform, but is a gradual and prudent accommodation of established institutions to the varying opinions, manners and circumstances of mankind' (*ibid.* 229). But the science of politics was only in its infancy and only exploratory sorties had been made into the field. Of these the most important was Smith's inquiry into the principles of political economy. But Stewart was very reluctant to use this brilliant but materialist inquiry as a foundation for his own science of politics. Political economy was only of interest to the moralist as part of a general 'system of commercial politics which aimed at the advancement of human improvement and happiness. It is this view of Political Economy that can alone dignify calculations of profit and loss in the eye of the philosopher' (Stewart xa, 59–60).

Stewart clearly believed that Smith's economics ought to be treated as he had treated Reid's metaphysics. That is to say, as a brilliant but flawed and incomplete sortie into a branch of philosophy which was of the utmost importance to the practical moralist and needed to be treated with the greatest care if citizens were not to believe that civic duties were merely extensions of market relationships. But Stewart failed conspicuously to create a pedagogically viable, neo-Ciceronian Science of Politics. As his posthumously published lectures on political economy show, the material was too complex and volatile to be easily contained within such a framework. As one of his former students Thomas Thomson later remarked,

> [Political Economy] is not a system of duties that is to be taught, but a great Political Science; – what you may almost call the science of legislation, where all matters relating to natural resources and power, and wealth are to be considered, and really forming no part of what I consider as genuine moral philosophy. (PP 1837, 35, 407)

The Pursuit of Virtue in Scottish University Education

Reid's and Stewart's failure to publish anything other than metaphysics inevitably meant that their philosophy appeared in the world as a vehicle of philosophical and moral education rather than as the self-standing comprehensive system of philosophy they had hoped it would become. Victor Cousin described it as 'une excellente préparation à une philosophie plus élévée' (Barthèlmy-Saint Hilaire 1895, iii, 232–3). One North American Reviewer put it more bluntly:

> Reid and Stewart were great philosophers, and it is impossible to rise from the study of their works without large improvement and gratitude; and nature undoubtedly formed them to be also great metaphysicians. They wanted not invention, wing, or acumen. But they fastidiously and conscientiously folded up their excessive powers, or only opened them to brood over the chaos in which the science of mind lay darkening beneath them. They struck out from the mass no brilliant revolving orb. This peculiarity, we apprehend, is the cause of a considerable depression of their original reputation, and has emboldened the critics to intrude upon Mr. Stewart's weary and honorable retreat, with asking, what has he done? An insatiable world is not content with seeing the old cumbrous rubbish removed from the path of science, though the labor is performed, like that of Virgil's swain, in ever so elegant a manner. (North American Review 1824, xix, 10–11)

In fact, the strength of Common Sense philosophy lay in serving so many different purposes. It could be used as an apologia for any form of religious belief. It could be used to combat any form of scepticism. Its introspective disciplines encouraged boys to think critically about philosophy and to cultivate self-reliance by processing their ideas against what they took to be the canons of common sense. But, in the last resort, the strength of common sense lay in the fact that it was a teachable system of philosophy. For this Stewart was responsible and it is for this reason that he is best thought of as the Scottish Ramus. Like Ramus his career began and ended as a pedagogue. Like Ramus, his conception of philosophy was geared to what was capable of being taught and that meant teaching what was within the capacities of students in their late 'teens (Ong 1958, ch.vii). But while Ramus had declared war on Aristotle, Stewart declared war on Hume, Smith and their circle and that extraordinary, secular and, we should say, sociologically sensitive enquiry into the principles of human nature, social organisation and history for which the Scottish enlightenment is so famous. Stewart set out to foreclose on this enquiry for ethical reasons and the success of his textbooks in the universities of the western world suggests that many universities were anxious to discourage such investigations as well. As it was, the pursuit of this investigation passed out of the salons and universities of Scotland to Prussia and to the lusher pastures of Hegel's Heidelberg and Berlin. For it was in those universities that the future of the Science of man was to lie.

REFERENCES

Barthèlmy-Saint Hilaire, J. (1895) *Victor Cousin: sa vie et sa correspondence*. Paris.

Chitnis, A. (1968) *The Edinburgh professoriate 1790-1826 and the university's contribution to nineteenth century society*. PhD Edinburgh University.

Cockburn, H. (1974) *Memorial of his time*. Chicago.

Cousin, V. (1857) *La philosophie écossaise*, 3rd edn. Paris.

Davie, G. (1953) *The Scotch metaphysics*. DLitt Edinburgh University.

Ferguson, A. (1766) *Analysis of pneumatics and moral philosophy. For use of students in the college of Edinburgh*. Edinburgh.

Fettercairn MSS. Cancelled proofs of the appendix to W. Forbes' *An Account of the Writings of James Beattie, LL.D.* (Letter to W.F. by Dugald Stewart), Box 25. National Library of Scotland.

Forbes, D. (1975) *Hume's philosophical politics*. Cambridge.

— (1982) Natural law and the Scottish enlightenment, in *The origins and nature of the Scottish Enlightenment* (eds R. H. Campbell and A. S. Skinner). Edinburgh.

Fraser, A. (1898) *Thomas Reid*. Edinburgh and London.

Grave, S. (1960) *The Scottish philosophy of common sense*. Oxford.

Hook, A. (1975) *Scotland and America 1750-1835*. Glasgow and London.

Horn, D. (1967) *A short history of the university of Edinburgh*. Edinburgh.

Howe, D. (1970) *The unitarian conscience; Harvard moral philosophy 1805-1861*. Cambridge, Mass.

Mackie, J. D. (1954) *The University of Glasgow*. Glasgow.

Martin, T. (1961) *The instructed vision*. Bloomington.

Moore, J. and Silverthorne, M. (1980) Gersholm Carmichael and the natural jurisprudence tradition in eighteenth century Scotland. Unpublished paper.

Ong, W. (1958) *Ramus; method and the decay of dialogue*. Cambridge, Mass.

The Pursuit of Virtue in Scottish University Education

PP (1837) *Minutes of evidence taken before the university commissioners, Scotland.* Parliamentary Papers, 1837, vol.35.

Phillipson, N. (1974) Culture and society in the eighteenth century province; the case of Edinburgh and the Scottish enlightenment, in *The university in society* (ed. L. Stone). Princeton.

— (1978) James Beattie and the defence of common sense, in *Festschrift für Reiner Gruenter* (ed. B. Fabian). Heidelberg.

— (1983) Adam Smith as civic moralist, in *Wealth and virtue; political economy in the Scottish enlightenment* (eds I. Hont and M. Ignatieff). Cambridge.

Reid, T. (1764) *An inquiry into the human mind on the principles of common sense.* Edinburgh.

Sell, A. (1979) Priestley's polemic against Reid. *The Price-Priestley Newsletter* no.3, 41-52.

Sher, R. (1980) Ideology, incentive and the Edinburgh chair of moral philosophy 1708-64. Unpublished paper presented to the Columbia University Seminar on Political and Social Thought, November 1980.

Sloane, D. (1971) *The Scottish enlightenment and the American college ideal.* New York.

Stewart, D. (II) Elements of the philosophy of the human mind, in *The Collected Works of Dugald Stewart* (ed. W. Hamilton), vol.II. Edinburgh, 1857.

— (VIII) Lectures on political economy. *Ibid.* vol.VIII.

— (xa) Account of the life and writings of Adam Smith, LL.D. *Ibid.* vol.x.

— (xc) Account of the life and writings of Thomas Reid. *Ibid.* vol.x.

Veitch, J. (1857) A memoir of Dugald Stewart. *Ibid.* vol.x.

COMMENTS BY RICHARD TUCK

I want to begin by addressing a question which arises directly out of Anthony Grafton's paper, but which bears closely on the papers by James McConica and Nicholas Phillipson. That is the question of when – and if – the sort of humanism that underpinned so much university teaching in the sixteenth century came to an end; the question of whether there was as Hiram Haydn suggested in a memorable title to an unmemorable book a 'Counter-Renaissance' in sixteenth- and seventeenth-century Europe. Grafton's answer is yes and no; he has shown persuasively that humanist academic culture of the type that George Buchanan stood for lasted much longer into the seventeenth century than we might have expected, but he has depicted that survival against a background of a New Philosophy which – he concedes – was broadly non-humanist. The story Grafton tells of Schurzfleisch, who concluded that

Richard Tuck

Descartes had turned to mathematics because of his incompetence at rhetoric, sums up both the survival of humanist ideas and their apparent inability to occupy the high intellectual ground of the modern world.

I would like to suggest that the academic culture of the seventeenth century was penetrated by *two* New Philosophies, and that while humanist relations with the one (represented by the mathematics and physics of Descartes and his successors) may have been lukewarm or non-existent, relations with the other were much closer, something that helps to explain the survival in the universities of a kind of humanism, especially here in Scotland. For alongside the new physical science went what Jean Barbeyrac at the beginning of the eighteenth century termed a new 'Science of Morality', whose history he (along with Pufendorf, Buddeus, Thomasius *et al.*) wrote. It was this modern moral science which features so prominently in the textbooks which Nicholas Phillipson has surveyed in his paper, and which many eighteenth-century Scottish writers seem to have seen it as their function to underpin, in philosophically different ways – just as eighteenth-century philosophers also wished to underpin Newtonian physics in various ways.

Let me just remind you of what Barbeyrac said about this Science of Morality in his *Historical and Critical Account of the Science of Morality* (1706). In a very unhumanist way, he was tremendously dismissive of classical culture; the ancient world had produced little that any self-respecting ethician could take seriously, and in particular Aristotle was a tremendous fraud. Only Cicero's *De Officiis* came close to what a modern reader might desire, and even that was flawed in various ways. The early fathers were no better (so that Christian humanist ideas were also spurned), and medieval scholastics in their devotion to Aristotle had produced a mishmash of conflicting opinions. Not until the time of Bacon and Grotius did things change. It was Grotius who first 'broke the ice' and created – at least *in posse* – a new moral and political science. After Grotius, the cleverest men of Europe set themselves the task of clarifying and rendering philosophically coherent the new science; Hobbes had the first go, though that was pretty alarming; Selden tried, but that was incomprehensible; then Cumberland, Pufendorf and Locke together got it straight, perfecting a moral science which held out the possibility of serving as a vehicle for teaching men their moral and civic duties.

I think this is not such an unreasonable history as might superficially appear. Barbeyrac made it clear that what rendered classical and medieval authors unusable for modern readers was their inability to answer the sort of *sceptical moral relativism* that Pierre Charron, the great late-sixteenth-century French sceptic, stood for which seemed to threaten morals, religion and science. And it is true that there are no sophisticated anti-sceptical tracts surviving from antiquity – most of what we know about ancient scepticism comes from defences of scepticism against Stoicism (in particular) rather than *vice versa*. It is also true that a strong version of moral relativism was not taken seriously as something to be advocated or attacked in the middle ages. Grotius genuinely broke the ice in the sense that his was the first work of moral science which accepted the force of the relativist's case and then sought to transcend it. Not for nothing was Carneades singled out for attack in the Prolegomena to *De Iure Belli ac Pacis*.

According to Grotius and his successors, the relativist is correct in holding that there is a far wider variety of moral beliefs and practices than (say) the aristotelians had ever envisaged – the classical virtues were local and European. Nevertheless they believed that this was compatible with a minimal universal content to ethics. All societies must exhibit two features (these are structural necessities, it might be said): men must have the right to defend themselves and to acquire possession in the necessities of life, and they must not wantonly injure one another (though they are always entitled to injure other people when their own survival depends on it, and they are not obliged to *help* one another). Upon these two principles a complex science could (they thought) be constructed, based on some new psychology and metaphysics of a Hobbesian, Cartesian or Lockean kind. Overall, it would be safe from relativists unlike an Aristotelian ethical and political science which had always been vulnerable to the observations of the sceptic.

It is clear enough that there was sufficient here to keep philosophers busy for a long time, and that much of eighteenth-century Scottish philosophical activity in the moral sciences is to do with this theory. The survival of Cicero's *De Officiis* as the crucial classical text, particularly as reconstructed along the lines of the modern science by Pufendorf (to which Phillipson has drawn attention), makes sense in this light – the eighteenth-century Scottish Ciceronians were not like fifteenth-century Italian Ciceronians. But this raises the question as to how far this new moral science was as much a rejection of earlier humanism as the parallel physical science of Galileo, Descartes and Newton seems to have been.

The answer of course is that it was not. Descartes certainly does not look much like an earlier humanist, and his whole enterprise looks different from that of Lipsius and the rest. But this is obviously not true of Grotius: if anyone represented the perfection of many humanist ideals in the early seventeenth century as delineated by Grafton, it was he. So what – if anything – changed?

I think two things are important here. One is that humanism had begun, as we all know and as McConica makes abundantly clear, as a reaction against the *a priori* and deductive arguments of the late middle ages – an *a priorism* expressed most extraordinarily in the speculative grammarians, but found in all areas of human enquiry. The humanists' rediscovery of the arguments of the classical Aristotle had helped their cause, for Aristotle was of course the great philosopher of practical activity as opposed to theoretical and speculative sciences. But an interest in an admiration for classical languages and ancient philosophy does not necessarily go along with this stress on the anti-theoretical, and when humanists of Grotius's generation tried self-consciously again to construct true human *sciences*, they would not necessarily abandon their humanism. On the other hand, they were bound to find (as Grotius himself famously did) that some late-medieval arguments were once again congenial, and it is in this context that the law of nature re-emerges as the major organising concept of ethics after a hundred and fifty years of neglect.

Second, the kind of unified sense of antiquity which we get in earlier humanists (and which McConica again illustrates copiously in his remarks on Erasmus) breaks up at the end of the sixteenth century. Lipsius is important here, for he was one of the first people (in his *Manductio ad Stoicam Philosophiam*) to be very clear about the precise differences between the ancient philosophical schools. The ideological pluralism of antiquity was much clearer by 1600 than it had been in 1500, aand it was possible for modern philosophers to choose among the ancient schools in a much freer way. Old-style humanism was unlikely to withstand the pressures of the approach – but again it must be stressed that the new moral philosophy was a new *kind* of humanism rather than a repudiation of humanism *as such*. (It might even be said that the same is true of the new physics – didn't Newton think that he was reconstructing the mathematics of Diophantus?)

So I would like to suggest that Grafton is right – humanism *did* survive remarkably well – but it did so only because of the attitudes which Phillipson has surveyed, that is, because there was a new moral science which had humanist roots and a sympathy for parts of classical antiquity, and which continued to need the humanist literary and linguistic techniques. But these techniques were at the service of a philosophy which was very different from that of the early-sixteenth-century humanists whom McConica has told us about.

I'd like finally and briefly to say something about the social and political context of all this. As Lawrence Stone reminds us there is a social history of academic intellectual activity to be told alongside the kind of story I have just been telling. The central fact about most European states by the end of the sixteenth century is that they had become fundamentally ideologically pluralist, to a quite unprecedented degree: the wars of religion had been fought to a standstill, and neither side had won. European statesmen were perfectly conscious of this, and aware that their job was primarily to preserve order within the state and to hold the ring for the competing ideologies. Scepticism of the late-sixteenth-century type was a natural response to this new situation. On the continent politicians such as Richelieu and even Oldenbarnevelt both fostered the *libertins erudits* and concurred with their judgements; 'in matters of state the weakest are always wrong' wrote Richelieu, chillingly, to Grotius, while 'to know nothing is the safest faith' said Oldenbarnevelt. (England, incidentally, did not reach this state of theological pluralism until the mid-seventeenth century.) The trouble was that the welfare of such liberal intellectuals seemed to be endangered by those whom they thought of as mad fanatics and the fall of Oldenbarnevelt and Grotius was certainly a dramatic warning of what could happen to them at the hands of the non-sceptics. So the most urgent issue for many people at the beginning of the seventeenth century was to find a moral philosophy which both accepted the necessity of radical ideological pluralism, but also showed how a degree of free intellectual enquiry could be protected by a strong state prepared to use violence against the violent fanatic.

It is this new context which explains why what has often seemed a kind of proto-Enlightenment, Erasmian humanism, did not in fact engender the Enlightenment (and it should be said that McConica has shown persuasively how this picture of Erasmus is a false one). The men of the late seventeenth and eighteenth centuries needed an ideology in which pluralism was deeply entrenched *alongside* a defence of state power and violence – and this was the true moral philosophy of the Enlightenment. It may also be the true moral philosophy for our own rather similar times.

REPORT OF THE DISCUSSION BY ANTHONY GRAFTON AND LAWRENCE STONE

The discussion of Stone's lecture and the papers by McConica, Grafton and Phillipson ranged so widely in time, space and subject that the discussion was inevitably discursive and hard to summarise. During the course of the day, however, certain themes began to emerge. It was agreed that colleges and universities in the early modern period had been particularly preoccupied with two things: social discipline and the inculcation of virtue – leaving aside for the moment what that word might mean. Like the medieval universities they also held a monopoly on the provision of vocational training for the three older professions of law, medicine and theology, except in England where common law was taught in specialised establishments in London. What the faculty taught in these or any other areas had to be something reducible to a science, that is to a body of laws which could be written down in textbooks and expounded in class. Euclid or Latin grammar or the syllogistic method of argument are all ideal for this purpose.

It was generally agreed that in the early modern period

Report of the Discussion

before the eighteenth-century Enlightenment, the present-day stated objective of a liberal education, namely a consciousness-raising experience aimed at creating the doubting and sceptical frame of mind commended by Sir Stuart Hampshire, was the last thing desired by pedagogues or parents, church or state. All parties sought an intellectual training which reinforced traditional belief systems and strengthened respect for established institutions. Accepting this paradigm, the first issue which provoked the most extended discussion was changing concepts in higher education of what was meant by 'virtue' – admittedly an odd idea for a group of historians to concern themselves with for the better part of a day. It became clear that if early modern European universities look to the modern observer like instruments for imposing social discipline on the refractory children of the elite, they looked to their inhabitants like instruments for instilling what they believed was virtue. It was agreed (with few dissenters) first that this aim holds true for all early modern universities and second, that it is not a concern of any modern ones in the West. The discussion thus pointed up at least one crucial change in the way in which universities have exercised their social and cultural function. Phillipson's paper, moreover, offered some welcome concrete information about the ways in which specific notions of virtue were concretely embodied in the eighteenth-century Scottish curriculum. But it also became clear that for most periods before quite modern times it is very difficult to establish the ways in which attitudes and ideas about what was regarded as good behaviour were actually passed on to students. Clearly we need to know much more both about the history of moral philosophy itself, and even more about the subtle and obscure history of the ways in which pedagogical techniques were designed to mould students' characters, as well as to fill their minds with wholesome learning.

A second theme concerned the role of state intervention in university constitutions and curricula. Discussion brought out both the immense differences between early modern and modern conditions and, more surprisingly, the immense variety of conditions that obtained in so limited an area as early modern England and Scotland. Schematically, one can range the forms of state intervention on a spectrum from the case of

Oxbridge, where rulers and ministers sought to concentrate executive power in the hands of a few of their loyal servants, solidly installed as heads of colleges, to that of Glasgow or Edinburgh, where a local patriciate tried at every turn to make the university express the city's ideas and fill its practical needs. Even in early modern times, all universities were subject to severe external controls, especially during the period of religious wars from 1520 to 1660, but some universities were national, some local, in their source of external control, finance, recruitment, support systems, and orientation. No simple taxonomy will meet all the twists and complexities of the cases. Even Cambridge, heavily controlled by Elizabeth and her ministers, harboured pockets of Puritan and Catholic resistance to royal policies and powers of appointment; even Edinburgh responded to pressures from the Scottish and English courts as well as to those exerted by the local burghers. The governing impression one was left with was one of an infinity of variations ill-adapted to the formulation of bold theory. The only viable generalisation is that external interference is greatest at times of international, political and ideological conflicts, such as those generated by the Reformation and Counter-Reformation and the French Revolution.

A third theme concerned how and why curricula succeed and fail. The papers showed that the educational reformers of early modern times tended to have equivocal and partial, rather than overwhelming, successes and failures. Erasmian humanism, for example, seriously influenced the universities but failed to reshape them in its own image in the early sixteenth century. And yet it lived on into the eighteenth century, in an attenuated form, long after it had ceased to be the cutting edge of intellectual advance or spiritual renewal. But they also made clear that the curriculum does come together and fall apart, attract and repel the parents and students at whom it is aimed, with differing success at different times. It also seems that once a curriculum is solidly established, it is extremely hard to change. Its practitioners rarely show the ability to adapt it to new conditions even when it is critically threatened by lack of student interest or intense outside competition.

Participants differed most on the question of how to account for the development of what one might call this curricular arteriosclerosis. Some, like Stone, tend to see the root cause of decay as a socio-psychological one; successful teachers simply attract too many pupils to deal faithfully with individuals and have too strong a vested interest in perpetuating their own power and their own forms of knowledge and discourse to be willing to adopt or adapt to new ones. This is a different way of stating the Kuhnian paradigm. Others stressed the innate conservatism of any curriculum, the tendency of teachers to advance those who are best at jumping through the traditional hoops and to resist suggestions that these latter be moved or replaced. Still others thought that it might be fruitful to treat curricula – at least those of pre-modern times – as having a sort of natural cycle of growth and decay, the latter taking place as social needs and cultural developments outside the universities render established texts, ideas and methods obsolete. Still others wondered whether curricula in decay provoke attacks from those who have ceased to share the underlying assumptions upon which they were once constructed.

These brief remarks convey only a sample of the substance and little of the flavour of the day's discussions. But they do perhaps suggest, as the discussions did, that university history continues to be a field ripe for the application of modern research strategies and tactics.

TWO

THE LIBERAL IDEAL
IN A SCIENTIFIC AGE

THE IDEA OF A UNIVERSITY:
NEWMAN TO ROBBINS

F.S.L.LYONS

'A University is a trust confided by the State to certain hands for the common interest of the nation; nor has it ever heretofore been denied that a University may, and ought, by the state to be from time to time corrected, reformed, or recast, in conformity to accidental changes of relation, and looking towards an improved accomplishment of its essential ends.'
(Hamilton 1853, 538)

This statement is not a government directive, nor even a warning shot from the University Grants Committee, but was made in Edinburgh, almost 150 years ago, by one of the most celebrated professors, Sir William Hamilton. It contains three assumptions, which in one form or another have overshadowed much of the discussion about the relations between state and university from his day to our own. The assumptions are:

1. That the state does indeed have the rights he assigns to it.
2. That the 'essential ends' – or, as Newman put it, the 'idea' – of a university can be generally known and agreed.
3. That the intervention of the state will necessarily work towards the realisation of these 'essential ends'.

The first assumption need not detain us long for it is clear that Hamilton was substantially correct. While the English universities were conspicuously less subject to the state than those of many other countries, there was a limit to their autonomy, and this was demonstrated by the pressure for reform in the middle years of the nineteenth century. Both the ancient universities, it is true, had made some tentative improvements before the commissions of 1850 began to investigate them, but much more needed to be done than they were willing or able to do for themselves. 'All experience proves', said the irrepressible Hamilton, 'that universities, like other corporations, can only be reformed from without', and in the larger sense he was quite right (Hamilton 1853, 448).

Yet the nineteenth-century state, for all the uproar caused by its intervention, was not unduly intrusive. It moved decisively, indeed, to end the Anglican monopoly in Oxford and Cambridge, but the main administrative changes it stimulated in the third quarter of the century, and especially the diversion of resources from the colleges to the universities, were designed to enable internal reform to proceed more effectively. More of this reform dealt with matters which now seem remote, but its importance for us is that it precipitated a debate about the idea and scope of a university which raised many fundamental and perennial issues – who should receive a university education, what form should that education take, what balance should be struck between specialism and generalism, between a liberal and vocational education, between teaching and research. I cannot here attempt a history of this debate, but I propose to look at two periods – c.1850 to c.1880 and 1945 to 1963 – when it was unusually intense and when profound changes were taking place in the universities themselves and in society's attitude towards them.

The central problem, particularly in the earlier of these two periods, was how to combine a liberal education with the need to equip men (and later, women) for life in the workaday world. But what was a liberal education? In its most famous form it was defined by John Henry Newman in the Discourses he gave in Dublin at the inception of the Catholic University in 1852. His first aim was to prove that a university could not be properly so called unless it had a faculty of theology. A cynic or an Irish critic — the two categories have been known to coincide – might surmise that an English convert, standing on a Catholic platform with the Irish bishops almost literally breathing down his neck, could, like Luther in rather different circumstances, 'do no other'. Newman's purpose, of course, went much deeper. Starting from one of Dr Johnson's more magisterial errors, that a university (*studium generale*) was a place of universal learning, he was concerned to establish the indispensability, even the primacy, of theology and to show that 'religious truth is not only a portion but a condition of general knowledge' (Newman 1959, 102–3).

Knowledge, he insisted, was an end in itself and 'that alone is liberal knowledge which stands on its own pretensions, is independent of sequel, expects no complement, refuses to be *informed* (as it is called) by any end, or absorbed into any art, in order to present itself to our contemplation' (Newman 1959, 134–5). 'I consider then', he argued, 'that I am chargeable with no paradox when I speak of a knowledge which is its own end, when I call it liberal knowledge, or a gentleman's knowledge, when I educate for it and make it the scope of university' (Newman 1959, 136–7).

Nothing has done more to distance Newman from our concerns than these and other similar passages. Yet to dismiss him as trying to create on the banks of the Liffey an ideal type which hardly existed on the banks of the Isis or the Cam is entirely to mistake his intention. It is in particular to miss the irony of that famous description in the eighth discourse of the gentleman, who has opted for a modesty rather than saving grace of humility and who, though the embodiment of propriety in all departments, has in his inmost core, no heart at all (Newman 1959, 217–19). But even if, in transcendental terms, a liberal education gave everything but the one thing needful, it was still necessary to explain what it could do for a man in *this* world, hence Newman's insistence that its essential purpose was the cultivation of the trained intellect, whose proper object was 'truth of whatever kind' (Newman 1959, 170). To achieve that purpose was for him the true business of a university, but he recognised that critics would demand, as they still do, some practical return for society's investment. 'This they call making education "useful" and "utility" becomes their watchword. With a fundamental principle of this nature, they very naturally go on to ask, what is there to show for the expense of a university: what is the *real* worth on the market of the article called "a liberal education..."' (Newman 1959, 171).

Newman's answer was simple – the whole point of a liberal education was that it had no market value. Yet this did not mean that he excluded professional studies from the university, as the sequel to such an education. 'General culture of mind', he argued, was the best preparation for professional and scientific study. Moreover, a cultivated intellect not only served its own purpose, it also fulfilled a social function, in that better men made a better world. And so he reached his conclusion. 'If then a practical end must be assigned to a university course, I say it is that of training good members of society. Its art is the art of social life and its end is fitness for the world ... a university training is the greatest ordinary means to a great but ordinary end' (Newman 1959, 191).

By thus defining a liberal education and attempting to relate it to society, Newman established the themes of the debate which ran through the next three decades. It was, however, a debate less about the validity of the concept of a liberal education than about its content and purpose. At one level it was about how to assimilate the rapidly growing body of scientific knowledge. At another level it was about whether such an education should still be thought of as training an elite – and whether those so educated ought to be limited to gentlemen, however that elusive term might be defined. At yet a different level it was about whether it was the university's function to 'liberalise the professions', as the saying went, and about which professions deserved to be liberalised and which must be left to take their chance outside.

Newman was, as it were, the silent point of reference to whom conservatives and radicals related in their different ways. And this was true both of Oxford and Cambridge. For Mark Pattison, probably the most formidable, if also the most cross-grained, of the Oxford reformers, Newman's doctrine contained most things necessary for salvation. 'The schooling given at Oxford', he proclaimed in 1868, 'has always involved the idea of culture for the sake of culture. It is therefore in direct opposition to the popular notion of education for success. It is founded on a totally different view of human life and its relation to the external world' (Pattison 1868, 135–6). But Pattison recognised that there was nevertheless a collision of interests. 'The conflict of claim', he wrote, 'is that between the special and the general. Every man has either to earn his bread, or at least to fulfil his function in life, through and in a profession or calling, and for this purpose he requires the special knowledge . . . proper to that calling. Every man is also a member of civil society, a participant in the human race, is a soul or mind capable of development or perfection of its own and for this purpose he may be the subject of a general or humane training . . . Every one of us is, consciously or unconsciously, working out this double problem, to combine specialty with generality of culture' (Pattison 1868, 258).

Pattison thought that Oxford had largely solved the problem by dividing the undergraduate course about equally between general and special studies, but special studies did *not* mean vocational training. Addressing the Social Science Congress at Liverpool in 1876, he was at his most Newmanesque. 'It is no

The Idea of a University: Newman to Robbins
part of the proper purpose of a university to be a professional school', he said'. 'Universities are not to fit men for some special mode of gaining a livelihood; their object is not to teach law or divinity, banking or engineering, but to cultivate the mind and form the intelligence. A university should be in possession of all science and all knowledge, but it as science and knowledge, not as a money-bringing pursuit that it possesses it' (Pattison 1876, 61–2).*

Nor was it essentially different at the other place. To William Whewell, Master of Trinity, the object of a liberal education 'is, not to make men eminently learned or profound in some one department, but to educe all the faculties by which man shares in the highest thoughts and feelings of his species. It is to make men truly men . . .' (Whewell 1845, 1074). Anticipating Newman, Whewell felt that liberal studies must come first, with specialist studies, if any, following later. His conception was that an ideal education should contain both 'permanent' studies – that is, where knowledge was already fixed for all time – and 'progressive' studies, where the field was still expanding. Classics and mathematics, in the best Cambridge tradition, were the key 'permanent' studies, 'connecting us with past generations and fixing in our minds the stable and universal principles of Language and Reason' (Whewell 1845, 6–7).

But Cambridge had its reformers too. In 1867 appeared *Essays on a liberal education*, in which a group of writers, mainly from within the university, launched a powerful attack upon the whole system. They were headed by Henry Sidgwick, who after dismissing the unimaginative grounding in classical texts which was the nearest most young men come to a liberal education, argued for a combination of what he called a 'natural' education, teaching what would be useful in later life, and a

*Pattison was not entirely consistent on this point. In 1872, in evidence to the Devonshire Commission, he was apparently all in favour, not merely of specialist studies in arts and sciences, but also in engineering and 'outlying technical branches'. And when in 1877, a year after his Liverpool speech, a member of the Selborne Commission asked him if he considered that 'the great object of a university ought to be to produce the greatest number of useful members of society, whereby the nation at large may be most extensively benefited', he answered 'Certainly'. He did not, however, have an opportunity to develop what he would have considered 'useful' (see PP 1872, q.3785 and Sparrrow 1967, 107).

F.S.L.Lyons

liberal education revivified by including some acquaintance with the physical sciences (Farrar 1867, 139). Another of the group, John Seeley, criticised particularly the cult of the Tripos, the examination mania with which Cambridge had done more than its fair share of infecting Victorian England.'The all-worshipped Tripos produces what in fact might be called a universal suspension of the work of education. Cambridge is like a country invaded by the Sphinx. To answer the monster's conundrums has become an absorbing occupation' (Farrar 1867, 163). From outside the walls, a third contributor, Lord Houghton, denounced the existing régime for its failure to include modern languages either with, or in place, of classics. The schools would not move until they got a lead from the universities and of that he saw little hope. The defenders of the status quo were in the grip of 'a powerful literary superstition', that the dead languages were essential to the education of a governing élite. Unfortunately, the middle classes had succumbed to the same superstition and would not abandon it for snobbish reasons. It would require an academic revolution to effect a change, he thought, but the principal obstacle to this was 'the extreme self-satisfaction with which not only our national pride, but the authority of our public institutions, regards the character of the present English gentleman. He is exhibited to us an ideal of humanity, which it is almost sinful to desire to improve or transcend . . .' (Farrar 1867, 378).

The discussion now became national. It continued to be about the definition of a liberal education, but that definition was changing with a changing world. While the debate still sometimes echoed Newman, it had to face the problem of how science, indeed modern knowledge generally, was to be given its place in the university curriculum. Nor could it avoid the complaint, made urgent by the growing evidence of foreign competition, that the universities were failing the nation by their almost complete disregard of technological education. Four statements dominated the argument. Three of them – those of John Stuart Mill, T.H.Huxley and Matthew Arnold – sought to redefine the idea of a liberal education in the light of these changing circumstances, but the fourth, by Lyon Playfair, was a peremptory demand that the universities should address themselves also to professional training.

Mill's position was outlined in his much-quoted Rectorial Address to the University of St Andrews in 1867. It was a curiously Janus-like position, looking before and after. He was, however, emphatic about the point which was agitating Playfair at that very moment. Universities, Mill said flatly, were not places of professional education'. Their object is not to make skilful lawyers, or engineers, but capable and cultivated human beings'. His assumption here was very close to Newman's and his conclusion almost identical. 'What professional men will carry away from a university is not profound knowledge, but that which should direct the use of their professional knowledge, and bring the light of general culture to illuminate the technicalities of a special pursuit' (Knight 1894, 20–1).

Where he diverged from Newman was in his insistence that the scope of a liberal education should be enlarged. He wanted it to be both literary and scientific and the dispute between these two components seemed to him as absurd as if one were to argue whether a tailor should make either coats or trousers, but not both. Admittedly, specialised knowledge was increasing very fast, but he felt that people underestimated the human capacity to learn. We may feel that Mill, with his appalling childhood, was hardly the best judge of the average man's power of assimilating knowledge, but his general point is one with which anyone involved in founding new universities, from Keele through to the 1960s, would have an instinctive sympathy – that there are grave dangers in teaching a student more and more about less and less. 'His state will be worse than that of simple ignorance. Experience proves that there is no one study or pursuit which, if practised to the exclusion of all others, does not narrow and pervert the mind...' (Knight 1894, 24–5). One should therefore know something of 'all the great subjects of human interest', but the main weight should be given to classics and the physical sciences, for reasons similar to those advanced years earlier by Whewell. 'As classical literature furnishes the most perfect types of the art of expression, so do the physical sciences those of the art of thinking' (Knight 1894, 44).

With the entry of Huxley into the debate the tone became sharper. Huxley, it is usual to say, represented natural science and modernity. This is true, but it is not the whole truth. There were moments when he was close to Newman, and other moments when he was even closer to Arnold, though to contemporaries they often seemed the two contending giants of the controversy. Huxley's point of departure was that life was a struggle, or rather, as he put it to a London working-class audience in 1868, a game with 'the player on the other side' hidden. Education was the business of learning the rules of this harsh game called life. 'Nature's discipline', he said, 'is not even a word and a blow, and the blow first; but the blow without the word. It is left to you to find out why your ears are boxed'. But man did not learn everything in this hard, haphazard school. He needed an 'artificial' education to make good the defects in Nature's methods. So, 'a liberal education is an artificial education which has not only prepared a man to escape the great evils of disobedience to Nature's laws, but has trained him to appreciate and seize upon the awards which Nature has scattered with as free a hand as her penalties' (Huxley 1895, 85–6).

Had such an education ever been attempted, he asked, and answered his own question with a resounding 'No'. Certainly not in the ancient universities. 'I believe there can be no doubt', he said, 'that the foreigner who would wish to become acquainted with the scientific, or the literary, activity of modern England, would lose his time and his pains if he visited our universities with that object' (Huxley 1895, 104). And that same year he told the Select Committee on Scientific Instruction, that it was useless to look to the universities for scientific thought until the system was turned upside down. 'At present our universities make literature and grammar the basis of instruction; and they actually plume themselves when they stick a few bits of science on the outside of the fabric. Now that . . . is not real culture, nor is it what I understand by a liberal education. The thing you really have to do . . . is to invert the whole edifice and make the foundation science, and literature the superstructure and final covering' (PP 1867–8).

This sounds very like Herbert Spencer's famous question and answer, 'What knowledge is of most worth? – Science' (Spencer 1861, 53). But Huxley was much more than an obsessive propagandist for science. In his Rectorial Address at Aberdeen in 1874, for example, he outlined a university curriculum which included, besides the various natural sciences, metaphysics, logic, moral and religious philosophy and also the

The Idea of a University: Newman to Robbins
social sciences. Mindful too, perhaps, of the Scottish tradition of 'the democratic intellect', he proclaimed that universities should be places where 'all sources of knowledge and all aids to learning should be accessible to all comers, without distinction of creed or country, riches or poverty'. In such universities, the very air the student breathed should be charged 'with that enthusiasm for truth, that fanaticism of veracity which is a greater possession than learning . . . for veracity is the heart of morality' (Huxley 1895, 204).

This is close to Newman, and like Newman at his most beguiling, drifts rather far from what the actual university might be like compared with its idea. He was more to the point when in 1880 he spoke at the opening of Mason College, which twenty years later was to become the University of Birmingham. Mason had laid three injunctions upon the college – there were to be no politics, no theology, no 'mere literary instruction and education'. Taking his cue from this last prohibition, Huxley turned upon the proponents of literary culture; treating Arnold as their spokesman, while exempting him from their chauvism. Arnold had not in fact written much about the universities and what he had written had arisen mainly out of his continental research tours which had left him, like many Victorians, with a strong feeling that they ordered these things better, or best, in Germany, with its powerful professorial tradition. Reviewing H. von Sybel's *Die deutschen und die auswärtigen Universitäten* in the *Pall Mall Gazette* of 1 June 1868 he had made an unflattering comparison. 'With us the universities are at best but continuations of the sixth form of Eton, Harrow or Rugby . . . In a German university, on the other hand, the aim . . . is *science* – the concentration of the spirit upon a definite branch of knowledge, the systematic study of this branch, and, finally, the sense of a first-hand, independent sure mastery of it' (Super 1964, 331). That same year his report, *Schools and Universities on the Continent*, came out in book form and in it he took issue with the purveyors of most of the fashionable nostrums:

> The aim and office of instruction, say many people, is to make a man a good citizen, or a good Christian, or a gentleman; or it is to fit him to get on in the world, or it is to do his duty in that state of life to which he is called. It is none of these and the modern spirit more and more dis-

cerns it to be none of these. These are at best secondary and indirect aims of instruction; its prime direct aim is to enable a man *to know himself and the world*. (Super 1964, 290)

Arnold's major statement of this theme, *Culture and Anarchy*, while it did not so directly concern itself with the universities, had all the same bearing on the controversy, or so Huxley chose to think. In his Mason College speech he seized on two of Arnold's propositions – that a criticism of life is the essence of culture, and that literature, 'the best that has been thought and said in the world', contained the essential basis for such a criticism. Huxley did not quarrel with the first proposition, but he sharply rejected what he took to be the implication that criticism of life was the function of literature alone, especially if by literature was meant the classics. 'I hold very clearly', he said, 'by two convictions. The first is that neither the discipline nor the subject-matter of classical education is of such direct value to the student of physical science as to justify the expenditure of valuable time upon either; and the second is that for the purpose of attaining real culture an exclusively scientific education is as least as effective as an exclusively literary education'. As for a criticism of life, 'an army, without weapons of precision and with no particular base of operations, might more hopefully enter upon a campaign on the Rhine, than a man, devoid of a knowledge of what physical science has done in the last century, upon a criticism of life' (Huxley 1895, 143–4).

At first sight this seems a dress-rehearsal, though a highly civilised one, for the highly uncivilised Leavis-Snow encounter a century later. But Huxley and Arnold had both too broad a sympathy for the totality of culture for either to claim a monopoly.* Huxley, indeed, conceded in that same Birmingham speech that 'an exclusively scientific training will bring about a mental twist as surely as an exclusively literary training' (Huxley 1895, 153–4). And two years later, in his Rede lecture at Cambridge, Arnold insisted that Huxley was quite

* Arnold, having read Huxley's speech, wrote to him to explain that when he had defined culture as 'the best that has been thought and said in the world', he had changed 'said' to 'uttered', so as to allow for arts other than literature, but had changed back to 'said', 'for the base reason that the formula runs so much easier off the tongue with the shorter word' (Bibby 1955–6, 381).

wrong in saying that he, Arnold, wanted to assert the pre-eminence of literature.* On the contrary, 'all learning is scientific which is systematically laid out and followed up to its original sources'. In that sense, a genuine humanism was genuinely scientific. To know Greek and Latin antiquity was to know the whole of that world. Similarly, if modern literature were in question, it would be modern life one would be studying, which would include 'what in modern times has been thought and said by the great observers and knowers of nature'. So, he concluded, 'there is therefore really no question between Professor Huxley and me as to whether knowing the great results of the modern scientific study of nature is not required as part of our culture, as well as knowing the products of literature and art' (Arnold 1885, 93–5). He still disagreed, however, with those who would make science the main part of education. In effect, he said, they left out of account an important part of the essence of human nature:

> ... When we set ourselves to enumerate the powers which go to the building up of human life, and say that they are the power of conduct, the power of intellect and knowledge, the power of beauty and the power of social life and manners, he [the man of science] can hardly deny that this scheme ... does yet give a fairly true representation of the matter' (Arnold 1885, 101).

Of course, he admitted, the natural sciences had already produced significant generalisations, such as Darwin's proposition that 'our ancestor was a hairy quadruped furnished with a tail and pointed ears, probably arboreal in his habits'. Yet, as Arnold pointed out, generalisations like that belonged only to one of his categories – intellect and knowledge – and men would still want to relate what the scientists told them to 'the sense in us for conduct, the sense in us for beauty. But this the man of science will not do for us and will hardly even profess to do'. On the contrary, he argued, the need for humane letters becomes actually greater as new conceptions of the universe emerge. 'If we know the best that has been thought and uttered in the world, we shall find that the art and poetry and eloquence of men who lived, perhaps, long ago, who had the most

---

* This lecture, with some changes for local audiences, formed one of the most popular of his *Discourses in America* and it is from the American version that my quotations are drawn.

limited natural knowledge, who had the most erroneous conceptions about many important matters . . . have, in fact, not only the power of refreshing and delighting us, they have also the power . . . of wonderfully helping us to relate the results of modern science to our need for conduct, our need for beauty' (Arnold 1885, 122–3).

It was, no doubt, assertion, not proof – or rather, perhaps, an affirmation of permanent values in an age of shifting beliefs and increasingly material preocupations. But, characteristically, Arnold could not resist adapting the theory of evolution to his own ends:

> And so at last we find, it seems, we find flowing in favour of the humanities the natural and necessary stream of things, which seemed against them when we started. The 'hairy quadruped furnished with a tail and pointed ears, probably arboreal in his habits', this good fellow carried hidden in his nature apparently something to develop into a necessity for humane letters. Nay more: we seem finally to be led to the further conclusion that our hairy ancestor carried in his nature, also, a necessity for Greek.
> (Arnold 1885, 135)

Was it then a drawn battle between the scientists and the humanities? Or was it shadow-boxing and not a real battle at all? It was, I think a genuine dispute, and at times a bitterly fought one, but so far as the idea of a university was concerned, it ended in an unspoken compromise. The traditionalists clearly had to give ground and in the last quarter of the nineteenth century both Oxford and Cambridge carried through reform after reform, in curriculum and in structure, which would have been unimaginable a generation earlier, and from which they emerged to face the modern world with an enhanced reputation and their supremacy unchallenged. Not only had pure science developed in both places, though more markedly at Cambridge, which as early as 1875 took a step towards the recognition of applied science by admitting engineering as a discipline, but the two universities almost *pari passu* had begun to demonstrate a greater awareness of the world outside. The admission of women in the 1870s was, however, incomplete, an example of this increasing adaptability. So too was the beginning of university extension lectures

The Idea of a University: Newman to Robbins
by Cambridge, followed soon by Oxford, in the same period. And at Oxford also, what has been called 'the new Oxford movement' was fostering from the 1880s onward a sense of social responsibility, partly inspired by T.H.Green's ethical teachings and partly by positivist influences derived from Comte (Richter 1964 and Kent 1978). This found expression, for example, in the university settlement movement of the 1880s and also in the development, early in the new century, of the university tutorial classes and summer schools from which the Workers Educational Association in part derived.

All this indicated a reaching out and to some extent a reaching down, though the process does not seem to have extended significantly to undergraduates. The admission of women apart, there does not appear to have been much, if any, change in the composition of the undergraduate body during the nineteenth century. The evidence is admittedly incomplete, but on the basis of some well-attested Cambridge figures the traditional categories – sons of the church, of other professions, of landowners – still accounted for the majority. Neither the poor, nor, interestingly enough, the new rich, made much impact on this charmed circle (Rothblatt 1968, 86–7; Jenkins and Caradog Jones 1950; Anderson and Schnaper 1953).

Yet outside the circle things were changing. Hard questions were being asked and the answers they evoked were radically to alter the idea of a university. The most important of these questions were being put, with increasing urgency from 1867 onwards, by Lyon Playfair. Playfair, in whose education St Andrews, Glasgow and Edinburgh all had a share, was one of those numerous Victorian scientists who had received their advanced training in Germany. His own scholarly career was intermittent, though he held the chair of chemistry at Edinburgh from 1858 to 1869, and his main claim to fame was as one of the great entrepreneurs and propagandists of science. From the time of his involvement with the Great Exhibition of 1851 until his death in 1898 there were few major developments in which he did not take a prominent part. His vision of science, however differed in one important respect from Huxley's and this difference prefigured the bifurcation in the idea of a university that was now about to take place. 'The primary business of universities', Huxley told the Cowper Commission in 1892, 'has to do merely with pure knowledge and pure art –

125

independent of all application to practice; with the advancement of culture and not with the increase of wealth or commodities' (P.P. 1894). Playfair, on the other hand, asked by the government a generation earlier to report on the dismal failure of the British entries at the Paris Exhibition of 1867, emerged with the absolute conviction that the weakness of Britain compared with her successful foreign competitors was that she lacked their programmes of advanced industrial, or technical, education (Ashley 1958, 111). To remedy this deficiency became for him, the great cause of his life.

A large part of his effort was directed towards trying to persuade the universities to re-establish the links with professional training which had been their *raison d'être* in earlier times, but training extended now to include the technological expertise which he saw as a necessity of modern civilisation. He wanted them not just to tack on technical subjects to their existing curricula, but so to adapt their arts courses as to enable students of those technical subjects to receive a liberal education. 'It is', he said, 'the power of liberalising the professions that distinguishes universities from technical schools' (Playfair 1889, 373). Naturally, this would involve a significant change in the meaning and content of a liberal education, but he faced this problem with equanimity. 'If liberal culture be, as it should be, made to bear directly on the training, and not remain a mere survival of an educational condition that is only known to us in history' (Playfair 1889, 374).

Nor was this just the demand of 'a few half-educated radical reformers'. It was the demand of a changed civilisation resulting from a combination of science, free trade and democracy. 'Unless our universities go with the stream, by fitting themselves to the changed requirements of modern society, need they be astonished if society soon gets accustomed to look upon them as venerable monuments of a past age?' (Playfair 1889, 377). He did not expect much response from Oxford and Cambridge – he got none – but he repeated his warning which was, in effect, 'adapt or perish'. 'Universities should understand that if they desire society to uphold their ancient rights, they must show themselves willing to extend modern obligations to society' (Playfair 1889, 384).

The Idea of a University: Newman to Robbins

With this ringing declaration of social need Playfair was in a sense drawing the outline of the modern debate. When that debate was taken up again in earnest after the Second World War (though it had never completely died away in the interval) the basis of the argument had been changed by a whole range of developments. The scientific and technological advances that contributed to these developments, or were sometimes called into being by them, are part of Dr Nuttgens' territory and I am anxious not to encroach on a subject he will handle so much more expertly than I. All I need to say here is that partly as a result of those advances in knowledge, partly because of the growth of 'applied' research conducted under government auspices or by industry itself, and partly because of the greatly extended need for science teachers following the expansion of secondary schooling around the turn of the century, the proliferating demand for science graduates had created a new situation.

That situation was beyond the capacity, or indeed the will, of the ancient universities to control, both because the demand was too great and because their thrust, such as it was, was so strongly in the direction of pure science. Neither, for a variety of reasons, could it be adequately met by the colleges established, mainly in London, in the earlier part of the nineteenth century, though it is right to add that the foundation of the University of London in 1826 marked, in G.M. Young's phrase 'the entry of a new idea' – that a university could be used to give a training in a specific profession – 'a novelty', he adds, 'to which the examples of Germany and Scotland both contributed' (Young 1936, 93 cited in Glass 1959, 31945). More and more, therefore, the satisfaction of industry's needs came to depend upon the creation in the large manufacturing centres of, first, colleges and then universities, beginning with the establishment of Owens College in Manchester in 1851 and continuing, in other large cities, mainly during the period 1870 to 1914. From the start they were a product both of need and of civic pride. They owed much to municipal initiative and support, much to the generosity of the large industrial entrepreneurs of their localities, something to the existence of medical schools in their midst, and in certain instances something also to the seed sown by the university extension movement (Armytage 1955; Sanderson 1972, ch.2, 3).

From the moment they emerged a different definition of the idea of a university began to be heard. The subjects in which they specialised were closely related to the needs of the industrial communities which had given them birth, their students belonged to those communities and expected to make their careers there, and from the outset there was a marked emphasis upon research, generally, although not always, related to the specific problems of specific industries. However, they were by no means technical colleges and nothing else. As they developed aspirations towards university status, they necessarily widened their range of subjects, and indeed, since the production of secondary school teachers was one of the main functions, an element of diversity was inherent almost from the start. Nevertheless, their guiding principle remained very much as the Reverend J. Percival of Firth College, the forerunner of Sheffield University, laid it down in 1873. 'The first object of a college in the centre of a great industrial population', he said, 'was that it should lay hold of the life of the industrial part of the people; that its education should start from the midst of their daily occupations, teaching them things which would help them in their occupations' (Sanderson 1972, 81–2).

Although most of the civic universities were well established by 1914, it was the First World War that first gave them a widely recognised national role. 'When the story of the scientific side of the war comes to be written', said *The Times*, 'it will be found that our modern universities have woven themselves into the very fabric of our national life in a way which had never been open to them before' (*The Times*, 9 Feb. 1916, cited in Sanderson 1972, 239). Oxford and Cambridge had also made substantial contributions and Imperial College, formed in 1907 from the mid-nineteenth century South Kensington science colleges, had particularly distinguished itself, but it was the civic universities which benefited most in terms of national satisfaction. After the war, the links with industry and with government-sponsored research continued and sometimes strengthened. It became widely accepted that the universities could help, not only with training scientists and engineers, not only with research, but also with the provision of graduates, from arts as well as from other disciplines, destined for the higher level of management.

The Idea of a University: Newman to Robbins

But soon the post-war euphoria faded and critics began to complain of what was coming to be regarded as an excessive involvement with industry. As early as 1927 Lord Rutherford had used his formidable authority to warn Bristol University that 'he would view as an unmitigated disaster the utilisation of university laboratories for research bearing on industry' (Sanderson 1972, 307). Other critics, the American, Abraham Flexner (1930, 255–6), and the English political scientist, Sir Ernest Barker (1932), for example, deplored the tendency in unmeasured terms. Barker in particular interrupted an otherwise bland account of the English universities (written in 1931) with the prophetic remark that England might be about to overvalue her universities by regarding them as a source of solutions for all sorts of ills. 'Those who know our universities best', he said, 'are haunted by the fear that democratic enthusiasm, as genuine as it is ill-informed, may result in an attempt to increase the quantity of university education at the expense of its quality' (Barker 1932, 96–7). It is easy nowadays to dismiss this resistance to technology as obscurantist, but underneath the patronising tone in which it was too often expressed, there was a genuine concern that universities, by committing themselves too wholeheartedly to the material needs of society, or of the state, could end by losing their freedom to pursue what knowledge they liked how they liked. But while the concern was justified, the dismissive attitude was not. The industrial and technological links established in the nineteenth century had for good or ill created an alternative idea of the university; the tragedy of the traditionalists was that although they could see it they could not come to terms with it.*

The gap between the two conceptions was widened by the Second World War, or rather, the balance between them was as a consequence much more heavily weighted in terms of social need. Once again the universities gave of their best and once again their indispensability was gratefully acknowledged. As

* For example, the historian, Sir Charles Grant Robertson who, as Vice Chancellor of Birmingham, vigorously defended the new disciplines and the new universities. 'The hardest task imposed on the universities today', he wrote, 'is to convince the nation as a whole that they are not laboratories of knowledge but – a very different thing – laboratories of life' (Grant Robertson 1930, 65).

F.S.L.Lyons

the UGC put it in 1948: 'The contributions which the universities were able to make in many fields of wartime activity won for them a new prestige and a place in the national esteem which it will be their ambition to retain in the period of reconstruction which has now begun' (UGC 1948, 16).

What this meant in practice was that the universities, having proved their value, would have to go on proving it by agreeing to an enlargement, certainly of their numbers, probably also of their functions. The stages by which these enlargements were achieved in the twenty years after the war are too familiar to need reiteration. It is enough to recall that full-time student numbers, which had been about 50,000 in 1939, had risen to just over 169,000 by 1965–6; that government expenditure on recurrent grants had risen from £7 million in 1946–7 to £22 million in 1956–6; and that non-recurrent grants, almost unknown before the war, stood at £80 million in 1965–6.

How was the idea of a university transformed between 1945 and the publication of the Robbins report in 1963 by this expansion and by the profound changes of attitude which it brought about? The debate had in fact begun before the war was over. In 1943 'Bruce Truscot' published his *Redbrick university*, which was partly an acute and sometimes mordant account of the anatomy of a civic university, and partly an attempt to redress the balance between the ancient and the modern universities.* Essentially, he demanded a levelling out of resources, so that instead of two large, wealthy, residential universities and nine poorer ones, mainly non-residential, there should be eleven of about equal size, all predominantly residential, with standards of admission about on a par, with individual institutions establishing themselves as the best in certain fields, and with a free interchange of students between them whenever that was in the students' interest (Truscot 1944, 37).

Apart from the fact that it failed to anticipate the great expansion after the war, much of this must have seemed impractical even at the time, though the proposals for centres of excellence and for student mobility were to recur in the Robbins report.

* In the 1944 edition entitled *Red brick university*, there is a note indicating that in the first edition the title was incorrectly given as *Redbrick university*, but as the text of the 1944 edition retains the familiar usage, *Redbrick*, I have done the same.

But the idea of a university underlying these suggestions was firmly traditional. 'A university' Bruce Truscot wrote, 'is a corporation or society which devotes itself to a search after knowledge for its own intrinsic value' (Truscot 1944, 45). In this definition 'a search after knowledge for its own intrinsic value' was for him the all-important phrase. Research would be combined with teaching, of course, and the two together would contribute to the formation both in teachers and taught, of character. 'For', he said, 'the discipline of conscientious teaching and application to learning cannot but make men better', an assertion which almost suggests that he had never seen the inside of a common room, if his sharp remarks about the indolence of certain Redbrick professors were not there to show that he had (Truscot 1944, 49). But what was novel, if also naive, about his book was its deliberate attempt to fuse two traditions which in modern times had been quite distinct.

In the event, the opening of the floodgates after the war made Bruce Truscot's reflections almost irrelevant. In the same year that *Redbrick university* was published, the white paper, *Educational Reconstruction*, argued that 'the aim of national policy must be to ensure that high ability is not handicapped by place of residence or lack of means of securing a university education' (cited in Glass 1962, 404). This was easier to proclaim than to achieve and twenty years later the Robbins Committee had still to lay down 'as an axiom' that courses of higher education should be available for all qualified and wishing to pursue them (Robbins Committee Report 1963, 8). But even if the post-war expansion was socially unbalanced, its size and speed put an immediate strain upon the universities, resulting sometimes in an almost panic-stricken loss of any clear sense of identity. This was the major theme of Sir Walter Moberly's much-discussed book, *The crisis in the university*, when it appeared in 1949.*

As chairman of the University Grants Committee from 1935

---

* Nowadays, we are told, the book would 'almost never be mentioned as relevant to the "crisis" defined in contemporary discussion ... because of its focus on the religious traditions of the universities' (Halsey 1968–9, 147n.11). This seems a slightly perverse verdict on a work which, though indeed written from a Christian standpoint, not only treated the Christian tradition as one among several, but also made it clear that it could no longer be resuscitated as the dominant tradition.

to 1949 Moberly had presided over the hectic first phase of the post-war expansion, and this experience undoubtedly coloured his book. In it he emerges as a humanist trying to come to terms with technology and not really succeeding. Admittedly, he wrote, technology had at least the merit of being in touch with contemporary culture, defined in Ortega y Gasset's terms as 'the vital system of ideas of a period' (1946, 44). Its aims were clear and straightforward – 'the conquest of nature for the satisfaction of human needs'. It had its own virtues – it was empirical, it was analytic, it had a sense of power, a sense of progress, and it was undeniably attractive to many students to whom opportunities for higher education were just being opened up. Nevertheless, he viewed it with undisguised alarm. 'We had the Classical-Christian university, which was later replaced by the liberal university. This in turn has been undermined, but not as yet superseded, by the combined influence of democratisation and technical achievement. What we have, in fact, today is the chaotic university'. The combined onset of democracy and technology were producing a new culture, quite different from that in which the universities had taken their familiar shape. 'It condemns liberalism as being aristocratic and fastidious, rather than equalitarian, detached rather than "mucking in" and as exalting a sterile scholarship rather han being frankly occupational and utilitarian. It regards "learning for learning's sake" as an idol to be demolished. In its light the Renaisssance humanist is as little a model as the medieval schoolman . . .' (Moberly 1949, 50).

Holding these views Moberly was unlikely to formulate an idea of the university in modern social terms. On the contrary, he argued that with an influx of new students coming into the system who lacked any inherited wisdom, it was more important than ever to insist on the traditional values. The university's distinctive responsibility 'is to be the university; that is, to be a place where the criticism and evaluation of ideas is constantly being carried forward . . . and where the intellectual virtues rooted in sincerity of mind are being fostered and transmitted' (Moberly 1949, 127). This implied not only the autonomy of the universities as institutions, but also that they should be the arenas in which the intellectual issues of the day were fought out. Yet, while freedom of expression was thus a necessity, that did not mean that universities were neutral on

The Idea of a University: Newman to Robbins

all issues. They should insist on certain fundamental values:

> Some of these basic values are academic; a passion for truth, thoroughness in pursuing it to the bitter end, a delicate precision in analysis, a judicial temper, a willingness to learn from all quarters, an uncompromising insistence on freedom of utterance . . . Other values basic for the university are those common to the whole community in which it is set. For British universities they include recognition of some absolute moral obligation . . . an ingrained respect for law and order, and an unshakeable conviction that 'people matter' (Moberly 1949, 298–9).

Whether one feels that he is here reiterating permanent truths or simply clichés that were already embarrassingly limp when he uttered them, one cannot escape the conviction that history had already passed him by. Moreover, his book suffered from a fundamental confusion. He seemed, as Michael Oakeshott pointed out, to want two conflicting things for the university – that it should provide guidance for the world and that it should also reflect and be shaped by the world. Failing to reconcile the irreconcilable, he had no convincing advice to offer about how the universities should relate to a society seriously transformed by technology (Oakeshott 1948–9, 515–42).

Of those who tried to address themselves seriously to that question in the pre-Robbins era, Sir Eric Ashby, as he then was, was perhaps the most notable. In his book, *Technology and the academics* (1958), he faced directly what was becoming the central issue in the redefinition of the idea of a university, how to combine the functions which had accumulated historically but were now jostling for supremacy, or in some cases for survival. As he saw them, the functions were fourfold – professional training in the old sense; the training of leaders; the preservation and advancement of knowledge; and, as he put it, to be a 'staff college' for technical specialists. Trying to marry these functions posed a dilemma which the universities must confront. 'On the one hand they cannot bring themselves to refuse the responsibilities laid upon them by society, nor the large financial grants which accompany these responsibilities. On the other hand they cling to their traditional organisation and curricula in the hope that the values for which the universities have stood since the Middle Ages may be preserved among the automatic factories and social planning and satellite-ridden atmosphere of the third millennium' (Ashby 1958, 68—9).

For him the absorption of the higher technology into the universities was the supreme example of the problem which had haunted them since the nineteenth century, the problem of how to reconcile the two antitheses of science versus humanism, and liberal (or general) versus specialised education. Both of these antitheses he regarded as false and unnecessary. The first, 'partly because scientists no longer regard science as an alternative to humanism or as inconsistent with it, and partly because much teaching and research in the humanities could not by any stretch of the imagination be regarded as humanism'. And the second, because the debate between specialism and generalism seemed to him to have lost sight of the essence of the matter, that 'liberality ... is a spirit of pursuit, not a choice of subject' (Ashby 1958, 75—7). So he now rephrased his alternatives more bluntly:

> Our predecessors in the 1860s would have understood our dilemma. for it is similar to their own; if the university repudiates the call of the technologists, it will not survive; if it repudiates the cultivation of non-practical values, it will cease to merit the title of university (Ashby 1958, 78).

His solution was not essentially different from that advocated by Lyon Playfair eighty years earlier. 'In order to adapt itself to an age of technological specialisation, the university must use specialised studies as a vehicle for a liberal education'. Out of this would come what he called 'technological humanism', that is, the habit of apprehending a technology in its completeness. If technology were so studied, with due regard for human and environmental problems for example, it could become a bridge between the humanities and science, on the ground, which some scientists might question, that technology was concerned with man and society, whereas in science the human element was eliminated as far as possible (Ashby 1958, 81—2). Sir Eric Ashby shared with many scientists the facile notion that for a marriage with the humanities to take place, it would be for the humanities to make the necessary adjustments, though this, he admitted, would be difficult, for the ironic reason that they had become too imitative of the sciences in their own disciplines.*A solution to the problem

The Idea of a University: Newman to Robbins
was urgent, however, because if the universities did not solve it they would soon be at the mercy of external forces beyond their control. But they must solve it in a way compatible with their continued existence as universities:

> The danger is not that universities will fail to respond adequately to the short-term demands of an age of technology: it is just the opposite danger: that in responding so readily and so efficiently they will run the risk of a self-disintegration through too facile an adaptation to tomorrow's world. Whether faculties of arts (as custodians of Renaissance humanism) can save universities from this danger of maladaptation is the major question arising from the expansion of technology in the universities today.
> (Ashby 1958, 88)

It was, as he said himself, the familiar antithesis between service-station and ivory tower, though by 1960 that antithesis was fast becoming out of date. Most universities were already part service-stations while still yearning to be part ivory towers. But to keep the two conceptions in balance was increasingly difficult, the more so because, as the Robbins Committe pointed out, there was no coherent system to which the universities could relate, 'if by system is meant a consciously co-ordinated organisation' (Robbins Committee Report 1963, 4). That committee's brief was to survey the whole range of higher education and to suggest at any rate the framework of a system for the future. The implementation and non-implementation of its recommendations lie outside the scope of this paper, but its ruling assumptions do concern us, since they permeate the idea of a university as it was conceived in a report which has been widely, perhaps excessively, regarded as a watershed in the history of the British higher education.

At the outset the Committee adopted certain aims and principles. They identified four aims which any properly balanced system should seek to achieve. The first was to provide instruction in necessary skills, and to obtain this they recognised was the main object of most young people coming to the university. 'Confucius said in the Analects that it was not easy to find a

---

* They were, he said, doing with grammar and documents what scientists and technologists can already do with formulae and instruments ... It is a sort of celibacy of the intellect [A. N. Whitehead's phrase], as inimical to a liberal education in arts as it is in science.

man who has studied for three years without aiming at pay'. This implied a concentration on specialist training, but the second aim was that 'what is taught should be taught in such a way as to promote the general powers of the mind. The aim should be to produce not mere specialists, but rather cultivated men and women'. Third was the aim of the advancement of learning, never indeed a monopoly of the universities, but still an essential function. And finally, there was what they called 'the transmission of a common culture and common standards of citizenship'. They emphasised this cliché, even though by the time they reported in 1963 such a common culture was as hard to discern as Confucius' man studying three years without aiming at pay. Their guiding principles were more widely drawn. They included, of course, the free availability of higher education for all able and willing to pursue it; equality of academic awards for equal performance; the removal of differentiation between institutions performing similar functions; mobility of students as between one institution and another; the free development of institutions within a framework of order and subject to due provision for a rational allocation of resources; and, above all, the maintenance of standards and the production of 'as much high excellence as possible' (Robbins Committee Report 1963, 6–10).

From all this it would seem that the Committee laboured to preserve a balance between the traditional view of the university and the concept of social need. Three of their recommendations had a particular bearing upon this balance. The first was that the Colleges of Advanced Technology should become technological universities and that five Special Institutions for Scientific and Technological Education and Research should be developed on the continental and American models. This last suggestion was only very partially realised, but with the elevation of the CATS, not only was the number of universities greatly increased, but the swing towards technology was accentuated, with the result that those institutions which had developed on traditional lines and wished to maintain traditional values, felt themselves more than ever on the defensive. The second recommendation, that the universities should supply some 350,000 student places by 1980–81, aroused an immediate outcry that this could not be done without a serious lowering of standards, that what the report itself described as 'the so-called pool of ability' simply was not there, in short that, in Kingsley Amis's immortal phrase, 'more means worse'. It is not possible to enter here into the statistical warfare that then developed, but it is obvious that whatever the projections might be, the universities were bound to be subjected in the coming years to extreme pressure of numbers arising from the combination of 'bulge' (the rise in the post-war birthrate) and 'trend', the tendency for children to stay on longer at school in the hope of obtaining a university place. When it becomes possible to view this influx with more detachment than at present, it may well turn out to have been the decisive factor tilting the balance finally against the survival of the traditional university in the modern world.

The third recommendation, it is true, may have swung that balance back again in some degree, though how far or how permanently it is difficult even to be sure. The Committee argued for an increase in graduate studies and to help this to come about wanted to see the emergency of a larger number and variety of broad, i.e., less specialised, first degree courses. As Lord Robbins himself said, universities in the future need not strive to be comprehensive in the old sense. They should pay more attention to graduate studies and make their undergraduate studies less overloaded. 'While I am all for the cultivation of an elite', he said, 'in my Utopia the elite starts in the graduate school rather than at the undergraduate level' (Robbins 1966, 90).

This broadening of courses had already begun in the new universities which were coming into being entirely without reference to the Robbins Committee, partly in response to government anxiety that the existing institutions would be unable to absorb the rising numbers caused by 'bulge' and 'trend', and partly because of vigorous local initiatives for a wider geographical spread of university opportunities. All the speakers in this section of the conference have been connected with this movement for the foundation of the new universities, and I, and I am sure Professors Gregor and Nuttgens also, can fully endorse the interdisciplinary principles set out so lucidly in the Sussex context by Professor Briggs (as he then was) in the essay, 'Drawing a new map of learning' (Griggs 1964, 60–80). My colleagues may well wish to refer to this themselves, but without wishing to trespass too much on their territory, I must make two brief comments. The first is that we were generally agreed in the new universities that the old antithesis between 'general' and 'specialised' education was outdated and must be rejected. Immense pains were taken in devising degree courses in which both specialisation and general education were seen as parts of a balanced and, we hoped, reasonably harmonious whole. And my second point is that both the planning and the teaching were a constant struggle against the ingrained specialism both of the undergraduates and the academics. Although in making our first appointments we succeeded in finding people with a genuine interdisciplinary bent, the time soon came when the supply of these splendid Renaissance all-rounders dried up and the old departmental specialists reappeared on our doorsteps; we had no option but to appoint them, sometimes with disintegrating effects. Therefore, although the new universities were and are a most interesting blend of the traditional and the innovative, representing an attempt to give the old idea of a university fresh life in a modern setting, the success of the endeavour was always, and is now more than ever, precarious.

The theme of expansion – as a *fortiori* the succeeding theme of contraction – brings us back remorselessly to Sir William Hamilton's dictum of the state having the power to correct, reform or recast the university. Historically, as we know, that power was used in the nineteenth century for limited purposes, although quite effectively within those limitations. Between the two world wars, and for about twenty years thereafter, the state was kept at a comfortable distance by the dual device of the 'bufffer' – the University Grants Committee – and the block grant which left the universities large freedom in disposing of the money allotted to them.

With the post-war expansion, increasing governmental intervention was inevitable. The Committee of Vice-Chancellors recognised this as early as 1946, when they accepted that 'the Government has not only the right, but the duty, to satisfy itself that every field of study is in fact being cultivated in the university system and that the resources which are being placed at the disposal of the universities are being used with full regard to efficiency and economy' (Briggs 1969, 97–107). If this possibly too abject kissing of the rod did no immediate damage, it may have been because the UGC was then the direct

The Idea of a University: Newman to Robbins
concern of the Treasury, which generally supported it in its dealings with the government and with the Public Accounts Committee (UGC 1968, 576–7). There was, after all, some point to the comment of Harold Dodds, President of Princeton, that '... the facetious observation that the Committee succeeds only because its members, the chief Treasury officials, and the Vice-Chancellors, are all members of the Athenaeum really expressed a deep truth' (Armytage 1955, 302). This cosy relationship was certain to change as times got harder, but, despite occasional earlier friction, it was not until after the UGC was transferred from the Treasury to the then Ministry of Education that the screw really began to tighten.*

Primarily, no doubt, this was a consequence of the academic situation. But although the full effects were not felt until some years after the limits of this paper, it was already obvious by the mid-1960s, with the growing involvement of government in university affairs, that what was at stake in the new circumstances was the old principle of academic freedom. By this was meant not so much the traditional freedom of the individual to teach and to pursue research and to publish, for this has not been seriously threatened except, latterly, in the fundamental sense that the freedom is curtailed, or ended, if financial stringency dictates that there is ultimately no job in which to exercise it. The fear rather was that the autonomy of institutions would be fatally impaired by the pressure of the state in demanding responses to immediate and not always correctly perceived needs, that were not necessarily those which universities, left to themselves, would have felt it part of their function to make. As long ago as 1949 Sir Walter Moberly had foreseen that the power of the purse did indeed give governments an irresistible instrument for controlling policy, but he commented, in words that now have a distinctly ironic ring: 'It has been an accepted maxim that any serious infringement of

---

* As examples one need only mention the UGC's sponsorship of the ill-conceived attempt in 1966–67 to elicit from academics a record of how they spent their time, a fatuity which was widely interpreted to mean that the UGC had 'changed sides', or the final success in 1967 of the prolonged pressure to have university accounts submitted to the Comptroller and Auditor-General; or the progressive collapse of the quinquennial grant system and the general near-paralysis of concerted planning from the late 1960s onward. For this see Caine 1969, 191–205.

university autonomy would be too high a price to pay for increased co-ordination and efficiency' (Maberly 1949, 227). The Robbins Committee, it is true, came out strongly in favour of autonomy and in 1963 this was still more or less intact. But twenty years on it is hard to avoid the conclusion that it is an irrretrievably lost cause (see Annan 1967, 24–43).

With the publication of the Robbins report in 1963 we arrive at a real divide across which the historian can as yet peer only dimly at a future which for his contemporaries is already of their past. All he can say in conclusion is that although the groves of Academe, like Prospero's island, are full of noises, three voices in particular seemed then to be especially audible.

First, the voice of those who still maintained that the universities must go on insisting that to play a functional role in society is not their primary business. One forceful exponent of this view, Michael Oakeshott, while conceding that universities cannot be entirely insulated, that there must always be some approximation to the world outside, wrote this in 1949:

> The doctrine that the university should move step by step with, or at the same speed and partaking in every eccentricity of the world's fashion, is a piece of progressive superstition and not to be tolerated by any sane man. Keeping up to date with the world is ... an ideal which is subject to two important qualificatiosns: the world must offer something which at least seems to be desirable as a model to be copied by an existing university, and the activity of approximation must be carried out in a manner that does not entail a loss of identity (Oakeshott 1948–9, 523).

Nor has the argument lost its edge since then. A decade after Robbins, Kenneth Minogue made precisely the same point. 'There is an important and neglected sense', he wrote, 'in which the belief that universities are ivory towers – an image seldom evoked these days without sneer or repudiation – is precisely true'. 'Universities', he also observed, 'can only preserve their identity if they steer by the academic; without it their increasing involvement with society makes them helpless pursuers of incoherent desirabilities' (Minogue 1973, 76, 60). This doctrine, of course, is immensely attractive to academics and probably still corresponds to what many would like to believe. The historian cannot predict what its fate will be, but he has to point out that a voluntary return to the chastity and poverty which this would entail (much greater poverty than is now being experienced) seems impracticable and would almost certainly be rejected in practice even by a majority of those who glibly subscribe to the doctrine.

Secondly, though more loudly in the late 1960s than ever before, was to be heard the voice of those who would regard the universities as citadels of privilege, bourgeois strongholds dedicated to upholding the capitalist status quo. Such critics would argue that progress could only be achieved, as one of them has stated, 'by breaking the domination of the whole educational system by universities which are dedicated to the academic ideal' (Robinson 1969, 92 cited in Minogue 1973, 54). Whether their domination was to be broken by mending them or ending them was not always evident, but at least it was becoming clear that the redefinition of the idea of a university in the post-Robbins era would have to take into account that one such idea is simply to have no university at all, at least in any of its traditional forms.

Finally, and still, as usual, the loudest voice of all, was the voice of those who would fall somewhere between these two extremes. Recognising that the university has shown great adaptability in the past, they have been fertile in suggesting ways in which it can still do so in the future (see, for example, Perkin 1974, 389–403). They would accept the view that the university had become so thoroughly involved with satisfying social need in an age which demands that service imperatively that there could be no going back. All that could be done would be to make the best of the situation as one found it. It would be a situation in which the old cry 'Hands off the universities' would no longer have any meaning. As Sir Eric Ashby put it, since nothing was more certain than that hands would be laid on the universities, it was for academics to seek to ensure that the hands of fellow academics would be prominent among the hands so laid. Only by that dangerous but necessary road of co-operation, the protagonists of that policy would say, could even an acceptable minimum of autonomy be salvaged (Ashby 1968).

That these, and doubtless many other, schools of thought will go on contending without resolving the issue is not only obvious and inevitable, it is also right. 'No consensual answer is possible', as has been said, 'perhaps because the university is no longer the citadel of the traditional mode ... but an arena in which the critics outside the Academy, have like the tiger (or Tyger) once outside the gates of society, found a place – deservedly – within. And the tension between past and future, mind and sensibility, tradition and experience, for all its strains and discomfitures, is the only source for maintaining the independence of inquiry itself' (Bell 1966, 149 cited in Niblett 1974, 168).

But at the end of it all, the independence of inquiry will depend upon the upholding of standards of integrity and excellence by individual scholars in individual institutions. Because, even if society at large has no common culture in the sense in which the Robbins Committee assumed it, there is still a common academic culture embracing the methods and the style by which knowledge must be preserved, transmitted and advanced, and the maintenance of this common culture remains the highest function of the university.

For all its vicissitudes, then, for all its diversity of outward form, the idea of a university as a place of vigorous and disinterested inquiry has shown remarkable tenacity and consistency. And it is fitting at the end of our inquiry that Lord Robbins should join hands with Newman in defining those of its activities which, as Robbins said, most of us would agree are good in themselves:

> To attempt to understand the world, to contemplate and analyse its values – these are activities which, even if they were never associated with practical advantage, would still lend dignity and meaning to life on this planet, and in our own day, with the visible crumbling of the ascendancy of so many of the more dogmatic creeds, it is perhaps in such activities, in such *milieux*, that the life of the spirit seems to flourish with least inhibition and with most intensity (Robbins 1966, 5).

So indeed it has flourished in this great University of Edinburgh. And we, who gather here to celebrate your four hundredth anniversary, do so, not only in a spirit of congratulation, but also with a sense of gratitude, that at a dark hour you have in your history given us a symbol of the capacity of the university to be a liberal place of learning – and to survive.

REFERENCES

Annan, Lord (1967) Higher education, in *Essays on reform, 1967: a centenary tribute* (ed. B. Crick). Oxford.

Anderson, C. A. and Schnaper, M. (1953) *School and Society in England*. Washington.

Armytage, W. H. G. (1955) *The civic universities*. London.

Arnold, M. (1885) *Discourses in America*. London.

Ashby, Sir E. (1958) *Technology and the academics*. London.

— (1968) *Hands off the universities?* London.

Barker, Sir E. (1932) Universities in Great Britain, in *The University in a changing world* (eds W. Kotschnig and E. Prys). Oxford. The essay had been published separately the previous year.

Bell, D. (1966) *The reforming of general education*. New York.

Bibby, C. (1955-6) T. H. Huxley's idea of a university. *Universities Quarterly* x.

Briggs, A. (1964) Drawing a new map of learning, in *The idea of a new university: an experiment in Sussex* (ed. D. Daiches). London.

— Development in higher education in the United Kingdom: nineteenth and twentieth centuries, in *Higher education: demand and response* (ed. W. R. Niblett). London.

Caine, Sir S. (1969) *British universities: purpose and prospects*. London.

Farrar, F. W. (ed.) (1867) *Essays on a liberal education*. London.

Flexner, A. (1930) *Universities, American, English, German*. New York.

Glass, D. V. (1959) Education, in *Law and opinion in England in the twentieth century* (ed. M. Ginsberg). Berkeley and Los Angeles.

— (1962) Education and social change in modern England, in *Education, economy and society* (eds A. H. Halsey, J. Floud and C. A. Anderson), 2nd ed. New York.

Grant Robertson, Sir C. (1930) *The British universities*. London.

Halsey, A. H. (1968-9) The universities and the state. *Universities Quarterly* xxiii.

Hamilton, Sir W. (1853) *Discussions on philosophy and literature, education and university reform*, 2nd ed. London and Edinburgh. Published originally in *Edinburgh review* (Jan. 1835), IX, No.122, 422-45, as part of the article 'On the right of Dissenters to admission into the English universities (supplemental)'.

Huxley, T. H. (1895) *Science and education: essays*. London.

Jenkins, H. and Caradog Jones, D. (1950) The Social class of Cambridge University alumni of the eighteenth and nineteenth centuries. *British Journal of Sociology* i.

Kent, C. (1978) *Brains and numbers*. Toronto University Press.

Knight, W. (ed.) (1894) *Rectorial addresses delivered at the University of St. Andrew's ... 1863-1893*. London.

Minogue, K. R. (1973) *The concept of a university*. London.

Moberly, Sir W. (1949) *The crisis in the university*. London.

Newman, J. H. (1959) *The idea of a university*. Image Books, New York.

Niblett, W. R. (1974) *Universities between two worlds*. London.
Oakeshott, M. (1948-9) The universities. *The Cambridge Journal* i.
Ortega y Gasset, J. (1946) *Mission of the university* (trans. H. L. Norstrand). London.
PP (1867-8) *Report from the Select Committee on Scientific Instruction, together with the proceedings of the Committee, minutes of evidence and appendix*, x.
— (1872) *Report of the Royal Commission on Scientific Instruction (Devonshire)*, xxv.
— (1894) *Report of the Royal Commissioner appointed to consider the draft charter for the proposed Gresham University in London . . . evidence, appendices and index*, [c.7425], xxxiv.
Pattison, M. (11868) *Suggestions on academical organisation*. Edinburgh.
— (1877) Address on Education, in *Transactions of the National Association for the promotion of Social Science . . . 1876*. London.
Perkin, H. (1974) Adaptation to change in British universities. *Universities Quarterly* (autumn), xxviii.
Playfair, L. (1889) *Subjects of social welfare*. London.
Richter, M. (1964) *The politics of conscience: T. H. Green and his age*. Harvard University Press, Cambridge.
Robbins Committee Report (1963) *Higher education, report of the committee appointed by the prime minister under the chairmanship of Lord Robbins, 1961-63*, Cmd.2154. London.
Robbins, Lord (1966) *The university in the modern world*. London.
Robinson, E. (1969) *The new polytechnics*. London.
Rothblatt, S. (1968) *The revolution of the dons*. London.
Sanderson, M. (1972) *The universities and British industry, 1850-1970*. London.
Sparrow, J. (1967) *Mark Pattison and the idea of a university*. Cambridge.
Spencer, H. (1861) *Education, intellectual, moral and physical*. London.
Super, R. H. (ed.) (1964) *The complete prose works of Matthew Arnold, IV. Schools and universities on the continent*. Ann Arbor.
Truscot, B. (1944) *Redbrick university*, 2nd edn. London.
UGC (1948) *University development from 1935 to 1947*. London.
— (1968) *University development, 1962-7*, Cmd.3820. London.
Whewell, W. (1845) *Of a liberal education in general*. London.
Young, G. M. (1936) *Victorian England*. Oxford.

LIBERAL EDUCATION: AN OUTWORN IDEAL?

IAN GREGOR

This is a paper written for a precise context. Its aim is to provide a link between the descriptive sketch which was drawn by Professor Lyons in his lecture 'The Idea of a University: Newman to Robbins' and the general discussion which that lecture is intended to provoke. My particular brief is to say something about the nature and fortunes of liberal education during this period. I have attempted to reflect on the general character of the debate which a discussion of liberal education invariably seems to provoke, and to take for particular illustration, the most recent and elaborate development of university education, the foundation, some twenty years ago, of nine entirely new universities – seven in England, one in Scotland and one in Northern Ireland. This is very much a working paper intended to emphasise and develop certain aspects of university education, as these will arise in the evolving discussion of the conference.

I begin with a moment in English fiction. It occurs in Hardy's novel *Jude the Obscure*, published in 1895. Jude, frustrated in his attempt to enter the groves of academe in the shape of the university of Oxford, finds himself gazing out of the lantern tower, high up in the Sheldonian theatre:

> He always remembered the appearance of the afternoon on which he awoke from his dream. Not quite knowing what to do with himself, he went up to an octagonal chamber in the lantern of a singularly built theatre that was set amidst this quaint and singular city. It had windows all round, from which an outlook over the whole town and its edifices could be gained. Jude's eyes swept all the views in succession, meditatively, mournfully, yet sturdily. Those buildings and their associations and privileges were not for him. From the looming roof of the great library, into which he hardly ever had time to enter, his gaze travelled on to the varied spires, halls, gables, streets, chapels, gardens, quadrangles, which composed the ensemble of this unrivalled panorama. He saw that his destiny lay not with these, but among the manual toilers in the shabby

purlieu which he himself occupied, unrecognized as part of the city at all by its visitors and panegyrists, yet without whose denizens the hard readers could not read nor the high thinkers live.

For anyone invited to reflect on the shifting currents in university education in the course of the last century, that description can hardly fail to have exemplary force. 'The unrivalled panorama', reveals to Jude, a world starkly divided; on one side, fine architecture, gardens, chapels, the great library – all enclosed by high walls; on the other, almost out of sight, a huddle of buildings and streets, 'a shabby purlieu', home to those whom the walls have excluded. 'The great library ... the manual toilers', the polarities of contemplation and action, privilege and dispossession, offer themselves to Jude, but the communication lines have been cut. The note of social criticism sounds sharply, and yet as we come to reflect upon it, it becomes less sharp, less obvious. If we were to ask whether Jude feels that the walls should be razed to admit 'the toilers', whether 'the unrivalled panorama' should be extended to include 'the shabby purlieu', then I think we would have to admit that neither Jude, nor his creator, would welcome the transformation.

It is easy to make a political point and say that Jude, for all his radicalism is at heart a supporter of the *status quo*. That may be true, but what is interesting about the passage is the way in which it goes beyond the political – or at least, the political in any immediate sense of that word. It exhibits a tension between a cultural awareness of what is embodied within that 'unrivalled panorama' and an awareness of the price that has to be paid for it, both literally and in terms of privilege. The lantern tower offers Jude a sharp lesson in the politics of learning.

At the heart of that lesson lies the notion of liberal education. The term provokes all the rallying challenges of educational controversy; the maintenance of standards or the defence of privilege; the free play of mind or the abdication of commitment; the criticism of the social order or its tacit endorsement; a preparation for action or the disparagement of action. Point and counterpoint – the list could be considerably extended, but the drift of the controversy is clear. What I would like to do is to enquire whether there is anything inherently in the notion itself that prompts this kind of debate. Certainly, this particular

Liberal Education: an outworn ideal?

debate about education has a curious air about it, as if it proceeds from certain logical assumptions from which it then begins to part company. Both sides impute a measure of bad faith, a concealed motive – but what if the very discussion about education itself, brings with it an ambivalence of attitude, a larger gesture than we can ever hope to convincingly argue for?

I want to look at three very different kinds of examples, to see if we can see this cross-grained effect in detail as it were. I have chosen these examples because although completely different in kind, and in scale, they all involve centrally the role of liberal education. The first is the general historical debate, which Professor Lyons describes in his lecture; the second is a local instance, an exchange of views published in *The Times* a few months ago; and the third is neither a large-scale general debate, nor a specific instance of it, but the role that certain ideas seemed to play when translated into a precise series of actions in the establishment of what are usually described as 'the new universities'.

The initial impression made by a sketch of the direction taken by university education in the period from Newman to Robbins is that for all the complexity of detail, the outline of the plot is stark and simple. The emphases are returned to again and again, and if the plot was to have a title it would surely be Academic Freedom v. Social Need. Contained within those phrases are others which time has worn smooth – knowledge its own end, social relevance, humanist ideals, vocational skills, the two cultures – but the essential conflict comes through insistently, powerfully, and almost without interruption. Let us catch the characteristic tones of the debate at an early stage. The auditors, on this particular occasion, are the students of St Andrews and they are listening in 1867 to their new rector, John Stuart Mill:

> There is a tolerably general argument about what a university is not. It is not a place of professional education. Universities are not intended to teach knowledge in order to fit men for some special mode of gaining their livelihood. Their object is not to make skilful lawyers, or physicians, or engineers, but equable and cultivated human beings ... Men are men, before they are lawyers, or physicians, or merchants, or manufacturers, and if you will

make them equable and sensible men, they will make themselves capable and sensible lawyers or physicians.
(Moberly 1949)

A year or so later they were to listen to the no less passionate tones of J. A. Froude:

You cannot learn everything, the objects of knowledge have multiplied beyond the powers of the strongest mind to keep pace with them all. You must choose among them, and the only reasonable guide to choice in such matters is utility... What I deplore in our present higher education is the devotion of so much effort and so many precious years to subjects which have no practical bearing upon life.
(Ashby 1958)

Here are pure and uncluttered instances of sentiments which are to be heard again and again – 'men are men before they are lawyers, physicians, merchants . . . if you will make equable and sensible men, they will make themselves capable and sensible lawyers or physicians'; 'the only reasonable guide to choice . . . is utility.' The liberal v. the vocational, the general v. the specialised – the battle lines are drawn and the only difference in a debate which has been remarkably consistent in sentiment and asperity for over a century, has been that the stakes have become higher, with the number of students vastly increased and with a corresponding increase in government outlay. We are not surprised then to find that a sketch of the debate with starts with Newman's *Idea of a University*, might well conclude with a meditation on the declining power of the UGC. In the early stages of the debate people like Mill and Froude, not to mention Huxley, Arnold and Playfair, were able to speak very much as individuals, where their contemporary equivalents would be circumscribed, or at least could not afford to forget, the economic resources available. But this is a complexity which colours, but does not alter, the fact that a reading of the numerous accounts of the developments in higher education will reveal a remarkable consistency in the articulation of the conflict.

The question must surely arise – why does the discussion not go stale? Why, when we hear the speeches of the latest successors to the positions occupied by Mill and Froude, do we not feel the tediousness of repetition? Let me add to that a further question. Why do we feel that any resolution to the

Liberal Education: an outworn ideal?

debate can only be provisional, temporary, and that this is not a debate which can ever, properly speaking, be resolved?

Of course, reconciling arrangements are made from time to time; the proponents of the liberal tradition have to come to terms with a state which, because it pays the piper, calls the tune; the proponents of a vocational tradition have to recognise that no vocation, however rigorously pursued, can exclude non-vocational considerations. But I would like to argue that 'reconciliations' however thoughtful, however desirable, however imaginative, are really side issues, in that the essential character of this debate should be recognised not as educational or economic, or political (though it is given substance by all these elements), but as mythological.

Let me say at once that far from using that term in a way that suggests something illusory, I intend by it something that reveals an inclusive truth about the nature of man and his relationship with the society in which he finds himself. Lest this sound too portentous, let me give an instance which makes modest my use of the word 'mythology' in relation to the education debate. It is the western film. Again and again we hear the familiar story, but again and again we are forced to pay attention. It is an unending conflict, because although local victories can be won, there is absolutely no 'right solution' because circumstances are always changing. So it is not right to talk of 'the latest successors of Mill and Froude', because what is always changing, however constant the argument may seem, are the cultural conditions out of which it came. The increase in student numbers, the enlarged role of the government, are not simply quantitative factors, they are qualitative – and the kind of debate between liberal and vocational education held (let us say) before 1945 and after that date is, in fact, quite different, though its central terms of reference may look the same.

So far I have been talking about the debate in a very panoramic way. I want now to reverse the perspective, and look at an exchange of views, again with the notion of liberal education at the centre, which took place in the columns of *The Times* only a few months ago. I cite this because it shows how very much the debate is still with us, and how it can find expression not in a formal context like the present one, but simply in the columns of a daily newspaper and be voiced by individuals who would not think of themselves as representing any large set of interests.

Under the heading 'Why politicians are all against real education', there appeared in *The Times* (4 January 1983) an article by Roger Scruton, Reader in Philosophy at Birkbeck. Deliberately provocative, Scruton argued that power and influence came through the acquisition of useless knowledge, and therefore it was one of 'the secret blows' dealt by politicians and those in authority to promote a concern for 'relevant knowledge' to preserve intact the sources of power. The uneducated can always be persuaded that there is a learning addressed to interests which they already have. The political danger attendant upon 'irrelevant subjects', Scruton argues, is that 'it brings an understanding of the human condition by forcing the student to stand back from it'. And he continues: 'A person with a classical or a literary education inhabits a transformed world . . . He is equipped not just to change the world, but to interpret it. Hence he will interpret it in his own favour and become master of it'. Scruton's *apologia* for irrelevance is a plea, journalistically heightened, for liberal education.

The measured reply to Scruton came from a member of the University of Edinburgh, in the form of a short letter by Professor Sir Michael Woodruff. Taking up Scruton's main point about relevant education – Woodruff begins by asking 'relevant to what?'. He then continues:

> In *The Idea of a University* John Henry Newman gets to the heart of the problem which Dr. Scruton wrestles with so unsuccessfully, when he says that the objective of (university) education is intellectual culture. This is not itself a branch of knowledge, but a healthy state of mind that can be developed only by study in some appropriate field.
>
> (*The Times*, 11 January 1983)

'Appropriate' subjects, he goes on, do not exclude the vocational and even in Newman's *Idea*, Medicine and Law have their place. 'One of the great challenges for those who teach in universities today is to find ways of giving students a general education in the context of their vocational studies.'

An eminently sensible response to Scruton's article and yet here is a specific example of a discussion at cross-purposes. Scruton is talking about culture and political power; Woodruff's sensible reply is about education and the necessity of a

Liberal Education: an outworn ideal?

balanced curriculum. This slide from one to the other characterises the whole debate about 'liberal education'. We can see the slide even within Woodruff's own letter. Beginning by citing Newman with approval, he invokes a key assertion of *The Idea of a University*, 'intellectual culture . . . not itself a branch of knowledge, but a healthy state of mind'. This leads him into asking how do we find an expression of such health? As soon as this becomes translated into 'giving a student a general education' we feel a contraction in the notion of 'intellectual culture'. The exchange between Scruton and Woodruff reveals the cross-currents involved in 'liberal education' between the culture and politics of a society on one side and its educational reforms on the other. Arnold realised this when in *Culture and Anarchy* he talked of culture as – 'getting to know the best that has been thought and said in the world' (the notion of 'general education'), but also he talked of culture as a means to get us out of your present difficulties (the notion of 'an interpretation of society'). When Eliot came to criticise Arnold in his *Notes Towards a Definition of Culture*, he took him to task for failing to distinguish between these different senses of the word 'culture'. While there is a distinction to be made, the senses are so closely related, that to go for the demarcation of meaning which Eliot asked for, is to rob the word of a necessary ambivalence.

I would like to illustrate the intimacy that exists between cultural assumptions and educational innovation in my third illustration touching on liberal education. What I have in mind is the foundation of the new universities in the 1960s – the most elaborate development in the university system in the present century.

In marked contrast to the foundation of the 'redbrick' universities there was no obvious social change that seemed to call for a corresponding change in the structure of higher education. There was no equivalent in other words to the developments in technology, the needs of applied science, the shift in population to expanding industrial towns – which made the creation of 'redbrick' almost inevitable. The reasons that are usually given for the 'new' university development, the rise in the number of people who wished to go to university, the need for a greater flexibility of the academic structure and a regrouping of subjects – seem, on the face of it, incommensurate with the lavishness of the enterprise. We might well have thought a more likely response to the situation – certainly, more economic – would have been a considerable expansion of those institutions already in existence, together with, let us say, the establishment of one new university, or conceivably, two, to allow for educational experiment and innovation. But nine . . . ?

I think we will find that this is a situation which is not really explicable in terms strictly of educational needs. It is a product of the cultural climate of the period – the period which not only gave us new universities, but Colleges of Advanced Technology, the progenitors of Polytechnics, and of course, it was a period too in which the whole debate about the comprehensive school was being fiercely joined. This kind of attention to education has, of course, its institutional concerns, it draws heavily on economic factors, but it is not to be defined within those terms, and the growth of the new universities is as much a product of the social and political images that a society has of itself, as it is of the need for educational innovation. Before speculating on this cultural and political hinterland out of which the new universities came, I should say something about the educational ideals which informed these institutions.

'The new' can best be thought of initially as a reaction against 'the old' – and 'the old', in this case, has to be understood, largely, as redbrick. At the heart of the impulse towards educational change, were worries about what constituted an academic discipline, or more precisely, what constituted an academic subject. Generally speaking, these were not questions that troubled the founders of those colleges, later to become redbrick universities. Dominantly scientific and technological in interest, taking their cue from the German universities, they had set research at the centre of their aims and duties, and in all faculties, it was the spirit of the natural sciences that dominated. 'Subjects' were self-declaring in their nature, the boundaries between one and another were clear and publicly acknowledged. When, at a later stage, other subjects were added and the faculties of arts and social sciences were developed, it was the influence of the natural sciences which prevailed and helped to shape the general academic scene. When the curriculum was broadened it was in the spirit of an

Liberal Education: an outworn ideal?

aggregation of specialisms. Although we think of redbrick universities being intimately connected to technological needs, particularly those of the area in which they were founded, it would be misleading to think of the education they provided as being utilitarian in spirit. Frequently, of course, that interest was served, but it was as a result of the severely specialist nature of the education which was provided, an education profoundly orientated round the needs of research. This was reflected in the administrative structure of the university – where the individual department exercised considerable autonomy, and where, within that department, the professor's role was absolute. It was an educational system which honoured and, in turn, sought to produce – the expert.

Time, of course, modified the redbrick spirit, but the emphasis on the specialism, on the department, on the lecture, on the professor, was integral to the academic and administrative structure. Moreover, these universities had grown up in large industrial cities, many of the students were drawn from the local population, and 'the university' was very much an institution which existed for formal academic instruction. In so far as the university catered for a student's life outside of that category – it was in places peripheral to the university, halls of residence and the students' union.

Different as the new universities were in their emphases, they were united in their opposition to the educational pattern which I have just outlined. A new re-alignment was sought between specialism and general education. Contextuality, in one form or another, became the desirable aim. It was no longer a matter of students *adding* one subject to another to obtain a breadth of interest, but of designing courses whose aim, more explicit than implicit, was to bring out the inter-relationships between one subject and another. To dramatise this inter-relationship, courses would be taught by more than one teacher, not as experts making specific contributions, but as collaborators engaged in a common educational enterprise. To achieve this degree of flexibility, the departmental structure had to give way to something much looser and the new administrative unit, often described as a school, had to accommodate within it several 'subjects'. Nomenclature altered from university to university, but a common aim prevailed, to heighten awareness of the inter-relatedness between subject and subject, and to seek an administrative structure best able to facilitate this.

These shifts in the curriculum had consequences both for the manner of teaching and the physical shape that the new universities took. The favoured mode of teaching – so far as the Arts and Social Science faculties went – was no longer the lecture, but the supervision or the seminar. This was symptomatic of a changed relationship towards 'the subject' – a change which emphasised that so far as the learning process was concerned, it was active participation that needed stressing rather than passive absorption. Throughout all these changes of emphasis we can see quite clearly that if the silent point of reference for the redbrick universities had been the procedures of the faculty of natural sciences, such a point of reference for the new universities was the faculty of arts and, at its centre, the notion of liberal education it entertained.

Nowhere does this emerge more clearly than in the considerations given to the architectural embodiment of the educational ideals. Unlike the redbrick universities which simply had to extend as best they could as the years went by, and as numbers increased, the new universities could think of themselves as a whole from the outset. How they did this varied considerably in detail – some, after all, were intended to be large, Warwick and Essex, some much smaller, East Anglia, York, Kent, Stirling – but this extract from the first planning paper at Kent (October 1962) sounds a note which was being echoed in many other such papers at the time:

> The lay-out should be conceived as a single whole. There should not be one area which is thought of as the place for teaching buildings to be developed solely for this purpose, and another possibly physically separate, to be provided for residence and planned only with this end in view. The issue here is a fundamental one. We want to get away from the 9 to 5 conception of a University, which is bound up with the idea that a student comes to hear lectures, to work in a laboratory or a library, to mix chiefly with those concerned with his own subject, and then to go back to his home or lodgings to do his private work and spend his leisure time in surroundings and company remote from the influence of the University.

That the 'new' university should be the antithesis of redbrick

Liberal Education: an outworn ideal?

could hardly have been expressed more clearly.

And what of the influence of Oxbridge? In some ways it was strong, not as a manifestation of nostalgia for an older tradition, but as a recognition that a central emphasis in Oxbridge had always been on undergraduate teaching, not postgraduate research, and once again this should be put firmly at the centre. Also, there was a recognition that the university should do everything it could to emphasise that it was an integrated whole, and although Jude's 'unrivalled panorama' might be only dimly reflected in the plate glass and untreated concrete of the new environments, the animating impulse behind them was not dissimilar. Indeed, an explicit acknowledgement of the debt to Oxbridge was made by Sussex, when in 1964, they published a symposium of essays on new development and aims under a title which deliberately recalled Newman – *The Idea of a New University*. But it would be very wide of the mark to see the new universities as latter-day copies of Oxbridge. The curriculum was often radical and innovatory, both in its detail and in its overall combination of subjects. It is especially different from Oxbridge in that, by definition, the new universities had no traditions to honour, no vested interests in their admissions' policy.

But different as they were from existing universities, the question still remains to be asked about the new universities, why was it that in the 1960s the spirit of liberal education should find this particular renaissance? Part of the answer lies in the reaction to redbrick ideals which I have sketched, but for another part of the answer I think we need to go outside of the educational world itself and see some of the social and political forces that were playing upon it. Behind every curriculum there exists an ideology, however obscurely glimpsed, and perhaps the twenty-year gap that exists between us and the creation of the new universities might allow us to see something, at least, of its outline.

We might begin by going back some fifty years, to North Staffordshire in the 1930s. Here there existed an extremely forward-looking and successful Adult Education Association, sponsored by the delegacy of the University of Oxford, under the chairmanship of the Master of Balliol, A.D. Lindsay, and having as its resident tutor, R.H. Tawney. It was out of this intellectual nucleus that the university college of North Staffordshire was born, later of course, to become Keele University.

The origin of Keele in the convergence of two unlikely streams, Oxford University and Adult Education classes, was decisive in giving the university its distinctive character. Deeply respectful of intellectual curiosity, it nevertheless felt strongly that such a curiosity was best expressed in a concern with contemporary social problems. In Lindsay's conception of Keele there was much that recalled Jowett's Balliol – a high philosophic idealism accompanied by a no less strenuous notion of social obligation. Part of the way in which this might be achieved was thought to lie in the judicious grouping of the curriculum, so that students were encouraged to think not only about a particular subject, but about the relationship between that subject and those which bordered upon it. It was in Keele that the new alignment between the specialism and its context, which was to become a common concern in all the new universities, was first given systematic treatment.

And yet for all its emphasis on interdisciplinarity, on small group teaching, on the necessity of residence, Keele existed in some isolation from those later developments which were to exhibit so many of the same features. The explanation has, I think, something to do with the changes which were occurring in Britain, during the period between 1949, when Keele received its Royal Charter, and 1961 when Sussex received its charter. Unlike the later foundations, the growth of Keele to university status was long and difficult and intimately connected with politics, both at a local and at a national level. That the university grew in the way that it did in the years following the war was largely due to Lindsay's persuasive advocacy with the Labour government during those years. The obligations were duly honoured. When in 1951 Herbert Morrison came to North Staffordshire, curious to find out why Labour had continued to maintain its strength in that area, he was told, without hesitation, that 'it was due to the new university college' (Gallie 1960). Whatever truth there may be in that claim, there can be no doubt that the austere idealism that went into the creation of Keele, was in tune with the mood of the Labour government which had created the Welfare State in the postwar period.

Keele provides an instance of institutional change and ex-

Liberal Education: an outworn ideal?

periment in the decade after the war, but in some ways a more powerful solvent in changing aims was taking place within the student body itself. This was the return of ex-servicemen. Here for the first time was a completely new kind of student. Frequently older than those who taught them, these students brought with them a maturity of outlook, a confidence in discussion, that transformed the teaching situation. It was open season for critical enquiry – and questions about 'relevance' and 'irrelevance', about methods of teaching, about the relationship of the university to the wider community, were a general subject of debate.

For both teacher and taught the decade 1946–56 marked a uniquely memorable experience, and when the progenitors of the new universities began to gather in the course of the succeeding decade, the experience of those years remained a major influence in their thinking.

The world into which the new universities were born was vastly different from that which had witnessed the origins of Keele. In full possession of degree-giving faculties from the outset, the new universities were happy recipients of generous government provision and the whole ethos reflected the economic well-being of the Macmillan government (1958–63) with its celebrated slogan 'You've never had it so good'. The large number of new university foundations would seem to have been tied up with the government policy to diffuse the national resources throughout the country. This was particularly noticeable when it came to the two new universities in Scotland and Northern Ireland, where a sense of political fairness rather than an overriding educational need, seemed a dominant motive in their foundation.

The siting of the universities has often provoked comment – on the edge of towns rather than inside them, and in small towns of historical and architectural interest. Again, the spell of Oxbridge has been suspected. However it may have appeared, the decisions about siting were the outcome of much more pragmatic decisions. The UGC had laid down as a condition that any new university had to have a site of not less than two hundred acres, and this determined that wherever they were, they would have to be on the edge or just outside of urban centres. In laying down this condition, the UGC was much exercised by the difficulties that redbrick universities were experiencing in trying to expand within the city limits, and at the same time retain some kind of physical identity.

It was in a number of more or less attractive settings that the new universities opened their doors. In the broadest outline the main educational emphasis resembled that which we have seen at Keele – inter-disciplinarity, new groupings of subjects, as largely residential as possible – and the spirit that prevailed was largely that of a liberal education. This was not to exclude the vocational interests which were vigorously present in every part of the university, but they were not its primary aim, any more than was the carrying-out of research, though no university, worthy of the name, could exist without it. That spirit of liberal education which had been fostered in the lean and austere days of Lindsay at Keele, had come to fruition in the economic hey-day of Macmillan's government in the early 1960s. It was not simply a matter of economics, however, there was a general desire to take risks, to make it new, together with a confidence that made talk of 'new maps of learning' not vainly pretentious. To read some of the books, written in the early 1960s, about the directions higher education should take, is to be made aware how remote that period seems from our own, and although the economy has had an indisputable part to play, it was more the occasion of the change, than its substance.

I have remarked throughout this paper in a number of disparate contexts that the notion of liberal education carries within it a sense of tension – whether we look at it in terms of a long historical debate, a local exchange of views, or as a presiding spirit in the foundation of new institutions. The time has come, by way of conclusion, to look briefly at the term itself in an explicit and analytic way.

Locked within it are two impulses, each contending for the upper hand. One of these is striving towards the communication of an idea, seeking its persuasive force, in arguing that if 'liberal education' attests to 'a good', then it is a good *for* something – to turn a fresh stream of thought, to sharpen judgement, to quicken perception. This impulse is defined, in Eric Ashby's words, as 'a spirit of pursuit, not a choice of subject'. In this perspective, the fruit of a liberal education can only be seen in the quality that attends its transformation. The other impulse is concerned precisely to resist such a trans-

Liberal Education: an outworn ideal?

formation. It takes its stand upon the notion that if liberal education is 'a good', it is not a good for something, it is good-in-itself. It draws on the classic argument that if all good is only good because it promotes other good, then we are launched on an infinite regress. For 'good' to have any meaning there must be something intrinsically good – and that, so far as liberal education is concerned, is the intellectual life. Within this perspective, what is valuable is not the spirit of pursuit, but the spirit of possession.

The idea of liberal education contains these contrary impulses and when the tension between them goes, the idea becomes impoverished. To insist on 'the spirit of pursuit', 'the frame of mind', is to become vulnerable to the charge which Henry Sidgwick (1867) once made of Matthew Arnold's classic *apologia* for a liberal education, *Culture and Anarchy*, 'culture is always hinting at a season which never seems to arrive'. It is an excessive preoccupation with means, never with ends. On the other hand, to become exclusively preoccupied with ends would seem to disparage action, to encourage self-regard, to celebrate a *mystique*. In terms of this particular paper, we have seen how a discussion of liberal education inevitably involves a wide spectrum of issues – the reform of the curriculum, 'relevant' and 'irrelevant' knowledge, the *idea* of a university as a good in itself, the images a society has of itself.

I talked at the outset of such issues belonging not so much to an educational debate as to a mythological one. In using that description I wanted to suggest that the contraries set up by liberal education on the one hand and vocational training on the other, while obviously capable of institutional expression, are best considered as ways of enabling us to think about education in general. To think of liberal education as 'an outworn ideal' is to misrepresent it, not so much because of the disparaging adjective, but because the phrase implies a state rather than a process, a concept rather than a temper of mind. 'Tension' rather than 'ideal' is the word to be associated with liberal education, an interplay of forces serving as a constant reminder that, in this instance, a politics of learning is also, and inextricably, a politics of culture.

REFERENCES
Ashby, E. (1958) *Technology and the Academics*. London.
Gallie, W. B. (1960) *A New University*. London.
Hardy, T. (1895) *Jude the Obscure*. London.
Moberly, W. (1949) *The Crisis in the University*. London.
Sidgwick, H. (1867) Culture: A Dialogue. *Macmillan's Magazine*, August.

COMMENTS BY ROBERT ANDERSON

Like other elusive concepts, liberal education is often best defined by looking at what it is contrasted with or opposed to. Professor Gregor speaks of 'the liberal versus the vocational, the general versus the specialised', and I would like to begin by suggesting that these are two distinct oppositions which may have different implications for liberal education, and that if Academic Freedom versus Social Need is the plot of the story, it is thickened by the fact that the academics themselves have had conflicting views which have changed over time. For to equate liberal with non-vocational education, to say that it is the education which forms the man rather than the specialist, is not necessarily to say that it must be based on a broad curriculum and embrace a wide variety of subjects. On the contrary, conservatives in the early nineteenth century usually claimed that one type of study – classics or mathematics – had uniquely liberalising virtues which made it in itself a complete preparation for life, while reformers concentrated on showing that other subjects could have just as liberal an influence. One could cite the debate about mathematics between Whewell and Hamilton in the 1830s as an example (Sanderson 1975, 68–73), while at Oxford in the 1850s the defenders of classical specialisation rejected even history as too 'professional' a subject for the liberal curriculum (Bill 1973). Today the claims of specialised subjects of all kinds have triumphed, but while teaching them we pacify our consciences by arguing that it is not the subject but the spirit in which it is taught which defines the liberal nature of university education, and that any subject properly taught can bring out the qualities thought desirable – the critical spirit, relativism and scepticism, and so on. This would seem to be the position of Professor Woodruff, arguing against the early Victorian conservative Roger Scruton.

But the Scruton view – that certain subjects have a unique

capacity to illuminate the human condition – seems to me quite different from the ideal of liberal education put forward by Mill in his famous St Andrews address, which was based on an encyclopedically wide programme of study which no university has come near to imposing in practice. Speaking in 1867, Mill was deeply influenced by Comte's views on the unity and hierarchy of the sciences, as the emphasis which he put on mathematics and logic shows; in another famous rectorial address, at Aberdeen in 1874, Huxley expounded a very similar ideal, though with a greater emphasis on the natural sciences. This encyclopedic, comprehensive definition of liberal education, however, enjoyed a comparatively short life, and it was to give way by the end of the nineteenth century to the German-inspired ideal of research and specialisation. Sheldon Rothblatt, who has done more than anyone to clarify the history of liberal education in this period, has suggested that it is the disinterested, objective pursuit of truth, based on research, which provides the working definition of liberal education in modern universities, though in uneasy alliance with a modernised version of the old anti-vocationalism (Rothblatt 1976).

Mill remarked that 'To comment upon the course of education at the Scottish Universities is to pass in review every essential department of general culture' (Knight 1894, 24), and when we think of general education we think naturally of the broad, uniform curriculum of Scottish tradition, with its subjects drawn from the three fields of language, philosophy, and science, a tradition restored to historical visibility by Dr George Davie in his remarkable book *The democratic intellect* (Davie 1964). The uniformity of the Scottish arts curriculum was not abandoned until 1892, but there was extensive debate about its future from the 1860s onwards, a debate inspired, I would argue, not so much by the 'Anglicisation' on which Dr Davie lays so much stress, as by 'social needs' and practical pressures which were common to England and Scotland, and which arose within Scotland in indigenous forms.

The ideal of liberal education has always been an ideal: in practice compromises with vocationalism have had to be made, and where something like the ideal has been turned into practice it has been because it met the actual needs either of a leisured class or of particular professions. So it was in

Scotland. The traditional arts curriculum was for training ministers and schoolteachers. Anyone else who went through it certainly got a remarkably broad education, but it would be wrong to think that the majority of the Scottish educated class did so. The freedom of study, the *Lernfreiheit* described in eighteenth-century Edinburgh by Professor Stone was still flourishing a hundred years later. In the 1880s the average attendance of arts students was two years (the full curriculum took four), and it was estimated that only one in five or six graduated, an estimate which statistics confirm (Grant 1884, ii, 120; Anderson 1983, 75). Alongside a minority who aimed at taking a degree, there were a large number of students who 'take what they or their friends think most useful for them in reference to professional objects' (Grant 1884, ii, 121); philosophy was a popular choice, but so were the sciences and various new subjects – economics, fine art, education – which had been introduced into the university by the foundation of chairs but which still had no place in the degree curriculum. Moreover, many of these students were part-timers, taking one or two classes while holding down a job in the city. For at both Edinburgh and Glasgow, where these tendencies were even more marked, the universities were situated in great cities and were non-residential, and this made their fundamental character, and their relations with the 'shabby purlieus' surrounding them, quite different from those of Christminster.

This system, under which the universities performed a diversity of educational functions, worked well for a long time, but by the 1850s the age of examinations was beginning, and formal qualifications became increasingly essential for the whole range of middle-class careers. The Scottish universities offered only one type of arts degree, and it now came under attack as too long, too inflexible, too exclusively attuned to the needs of the clergy, too esoteric, with its compulsory Greek and mathematics, for the average professional or commercial man. After 1858, 'social needs' could be expressed directly through the General Councils, bodies representing the graduates of each university. For another consequence of the urban character of the Scottish universities was that they were surrounded by their own graduates, who as leading figures in civic life were not slow to criticise the deficiencies of their *alma mater*. Between the 1860s and the 1890s the General

Councils played a leading part in controversies over university reform, and the election of Huxley as rector of Aberdeen in 1872 was part of a bitter conflict in that university over the place of science in the curriculum. One of the most articulate reformers of this period was Lyon Playfair; Professor Lyons has cited the speech of 1873 in which he said that the universities must adapt to the demands of modern society or be passed by, a speech which was made in the context of Scottish university reform. Playfair's argument was that by holding to the old rigid curriculum the universities were missing a vital opportunity to extend their social influence. Their business was to 'liberalise the professions', and they had much to offer the middle classes, but they would not attract those aiming at the professions unless they could provide flexibility and choice in the general or liberal part of their training (Playfair 1889, 373–7). The chief demand therefore was for options within the curriculum. The full story is complex; it is perhaps enough to say that more choice and specialisation were introduced in 1892 (though the move to specialisation was not as great as Dr Davie claims), and that this led to a great increase in the numbers actually graduating; by the 1900s the modern pattern of full-time study leading normally to a degree was established. In other words, the old general curriculum only survived so long because few wanted to take it; once the majority of the universities' clientele became interested in degrees, a compromise with vocationalism had to be made.

I would add two caveats at this point. First, we should beware of laying too much emphasis on the needs of science or industry as a stimulus to reform. These fields provided few salaried posts for graduates in the nineteenth century: it was the growth of the professions, commerce, schoolteaching, and the civil service which really generated change, in secondary schooling as well as in universities. My second caveat is indeed that the history of universities needs to be studied in conjunction with the history of secondary schools, though for the modern period it rarely has been. In Scotland secondary schools were under-developed, for various reasons, and the universities had partly taken their place. In the mid-nineteenth century the usual age of university entry was fifteen or sixteen. But from the 1870s secondary education developed rapidly, and by 1890 the age of entry had risen to seventeen or eighteen

(Anderson 1983, 301). Liberal education, it could be argued, was now given in the schools, and this freed the universities to specialise as they could not before.

In the last part of his paper Professor Gregor opens up a fascinating subject, the history of the new universities of the 1960s, and he is surely right to say that their creation is something which needs to be explained. He sees their curricular innovations as a reaction against the departmentalised specialisation of the civic universities; no doubt they were also intended to correct the excessive specialisation of the secondary schools, something which, although now regarded as traditional, was in fact quite a recent development. But beyond that, the foundation of these universities was clearly, as Professor Gregor says, a moment in British culture. He evokes the mood of 1945, the high-minded idealism of the post-war years, Keele and A.D. Lindsay. Perhaps we should also take into account those two classics of the 1940s, *Red brick university*, by the pseudonymous Bruce Truscot, and Sir Walter Moberly's *The crisis in the university*. In his lecture Professor Lyons rather depreciated the influence of these books, but for a long time they were where you turned if you were looking for ideas about university education. Reading them today suggests several reflections. One is that Truscot casts doubt on the view that research and specialisation were paramount in the civic universities: he was scathing about the neglect of research by professors, and the main purpose of his book was to recall redbrick to the scientific and scholarly ideal. Today research is taken for granted as a central task for the university teacher in a way that does not seem to have been the case when Truscot was writing, and the generation of academics appointed to the new universities was surely very representative of this new commitment.

A second point is that both books reflect an age, which now seems remote, when Christianity was a live force in British intellectual life, and suggest to me that Eliot, with his special brand of cultural conservatism, should be placed in the plate-glass pantheon along with Tawney, Lindsay – and perhaps Leavis? At any rate, the inspiration seems an essentially literary rather than scientific or technological one.

Thirdly and finally, both books strongly recommended the residential ideal, and helped to establish the idea of the 'community of scholars and pupils' which appears so often in British definitions of the nature of a university. As Professor Gregor shows in his quotation from the planners at Kent, the redbrick universities were especially condemned for their nine-to-five character. From this point of view, the residential new universities might be seen as the culmination of the collegiate, tutorial strand in the reform of Victorian Oxford and Cambridge, but also of those wider tendencies of modern society which have made educational institutions into worlds apart, places of intensive socialisation. Historians have made us familiar with the 'invention of adolescence' (Musgrove 1964; Gillis 1974). The invention of the student was an equally important nineteenth-century phenomenon; it was especially striking in Scotland, where the whole apparatus of 'corporate life' – Students' Representative Councils, student unions, athletics, student journalism – sprang up quite rapidly in the 1880s (Anderson 1983, 330). The irony of the new universities was that they embodied the triumph of the residential ideal at the very moment when it was losing its magic for students. No sooner were the colleges built, the high tables installed, the gowns and scarves designed, than the youth revolution of the 1960s struck, with results which Professor Stone has traced for us. British universities seem to have adapted well enough to that change. Today they perhaps face a more radical challenge, and will need to depart from their concentration on giving a full-time education to the eighteen-plus age-group. In Scotland at least, that concentration is itself a relatively recent phenomenon. One lesson of university history is that universities in the past have performed very diverse tasks, and if the ideal of liberal education is to have a future we must seek to identify it with the fundamental intellectual tasks of the university rather than with historically contingent ways of life or social functions.

REFERENCES

Anderson, R. D. (1983) *Education and opportunity in Victorian Scotland. Schools and universities.* Oxford.

Bill, E. G. W. (1973) *University reform in nineteenth-century Oxford. A study of Henry Halford Vaughan, 1811-1885.* Oxford.

Davie, G. E. (1964) *The democratic intellect. Scotland and her universities in the nineteenth century,* 2nd ed. Edinburgh.

Gillis, J. R. (1974) *Youth and history. Tradition and change in European age relations, 1770-present.* New York.

Grant, A. (1884) *The story of the University of Edinburgh during its first three hundred years.* London.

Knight, W. (1894) *Rectorial addresses delivered at the University of St Andrews . . . 1863-1893.* London.

Moberly, W. (1949) *The crisis in the university.* London.

Musgrove, F. (1964) *Youth and the social order.* London.

Playfair, L. (1889) *Subjects of social welfare.* London.

Rothblatt, S. (1976) *Tradition and change in English liberal education. An essay in history and culture.* London.

Sanderson, M. (1975) *The universities in the nineteenth century.* London.

Truscot, B. (1951) *Red brick university*, new ed. Harmondsworth.

TECHNOLOGY AND THE UNIVERSITY

PATRICK NUTTGENS

On 7 November 1855 the first – and only – Professor of Technology in the University of Edinburgh delivered his inaugural lecture under the title *What is Technology?* It is a remarkable lecture, not only because of its subject, which was still new at the time, but also because George Wilson was a remarkable man (Balfour 1860).

He was born in 1818, studied at the High School, entered the University of Edinburgh in 1832 and like many of the leading scientists of his time qualified in medicine. Like many of them also he turned to chemistry, worked as an assistant in the University and spent a year or two in London before returning to Edinburgh. He had extraordinarily bad luck with his health. In 1843 he had his foot amputated, before the days of anaesthetics – 'a very painful and sometimes tedious' operation, said one of his colleagues; he himself said later that he watched the operation 'with fascinated intensity'. But what gave him great local distinction were the public lectures he started in 1840; they became famous for his ability to illustrate difficult points and make science comprehensible to a lay audience.

He was appointed Regius Director of the Industrial Museum (about to be built beside the university in Chambers Street) in 1855 and Regius Professor in Technology in the same year. He held the chair for only a few years, for he died in 1859 at the age of 41. By that time he had assembled the basis of the collection for the Museum of Science and Art as it was first known. His lectures in the university were not included in any curriculum of study (except, for some reason, that of the Highland Society) but were widely attended. His inaugural lecture contained many of the themes that were to recur again and again and continue to the present day.

'The word *Technology*', he said at the start of the lecture, 'appears to have been first explicitly employed, in the sense in which it concerns me, in 1772, by Beckmann, the famous author of the *History of Inventions*, who was for many years Professor of Economy in the University of Gottingen. Availing himself of the liberty conceded to professors in German universities, to lecture on any subject within their Faculty, he chose the Industrial Arts as the topic of a series of prelections, and entitled the science of these arts – *Technology*' (Wilson 1855).

The word had come to comprise the systematic definition (logos) of the rational principles upon which all processes employed in the arts (technes) were based. So for Wilson, 'Technology, in the sense I have to deal with it, implies the Science, or Doctrine, or Philosophy, or Theory of the Arts. Its object is not Art itself, i.e. the practice of Art, but the principles which guide or underlie Art, and by conscious or unconscious obedience to which, the artist secures his ends'.

The utilitarian arts with which technology is concerned are those which are indispensable, essential to man's physical existence. 'The most degraded savage must practise them, and the most civilised genius cannot dispense with them.' He discusses at some length the distinction between the Fine and the Industrial Arts. 'We concede to the former the special title of Fine or Noble Arts, because their ends are high, their students are few, and excellence in them is rare; and we acknowledge the latter to be Common Arts, whose ends are humble, whose students are countless, and excellence in which is, in many respects, universal. We have few great artists; we have many skilful artizans'.

Although Wilson was rather apologetic about the clumsiness of the word *technology* he said he could suggest no better. '*Applied Science*', he pointed out, anticipating an argument which is still unresolved, 'is a misnomer; for *applied science* is but a clumsy circumlocution for art or practice, as Theorised or Generalised Art or Practice would simply signify science'.

The meaning of technology (even though, it may be noted, Beckmann had written a textbook on it which went into six editions by 1801 (Armytage 1965)) remained a challenge. A woman friend of Wilson's had joked that if he was ever made a professor she would work a cushion for his chair. This happened and in thanks he sent her a poem of 27 verses, of which these are four:

> The Queen of England in her might
> She made a wondrous chair;
> She beckoned to a Scottish wight,
> And said, 'Ho! Sit thou there'.

Technology and the University

> The Scottish wight, he bowed his head,
> And stammered an apology;
> 'Nay, Sit thou there!' the Queen she said,
> 'In my Chair of Technology'.
>
> It was a strange, unheard-of Chair,
> And every part was new.
> The wood that made it was so rare,
> No one knew where it grew.
>
> And through the land the people went
> And stopping at each college, 'Hey!'
> They called, 'Oh! tell us what is meant
> By this Chair of Technology'.   (Jessie Wilson 1860)

George Wilson's early death left their questions in the air. Although the chair was discontinued by the University 'to repair the blunder of establishing in 1855 through Government intervention, a hybrid Professorship in Technology' (in the words of one of its historians, Logan Turner 1933) Wilson had already articulated many of the problems attending the place of technology in the universities. It was indeed an unsatisfactory Chair because Technology is not really a subject but a category of subjects and activities; as far as I can tell, no other university attempted to found a chair in it, however many branches of technology they might later establish and teach.

But his definition of technology was the precursor of others that emphasise its nature as a systematic approach to the practical arts. The latest edition of the *Encyclopaedia Britannica* defines technology as 'the means or activity by which man seeks to change or manipulate his environment'. In that process the relationship of science and technology is important; and the University of Edinburgh can be seen as an exemplar of the changes and development in those areas. Before coming back to technology in Edinburgh — in the form of engineering — I want briefly to look at the situation of science.

If, as Eric Ashby maintains in his valuable book on *Technology and the Academics* (Ashby 1958) scientific thought, which by 1800 was already consolidated in the foundations of modern physics and chemistry, and scarcely influenced the universities of England, it had had a greater effect in Scotland, though even there as much through popular lectures like

Anderson's 'anti-toga' lectures in Glasgow as through anything in the universities.

What distinguished the Scottish universities was the pre-eminence of medicine and the medical schools. Ashby points out that most of the Scottish professors at that time were part-time teachers, whose main preoccupation was medical practice. It was thus through the interaction of medicine with physics and chemistry, especially chemistry, that much of the teaching of science became available throughout the university, and because medicine dealt with real cases gave the Scottish universities a practical character and link with society at large. Edinburgh had already founded a chair of Anatomy in 1705 and a chair of Chemistry in 1713, without which scientific medicine could not have developed. By 1800 it had one of the best medical schools in Europe and the teaching of science was part of that provision.

The impact of medicine was one side of the impact of scientific scholarship in Scotland. The other was the profitable activities of the physicists and their colleagues. Of no academic was this more true than of William Thompson, Lord Kelvin, perhaps the major figure in the story and most influential in his training of leaders in science and engineering in the nineteenth century (Sanderson 1972). He was appointed to the chair of Natural Philosophy in Glasgow in 1846 and was involved not only in research into electricity but in practical projects such as the laying of the Atlantic cable.

The man who wrote most copiously about the needs of the country in science and especially technology was Lyon Playfair. Playfair, later Sir Lyon Playfair and then the first Baron Playfair, 1818–98, saw himself as a missionary to bring chemistry into relation with the industries of the country, which had for too long been carried out by rule of thumb (Roderick and Stephens 1978). He was educated at St Andrews and then studied under von Liebig in Giessen University where he gained his PhD. He taught at the Royal School of Mines and was appointed to the chair of Chemistry in Edinburgh in 1858, a year before George Wilson's death; in 1869 he became MP for the Scottish Universities and later Postmaster General and Vice-President of the Council of Education.

At the time of the Great Exhibition of 1851 he had toured Europe at the request of Prince Albert to study technical edu-

Technology and the University

cation at first hand and delivered on his return a scathing condemnation of the failure of England to develop technical education, in marked contrast to continental countries – particularly France and Germany. The accuracy of his warnings was clearly shown when in contrast to 1851 the British exhibitors at the Paris Exhibition of 1867 failed to carry off more than a handful of prizes.

Playfair's work in Edinburgh introduces a new dimension into the implications of developing technology. He gives a neat discourse in his inaugural lecture of 1858 (Playfair 1858) on the different roles of the lecturer and tutor, with emphasis on the value of the latter: 'the teacher and the taught then get into an intellectual grapple, and, as the former should be the stronger man, he is enabled to drag the mind of the student from the dark holes in which it may lurk to the broad light of day'. Whether or not he succeeded in dragging his students' minds from their dark holes, he effectively extended the discussion. What he added to it while he held the Chair in Edinburgh and in the following years as a Member of Parliament was a recognition, however tentatively expressed, that the advent of technology into the university required the re-consideration of the very nature of the university as a community of teachers and scholars.

In the address to the Philosophical Institution of Edinburgh in 1872 on *Teaching Universities and Examining Boards* (Playfair) he starts the argument by quoting a blunt statement by the Chancellor of the Exchequer that 'What I mean by a University is an Examining Board' – and 'the fewer the better' – reviews the provision and the nature of universities in France, Belgium, Germany and Italy and refers to London University as a 'useful and faithful examining board supplementary to the other universities of the country'. He explains how 'it is desirable to keep together the teaching and examining functions of Universities as of old, and how it is that examinations alone fail to produce a large educational, though . . . they do produce a directive effect. A combined University, when well conducted, aims and succeeds in producing an *educated* man; an Examining Board can only be assured that it has produced a *crammed* man. It is the curriculum of the University, not the examination, which educates the man'. Epictetus was right when he pointed out that though sheep eat grass, it is wool not grass that

171

grows upon their backs. He quotes Cambridge as an example of the worst practice, in that the Colleges do the teaching and the university does the examining, so that the 'intellectual training has passed away from the professors and preparation for degrees is undertaken by private coaches'.

Having established the case for the unity of teaching and examining he concludes with an important comment upon the nature of the Scottish universities and quotes the Vice-President of Queen's College Belfast that 'few, except those conversant with the practical arts, are aware of the immense advantages England herself has derived from them, particularly in the great northern seats of industry. It may indeed be said, without exaggeration, that England would long ago have been forced to establish Universities after the Scottish or German model, for the use of the middle classes, if the Universities of Scotland and Germany had not furnished her with a large supply of men well versed in the sciences connected with the useful arts'.

In an address a year later to the St Andrews Association (Playfair 1873) on *Universities in relation to professional education* Playfair returns to the theme in a delightfully unscientific manner. 'The skull of a man is a close and rigid cavity, which can only hold an average quantity of brains; it is not a vulcanised Indian-rubber bag, capable of swelling out at each pressure applied to it. We must put into this space of fixed dimensions a continually growing quantity of knowledge; and you cannot be astonished if you find a disposition to reject that which is useless for that which is useful'. He sees a widening gap between the universities and the professions.

'The Universities allowed profession after profession to slip away from them, because they could not escape from their mediaeval traditions. Nothing is more strange, for instance, than their abandonment of the teaching profession, which was of their own creation, while the older professions were rather the creation of the creators of the universities'. The universities must resume their old function of liberalising the professions. 'It has, therefore, been a source of pride and gratification to me to see my own University of Edinburgh developing courses of engineering and agriculture, and opening its degrees to technological professions'.

If technology had been considered a hybrid affair in 1859 the same did not apply to engineering – that is, engineering as such rather than the functional divisions into which it was much later divided. The world's first chair of Engineering was established at Glasgow in 1840 though there had been lectures in the principles of Engineering in Cambridge since 1796. It was unpopular with academics from the start. The first Professor, Lewis Gordon, one of Kelvin's many protégés and a practical colleague who had made the Atlantic cables at his Birkenhead factory, was not even supplied with a classroom at first and for a long time the subject remained in the Faculty of Arts.

The establishment of the Regius chair of Engineering in Edinburgh in 1868 was especially significant in a number of ways. Within a few years the university created science faculties and science became pure science, consciously veering towards the theoretical in the 1880s. Engineering thus became one of the main links between the university and the outside world (Sanderson 1972). And it was symptomatic of the practical bias of the subject that the first professor should have been another disciple and colleague of Kelvin, recommended to him by the Glasgow professor with whom he had worked in his Birkenhead factory.

Fleeming Jenkin was an expert in electrical telegraphy. He took up the chair in 1868 and delivered his inaugural lecture on the subject of *The Education of Civil and Mechanical Engineers in Great Britain and Abroad* (Fleeming Jenkin 1868). Both he and his two successors took the opportunity in their inaugural lectures of reviewing the development of education for engineering and relating it to engineering as a whole; and those inaugural lectures therefore form the basic material for the next part of this paper.

Jenkin refers straight away to Lyon Playfair and comments that a Professor of Engineering in this country still has to create the system of instruction which in other Faculties needs only to be developed and improved. He looks abroad, especially to France, where the contrast in the position of the engineer is greater than in any other country. To an English (or Scottish) academic the list of their studies is frightening – a mass of theoretical teaching before any practical experience takes place at all.

This is at the heart of the problem of educating engineers and

Jenkin comes back to it for most of the paper. If on the continent the path to the profession of engineer lies through the colleges, in England the path is a system of apprenticeship through the office or workshop of a civil or mechanical engineer. He recognises that the two systems cannot well be combined. 'The foreign plan requires a young man to study in a college till the age of about twenty-three, when it is too late for him to think of entering an office or workshop for three more years, paying a heavy premium and receiving no salary'.

His tour of inspection had led him to marvel at the combination of theoretical with practical knowledge evinced by the German professors. He makes a withering comment upon the British system in which young men are recruited who are ignorant of algebra, shaky in their arithmetic and ignorant about what happens in mechanical workshops. 'They really seem to think that a little turn for making toy-models shows a bent for mechanical engineering such as will justify them in expecting success'. Abroad, competitive examinations keep out incompetent men; in Britain they are weeded out by the struggle for existence.

Taking a critical view, Jenkin comes to the conclusion that 'a gentleman of fair education and intelligence, after working for three years in a civil engineer's office, is, for subordinate positions as a civil engineer, a more useful man than the pupil of a foreign school'. For a mechanical engineer the case is different, for a sound knowledge of mathematics, mechanics and physics is of the greatest importance; he would therefore prefer a foreigner. And of course different qualities are required as engineers rise in the profession. Ultimately, with all the qualities he may be expected to have – in theory and business and the law of contracts and the ability to choose subordinates – he must be a man of great *Common Sense*. Our defect is simply the 'want of a good knowledge of the theories affecting our practice'. Students should get some knowledge of theory before their apprenticeship begins. If they could do this the British system would be superior to the foreign one.

But here comes the crucial recommendation. Jenkin was sure that in ensuring this balance of understanding of theory without sacrificing the traditions of practice it would be 'better done at a university than in any new special schools' and he warns against the foundation of polytechnic schools in rivalry

Technology and the University

with the university as happened on the Continent. At Zurich, he says, 'the polytechnic school dwarfs the university; and in French universities, the scientific teaching has fairly been extinguished by the polytechnic school'. Hardly a student of science, he says, attends a class in the universities.

Fleeming Jenkin's successor was George Frederick Armstrong who devoted his inaugural lecture in 1885 to *The Progress of Higher Technical Instruction* (Armstrong 1885). He noted the humiliation of Britain at the Paris Exhibition of 1867 and had no doubt that if you asked on the Continent what was the reason for their victory, they would reply 'Our systems of general education, and the training of our technical schools'. In that development he recognises the historical importance and the dominance of the École Polytechnique in Paris, 'the commencement of an era in the history of applied-science teaching in Europe'. But what is especially significant is Armstrong's insistence upon a remarkable and far-reaching principle which he says has from the first dominated one of the most famous schools that followed the École Polytechnique, the non-government Central School of Arts and Manufactures established in 1829 to train engineers for private enterprise. The principle is expressed in the original prospectus.

'Industrial science is one, and therefore all the courses of the school form but one and the same. Arts apparently widely differing from each other and often employing very different methods, make use of analogous operations; and the general education of the school will teach how to transfer into each process of manufacture the improved methods used in others'. All the famous schools on the Continent – the Polytechnics of Carlsruhe, Zurich, Dresden, Lausanne, Vienna, Prague, Hanover, Brunswick, Berlin, Stuttgart, and Munich – had been organised on that model.

Looked at from the perspective of today that principle has an importance that we cannot afford to overlook. The challenge that we face in today's polytechnics concerns the possibility of teaching transferable skills and of discovering a unity in industrial science which would give a core to the scholarship of a polytechnic that would put it on a level with a university.

From the Continent Armstrong turns his attention to America whose schools of engineering, he says, are in no way inferior to the best in Europe. As in them, a student receives the

Patrick Nuttgens

whole of his professional training, theoretical and practical, prior to seeking employment as a paid manager or assistant. Private individuals had given huge sums for the provision of technical education for such professions as Engineering and Metallurgy; and universities like Cornell had been founded in which technical instruction took a foremost place. His list of outstanding schools, which includes the Massachusetts Institute of Technology 'one of the very best schools in the country', makes anything in Britain at the time look derisory.

Armstrong emphasises that after a severe entrance examination in subjects of general education and culture, the American students are not permitted wholly to abandon the study of Literature and Philosophy. 'These and especially Modern Languages are made a part of the regular curriculum, so that ethics and culture are from the first to last made to progress together towards a common goal – a principle of education which is not without its lessons for us in this country, when we are engaged in the evolution of corresponding systems of technical instruction'.

It may be remarked that we have still not resolved that problem. One of the oddities in this country is that whereas students taking a lower course in engineering have been obliged to pass an examination in general (or complementary or liberal) studies, no such obligation is usually imposed upon the university student.

A final dimension to the themes that I am here assembling was introduced by the third professor of Engineering, T. Hudson Beare, whose inaugural lecture in 1901 was on *The Education of an Engineer* (Hudson Beare 1901). Beare thought that if in the last sixteen years the country had made huge strides in the technical education of artisans, the education and technical training of the chiefs in the industrial struggle had been seriously neglected. He gave examples of the capture of industries from Britain by the Germans and cited brewing and dyeing as two cases where the application of scientific method and research by the Germans had displaced us from our markets while we carried on in the old empirical haphazard methods which had served in the past. Shipbuilding was an even more critical case for Scotland; the Germans had expanded that industry while we had contracted it.

Why was that? The reason was that German engineers 'had

Technology and the University

received their education in institutions in which research is in the very air'. 'We seem to fancy', he goes on, 'that if we only teach the man who is to wheel barrows of stuff to and fro to the furnaces how to analyse the materials he is wheeling, or to teach the man who will all his life drill holes in the steel plates from which the ship is built, how to make a simple mechanical drawing, that we have taken every step that is necessary to put us on an equality with our pushing rivals across the North Sea, or those still more pushful ones across the herring pond'. We need men who are as continually employed in research as their teachers were in the college or school.

He then goes on to worry about the development of the alternative system, as Jenkin had done before. In Britain that meant the emergence of institutions like the Heriot-Watt College, 'of the very first rank', with its lecture rooms and laboratories crowded night after night with hundreds of students, which compared favourably with anything on the Continent or America; but the universities and the secondary schools had fallen short in education for the middle-class man who would in due course be running industrial enterprises. Most school education was the very reverse of what was needed as a preparation for technical studies. 'Public and secondary schools must devote as much attention to preparation for the science schools as they do for the literary schools. In Germany by contrast the professors are not burdened with students absolutely unfit for the instruction they are receiving.'

Beare was another who saw the necessity of apprenticeship or pupillage; he could see no way that a future engineer could learn in college about the control and direction of large bodies of workmen; practical training was irreplaceable. He pointed to the glaring contrast between the numbers (proportional to the population) taking up engineering in America and the paltry number in Great Britain – the total number of engineers in Britain being trained in colleges or universities was smaller than the number attending the technical school in Munich.

The instruction should be given by people who were themselves engineers or trained as engineers; the course should start as one course and after two years branch into specialisms. The co-operation of the University with the Heriot-Watt College was essential. He saw civil engineering as the province of the university and mechanical and electrical engineering as that of the Heriot-Watt.

The problems – and the challenges – raised by the three Edinburgh professors reflected a profound change in the scope and meaning of technological education and thus of education as a whole in the nineteenth century. To understand that change it is necessary to refer back to the institution that influenced the whole scene. That was the École Polytechnique – one of Napoleon's most lasting innovations – set up in Paris in 1793 (Armytage 1965). It shaped the educational scene on the Continent during the nineteenth century and gave rise to serious anxieties among the universities of the United Kingdom. It challenged their conventions and opened up a new prospectus for the world of action as well as scholarship, and helped to shape the mass of institutions not only in France but in Germany and ultimately America.

The ancestor of the École Polytechnique was the École des Ponts et Chaussées set up in 1748 to train builders of roads and bridges. The Polytechnique had a wider remit. It had to provide engineers for the Revolutionary armies and give officers a training in pure science. It began as a Central School of Public Works with subsidiaries (écoles centrales) in each provincial capital, to feed industry and the armies with technical personnel. Its students were admitted by competitive examination and were taught by some of the most outstanding mathematicians, physicists and chemists of the day. Two years of basic science were topped by a third devoted to engineering.

That brief account does not indicate the profound effect the school had in its time, nor the fundamental reorientation of studies of which its leaders were confident and proud. 'Its physico-centric curriculum produced a new kind of man appearing, according to Professor Hayek, for the first time in history. Having never learned to interpret human life or growth in terms of mankind's literary past . . . they tended to see life in scientific terms' (Armytage 1965).

They believed they were forming a new type of person who would organise society on scientific lines. The polytechnique would spread ideas through society; as apostles of the religion of industry and the inventors of machines, that would reduce human drudgery. Its graduates became in effect the governing elite and major figures in civil life.

Here was the fertile seed of a movement that formed the new

Technology and the University

breed of technocrats. It was to influence education all over the world. Immediately it was the model for the new universities of Berlin in 1810 and Bonn in 1817, founded to promote the advancement and extension of science (Armytage 1965). They took the development further. Berlin in particular promoted the idea of the university as a centre for research; students were there to discover new knowledge rather than just receive instruction. That attitude was in due course to move to America.

That was at the university level. The ideas of the Polytechnique were extended to a wider community through the huge growth of German polytechnics from 1851 – the *Technische Hochschulen*. They were upgraded technical schools that had started in the 1820s and 1830s; they now had the status and character of universities. There were nine in Germany by the end of the century, in places such as Berlin, Dresden, Stuttgart, Munich and Hanover, established specifically for the purpose of 'affording higher instruction for the technical professions in state and community service, as well as in industrial life, and of cultivating sciences and arts which are intimately connected with the field of technology' (Emmerson 1973).

The implications of this were clear. Technological education could be, and must be, of the highest status. It required special institutions of university rank that would not just specialise in science and technology but would see them as the centre of a whole education and culture. But the new development was not just a matter of organisation or status. The German universities and *Technische Hochschulen* taught a different kind of learning. That was *Wissenschaft* (Ashby 1958).

The fact that the English universities were little influenced by the continental excitement of a new map of learning may be not unrelated to the fact that *Wissenschaft* does not translate easily into Engish. It does not mean science, nor just knowledge. It covers, in Ashby's phrase, the 'objective and critical approach to all knowledge'. The foundations of this empirical approach to knowledge were laid in Germany not by scientists but by humanists in the universities. They took the scientific spirit from France and brought it into the core of the university's life. The university became what it had been in medieval times – a cosmopolitan place for the influx of scholars. Its pattern was changed for ever. It was now the centre for research.

Meanwhile in England and Scotland a different institution was being developed – essentially to meet the same needs, but at a humbler level – which was in the long term to become the start of an alternative tradition in education. That was the formation of the Mechanics Institutes. Unlike the French colleges they – the first technological education in Britain – were started, as Ashby points out (Ashby 1958), not for the sons of managers in industry, but for that small minority of the working classes who could read and write: the craftsman, the foreman, the mechanic.

They started in an irregular way in Glasgow where the professor of Natural Philosophy, John Anderson, known as Jolly Jack Phosphorus, who like many another academic spent much of his time quarrelling bitterly with his academic colleagues, started in 1791 to give public, 'anti-toga' lectures to all sorts of workers and left what money he had in his will to the people of Glasgow for the setting up of a rival university 'for the Improvement of Human Nature, of Science, and of the country where they live'. It became, not a university, but Anderson's Institution in 1796. Its first professor of Natural Philosophy, Dr George Birkbeck, gave lectures attended by several hundred artisans. Then in 1804 he moved to London and formed the London Mechanics Institution, later Birkbeck College (starting the trend now known as 'academic drift'). The mechanics' class in Glasgow broke away and formed the Glasgow Mechanics Institution in 1823 (Roderick and Stephens 1978). By that time, in 1821, the Edinburgh School of Art had been set up, which is considered to have been the first genuine mechanics institute.

From Edinburgh, Glasgow and London the movement spread through the kingdom. There were a hundred by 1826, two hundred by 1840, and over six hundred by 1850, with over 200,000 students. The Society of Arts, now the Royal Society of Arts, set up specifically in 1754 for the promotion of the arts, manufactures and commerce, established examinations and diplomas. For the institutes were there to meet the vocational needs of the artisans, and even if the promoters and employers saw many other advantages in them – like better workmen, and the alleviation of the miseries of the working classes – they were seen by their inventors, like Birkbeck, as liberating agencies for enriching the ordinary man's understanding.

Technology and the University

The mechanics' institutes might have been the germ of a national system of vocational education. The fact that it never happened seems to reflect something in the national mood, or perhaps the overall dominance of the universities. In any case the tradition started by the mechanics' institutes had to go through many changes before it reached some kind of maturity in Great Britain. The Mechanics' Institutes, nearly all of which started in the 1820s as evening schools, became Colleges of Technology. The Colleges of Art grew out of the Schools of Design started in 1836, following the recommendations of the Select Committee of 1835 to train designers for industry. The Colleges of Commerce were developed from the evening classes first established in the nineteenth century to train book-keepers and secretaries, then accountants and business managers. The Teacher Training Colleges, later Colleges of Education, started as training schools usually in the late nineteenth century to provide teachers for the elementary schools after Forster's Education Act brought schooling within reach of everyone. It was the amalgamation of all those colleges during the seventies of this century that created the present polytechnics.

There are certain features about this development that are in marked contrast with the Continent. None of the schools were places of privilege. They were mostly originally part-time. They had to be local, if only because of the part-timers. They taught, not a liberal education, not even research, but how to do a job. In short it is a tradition in education, rarely given the recognition it deserves, based not on the lecture room or classroom but on the workshop and the studio. And it makes no distinction between education and training.

It was essentially the same tradition that led after elaboration in the latter part of the nineteenth century to the formation of the civic universities (Armytage 1955; Sanderson 1972). Owens College in Manchester had been founded in 1851, modelled on Oxford and Cambridge. In 1880 it became the first leg in the tripod that became the Victoria University; Liverpool joined it in 1884, Leeds in 1887. They were eventually disentangled and given their own charters in 1903. By that time other universities had been founded – Newcastle, Dundee, Bristol, Birmingham, for example – in the great industrial cities and towns. They had a lasting effect in at least two ways.

First, they resulted in more working-class students obtaining a higher education. They were the sons of merchants and members of the lower mercantile and artisan classes. In the evening classes about four-fifths of the students belonged to the working class (Armytage 1955; Sanderson 1972). The second, more academic change was that the new civic universities, led by the Victoria University in Manchester, absorbed the idea of *Wissenschaft* by the end of the century. Ashby regards the change as a profound metamorphosis. 'They recovered something they had lost for many generations, for they regained equilibrium with the intellectual climate of their age' (Ashby 1958).

The recovery of that equilibrium involved a fundamental change in the ethos of the university. For the new intellectual climate was not only one based upon science rather than the classics and literature. It was also based upon technology, the activities of an industrial society responsible for the wealth and thus ultimately for the survival of the universities. If the fostering of science had been the main innovation of the universities in the late eighteenth and early nineteen centuries, the acceptance of technology, essentially through the establishment of courses in engineering, was the achievement of the late nineteenth century. It happened notably in Scotland, partly because of the influence of the practical work in Glasgow and Edinburgh pioneered by Lord Kelvin. But even that in its way reflected something deeper and more lasting in the Scottish character and the character of its universities. That was what in G.E.Davie's phrase has come to be known as *the Democratic Intellect* (Davie 1961). It was a tradition not only in thinking; Scotland having far more places in universities than England in relation to their populations, it could offer places to a much wider social range (Sanderson 1972).

The civic and the Scottish universities thus had firm links with local industrialists and taught skills that were needed by them. In return the civic universities made their own contribution to industry. Electrical engineering was an obvious case where the universities were crucial to the activity. But their contributions were much more diverse and often humble – in chemicals, metallurgy, textiles and also soap, beer, sparking plugs, gas fires and radio. It was a contribution that became more obvious and urgent during the Great War. By that time it

Technology and the University

had been bitterly noted that in contrast with Germany this country was using its graduates as manpower to perish on the battlefields rather than using their skills if only for the production of armaments. There was no better case of university co-operation than Edinburgh where the government factory at Craigleith was operated by the Professor of Chemistry, Sir James Walker, who organised the staff and students of the Chemistry department to produce TNT with record efficiency (Sanderson 1972).

In the last fifteen years, we have, in an embryonic way, recreated the problem described with such vigour by Fleeming Jenkin, by establishing polytechnics throughout the country, if without the resources to do the job properly. But their existence raises again the important question about both the provision of training for an advanced technological society and the effect that must have upon the nature of the university. Should the university be the comprehensive repository of all the disciplines that add up to the corpus of education? If so, it must include technology. Or should, as happened to great effect in France and Germany and then America, technology be the specialist business of major institutions?

Charcteristically, in a nation that drifts into odd positions, we have adopted neither the one nor the other. The new polytechnics are not predominantly technological, whatever their title may suggest. The Colleges of Advanced Technology, designated as such in 1958, which undoubtedly would, if different counsels had prevailed in government in the 1960s, have been the leading polytechnics, were elevated to university status in 1965 following the Robbins Report and, with one exception, dropped the name Technology from their titles as soon as they respectably could.

In that process the great colleges of technology like the Royal College of Science and Technology in Glasgow (now Strathclyde University) and the Heriot-Watt College in Edinburgh (now the Heriot-Watt University) grew into a different shape and sometimes moved to rural sites, away from the environment of work. Should the polytechnics follow suit? Would that represent a downgrading of technology and another case of what has come to be known as *academic drift*? (Burgess 1978). The problem revolves around technology, which is not, as George Wilson said, simply applied science. Science is held in the loving embrace of the universities; technology still sits uneasily in the groves of academe as urgent reality presses on it, finances it and demands to be faced.

But that might be the very reason why the modern university cannot afford to undervalue technology. As the means or activity by which man seeks to manipulate his environment, it must be crucial to the university if the university is to justify its name. If Armstrong was right and industrial sciences can be considered as one, the understanding of technology as a whole might be thought to be the very stuff of any understanding of the modern world. As such, the university is a paradigm of the problem of technology in the modern world. If it is important to the world's future (which it is) the university cannot ignore it. Perhaps it should be not just within the university but the very basis of the teaching and research upon which the university rests.

On the other hand, in an age of mass education, of equality of opportunity and of large populations, institutions may become too big for comprehension and for adventure. If the subject or the activity is not being pushed ahead, in which way is it contributing to an education? Perhaps it is better after all to split institutions up, or keep them small and more single-purpose. The establishment of the new polytechnics changes the situation in any case and means that there are now major institutions of higher education – many of them considerably larger and more diverse than many universities – concerned with the world of action, with the arts of doing and making and organising, rather than with learning for its own sake.

The argument discussed by the Edinburgh professors is unlikely to be settled in a hurry. Maybe it is one of the glories of a university that it can and must continually argue about such things. For it is not one thing itself, but a multipurpose organisation. Perhaps it will be the end of the university when it ceases to argue about its own meaning.

REFERENCES

Armstrong, G. F. (1885) *The Progress of High Technical Instruction*. Edinburgh University Library, Edinburgh.
Armytage, W. H. G. (1955) *Civic Universities*. London.
— (1965) *The Rise of the Technocrats*. London.
Ashby, E. (1958) *Technology and the Academics*. London.

Technology and the University

Balfour, Professor (1860) *Biographical Sketch of the late George Wilson*. Private printing. Edinburgh University Library.

Beare, T. H. (1901) *The Education of an Engineer*. Edinburgh University Library, Edinburgh.

Burgess, T. (1978) *New Ways to Learn*. Cantor Lecture, Royal Society of Arts.

Davie, G. E. (1961) *The Democratic Intellect: Scotland and her Universities in the 19th century*. Edinburgh.

Emmerson, G. S. (1973) *Engineering Education*. Newton Abbot.

Jenkin, Fleeming (1868) *The Education of Civil and Mechanical Engineers*. Edinburgh University Library, Edinburgh.

Playfair, L. (1858) *Inaugural Lecture University of Edinburgh*. Edinburgh University Library.

— (1872) *On Teaching Universities and Examining Boards*. Address to Philosophical Institution of Edinburgh. Edinburgh University Library.

— (1873) *Universities in relation to professional education*. St Andrews Graduate Association.

Roderick, G. H. and Stephens, M. D. (1978) *Education and Industry in the 19th century*. London.

Sanderson, M. (1972) *The Universities and British Industry 1850-1970*. London.

Turner, A. L. (1933) *The History of the University of Edinburgh 1833-1933*. Edinburgh.

Wilson, G. (1855) *What is Technology?* An Inaugural Lecture. Edinburgh University Library, Edinburgh.

Wilson, J. A. (1860) *Memoir of George Wilson*. Edinburgh University Library.

TRADITION AND INNOVATION IN BRITISH UNIVERSITIES
C. 1860–1960

ASA BRIGGS

'It has been truly remarked,' wrote Herbert Spencer at the beginning of his essay on Education, published in 1861, 'that in order of time decoration preceded dress.' It was a characteristic beginning to a Spencer essay which, like most of his essays, was lacking in specific examples. The most significant point is that Spencer had virtually nothing to say in his essay about universities. Almost as significant is that the little that he had to say was wholly unfavourable. Spencer would not even admit, as many critics of universities did, that what was taught in them represented 'tradition', however ossified. 'If we inquire what is the real motive for . . . a classical education,' he claimed, 'we find it to be simply conformity to public opinion. Men dress their children's minds as they do their bodies, in the prevailing fashion. As the Orinoco Indian puts on paint before leaving his hut, not with a view to any direct benefit, but because he would be ashamed to be seen without it; so a boy's drilling in Latin and Greek is insisted on, not because of their intrinsic value, but that he may not be disgraced by being found ignorant of them – that he may have the "education of a gentleman" – the badge marking a certain social position, and bringing a consequent respect' (Spencer 1911, 1–2).

Spencer was one of the great majority of Victorian Englishmen, even of highly articulate Englishmen, who had no university education, but in his case he stayed out of university not of necessity but of choice. His father was a schoolmaster, and his uncle, a clergyman, offered to send him to Cambridge. Spencer refused. What higher education he received, therefore, was largely the result of his own reading. So, too, of course, was John Stuart Mill's. And while Mill, who had published his essay on Liberty two years before Spencer's essay on Education, was far more sensitive to the significance of tradition, even of tradition of which he disapproved, he was just as hostile as Spencer was to endowed universities. 'Unfortunately,' he had written in 1852 in a dismissive article on Dr Whewell, the Master of Trinity College, Cambridge, 'it is not in

Tradition and Innovation in British Universities
the nature of bodies constituted like the English universities, even when stirred up into anything like mental activity, to send forth thought of any but one description. There have been universities (those of France and Germany have at some periods been practically conducted on this principle) which brought together into a body the most vigorous thinkers and the ablest teachers, whatever the conclusions to which their thinking might have led them. But in the English universities no thought can find place, except that which can reconcile itself with orthodoxy' (Mill 1969, 167).

Mill had more than religious orthodoxy in mind, although Pusey would have been a better target than Whewell; and it was Whewell's attack on Bentham which most disturbed Mill. Two years after Mill, Pusey wrote explicitly that 'the problem and special work of a university' was 'not how to advance science, not how to make discoveries, not how to form new schools of mental philosophy, not to invent new modes of analysis, not to produce works in Medicine, Jurisprudence, or even Theology, but to form minds religiously, morally, intellectually, which shall discharge aright whatever duties God, in his Providence, shall appoint to them' (Richter 1964, 61). There was more abundant evidence of dislike of what was new in this forthright statement than of an appeal to an older tradition or traditions. Yet there was something new in the tone of the statement itself. When fifteen-year-old Bentham had been made a Senior Commoner at Queen's College, Oxford, in the eighteenth century, Queen's was certainly not like that, as Bentham's often amusing letters show. He was not an easy conformist and in one of his first letters home he tells how after intending to fast in order to prepare for the Sacrament, 'it would not do, for I began to grow sick for want of victuals; and so was forced to eat a bit of breakfast' (1968, 21). Bentham was also prepared to show far more spirit than Spencer would have done in the same position. Hoping to see the transit of Venus in 1761, he broke College rules to gain access to a telescope which the Fellows had appropriated to themselves:

> Whatever belongs to the College far from being for the free use of all the individuals belongs only to the Fellows. Instead therefore of letting the under-graduates have the use of the Telescope, the Fellows had it only to themselves, so that we had no hopes of seeing this remarkable

Phaenomenon which it was allmost impossible we should ever have an opportunity of seeing again in our lives as it will not happen again this 160 years or more. But I and two others of my Acquaintance thinking it unreasonable that we should not see it . . . stole up the common-room stairs and marched up to the leads where the Fellows had brought the Telescope for the convenience of observing the Phaenomenon. There we found only Dr. Dixon and a Master of Arts of his hall, by good luck as the Fellows were gone to prayers, who very obligingly offered to show it to us, but unluckily the Sun just then happened to pop his head under a cloud, and we could not get to see it again 'till the senior Fellow Mr. Knaile came up thither, who seeing us there behaved civilly enough, as he could not then very well turn us out again. (Bentham 1968, 46)

This anecdote relating to a year which is just one century before the date in my title is worth telling if only because it brings out the important point that whatever the state of universities and their attitudes towards 'innovation' and 'tradition' there are ways round the system for the bright and active, whether or not they are influenced primarily by social or educational considerations.

There were, of course, many changes in the university scene both in England and Scotland between 1761 and 1861, notably the setting up of the 'Godless College' in Gower Street, London, with which Bentham is now most associated, a college very different from Queen's. (He does not seem to have subscribed money to its foundation, although he bequeathed it his skeleton, wax head and clothes). The influence of Scotland on the new institution was greater than the influence of Bentham, since many of its most important sponsors, like Brougham, had studied at Edinburgh, as had most of the new Professors. There was not a single graduate of Oxford. As the historian of University College has put it, 'the extended range of the subjects of University study, the lecture system, the non-residence of the students, their admission to single courses, the absence of religious tests, the dependence of the professors upon fees and the democratic character of the institution, were all deliberate imitations of Scottish practice' (Hale Bellot 1929, 8)

Within England this was real innovation, innovation through reaction and deliberate contrast. And texts from Scotland, like George Jardine's *Outlines of a Philosophical Education* (1818), were employed in the defence of innovation, 'We do not in this part of the Kingdom,' Jardine had written, 'attach to classical learning that high and almost exclusive degree of importance which is ascribed to it elsewhere, thinking it of greater consequence to the student to receive instruction in the elements of science both physical and mental, than to acquire even the most accurate knowledge of the ancient tongues' (Davie 1964, 10). When this approach was challenged in Scotland itself in 1826, Francis Jeffrey offered the second basic argument in favour of the Scottish tradition. While admitting that 'our knowledge, though more general, is more superficial than with our neighbours', Jeffrey claimed that this was a 'great good on the whole, because it enables relatively large numbers of people to get . . . that knowledge which tends to liberalise and make intelligent the mass of our population' (Davie 1964, 27). Education was not decoration: it was enlightenment.

The story of Edinburgh and other Scottish universities between 1826 and the Universities (Scotland) Act of 1858 raises almost every issue related to tradition and its erosion, and innovation and its decline. Of the many issues, the increasing power of the State to intervene is one, and in general it seems to have been used neither to support tradition nor to encourage innovation but to tighten order. Sir William Hamilton suggested, indeed, in 1826 that the proposals of the Commissioners left unreformed those things which should have been reformed and reformed those things that ought not to have been reformed. And whatever may be said of the domestic management of arts or medicine at Edinburgh – no new chair was founded in arts between 1761 and 1861 – it was certainly an odd governmental decision to abolish the Chair of Military Surgery in 1856 just when the need for such a chair had been demonstrated, amid considerable publicity, during the Crimean War.

When John Stuart Mill gave his famous Inaugural Address at St Andrews in 1867, he did not touch on these matters. Indeed, he argued less in terms either of distinctive tradition or of deliberate innovation than in terms of what was coming to be a kind of conventional wisdom about universities which transcended boundaries. 'The proper function of an University in national education is tolerably well understood,' he began. 'At least, there is a tolerably general agreement about what an University is not. It is not a place of professional education. Universities are not intended to teach the knowledge required to fit men for some special mode of gaining their livelihood. Their object is not to make skilful lawyers, or physicians, or engineers, but capable and cultivated human beings . . . Men are men before they are lawyers, or physicians or merchants, or manufacturers; and if you make them capable and sensible men, they will make themselves capable and sensible lawyers or physicians' (Mill 1867, 5–7). By 1867, this was an acceptable approach to many people not only in St Andrews – or in Edinburgh – but in Oxford and Cambridge.

In England, when the issue of reform was raised during the 1850s, particularly in relation to Oxford and Cambridge, the argument inside universities was at least as interesting as the public debate in Parliament. Nor had conventional wisdom quite hardened by that time. The decade opened with the important Examination Statute of 1850 in Oxford which raised the whole question of college tuition and ultimately of professorial tuition (the two were, of course, to be forced into contrast) as well as of the reform of the curriculum. The claims of innovation and tradition were deliberately pitted against each other. The historian E. A. Freeman, for example, opposed the setting up of a new History School on the grounds that it was impossible to combine the traditional education offered in Oxford with the specialisation demanded by the Statute, while the reforming Master of Pembroke, Francis Jeune, wanted to go further and bring in political economy, originally a Scots speciality. 'Political economy we greatly desire,' he wrote to the Professor of History, 'and have urged on the Board but have always been scornfully refused. Now even Adam Smith stinks in their nostrils. I fear he must be adjourned' (Bill 1973, 83). Eventually a revised Statute was carried in 1850 creating a combined School of History and Jurisprudence and including a paper on Adam Smith. Compulsory classics was the price of such compromise. And all this internal change preceded the setting up of the Royal Commission to enquire into the state, discipline, studies and revenues of the University of Oxford.

The subsequent interplay of internal and external opinion, to a limited extent public opinion as well as opinion in the Royal Commission or in Parliament, demands detailed examination;

Tradition and Innovation in British Universities
and while a simple dichotomy between 'internal' and 'external' influences' on the development of universities is not more satisfactory than such a simple dichotomy applied for so long to the history of science, three points stand out in the university story. First, there was a continuing difference of opinion within the University. There were not only 'liberal' Fellows and 'conservative' Fellows, but 'liberal' Colleges and 'conservative' Colleges. Second, the Press, particularly the periodical Press, of increasing importance in national life during the 1850s and 1860s, spotlighted what it took to be the main issues. (The *Morning Post*, for instance, dismissed the Oxford curriculum as a collection of odds and ends swept together 'for no better reason than that there was no room for them elsewhere' (Bill 1973, 80).) Third, it was not only Benthamites who were suspicious of endowed Colleges. Walter Bagehot, for example, wrote of Oxford in the same year as Mill was criticising Cambridge (1852) that 'badly as the University has observed her statutes, her very laxity seems scrupulous when compared with the scandalous evasions of her Colleges' (1974, 340).

Bagehot, educated at London, was not in general unfriendly to Oxford – nor Cambridge – but he noted acutely that the kind of education offered there was even in its ideal form unsuited to more than a few people, and that for this reason the social role of the university was not easy to defend. 'The canon law is gone by, the medieval theology is food for inferior animals,' he wrote of the curriculum *after* the first reforms. 'The finer classic – the lighter thoughts – the more delicate fancies – the most evanescent shades of meaning and of language, these are what we now call scholarship. We cannot expect to train any great number of persons in any age to spend their lives on these' (1974, 340).

In his own way, Bagehot was as damning as Spencer when he dissected Arthur Hugh Clough's argument that 'universities are and ought to be, and must be, mere finishing schools for the higher classes.' (He was even more sarcastic about Robert Lowe's opinion that universities should prepare undergraduates for going to Australia.) 'The gentlemen of England educated at many schools, ... come to College for a year or two to learn one another's faces and names ... and derive from the society of one another – from wine parties – from the common *et ceteras* of college life – a certain cultivation, certain friendships, certain manners, which are a step in advance of what in each kind they previously possessed, and give them besides an excellent start in English life. The gentry of England are thus it is said "finished". They take the social type which is to last them for life. But surely this is hardly a sufficient reason for so great colleges, scarcely a sufficient account of such large structures and such enormous revenues' (1974, 343). Much later critical comment scarcely moved beyond this point.

Bagehot was not impressed by Carlyle's dictum that 'the true university of today is a collection of books': he held that the proper object of a university education was 'to train intellectual men for the pursuits of an intellectual life', as, indeed, did Mill and defenders of the old Scottish system. And Mill would have agreed also with Bagehot's proposition that by contrast the real education for every practical pursuit was 'specific'. Both men thought that reforms of university structure, if not of curriculum, would have to come from outside the universities. Yet both were convinced that change was inevitable. As Bagehot put it succinctly, 'the University is part of the nation; it has changed, is changing, and will change, with the nation.' He was not unaware of the fact, however, as he remarked years later in an essay on 'Matthew Arnold and London University' that since he was an outsider to Oxford, he was dealing in images as much as in facts, in what Arnold called 'unreal words' and that he was missing 'shades and touches' – and perhaps much else which could only be known from within. Few later critics who shared his general stance would have been so generous (1974, 361, 386).

From within, the university picture became more rather than less complex during the 1860s as groups of reformers with a variety of motives emerged, their outlook radically different from that of Pusey. Some, indeed, were directly influenced by Mill, a few by Comte. And while it now began to be possible inside the university to develop a 'high' view of tutorial teaching, to generate a strong pressure for a German-style professoriate and, above all, to proclaim the conception of a 'community of scholars', it also began to be possible, at least for radicals, to look outside the university altogether and to dream of a new alliance between brains and numbers in order to secure political change. By the time of the passing of the

Tradition and Innovation in British Universities

Reform Bill of 1867, the case was being regularly (and eloquently) presented that an enlightened university elite was a necessary agency in the making of democracy, not antithetical to it. This sense of strategy had little in common either with that of the Scottish 'democratic intellect' or with that of associates in Clough's finishing school. In John Morley's words, 'the extreme advanced party' was 'likely for the future to have on its side the most highly cultivated intellect in the nation, and the contest will lie between brains and numbers on the one side, and wealth, rank, vested interest, possession, in short, on the other' (Kent 1978, 34).

The picture in Cambridge was not dissimilar, although there were fewer links with the outside world of politics. 'A new group of dons emerged there in the twenty years preceding the statutory reforms of 1882' (Rothblatt 1968, 227), who placed more emphasis on scholarship, more on teaching as a career, much on the 'idea of the College'. Indeed, Whewell's death in 1886 marked the end of a generation, and within a few months Henry Sidgwick, a key figure in the new generation of the 1860s was writing 'We are in a considerable state of agitation here, as all sorts of projects of reform are coming to the surface, partly in consequence of our having a new Master – people begin to stretch themselves and feel a certain freedom and independence' (Rothblatt 1968, 212). For him, innovation was a cultural phenomenon out of which a new tradition would emerge. Indeed, much of the very sense of 'traditional' Cambridge that was transmitted to the twentieth century can be traced back only to Sidgwick.

By then, however, there had been many realised national reforms which had long-run implications for the development of higher education in the twentieth century. First, the Test Acts went in 1871, opening up all teaching posts in Oxford and Cambridge regardless of religion. One gap between them and London narrowed. Second, the marriage of dons narrowed the gap between dons and the rest of the population, while changing the characters of the colleges. Third, an extension movement developed which took both Oxford and Cambridge far away from their colleges into industrial towns and cities, widening contacts if not extending access: this was based on the conception of a 'peripatetic university'. Fourth, the higher education of women had been begun – significantly in a wide range of very different institutions. Fifth, school education had been grasped as a national issue and compulsion had been introduced at the elementary level. It was a very elementary level, and the provision seemed at first to have little to do with ultimate access to higher education. Sixth, new universities had emerged which incorporated science and technology into their curriculum. Seventh, there was a great expansion of professional education, with a proliferation of examinations and diplomas. Eighth, an embryonic University Grants system came into existence in 1889.

Each item in this list could be singled out for detailed treatment. In particular, however, the new 'civic universities' obviously must figure in any focused account of innovation and tradition. Owen's College, Manchester, founded in 1851, had a difficult early history, though it quickly established an *ethos*, if not a tradition, of its own, closely bound up with a lively industrial city. The kind of idea behind it had been expressed a quarter of a century earlier in Leeds, where Yorkshire College was founded in 1874, for it was in 1826 that John Marshall, President of the Leeds Philosophical and Literary Society, had put forward a scheme for a university with no religious tests, with children living at home, which would teach 'the whole circle of literature, the sciences and the arts', and would conceive of higher education not as a finishing school but as 'a preparation for active life' (Shimmin 1954, 3).

There would have been few quarrels with this approach in any of the new institutions which emerged late, not early, in the history of English industrialisation, during the critical decades of the 1870s and 1880s – University College, Bristol (1876), Mason College, Birmingham (1880), and University College, Liverpool (1881). Yet in all of these places there was as much emphasis on continuing tradition as on innovation. Thus, in Birmingham, where new departments were established in subjects which were not taught in Oxford and Cambridge, Joseph Chamberlain, who was well equipped to judge what was educationally 'relevant' to the interests of Birmingham industry, could tell his own Court in very different language, that 'to place a university in the middle of a great industrial and manufacturing population is to do something to leaven the whole mass with higher aims and higher intellectual ambitions than would otherwise be possible to people engaged

Tradition and Innovation in British Universities
entirely in trading and commercial pursuits' (Vincent and Hinton 1947, 20–1). From the start, but not, of course, for the first time ideal and reality were placed in a somewhat uneasy relation to each other in the great provincial cities.

The detailed histories of individual 'Redbrick' universities, as they came to be called, have much in common, although the differences between them are as illuminating as the differences between Oxford and Cambridge colleges. In general, however, they were drawn into innovation only in piecemeal fashion at the departmental level — after the first pioneering years they became very departmentalised — and they made few experiments in modes of teaching. Their relationship with Oxford and Cambridge remained important, for while they drew a significant proportion of their staff from them — James Bryce, for example, taught at Manchester for six years — they were conscious of the fact, too conscious indeed, that they seemed unprepossessing when compared with Oxford and Cambridge Colleges. As a Vice-Chancellor of the University of Leeds put it in the 1950s, for his own *alumni*, 'Naturally a young university sought to learn from the long and valuable experience of the older universities, but it had to avoid the danger of attempting to ape them.' The sense of themselves as universities was a cultural matter, therefore, inextricably bound up with the sense of the cities to which they belonged and, indeed, of the whole industrial environment.

There were enough new universities, however, to constitute an interest, though they were not created as a *bloc* and a fascinating brief account of the difference between them and the German universities was given during the First World War by Sir Michael Sadler, who was to become Vice-Chancellor of Leeds. While praising German 'energy' in creating universities, he noted in them the presence of 'base political intrigues' which were absent in Britain. Moreover, he went on, while the German universities, 'together with their younger sisters the Technical High Schools', were 'very liberally financed by governments — by way of business investment as well as for reasons of intellectual policy' — they were staffed by men who were 'sensitive to the behests of the authorised Government, even to the point of accepting their ethical judgements' and were 'the workshops of professors who never forgot that they are the sworn servants of the Government they serve.' In Great

Britain, on the other hand, Sadler explained, 'the older professions of law and medicine' retained (with some modifications made by modern statutes) 'the mediaeval characteristic of corporate autonomy'. The result was that in Great Britain (1) the Universities were not the sole road of entry to the older or newer professions; (2) the State had never yet 'felt the interest of the national revenue to be directly concerned in the development of the scientific power and equipment of the Universities or higher technical schools'; (3) 'the habit of mind of a British professor was by social custom independent of State influence; and (4) the British educational institutions, and especially the English, whether of University or of secondary rank, had retained in a large degree 'the mediaeval tradition of self-government and the mediaeval freedom to adjust themselves insensibly to the needs and preferences of particular social groups.'

The extent to which new universities had established their own more recent traditions by the 1920s is well brought out in a popular book of 1928, *The New Universities*. It begins not with the Senate Chambers – and all the new universities had Senates and Councils – but with the Union, has much to say about 'home and vacation', and while it denies the claim that 'the civic university loses because it is not detached', a claim of some supporters of Oxford and Cambridge – 'the very life of the city brings life to the university' – it suggests, first, that relationships between academics and students are wrong, and, second, that it is not easy to see how they can be improved. 'The student very often regards the lecturer as a schoolboy regards his master or as a workman looks upon his employer. They do not often feel as partners in a common adventure for the discovery of knowledge.' Throughout there are glances back to 'Oxbridge', often an idealised version of it.

Innovation at the departmental level is difficult to ferret out in 'Redbrick' universities before 1939, though there are many examples of new development in Manchester and many instances of innovation in research, with no cultural connotations in almost all universities. An excellent example comes from the University of Leeds. The first lecturer in textile physics, appointed in 1928, W. T. Astbury, was concerned with the fine structure of the wool fibre, a subject of direct economic importance in the West Riding of Yorkshire, and by 1933 a skeleton structure of the wool molecule had been established.

Tradition and Innovation in British Universities
But textiles were then left behind as Astbury and his colleagues concerned themselves with other proteins, and in 1945 Astbury went on to become Professor of Biomolecular Structure. What started as applied science in a field taught only in a few civic universities passed, therefore, into pure science and into applied science in quite different fields. Yet tradition had a part in this story too, for it was an ancient London Livery Company, the Clothworkers, great benefactors of the University of Leeds, who provided the first funds for Astbury's research. The State did not figure in the picture at all.

The report of the Barlow Committee of 1945 reflected an increasing attention to universities on the part of the State after the Second World War and reported the willingness of the civic universities to increase their numbers in the national interest by 86 per cent in ten years. And a year later the University Grants Committee had its terms of reference widened to include the clause 'to assist, in consultation with the universities and other bodies concerned, the preparation and execution of such plans for the development of the universities as may from time to time be required in order to ensure that they are fully adequate to national needs.' Lord Murray of Newhaven, who was to serve as Chairman of the UGC from 1953 to 1963, has described this statement as 'the first open recognition that national needs should be a factor in the development of universities in Britain.' It was singled out also by Sir Frederick Ogilvie in a pamphlet on *British Universities* published by the Bureau of Current Affairs in 1948. 'The Committee', he said, 'has swallowed its scruples about earmarking and has allotted large sums specifically for the development of medicine and the social sciences' (Ogilvie 1948).

When the UGC went on in 1947 to make its first non-recurrent grants to universities to meet their capital needs and their needs for scientific equipment – and the power to decide on the distribution of these capital grants clearly increased the influence of the UGC – the Vice-Chancellors' Committee, a body which had first come into existence very informally in 1918 but which was never concerned with innovation as such, welcomed the new dispensation. 'The universities entirely accept the view that the Government has not only the right, but the duty to satisfy itself that every field of study which in the national interest ought to be cultivated in Great Britain is in fact being cultivated in the university system and that the resources which are placed at the disposal of the universities are being used with full regard both to efficiency and economy' (Berdahl 1959, 76).

The emphasis was on meeting needs, not on innovation, and it was in this mood that in 1948 Nottingham University College, an offshoot of London, was given full university status. The first real innovation was the setting-up in 1949 of the new University College of North Staffordshire, an institution which deliberately set out to look at university education in a new way. The second was the long sequence of decisions, first taken within the Ministry of Education in 1953, which led in 1956 to the designation as Colleges of Advanced Technology (CATS) of a number of local technical colleges of high standing, financed from 1962 onwards not by local authorities but by direct Ministry of Education grants. They were to be granted charters as full universities from 1964 onwards, thereby broadening the base of the community of universities and widening the scope of the UGC.

The third was the decision taken by the UGC in 1958 to sponsor seven brand-new universities, not upgraded institutions nor institutions subjected, like North Staffordshire, to an initial period of tutelage, but from the start autonomous and free. One new university would have been incremental, as North Staffordshire was; seven changed the dynamics of the system, indeed, helped to foster the sense of a system. This was a crucial decision taken in steps, without a debate in Parliament, five years before the Robbins Report on Higher Education – and taken essentially on the same basis, to begin with, as the decision taken to increase university numbers after the Barlow Committee had reported on 1946. The steps were: inquiries to existing universities about the targets they wished to achieve; estimates of national 'shortfall'; and determination about the extent of new provision. Had existing universities been willing to increase their numbers sufficiently to meet the shortfall, there might well have been no new universities at all, although in 1946 the Barlow Committee had recommended the foundation of at least one new university and several university colleges.

At first the language of the UGC was remarkably cautious, when contrasted with the Barlow Report. 'It is clear that the

Tradition and Innovation in British Universities
situation contemplated by the Barlow Committee does not immediately arise. In these circumstances the establishment of new institutions could no longer be regarded as a necessary means to the policy of expansion, and we have acted on the opinion that, in present circumstances, with shortages of qualified staff and with restrictions on building, greater progress can be made by concentrating the limited men and materials upon the development of existing institutions than by scattering them over a wider field' (UGC 1948, 41–2). By 1954 and 1955, however, when the UGC began to consider a shift in its policy under the leadership of Keith Murray, it could go back to the word 'immediately' in the first sentence of the earlier statement and use it in a way familiar to all members of committees, as a link word across time. The argument in 1957–8 for creating new universities now looked simple. Existing universities, which it was assumed were quite free separately to determine what their maximum rates of growth and maximum future targets would be, could not or were not willing together to meet the demand for additional university places by 1970, 'irrespective of questions of finance.' The UGC, therefore, felt that it had the duty to assess future total national demand for university places. The national assessment was based on demographic factors – 'Bulge' – and socio-educational factors – 'Trend' – and the appreciation of the need for action was reinforced by its knowledge that the government itself, pressed by representatives of secondary education, was disturbed that unless more university places were provided, a sizeable number of those qualified to go to university on current standards would not have a chance of securing a place. Nonetheless, from 1954 onwards, there was protracted debate inside the UGC (a very English debate) about the quantitative estimates of 'Bulge' and 'Trend' and about how speedy expansion should be. Even as late as 1956, when it was decided to support proposals being made locally in Sussex for a new university to be located in Brighton, there was no commitment to a whole cluster of new universities. It was not until 1960 that York and Norwich were also accepted as new university sites, and the Treasury was informed that three or four more new universities would be necessary. The setting-up of a UGC Sub-Committee on New Universities in April 1959 enabled the UGC to examine and choose between local bids for universities: it attached import-

ance from the start to local enthusiasm and interest. In May 1961 Essex, Kent, and Warwick were approved, and in November Lancaster.

If in retrospect it appears that the UGC was holding back, it is instructive to examine a paper on 'a policy for University Expansion' prepared by the Association of University Teachers in 1958. 'There is no walk of life,' it stated in an admirable prologue, 'in which Britain has a surplus of able men, and the effort of university education should be to develop to the maximum the innate ability of the individual.' Yet it was cautious about the rate of expansion and unimaginative in its practical suggestions. 'If student numbers were increased in relation to the numbers of teachers in such a way as to make research difficult and personal knowledge of students impossible,' it would not be worthwhile. Nor would it be worthwhile 'if the universities felt themselves bound to produce a large number of specialists, e.g. engineers or nuclear physicists, fully trained to meet an industrial requirement.' 'A university will do no service to itself or to society if it permits its essential character to be overwhelmed by arguments of expediency.' The AUT supported Brighton as a new location, but there was an element of bathos in its report of a 'special suggestion ... the establishment of a university near Leatherhead, because so many research associations have laboratories at Leatherhead.' There was no clarion call either in the sentence 'The founding of new universities should be made the opportunity to encourage some variety in organisation and methods of teaching, though a reasonably uniform standard of merit should be sought in the awarding of degrees.' This statement stopped well short of the views of Sir Keith Murray and many members of the UGC. Nor would they have easily accepted the further statement that 'it is true in the last resort that an established university has more scope for improvisation than has a new college' (AUT 1958).

The framers of brochures on new colleges and universities had ample scope for generalisation, and the New Universities Sub-Committee of the UGC had to consider their claims one by one. The sites included Bournemouth, Whitby, Stevenage, Chelmsford, Falkirk and Cumbernauld, and the items in each prospectus ranged from residential accommodation to the philosophy of general education. The act of choosing sites took the UGC outside the realm of applied mathematics. So too did a growing concern for innovation both in teaching and research which was already beginning to be expressed in many circles. Yet one other point must be made about the mathematics behind the critical decision to create new universities, since it has never been made clear by otherwise knowledgeable commentators in Britain itself. It was assumed by the UGC that in the short run there could be only limited growth in the new universities and that the main thrust of immediate expansion should be met in the existing universities, some of which, notably Hull and Leicester, had grown rapidly since 1945 (Hull 800 per cent by 1958; Leicester 1,100 per cent). 'We did not face a choice between expansion of the existing universities and creation of new ones', the UGC reported faithfully in 1964. 'It was clear to us that both were needed.' This was the last bit of mathematics, and qualitative as well as quantitative questions quickly entered into the argument: indeed, they were part of the texture of the argument inside the UGC itself. 'We also had in mind the need for experimentation' (UGC 1964, 100).

After Southampton, Hull, Exeter, and Leicester had followed Nottingham in passing from university-college status to full university status between 1952 and 1957, the UGC recognised that an epoch had ended, and that any new universities now brought into existence should start freer than North Staffordshire had done. The 'newness' of the institutions and the fact that they were not upgraded institutions with a history was of their very essence. 'New institutions, starting without traditions with which the innovator must come to terms, are more favourably situated for such experimentation than established institutions' (UGC 1964, 93). The formula that was devised for the creation of new universities – local initiative; competitive bidding to the UGC; formulation of academic plans by UGC-appointed Academic Planning Committees; granting of charters – encouraged not only innovation but diversity, well expressed in prospectuses which read like manifestos. Thereafter, each new university appointed its own faculty, devised its own curriculum, its own approach to teaching methods, and its own governmental organisation – and there was to be innovation here, particularly at Sussex – although the Privy Council (via the UGC) had to approve of each charter and the UGC itself could influence the 'mix' of subjects taught and the rate of growth. It would be completely wrong to concentrate on the controls of the UGC and to underplay the initiatives of the decentralised planning groups, who were often far more sensitive to the role of applied science and technology than the UGC itself. The diversity was accentuated by the fact that from the start the new universities never worked together as a *bloc* or attempted to bargain together to strengthen their position *vis-à-vis* older universities. Between 1961 and 1968 they moved on separate lines, although they obviously had common problems and sometimes produced common solutions or at least what looked like common solutions to fundamental problems in university education.

The extent to which the innovations introduced by the new universities were successful would demand a different study. So, too, would the extent to which they created new traditions. It would need further study also to examine the impact of both academic and cultural innovations on other universities, Oxbridge and Redbrick. Three points, however, stand out. First, the State was directly involved in the process only late. The Robbins Report came *after* the crucial decisions had been taken by the UGC, though it influenced the supply of resources available to it. Second, there was relatively little pressure from below – either from students or would-be students, although early enrolment rates revealed preferences for courses which broke with existing patterns and for places which shared the characteristics neither of Oxbridge nor of Redbrick. Third, some, at least, of the makers of the new universities were interested not only in their own subjects but in the 'idea of a university', and when they turned to curricular reform they were not satisfied with recent attempts to change the single-subject curriculum (for example, by the introduction of combined degrees). They wanted to go further with what I myself called 're-drawing the map of learning'. The sciences were not neglected in this process – indeed, some of the crucial new ideas were stimulated by recent developments in biological sciences. Nor was technology. The transformation was not only to be a transformation in the humanities or in the social sciences. Above all the idea of innovating, not imitating, was to shape the developments of the 1960s. By the end of the decade, however, there were signs that the State wanted to intervene more, that students had their own conceptions of what they wanted from a university, and that it was more difficult to inspire a second round of new university academics than it had been to mobilise the first.

REFERENCES

Association of University Teachers (1958) *Report on a Policy for University Expansion*. London.

Bagehot, W. (1974) *The Collected Works of Walter Bagehot*, ed. N. St. John-Stevas, Vol.VII. London.

Bentham, J. (1968) *The Correspondence of Jeremy Bentham*. Vol.I: *1752-76*, ed. T. L. S. Sprigge. London.

Berdahl, R. O. (1959) *British Universities and the State*. London.

Bill, E. G. W. (1973) *University Reform in Nineteenth-Century Oxford. A Study of Henry Halford Vaughan, 1811-1885*. Oxford.

Davie, G. E. (1964) *The Democratic Intellect. Scotland and her Universities in the Nineteenth Century*, 2nd edn. Edinburgh.

Hale Bellot, H. (1929) *University College London, 1826-1926*. London.

Kent, C. (1978) *Brains and Numbers: Elitism, Comtism, and Democracy in Mid-Victorian England*. Toronto.

Mill, J. S. (1867) *Inaugural Address delivered to the University of St. Andrews, Feb. 1st 1867*. London.

— (1969) *Essays on Ethics, Religion and Society*, ed. J. M. Robson (Collected Works of John Stuart Mill, Vol.x). Toronto.

Ogilvie, F. (1948) *British Universities*. London.

Richter, M. (1964) *The Politics of Conscience. T. H. Green and his Age*. London.

Rothblatt, S. (1968) *The Revolution of the Dons. Cambridge and Society in Victorian England*. London.

Shimmin, A. N. (1954) *The University of Leeds: the First Half-Century*. Cambridge.

Spencer, H. (1911) *Essays on Education etc*. Everyman edn. London.

University Grants Committee (1948) *University Development from 1935 to 1947*. London.

— (1964) *University Development 1957-62*, Cmnd. 2267. London.

Vincent, E. W. and Hinton, P. (1947) *The University of Birmingham. Its History and Significance*. Birmingham.

COMMENTS BY ROBERT ANDERSON

Both Dr Nuttgens' and Lord Briggs' papers are about 'tradition and innovation', and both can be related to the topical, important, and complex debate about whether universities have contributed, and if so how, to what Martin Wiener has called 'the decline of the industrial spirit', in a book which is only the latest instalment in controversies which have raged periodically ever since the 1850s (Wiener 1981). Has Britain lagged behind other countries in scientific and technical education? Have the universities, and the English public schools, played an insidious role in imposing the gentlemanly values of the old landed and professional elite on the rising industrial and commercial bourgeoisie, so denaturing them and weakening the entrepreneurial spirit? Would Britain have done better to emulate continental countries by concentrating technological education in separate institutions?

Dr Nuttgens' analysis of the very interesting series of inaugural lectures by Edinburgh engineering professors certainly shows that the technological spirit could find a home in the university; he could also have quoted Sir David Brewster, who as Principal of the University in 1864 was declaring that 'The history of civilisation is the history of the applications of science and the arts to the material wants of our species', and thought technology a proper university subject for that reason (Brewster 1864). In fact the Scottish universities seem to have had very little academic prejudice against utilitarian subjects (if more did not appear, the reason was shortage of money), and it is striking that the engineering professors devoted their lectures not to proving the respectability of engineering as a university subject, but to persuading the engineering profession itself that theoretical as well as practical training was needed. They were only able to get their classes established by working with the existing apprenticeship system, for in the 1860s and 1870s most of their students in Edinburgh and Glasgow worked in engineers' offices or workshops during the day and came to lectures in the early morning or evening. This was soon found unsatisfactory, but the fact that the Scottish university year lasted only six months allowed the development of what Armstrong in the 1880s called the 'half-time system'; by the 1900s, and perhaps earlier, the term 'sandwich system' was in use (Armstrong 1885, 25).

Fleeming Jenkin, as Dr Nuttgens shows, wanted engineering taught in the universities rather than in special institutions. But it inevitably remained a small part of their activities, and whatever the merits of the teaching, Britain was by the twentieth century simply producing far fewer engineers than her continental rivals (Ahlström 1982, 13–14). Dr Nuttgens is sympathetic to the idea of separate schools like the *grandes écoles* in France or the *Technische Hochschulen* in Germany, enjoying high prestige and standing for a distinctive principle, the unity of industrial science. I sense some ambiguity, however, about whether their aim should be to turn out a technocratic elite, apostles of the religion of industry, or to be universities of the people, the heirs of the Mechanics' Institutes.

Historically, this question is by no means simple. It is not difficult to pile up evidence for anti-industrial attitudes in Britain, as Wiener does, but there is another side to the picture represented, for example, by the development of science in modern Cambridge, the foundation of the civic universities, or the organisation of Imperial College in the 1900s, based directly on the German model. Michael Sanderson takes a generally favourable view of the contribution of British universities to industry in his important book on the subject (Sanderson 1972), though no doubt it is true, as Lord Briggs says, that practical research tended to drift in a pure direction. It is important to distinguish here between pure science, which soon took its place in the tradition of liberal education, and applied science or engineering which, like commerce, had more trouble in establishing a university foothold.

Nor are the continental parallels so simple. Clearly the *Technische Hochschulen* contributed largely to modern Germany's impressive economic achievements. But did they really enjoy high social or intellectual prestige? Historical opinion suggests not, for these schools and the secondary schools which corresponded to them had a long struggle to establish their parity with the old universities and with the classical *Gymnasien*, a struggle which achieved partial success only after 1900 (Ringer 1979, 36–40). More generally, the gulf between *Bildung* and *Besitz*, between the professional and bureaucratic bourgeoisie and new wealth, was notoriously wide in Germany, a society where aristocratic and military values prevailed in public life over material, entrepreneurial ones.

Literary culture retained its dominance, and Fritz Ringer, the leading authority in this field, has spoken of the 'antithesis between technology and culture that was so visibly embodied in the German system' (Ringer 1978, 168). One consequence of having a separate technological sector, it may be noted, is that the more traditional institutions are then free to ignore technology and to cultivate their superiority to it.

In introducing his paper, Dr Nuttgens made the interesting suggestion that technical education can only flourish where there is a sound basis of universal primary schooling. This certainly works for Germany, but it does not seem to for France, where until the 1880s the development of popular education lagged rather behind England, and well behind Scotland. Elite institutions like the *Ecole polytechnique* could co-exist with the neglect of mass education. On the other hand, the significance of that school for industry should not be exaggerated. It was constantly criticised for its excessively mathematical and theoretical bias, and throughout the nineteenth century the majority of its graduates went into the army, not into industry (Shinn 1980); the *Ecole centrale* of 1829, which Dr Nuttgens mentions, was founded as a more practical alternative to it.

Moreover, the surrender of the bourgeoisie to 'aristocratic' values, the attraction of the professions and the civil service for commercial and industrial families, and the decline of the entrepreneurial spirit have long been favourite themes for historians of nineteenth-century France. Perhaps European societies were not all that different in this respect. Everywhere a new entrepreneurial and managerial class had to establish itself alongside powerful landed and professional classes, and it is not surprising that the values of the latter had a strong attraction. In Britain, educational institutions certainly encouraged the formation of a homogeneous national elite, whereas in Germany, it could be argued, the industrial class were forced by their social exclusion to stick to their own money-making values. Whatever the economic outcome, the British experience had its virtues for social and political stability (Ringer 1978, 169). All this merely emphasises that the function of universities or schools cannot be understood in isolation from the cultural and social context in which they are embedded.

Finally let me mention some concepts which may guide the

discussion. One is elites – and I have just referred to competing elites, or division within elites, as a historical problem. Forming elites is obviously a basic task of universities, but it can take different forms. Do they merely act as a 'finishing school' for a social elite already defined by birth? Should they produce a creative Saint-Simonian elite of technocrats and experts, inspired by the vision of a more productive and efficient society? Or perhaps an elite of cultivated intellect, an 'aristocracy of intelligence amid a people which wants no other sort of aristocracy' (Anderson 1971, 124)? The words are those of a French minister of education in the 1860s: the idea that intellectuals were the natural and legitimate leaders of a democracy was a popular one among French liberals and Republicans, and is obviously similar to the alliance of 'brains and numbers' cited by Lord Briggs. And as he says, it is to be distinguished from the ideal of a broad-based meritocratic elite, created by a democratic educational system which seeks out talent wherever it may be found. A parallel may be seen here between Napoleon's doctrine of the marshal's baton in every soldier's knapsack and the Scottish ideal of the lad of parts; Lyon Playfair, indeed, who expressed more clearly than anyone the nineteenth-century liberal theory of meritocracy, made this precise connection in a parliamentary speech in 1871 (Anderson 1983, 108).

The second concept which may be useful is culture, using the word in the sense which links systems of values with the social groups which hold them and with their sense of group identity. Both these papers have shown how the civic universities, and other new institutions in the nineteenth century, were seen to represent an industrial culture or ethos; though here too there were ambiguities, for often one of their purposes was to supply 'the means of placing alongside of our material prosperity an enlargement of mind and an elevation of character, and of ennobling and purifying the spirit of trade by the influence of culture and scientific knowledge' (Anderson 1983, 82). This quotation, which uses 'culture' in another, more Arnoldian sense, is from the founders of University College, Dundee, itself celebrating its first centenary this year.

Then there is the question of metropolitan versus provincial culture. It would be interesting to ask whether the foundation of the civic universities represented the assertion of a specifically provincial culture, and also why, despite the local element in their foundation, this was plainly not the case with the new universities of the 1960s. The idea of universities as a national system, the way in which it is seen as a positive virtue for students not to use their home university – these are recent phenomena, and part of a more general delocalising of British culture.

One could also apply a cultural interpretation to the religious disputes, about tests or the relation of the universities to national churches, which bulked so large in Victorian controversy. They have hardly been mentioned today. Nor have questions of national culture within the British Isles. In Wales, the foundation of the national University was intimately linked with the progress of national sentiment, while the little I know of Irish university history suggests that it was a central element in the clash of rival cultures in that country. In Scotland these issues never had quite the same salience, partly because the university system was already firmly established, partly because the Scottish middle class managed to combine a certain cultural nationalism, which included pride in the distinctiveness of the educational system, with a strong sense of British identity.

Michael Sanderson criticises the University of Wales as 'a pathological example of the dangers of disengagement between the universities and industry' (Sanderson 1972, 122). One sees what he means, and yet in a way this is to miss the point. In creating a university which would turn out ministers and schoolteachers, and safeguard a distinctive literary and religious culture, the Welsh had aims and preoccupations of their own. We should beware of letting our own preoccupations with science, economic growth, or industrial decline distort our understanding of a university history which often centred on problems of a very different kind.

REFERENCES

Ahlström, G. (1982) *Engineers and industrial growth. Higher technical education and the engineering profession during the nineteenth and early twentieth centuries: France, Germany, Sweden and England.* London.

Anderson, R. D. (1971) Secondary education in mid nineteenth-century France: some social aspects. *Past and Present* 53, 121-46.

— (1983) *Education and opportunity in Victorian Scotland. Schools and universities.* Oxford.

Armstrong, G. F. (1885) *A lecture on the progress of higher technical instruction at home and abroad in relation to the education of engineers.* Edinburgh.

Brewster, D. (1864) *Introductory address at the opening of session 1864-5.* Edinburgh.

Ringer, F. K. (1978) The education of elites in modern Europe. *History of Education Quarterly* 18, 159-72.

— (1979) *Education and society in modern Europe.* Bloomington.

Sanderson, M. (1972) *The universities and British industry, 1850-1970.* London.

Shinn, T. (1980) *Savoir scientifique & pouvoir social. L'Ecole polytechnique, 1794-1914.* Paris.

Wiener, M. J. (1981) *English culture and the decline of the industrial spirit, 1850-1980.* Cambridge.

REPORT OF THE DISCUSSION BY F.S.L.LYONS

The proceedings were opened by Professor Gregor with an elegant gloss upon his paper 'Liberal education – an outworn ideal?' He went beyond the scope of his original paper to emphasise the contemporary pressures threatening the continued existence of a liberal education in any traditional sense. To illustrate them he cited the 'thirteen points' dealing with the future of universities which had formed part of the programme of Mrs Shirley Williams when Secretary of State for Education and Science. It would have been extremely interesting to have had Mrs Williams' own thoughts on these points in the light of recent developments, but of course this was not possible because of her enforced absence on election business. Doubtless she might have contested what many thought one of Professor Gregor's most telling points – that the real continuity of pressure to change the universities comes from permanent civil servants rather than from transient ministers and that whoever might be in charge of the DES in the immediate future, more might yet be heard of the thirteen points in one form or another.

Sir Stuart Hampshire returned the discussion to its historical roots by asking when exactly it was that the idea of a liberal education first established itself in Britain. He never received a precise answer to this question – perhaps precision is impossible in such matters – but, while critical of the vague rhetoric which the term 'liberal education' so often seemed to engender, he left us in no doubt that he thought there was a place for such a concept and remarked especially on the value for young minds of coming into contact with the 'learned man' of the kind universities used to produce prodigally and still do sparingly.

Dr Anderson, in a thoughtful and weighty contribution, reminded us that a liberal education need not involve a broad curriculum, thus echoing Lord Ashby's dictum, quoted by Professor Lyons in his lecture, that liberalism is a spirit of pursuit not a choice of subject. Dr Anderson spoke convincingly about the Scottish experience and partly, though not wholly, connected with this he reminded us that a main agency in moving the emphasis away from a liberal education was less often science and technology than commerce pressing for, and getting, a strong business studies presence in modern universities.

This led naturally on to Dr Nuttgens' contribution, which was a witty and acute analysis of the present state of technological education, based in part on his own experience as Director of the Leeds Polytechnic. One of the striking differences between the technological and the more traditional university sectors which he brought out very clearly was the extent to which, in the former, courses were still to a large degree related to the specific kinds of employment that, in happier times, the successful student might expect to enter. This apart, however, Dr Nuttgens' approach was in all senses so humane that the conference might have been forgiven for underestimating – as it may have been tempted to do – the real differences, of function as well as of aim, which separate universities from purely, or mainly, technological institutions.

The general discussion turned increasingly towards the new universities of the 1960s and to those who had helped to found them, or who still thought of themselves as working in them, it was a strange sensation to feel that the rest of the conference was apparently intent on considering them as historical, if not historic. Historic, however, is the world for Lord Briggs' contribution to this theme. He spoke with the particular authority of one who had been a member of the UGC's committee on the new universities and the conference listened, fascinated, to his account, not only of the creation of the University of Sussex, but also of the whole process whereby the six English sequels to Sussex emerged from a welter of bids and counter-bids. This, as all realised at the time, was a genuine contribution to oral

Report on the Discussion

history – fortunately, it was recorded.

General discussion continued with Dr Anderson's comments on the drift of the debate so far, and in almost instinctive response to this speaker after speaker returned to the theme of technology and the place of engineering in the British universities. There was, however, no clear-cut answer to a question Professor Stone had raised earlier in the day – why engineering and allied sciences had been so ill-regarded for so long in the educational system in Britain and why no internationally famous institution like MIT had yet emerged. The conference circled round this question a little uneasily, but more time than was available would have been needed to locate the answer in the history of Victorian society as much as in the history of education.

The point was made, however, that the last twenty years or so have seen a great change in this regard. Indeed, the conference itself testified to this by linking its obvious affinities for a liberal education with a sensible realisation that technology was the wave, if not of the future (which looked thoroughly unpredictable and rather bleak to most of us) at any rate of the present. And on this harmonious note the proceedings drew to a close.

THREE

BRITISH HIGHER EDUCATION AND THE UNIVERSITY SYSTEM

HIGHER EDUCATION:
THE CONTENDERS

HAROLD SILVER

Eric Ashby, frequently and understandably given to biological analogies, compared universities to biological organisms, both having as their function to survive. Universities, however, he explained also had purpose (Ashby 1958, 68). This argument may have seemed circular to some of us of late, given that our main purpose has sometimes appeared to be to survive. It is good to know that Edinburgh University is prepared to lift its head long enough from its history and its present problems to ask questions about both, and about the future. I should like, however, to extend the discussion beyond that of *universities* in society.

A crucial difference between our understanding of higher education since the 1950s and everything that went before is in the kind of questions that we are able, but also willing, to ask. Social and behavioural scientists and educationists of many descriptions have, especially in the past quarter of a century, wanted to know who enters higher education, and why, correlations between access and social background, between school performance and later achievement. They have investigated learning, success and failure, choice, methods of admission and assessment. They have even asked students their opinions, and increasingly frequently those of employers of graduates. We have an economics and sociology of recent higher education, we have research into higher education vocabularies unknown even twenty years ago — Expectations of Higher Education, Higher Education and the Labour Market ...

Writing about British universities and the state at the end of the 1950s, Berdahl concluded that further encroachments by the state on the autonomy of the universities were unlikely — and he was, of course, proved to be wrong (Berdahl 1959). It is not only the role of the state, but also the landscape of higher education, that has changed. One of the main novelties under recent scrutiny has been the emergence and awareness of the 'system' or 'systems' of higher education, and attempts to define what Ashby in 1974 called the 'inner logic' of the different sectors (Ashby 1974, 138). In England and Wales, with new universities, thirty polytechnics and some sixty colleges and institutes of higher education – and the equivalent Scottish colleges – new complexities of scale and style and – who knows? – perhaps even function and purpose, have needed attention. The polytechnics, mainly urban, with traditions inherited from their progenitors of technical and applied studies, part-time students, and other self-conscious characteristics, suggested a new range of higher education images from their creation in the late 1960s. The colleges and institutes of higher education, mainly smaller, often out of traditions of teacher education, residence and strong student support services, stretched the new definition of 'higher education' even further from the mid-1970s. Once upon a time there had just been universities. As little as twenty years ago ('little', of course, to an historian) books were still being written and debates being conducted in which higher education was equated with universities, and according to which other institutions – even if promoted – would remain a rank or two below the universities. Inside the universities those perceptions remain – but I shall return to the contemporary viewpoint. The point for the moment is that in all this expansion and diversification there has been much to discuss and to research.

But what about questions asked of the first half of this century, the nineteenth century, and before? It is not easy to generalise about the ways historians have approached the history of Edinburgh or St Andrews, Cambridge or London, Harvard or Virginia, still less about the national and cultural contexts, traditions of ideas and social purpose, in which they have tried to situate and explain the patterns and the differences. But, and always with exceptions, historians have asked their questions mainly about provision, about the relationships between provision and ideas and intentions, provision and providers, provision and national economics and international relationships, the motives for and forms of provision, the debates about what to provide. That may be less true of historical work on medieval or Enlightenment Europe or some American work on Revolutionary or Great Awakening times – in such cases the experience of the scholar attracting interest. It is largely true, however, of the way historians have approached the nineteenth century. In the last century or so they have conducted their explorations largely in the frame of institu-

Higher Education: the contenders

tional and curricular responses to 'industrialisation', 'modernisation', scientific and technological advance, the interests of new classes and new professions. The record is predominantly focused on the most public spokesmen for the liberal defence and the scientific prosecution, with obvious differences to explain between England on the one hand, and Scotland, continental Europe and the United States on the other hand. Our understanding of the last century and a half of torment – particularly in England – about a liberal education and its alternatives remains substantially conditioned by the interpretations of John Stuart Mill or Cardinal Newman or Matthew Arnold, with sideglances at the more moderate spokesmen for science, and encompassing perhaps the *Edinburgh Review* and *Blackwood's Magazine* and the reports of the relevant royal commissions.

What we know about the nineteenth century, therefore, is a function of the questions historians have asked – and on the whole they have not asked questions about the nineteenth-century universities in their communities, the employers rather than the founders, the experience of students rather than parliamentary controversy and reluctant reform. It may not be easy but, for example, Michael Sanderson in the one case and Sheldon Rothblatt in the other, have shown the directions and the possibilities (Sanderson 1972; Rothblatt 1976a, 1976b). We know little, however, about how the emergent professions, industrial, managerial and commercial occupations viewed the universities and their functions, their procedures and standards. We know next to nothing about student expectations or opinion, about liberal values as interpreted within the new institutions, as translated into practice by academics and in their encounters with students. Historians have certainly shown little curiosity about the views and activities of those seeking to challenge, to re-interpret or to adapt the liberal traditions under debate – the industrialists, the European- or Scottish-trained scientists, the technical staffs of the new English university colleges, universities and late-nineteenth-century polytechnics. The very conception of a university, as autonomous and hermetic as possible, has made such questions irrelevant. The history is therefore resistant to non-institutional implications – except as seen from elevated positions. It is very often a history in which the contenders for truth or for position include few or no students, and only those intellectuals with access to the pulpit or the publishing house. Historians are capable of easy and wild assumptions about how policy is made and how institutions receive and interpret messages and act, or decline to act, on them.

These historical deficiencies help to define our version of the past and the dilemmas of our present. But we do not have a ready made 'history' that tells us how to discern, let alone to solve, the problems of the dichotomies and polarities which have been under discussion here, as often before. There is not a history which tells as how to handle, for example, the conceptual and practical difficulties of the 'vocational' and the 'liberal', the 'specialised' and the 'general', and overarching all of these past and present debates, the question of the relationship between the university and whichever wider canvas you prefer to use – government, the state, society, the world outside. At the same time as interpreting those relationships, there is a confusing history to be interpreted also.

Having defined the near-impossibility of the task, let me try to stand for a while at some intersections of what we ask of the present and what we think we know of the past. I would like to select a small number of the directions in which universities and others have to look in determining their future courses of action. The worst now is reflex action to protect oversimplified histories.

We continue to agonise in the present about the dichotomies to which I have referred, and they are a good place to start. In the past thirty or so years we have located those dichotomies in the strains of expansion and of contraction. In the 1950s and 1960s we were familiar with controversies about the universities and the world outside – Kingsley Amis and his team versus A.D.C.Peterson et al. on 'the threat of the practical' (Peterson 1961, 17; Amis et al. 1961, 21), debates about two or more cultures, technology as humanism (Ashby 1958, 81–5), or, in terms peculiar to England, as low-status intrusion – with the UGC and others valiantly attempting to define the controversy out of existence (UGC 1950, 3–4). We went on looking over our shoulders at the world as explained to us between the wars by, among others but outstandingly, Abram Flexner, distinguishing between professions, which belong in a university, and vocations, which do not. A case could be made, he told us in 1930, for a university faculty of law and medicine, but 'certainly not at all for business, journalism, domestic "science", or Library "science"'. In the British universities, which he rather liked, he discovered nevertheless

> such short-sighted and absurd . . . excrescences as the School of Librarianship and course in Journalism at University College, London, the Department of Civic Design at Liverpool and the work in Automobile Engineering at Bristol. This technical development is slight, as compared with that in America, but is none the less deplorable and, we may hope, the defects of youth, for it is of neither liberal nor university quality. (Flexner 1930, 255–6)

What a battle, thirty years later, Ashby and others had to wage! And, in whatever versions, and with whatever publicity, the problem has accelerated as the world has pressed in upon the universities and upon that newly diversified artefact labelled higher education. *The Sciences, the humanities and the technological threat* is a book title only eight years old (Niblett 1975), and in it 'technological totalitarianism' is firmly confronted (*ibid.* 19). As the technological and the economic have become more salient, as expansion and national planning for it or for its opposite thrust institutions more firmly into dependence on the state, so have the meaning and the relevance of the 'liberal' become more elusive. In a powerful American book on the subject Earl Cheit summarises a view increasingly explicit among many academics on both sides of the Atlantic:

> Now colleges and universities are no longer defined by liberal education. Liberal education lacks the power to define. It lacks coherence; it lacks definition itself. Liberal education has become splitered, specialized, and, to some extent, eroded. (Cheit 1975, 136)

Behind that comment lies the curriculum search of Harvard and other American institutions, lies the difficulty of understanding, let alone defending, the binary policy in Britain, lies the confusion of a recent past about where to put, and what to offer, an increasing number of students, and of course, where to put the 'excrescences'. Revise or abandon the liberal? Liberalise the vocational, as became official British policy in the late 1950s, or vocationalise the liberal – as David Hawkins persuasively suggested to us in the United States (Hawkins 1973)? And then, having botched up some answers – how to sustain them in contraction and a disappearing age participation rate?

I spent some years teaching 'liberal studies' as an additive to technical and science students and am still, much though I enjoyed it, not sure with what justification. I am not as sure as I once thought I was that Ashby was wrong to argue that brewing – and by implication almost anything else – can be a liberal education if properly approached. I am certainly not sure that a core study of great books *à la* Hutchins or Lord James, or a compulsory core study of the 'civilising' disciplines, is a useful approach to education after school. There are, of course, important national differences here, and knowing Scottish attempts to defend its tradition of broader curricula, or to reconcile that tradition with the pressures on all of us to narrow, to refine and to specialise, I am reluctant to pursue that discussion here. Nevertheless, the actual or potential danger of losing purchase on familiar models of the liberal remains a matter of anxious debate – especially when the contenders for influence and position outside the institutions appear to threaten to impose new and unacceptable conditions and values – though of course there is nothing new in that. What we have to be sure about is that we know clearly what we do before we defend it. Alain Touraine recently suggested that the idea of general culture needed to be 'unequivocally defended', but by 'reviving it, to start with' (Touraine 1980, 193). Are we sure whether teacher education, and if so all of it or some of it, and by implication the mission of the colleges where it still forms a significant fraction of their work, are easily identifiable as 'vocational'? The Committee of Directors of Polytechnics thought so when one of their spokesmen told a Commons committee that 'we have also had the colleges of education that have been highly motivated vocationally and in a sense have existed in order to meet the needs of a particular profession' (House of Commons 1972, 135). On that basis I am scarcely able to find a course of study in higher education that does not have some major element of the vocational or the professional – the vocabulary here is difficult to disentangle (and certainly before the late nineteenth century the argument would not have had much meaning). Theology, architecture, medicine, the law . . . raise intractable problems of definition in the context of vocational motivation and the needs of particular professions. As, indeed, do all those courses of academic study

Higher Education: the contenders

which have in the past pointed towards employment in academic life.

Amidst the pressures we face, therefore, is this complex question of what it is to which we are wedded, in the face of strong pressures for change, including for change in the focus of policy- and decision-making. If the universities and others are going to have to accommodate such pressures from various directions, they will need to understand them — and, as I shall suggest, that is far from easy, but they will also — in circumstances that I shall also suggest — retain choices. I do not agree, for example, with the conclusion reached by the Committee of Directors of Polytechnics at the end of their evidence to a Commons select committee some three years ago:

> Traditions of academic freedom and of permitting local judgments on nationally allocated educational expenditure must both bow to the over-riding need to achieve greater national purpose and prosperity. (House of Commons 1980, 122)

That seems to me to be abandoning too many fields, unnecessarily, to too many enemies. I prefer the kind of conclusion reached by Maurice Peston that the role of higher education is likely to increase in relation to the economy, but the task of becoming more responsive to national needs can best be accomplished by the institutions taking the initiative themselves (Peston 1979, 131). If that, baldly put, begs a lot of questions, it points in the right direction.

The problems of curriculum, of the profile of teaching and of research, and the traditions and values associated with them, are inextricable from another set of problems to do with institutions, with the expansion of the system since the Second World War, and with the reasons both for that expansion and for the forms it took. I will not re-enter that general discussion except to extract one component, the purposes and implications of the expansion. Broadly speaking, in Britain I do not believe that we gave the implications for higher education much serious attention. We had a silly debate about whether more means worse, and Robbins attempted — in less than four pages of the report — to discuss aims and principles. We discussed, hotly, a 'pool of ability', academic governance, and student participation, and occasionally such matters as whether the elevated Colleges of Advanced Technology should be technological universities or plain universities. We did not much care how many new universities were in suburbs or green fields, and there was little debate about the UGC preference for sites not less than two hundred acres. There was discussion of and report on degrees broad and narrow, single-honours and modular, on what a Nuffield research group rightly called *the container revolution*. Having aired our prejudices about numbers and size and structure or even democracy, most of us went on doing what we thought we knew how to do best. We did not really discuss higher *education*. If that sounds unduly cynical, may I summon two witnesses in my support – only two, but two worth calling.

Richard Hoggart, then still a university teacher, said in a lecture in 1965 (the date is important): 'Like most people in the educational world, I am engaged almost to the point of preoccupation with expansion and its effects – and don't get enough time to think about them' (Hoggart 1965, 3). That may seem light years away now, but it is how it was in most places and for most people. If the history of the nineteenth century cannot be written confidently around Newman and Arnold, neither can the history of the past quarter of a century be written around the new universities and the Robbins report. That things were happening at Falmer or the outskirts of Norwich, or that the UGC was publicising them, did not alter the basic national picture, and a host of good intentions did not alter the realities of institutions accomplishing much expansion and little thought. In most places, as with Hoggart, there was not the time. More important, I doubt if there was the will.

Sir Frederick Dainton, from a quite different point in the higher-education spectrum, wrote a note on science in higher education in the period 1945–60, though what he says has implications well beyond that date. He describes the rapid growth in the proportion of the gross national product placed at the disposal of scientists, and he asks:

> So what did the scientists in universities do? They enjoyed a bonanza. With money and research students in plentiful supply they 'pursued research', winning approbation whatever the quality of the product . . . possibly because would-be critics were bemused by the sheer quantity. There was no need to change courses; all that was necessary was to produce more chemists, physicists or

whatever, cast in the same mould as their teachers, acquainted with as much of the latest rapidly growing information as students could tolerate through an undergraduate curriculum determined in its essentials by research scientists using primitive pedagogic methods.
(Dainton 1975, 36)

And not just scientists, of course. And the world did not stand entirely still. The Hale Committee on university teaching methods did, in 1964, point to weaknesses and suggest remedies, including operational research, training and experiment (UGC 1964). Dainton tried to move the schools and Swann to move the universities to think about new approaches to science and technology – and of course Swann included Stirling and Edinburgh in the list of commendations (Council for Scientific Policy 1968; Committee on Manpower Resources for Science and Technology 1968, 77). Things did happen, but Hoggart and Dainton were basically right.

If we plunged into expansion without too much concern about the validity of what we were expanding, the same is true for the institutional implications. This is particularly the case of attempts to describe, let alone to define, differences amongst the sectors of institutions which, in the late 1960s and 1970s, entered the newly named territory of higher education. How complex that territory became is something which – if I may be autobiographical for a moment – I encountered at close quarters. I taught in a College of Commerce, which was a College of Further Education, and which became part of Hull College of Higher Education. I then taught in a Technical College which is now Huddersfield Polytechnic. I then moved to a College of Advanced Technology, which then became a school of the University of London (having almost, in combination with what is now Hatfield Polytechnic, become an independent university in Hertfordshire). I then became principal of what started life nineteen years ago as a Teacher Training College, became a College of Education and was, when I arrived, a College of Higher Education. As a guest speaker I am often introduced as principal of the Bulmershe College of Further Education, the Bulmershe Institute of Teacher Training, and every variant you can imagine. Since Bulmershe has almost nothing but degree-level students, including masters' and PhD students, my visitors from Japan or Kuwait want to know how we differ from a university and – even whilst explaining the Council for National Academic Awards – I am hard put to tell them. My point is not that we have indulged in troublesome, unsystematic or unnecessary developments. The point is that we have not really thought about and discussed the educational implications of what we have been doing. On the rare occasions that purposes have been declared, they have not been the subject of serious debate – least of all in the universities. The invention of the binary system, as Peter Scott has rightly shown us, combined two parallel and conflicting motives. Were we seeking to build a bright new technological future, or were we protecting the universities from too many encroachments on their traditional pattern of activities? The history is at least ambiguous, and if Scott is right in suggesting that 'the binary policy was never intended as an instrument of radical change in higher education' we are guilty of never having seriously debated why not, or what would be (Scott 1981, 3–9; Scott 1979, 7).

In terms of the institutions rather than the system, the difficulties of definition are enormous. By what criteria do you judge the difference between a university and a polytechnic or its Scottish equivalent? If one takes such criteria as research and teaching, part-time and full-time students, the curriculum and its content, size, students' motivation, either the overlap between them is too great to make sense, or there is – in Maurice Peston's words, 'no reason *a priori* why (one) sector should have certain characteristics' (Peston 1979, 130). The polytechnics, even given their own differences from one another, have often laid claim to a common concern for vocational content in their courses – but the claim is equally valid for some if not all of the British universities, according to how you resolve the ambiguities of the definition. There is certainly considerable overlap in curriculum, research is as much a commitment of the polytechnics as it is of the universities, and no institution or kind of institution has a monopoly of good or bad teaching, of part-time students, or of anything else I can detect (Silver 1980, 55–63). The polytechnics, needless to say, have had to overcome resistance and ignorance. Sir Lawrence Bragg once considered it impossible for the higher technological education to take place in 'any institution which is under the direct tutelage of the Ministry of Education or the

Higher Education: the contenders

local education authorities' – which were competent only to control technical schools serving local interests' (Bragg 1949, 75) – a view that has not entirely disappeared over thirty years and many developments later. With that hurdle surmounted, the question then had to be faced of whether the Colleges of Advanced Technology and the polytechnics could or should teach in areas considered traditional to the universities. There were questions as to whether they should conduct research at all, and if so in more than narrowly specified areas. The very existence of their degree work, of their postgraduate teaching and research, was widely ignored or misrepresented. As with the development of state colleges and community colleges in the United States, there were attempts to view the universities as 'critical' and the rest as 'service stations', and – however the relative positions were allocated – the universities as first-tier, and the others as second- and third-tier (Trow 1982, 23). And then, of course, when the colleges and institutes of higher education entered the picture in the 1970s, there was not only massive misunderstanding of their roles and standards within the universities, but also self-defensive positions by the polytechnics, alarmed at having to protect their tenuous hold in higher education against a new wave of immigration. It all sounds a bit like Boston in the nineteenth century.

Critics of all of these policies and outcomes have argued that if the intention was to create, in the polytechnics particularly, a British higher-education sector somehow similar to the technological institutions which emerged in nineteenth-century mainland Europe or in the United States, the policy signally failed. It is not only the directors of the polytechnics who have argued that they have been underfunded to achieve such a purpose. In 1950 the UGC described the continental system of establishing technology outside the universities in high-status institutions, and the American system of establishing a 'great range of work both in technology and in technical studies' inside the universities (UGC 1950, 4). It could be argued that the way decisions were implemented in the 1960s and 1970s achieved the worst of both worlds.

My contention is that it is impossible to discriminate between the university and other sectors of higher education on the basis of defensible criteria. You can, of course, discriminate in resourcing and thereby introduce or strengthen differences of quality and inevitably of standing. The transfer of the UGC to the Department of Education and Science, however, together with the search for new forms of accountability, the likely and growing similarity between the National Advisory Body for the maintained sector and the UGC in their agency functions on behalf of government — all of these have eliminated major differences with regard to institutional autonomy, public accountability and outside influence or control. This does not mean that institutions enjoy, can or should enjoy, parity of prestige. That is a different and a long story, but it would be helpful to consider for a moment two related aspects of how the different sectors of higher education are viewed by two constituencies — by employers and by students. These now seem to me, in any judgments universities and other institutions may make about their responses to social and political pressures, crucial points at which to try to achieve greater clarity.

First, what is it that employers want of higher education? Do they want different things of different kinds of institution? Without attempting to summarise the available research I would like to underline how uncertain or contradictory or ambiguous are the declared expectations of employers. Again, there are national differences, and Michael Sanderson in particular has described the nineteenth- and twentieth-century involvement of Scottish professors and their research in engineering, electrical physics and shipbuilding, for example (Sanderson 1972, 389—90). With the slow growth of willingness by English employers to employ graduates — in many cases the reluctance not being overcome until the past quarter of a century — no unanimity or even clear pattern has emerged in the qualities employers seek in the graduates they employ. There have been pressures for greater specialisation, and especially for greater practicality in higher education courses, the outstanding example being the argument of the Finniston report on engineering in favour of students gaining 'an understanding of engineering practice within the working environment' (Committee of Inquiry 1980, 84). Employers in certain industries, or more precisely those who do the recruiting at certain levels in certain firms or services, have a clear picture of the particular skills they require of certain graduates in certain situations. But that is only part of the story. There are also employers who want something very much less specific from graduates, in order to complete the specific requirements themselves. The history of the past couple of decades seems consistent in the strength of this employers' lobby, whatever the particular stage of technological development. It is less than twenty years since *The Times Review of Industry and Technology* reported that some firms took graduates because 'bright people nowadays go to university'. A representative of a steel company at that time said: 'If there were other alternatives we would go for them' (*TRIT* 1964, 83). A year before, in a debate preceding the publication of the Robbins report, the chairman of the English Electric Company called for encouragement to be given 'to a general education with a proper balance between science and the arts', and the chief education officer of ICI hoped that the problem of overspecialisation would be tackled (*TRIT* 1963, 73–4). At the beginning of the 1970s the chairman of Shell Transport and Trading and of Shell International explained that 'tomorrow's executives will have to be competent in a much wider field than at present, and in Shell we are applying more scientific methods in order to find them in good time and then equip them for their future responsibilities' (Barran 1971, 122). There are of course many interpretations of what constitutes a broad education, but Sir David Barran's 'then' is important and not untypical. The Swann report on the employment of scientists, engineers and technologists argued in 1968 for 'a more general scientific or technological education with specialism grafted on later', and specifically for a broad first degree to be followed by 'continuing education and training, beyond graduation and throughout the career' (Committee on Manpower Resources 1968, 75–9). Touraine, looking at the international crisis in university education in 1980, suggested that big firms in fact prefer future employees to have a general knowledge precisely because the firms 'prefer to supervise the training of members of their staff ... so that they themselves remain in direct control of what is most closely connected with their own particular operational system' (Touraine 1980, 192). At an OECD conference last year a Japanese representative concluded, in Maurice Kogan's words, that 'Japanese industry probably prefers students with general knowledge and vitality to people with specialised knowledge'. Kogan underlined that in both Japan and Britain 'the stereotypes of industry knowing what it wants and students and higher education failing to meet industry's expectations must be seriously modified' (Kogan 1982, 5).

There is continuing evidence that many employers have no clear view of any relationship between undergraduate studies and the requirements of graduates in employment. Evidence from the employers themselves to parliamentary committees and elsewhere reveals constant stress on personality characteristics, extra-curricular activities and general education, together with diverse views about and interpretations of specialisation and broadly-based study. The Fulton committee on recruitment to the civil service reflected but certainly did not end the debate about a change from the recruitment of 'generalist' administrators and 'intelligent all-rounders' to the recruitment of people to 'do a specified range of job in a particular area of work, at any rate during their early years' (Committee on the Civil Service, 1968, 78). There is evidence from within the CNAA, from the Expectations of Higher Education project based at Brunel University, and elsewhere, that the confusion amongst employers about what they want – even in highly specific areas of expertise – is no less now than it has been. The range of views is likely to remain as wide as ever, the interpretation of vocabularies just as confused, and the job of higher education in reading the signals – whilst crucially important – no less difficult.

If the employers' expectations are so complex and uncertain, in a sense those students seem more clear. The findings of the available research seem very similar for Britain and other countries. In explaining their presence in higher education students over the past couple of decades have tended to use more rather than less vocational arguments. The figures and the arguments are consistent and revealing both of secondary school and of higher education students. As one researcher put it, some 80 to 90 per cent of sixth formers (in this case aspirants to a university or a college education) tended to 'eschew the "academic" and espouse the "applicable"' (Cohen 1970, 70). Another researcher found that students expect priority to be given to a combination of intellectual and vocational goals (Oxtoby 1971, 88). Other researchers found that *in a sense* (the phrase is important) vocational goals are relevant to all students (Brennan and Percy 1976, 150). The question is, in what sense? The researchers in this field have tried to break down the question and explore students' perceptions of more or less specific vocational goals, and although there are obvious differences between, say, engineering and English students at the level of specific expectations and links between courses and precise job destinations, there are consistent vocational emphases across the whole range. Researchers have therefore suggested a clash between the practical/vocational orientation of a majority of students and the academic/research orientation of a majority of teaching staff. What students expect is therefore not what they often find. One research conclusion is that students expect better teaching than they get, expect a greater relationship than they find between the staff's research and the quality of their teaching, and even where students expect to participate in the academic culture of the institution and try it, are frequently disappointed and opt out (Percy and Salter 1976, 466). On the reverse side, therefore, staff expect students to achieve excellence by criteria students often do not share or understand (ibid; Silver 1983a, ch.8).

There are other elements in what students expect, including of their subjects and institutions. They see hierarchies in both — for instance, a higher status for science than for technology (Hutchings 1963; Hutchings 1967) and often have somewhat uncertain expectations of differences between, in particular, universities and polytechnics. Not surprisingly, parents also see disparities between expectations and realities. One project which looked at parents' goals for their children's university life discovered three main goals. The parents thought that universities should *a*) work students hard, in a few specialised subjects, with 'a supporting cast of academic counsellors'; *b*) provide career guidance, and *c*) develop skills for dealing with other people. Among their lowest priorities was learning for its own sake. Parents were, however, least satisfied that universities were catering for the parents' highest priorities (Child *et al.* 1971).

It may be that with many students and their parents their vocational target is no more precise than getting 'a more interesting job', or that employers aim to detect something as vague as 'qualities of leadership', but questions are being asked of these and other constituencies, and of the institutions' responses. These attitudes and expectations are difficult to discover, to interpret and to respond to — given the basic conceptual ambiguities. But while we are locating change in the economy, in technology, in various public agencies, interests and positions, there are also publics whose involvements can and must be made explicit and taken into account.

These are just some of the contenders in the higher education arena. There are others, but let me try to summarise the implications I see for the universities in the social situations I have discussed.

First, universities are inevitably going to continue to be drawn into debates about the relationship between their curriculum and structures and processes and methods on the one hand, and employment, the professions, the labour market, on the other hand. If their autonomy appears undermined by this, then it is no good looking for solutions in Newman or Flexner. If there are traditional values that appear to be at stake, then these will need to be scrutinised and redefined, knowing how relative they in fact look across national boundaries and across time. Employment is not part of the world outside, it is in the motives, aspirations and expectations of students inside. Without suggesting that there are prescriptions which follow, I would argue that universities will need increasingly clear understandings of the relationships between what they offer and how it is perceived by the largest possible range of constituencies and contenders. In contraction, expansion or steady state, the learning/employment relationship is bound to attract increasing attention. I am not predicting how universities will or should react, I am describing a situation in which their functions, their definitions, their activities, have become negotiable.

Second, I would select as a priority in that process a much clearer understanding by universities of the world outside as it is brought inside in the shape of students. I believe now as I did in the 1960s that students were at that time being radical about the wrong things. Leaving aside the wider political concerns of some students, in relation to their own institutions student debates about university government and membership of senates and academic boards and so on were either wrongly targeted or unduly narrow. What students really needed was to be seen as members of their institutions, as integral, as counting in some coherent and fundamental sense, not as customers, as guests. To return to one of my earlier points – the history of

Higher Education: the contenders

universities is very often a history without students, except as statistics. Psychologists and sociologists and others have shown us much more clearly in recent decades that students are there, with analysable characteristics, as participants in processes. The history of universities needs to become also a history of adolescence, of student expectations of academic, social and adult life – including employment. You cannot talk about the purposes of universities in modern society, in my view, without asking what students want of them, and without discussing the implications for the institutions. It is not enough, and it certainly will not be in the future, to assume we know, to identify students with the institutions' unchallengeable values and purposes. They need to be asked, as do all the partners and contributors who have historically been, not silent, but not heard.

Third, universities will have to learn far more clearly than they have done so far, that society has altered the landscape of higher education without consulting them, and the world out there now contains two major components with which they are still fairly unfamiliar: a hundred or so institutions which are not universities but which are doing things barely, if at all, distinguishable from what universities do; and the need to think in terms of a national system, or at least pattern, of high education, with consequences that need sustained discussion. I have been in no small number of places where it is totally clear that university staffs do not understand that the newer institutions now share the landscape with them, share an interest in good teaching and research, provide courses which require students to enter with similar profiles and to reach similar destinations, share the same system of external examiners, the same anxiety to exert institutional control over the curriculum, over staff development, over the whole range of institutional operations. Many university people do not begin to know what polytechnics and colleges actually are and do, and the nature of their share in the new, if still incoherent, structure called 'higher education'. Approximately one-third of all undergraduates in this country are reading for degrees not of universities but of the Council for National Academic Awards, in polytechnics and colleges. In defining themselves universities are now doing so in competition for students and resources in a total system, and most discussions of universities have little meaning unless they are located in that wider context.

One disincentive to considering the whole pattern of higher education has been the underlying anxiety about autonomy *vis-à-vis* government. Are we, by admitting the existence of a 'system', weakening the UGC, lessening university autonomy, increasing the power of national and local government, streamlining higher education ready to be controlled all the more tightly by the exchequer, the needs of national finance and economics, the busybodies of politics, industry and commerce? These dangers are no less real today than when our Victorian spokesmen worried about them or than when Thorstein Veblen in the United States railed so splendidly against them. The Americans are tormented by them – with Burton Clark and others explaining how inefficient is European-style central control of higher education, and a flurry of academics and administrators agonising over creeping or rampant dependence on or interference by the federal government since the mid-1960s (Altbach and Berdahl 1981; Bok 1982). In Britain we have experienced, in different ways, the same phenomenon. Edward Shils has recently talked of the United States and British governments moving 'steadily forward towards making the universities the instruments of their social ideals of efficiency, of justice and of the pre-eminence of government over all other institutions' (Shils 1982, 483). Shils starts from the point that 'the autonomy of universities in the face of governments has been genuine but it has never been complete' (*ibid.* 437), and it is important that without hysteria and blinkers we should look both at the history of that incompleteness, and at the nature of the experience of non-university institutions that are now part of the landscape.

There are interpretations and solutions that have been canvassed but little discussed, and are feasible even within present difficult realities. Peter Scott has argued for the acceptance of between eighty and a hundred universities (Scott 1979, 22–5). Robbins argued twenty years ago, after the report, for 'more and more university institutions with limited areas of activity' (Robbins 1966, 9). Charles Carter wants more higher education but fewer universities, each a centre of excellence (Carter 1979). Some polytechnic directors have proposed chartered status for their institutions in parallel with the universities. My own preference has been, not for a large number of separate new universities, but one new federal National University, incorporating polytechnics, the main colleges, the CNAA and the Open University (Silver 1983b). My point is that we are inevitably, with the trends of the past few years, and with the emergence of the National Advisory Body or whatever succeeds it, in a new world, a world of imperatives which we cannot, and which I would not wish, to escape. An opportunity for the would-be controllers is also an opportunity for those intended to be controlled – as social control theories seem to ignore. Establishing a coherent pattern of relationships, whatever they are, in higher education may be a temptation for some to use their razors on us – though the absence of that pattern has by no means deterred them hitherto! It is also a chance, however, for us to make something acceptable of our present unsystematic system, to relate and to respond on the basis of better understandings of our present and our future than we have at the moment.

I was invited to consider 'the university in society', but the third implication of my discussion is that we need to pay a great deal of attention to 'higher education in society', or to 'the university in higher education and society' – whichever you prefer. There are historical and contemporary components to that argument. Without attention to them the issues facing universities seem to me narrowly defined, intractable, and in the end insoluble.

REFERENCES

Altbach, P. G. and Berdahl, R. O. (eds) (1981) *Higher education in American society*. Buffalo.
Amis, K. *et al.* (1961) The threat of the practical. *The Observer weekend review*, 26 February.
Ashby, A. (1958) *Technology and the academics: an essay on universities and the scientific revolution*, edn of 1963. London.
— (1974) *Adapting universities to a technological society*. San Francisco.
Barran, D. (1971) Industrial requirements from the universities, in *University independence* (ed. J. H. M. Scott). London.
Berdahl, R. O. (1959) *British universities and the state*. London.
Bok, D. (1982) *Beyond the ivory tower: social responsibilities of the modern university*. Cambridge, Mass.
Bragg, L. (1949) The place of technological education in university studies, in Association of Universities of the British Commonwealth, *Conference of the home universities: report of pro-*

ceedings. London.
Brennan, J. L. and Percy, K. A. (1976) What do students want?, in *Proceedings of the second congress of the EARDHE* (ed. A. Bonboir), I. Louvain-la-neuve.
Carter, C. (1979) Not enough higher education and too many universities? *The three banks review* 123.
Cheit, E. F. (1975) *The useful arts and the liberal tradition*. New York.
Child, D. et al. (1971) Parents' expectations of a university. *Universities quarterly* 25, 4.
Cohen, L. (1970) Sixth-form pupils and their views of higher education. *Journal of curriculum studies* 2, 1.
Committee of Enquiry into the Engineering Profession (1980) *Engineering our future*. London.
Committee on the Civil Service (1968) *Report of the committee, 1966-68*, I. London.
Committee on Manpower Resources for Science and Technology (1968) *The flow into employment of scientists, engineers and technologists*. London.
Council for Scientific Policy (1968) *Enquiry into the flow of candidates in science and technology into higher education*. London.
Dainton, F. (1975) A note on science in higher education: the era of certainty 1945-1960, in *The sciences, the humanities and the technological threat* (ed. W. R. Niblett). London.
Flexner, A. (1930) *Universities: American, English, German*. New York.
Hawkins, D. (1973) Liberal education: a modest polemic, in *Content and context: essays on college education* (ed. C. Kaysen). New York.
Hoggart, R. (1965) *Higher education and cultural change: a teacher's view*. Newcastle-upon-Tyne.
House of Commons (1972) *Minutes of evidence taken before the expenditure committee* (education and the arts sub-committee), memorandum of evidence by the Committee of Directors of Polytechnics, examination of witnesses (N. Lindop). London.
— (1980) *Minutes of evidence taken before the select committee on education, science and arts*, memorandum submitted by the Committee of Directors of Polytechnics on the planning and control of higher education. London.
Hutchings, D. (1963) Sixth form scientists in search of an image. *Universities quarterly* 17, 3.
— (1967) *The science undergraduate: a study of science students at five English universities*. Oxford.
Kogan, M. (1982) Expectations of higher education within the policy setting, introductory paper at OECD conference on higher education, Hatfield (mimeo).
Marx, L. (1975) Technology and the study of man, in *The sciences, the humanities and the technological threat* (ed. W. R. Niblett). London.

Niblett, W. R. (ed.) (1975) *The sciences, the humanities and the technological threat*. London.

Oxtoby, R. (1971) Educational and vocational objectives of polytechnic students. *Universities quarterly* 26, 1.

Percy, K. A. and Salter, F. W. (1976) Student and staff perceptions and 'the pursuit of excellence' in British higher education. *Higher education* 5, 4.

Peston, M. (1979) The future of higher education. *Oxford review of education* 5, 2.

Peterson, A. D. C. (1961) Degrees for living. *The Observer weekend review*, 8 January.

Robbins, Lord (1966) *The university in the modern world and other papers on higher education*. London.

Rothblatt, S. (1976a) *Tradition and change in English liberal education: an essay in history and culture*. London.

— (1976b) The past and future freedom of the British university. *Minerva* XIV, 2.

Sanderson, M. (1972) *The universities and British industry 1850-1970*, London.

Scott, P. (1979) *What future for higher education?* London.

— (1981) From binary to pluralism: opening address to the residential conference of the Standing conference of principals and directors of colleges and institutes of higher education, Stoke Rochford (mimeo).

Shils, E. (1982) Great Britain and the United States: legislators, bureaucrats and the universities, in *Universities, politicians and bureaucrats: Europe and the United States* (eds H. Daalder and E. Shils). Cambridge.

Silver, H. (1980) Enforced conformity or hierarchical diversity?, in *Education beyond school: higher education for a changing context* (ed. N. Evans). London.

— (1983a) *Education as history*. London.

— (1983b) A national university – the next step? *The Times higher education supplement*, 22 April.

Times review of industry and technology (1963) Robbins: the great debate, in 1, 8 (contributions by Lord Nelson of Stafford and F. H. Perkins).

— (1964) Does industry know what it wants?, in 2, 10.

Touraine, A. (1980) Decline or transformation of the universities? *Prospects* X, 2.

Trow, M. (1982) *Defining the issues in university-government relations – an international perspective* (Center for studies in higher education, occasional paper no.27). Berkeley.

University Grants Committee (1950) *A note on technology in universities*. London.

— (1964) *Report of the committee on university teaching methods*. London.

THE LEVERHULME PROGRAMME OF STUDY INTO THE FUTURE OF HIGHER EDUCATION: FUTURE PROSPECTS

GARETH WILLIAMS

The 1970s was a bad decade for British higher education. It undoubtedly went down in political esteem. However, the most obvious quantitative indicator of its decline is that the proportion of school-leavers entering higher education, which had risen explosively in the 1960s, stopped growing. Indeed, between 1972/3 and 1980/1 it fell from 14.2 per cent of the relevant age group to 12.7 per cent. This decline is often ignored in debates about future prospects for higher education.

In 1978 the DES drew attention to the prospect that from the early 1980s the size of the age group from which most students come would start to fall – slowly between 1984 and 1989, and then very rapidly indeed for about seven years (DES 1978). In 1996 there will be about thirty per cent fewer eighteen-year-olds in Britain than there are today. A declining age group combined with a stagnating participation rate raises the spectre of excess capacity.

Many of those who commented on the DES document claimed that higher education could attract a large new clientele from adults and from school-leavers in social groups with low participation rates at present. Few ideas were forthcoming, however, about how such new students would be attracted, or whether it was desirable that they should be, or whether public funds should be used to encourage them to do so. There is some reason to doubt whether the main thrust of efforts in continuing education of adults can or should be in the area of higher education (see Williams 1983).

In 1980 an SRHE working party expressed the view that

> The fundamental problem facing post-secondary education during the next two decades is not demography but loss of confidence: loss of confidence by school-leavers in the private benefits of higher education, loss of confidence by politicians in the social benefits and often a loss of confidence by academics in their own sense of purpose.

The Leverhulme Programme: Future Prospects

These problems may be exacerbated, but they are not created, by public expenditure constraints ... (Williams and Blackstone 1983)

Student numbers are certainly not the whole of higher education policy. However, in the twenty years since the Robbins Report (1963) the numbers game has dominated higher-education policy-making and it is difficult, even for a government that rejects the Robbins principle, to ignore the effects of student demand. National higher education policy in the 1980–3 period was probably influenced as much by what the government saw as the likelihood of excess capacity within a decade as by the general policy of restraining public expenditure.

Any projection of the future must contain a substantial element of speculation, and it does no harm to remind ourselves that during the past twenty years there have been some dramatic mistakes in forecasts of the demand for higher education. The two most important projections during the period were contained in the *Report of the Committee on Higher Education* (Robbins 1963) and in the revision of the Robbins projections published in the 1972 Education White Paper (DES 1972). The former underestimated by 100,000 the number of full-time students in 1971, and the latter overestimated by 200,000 the number by 1981.

Nevertheless, to ignore the implications for future policy of trend projections is even more irresponsible than to accept them uncritically. To show that past projections have not been borne out by events is not to prove that the projections were not worth making. The Robbins projections in particular did much to create the political climate that made it possible for them to be exceeded by a considerable margin during the following ten years.

The fall in the eighteen-year-old population is inevitable. All the remaining constituents of any projection of the demand for higher education are to some extent speculative. One large speculative element is the proportion of these eighteen-year-olds who will seek to enter higher education. This figure fell away for several years after 1972, partly because the decline in opportunities to undertake teacher training was not accompanied by a corresponding willingness to take up available places elsewhere. In 1980 the age participation rate started to rise slowly, and by 1982/3 it had reached 13.5 per cent. In the most recent official projection (DES 1983) government statisticians indicate a belief that this recovery will continue but that there is little probability of participation rates rising substantially above their 1970 level.

Many commentators derive comfort from the rising proportion of births in middle-class families. In 1964 seventeen per cent of all births were from families in which the main income earner was classified as belonging to Social Class I or II. In 1970 the figure had risen to 21 per cent, and in 1977 it was 28 per cent. Farrant (1981) shows that in 1977 the age participation rate for Social Classes I and II was 29 per cent, while that for Classes III, IV and V combined was 8 per cent. If we apply these proportions to the birth patterns of 1970 and 1977 (which cohorts will be ready for entry into higher education in 1989 and 1996, respectively), we would find an overall age participation rate of 14.5 per cent by 1989 (allowing for the rise of 10 per cent in participation rate between 1977 and 1982). This corresponds to the midpoint of the 1983 DES projections. A similar calculation for 1996 gives a participation rate of 16 per cent, which is about the same as the DES higher projection. It appears that while current DES forecasts are not ambitious as regards participation rates, there is no reason to suppose that the 'social class effect' by itself will raise them sufficiently to prevent a decline in the higher education population. Furthermore, there must be some doubts as to whether the 'new' members of white-collar families will have the same patterns of educational behaviour as the more established members. It is therefore unlikely that the social class effect can completely overcome the effect of the decline in the age group. The Royal Society (1983) adopts a rather similar procedure to make estimates for universities only and is able to show that up till the end of the present decade the 'social class effect' could avoid excess capacity in the university sector before 1990. By the 1990s higher education institutions will need to attract more students from within either or both of the main social class groups if they are to avoid excess capacity.

In 1982, after a thorough review of the then-available evidence, Farrant concluded that, '... within the limits of policy initiatives likely to be taken by either the present government or its successor, there is little prospect of averting a decline in the total size of the higher education system by 1990' (Farrant

The Leverhulme Programme: Future Prospects
1981). There seems no reason substantially to revise this judgement. The rest of the 1980s is at best likely to be a period in which higher education can have a breathing space and an opportunity of adaptation without growth to prepare for the much more severe demographic trends of the 1990s.

The current crisis of higher education is not, however, simply a matter of quantitative prospects. I believe that a fundamental weakness of British higher education is that it is producer-dominated – something it has in common with many of our great institutions. We have in this country, quite rightly, a firm belief in the value of academic freedom. In matters of scholarship and learning, professional academics know best, and the opportunities for politicians and other outsiders to intervene are kept to a minimum. This can be seen as one manifestation of a phenomenon that is fairly general in Britain, that is, the important role of professional expertise in matters of resource allocation. We have it in medicine, we have it in the law, we have it in the BBC and we certainly have it in education at all levels. The producer knows best, because he is the expert. In passing, I would like to suggest the thesis that the criticism of the present-day civil servant as a dilettante amateur is wide of the mark. Surely *Yes, Minister* has given the lie to that. The Civil Service consists of professional public administrators with their own in-group language (often consisting of public-school cricketing metaphors), and they are more than a match for any politician or outsider (such as Fulton 1968) who tries to upset their highly developed system of professional self-regulation.

I suspect that our very specialised system of secondary and higher education may have something to do with this producer domination in that very few people have the kind of knowledge that enables them even to begin to evaluate the arguments of anyone outside their own particular area of expertise. There is no doubt that this stress on professional self-regulation can result in technical excellence which it is ungracious to criticise. It leads to Concorde, it gives us a very high level of integrity amongst our public servants, it leads to the well-known phenomenon of Britain being in the forefront in the early stages of much new technology, it breeds Nobel prize-winners, it means that in a particular area of knowledge the English graduate after three years of study has reached a level comparable to that achieved after five or six years of study in many other countries. It is not so clear, however, that this professional self-regulation results in equity or that it leads to commercial success. That is the conceptual starting point of the problems confronted in the final report of the SRHE-Leverhulme Programme of Study. We have a higher education system which in many ways is excellent, but it is a system dominated by the ethos that the professional knows best and should not be interfered with. For sixty years the universities have been, on the whole, generously financed by government on this assumption.

The implications of such professional self-regulation in a period of adaptation without growth were at the centre of many of the debates of the Leverhulme study, and they provide the central theme of the final report. The aim was to find ways in which the undoubted advantages of this professionalism can be maintained while at the same time encouraging people in higher education to be not only professionally responsible but also responsive to the needs of society outside the walls. In some ways we were helped in this task by the decline in the birthrate and the stagnating participation rates because they draw attention to the fact that it is in the self-interest of universities and colleges to respond to the needs of the society they serve.

The ideas that underlie the final report of the SRHE-Leverhulme study, *Excellence in Diversity*, are expounded at grreater length in the accompanying book *Response to Adversity* (Williams and Blackstone 1983). On the title page of that book there is a short extract from Francis Bacon's essay *Of Adversity*: 'Prosperity doth best discover vice, but adversity doth best discover virtue'. The adversity which higher education is likely to continue to experience might be a goad to us to be responsive to the needs of society in a way in which we were not during the prosperous years of the 1960s. Except in the very narrow sense of catering for a certain kind of school-leaver, it cannot be claimed that our universities became much more open to the needs of society as a result of the post-Robbins expansion. This is understandable: no successful enterprise is easily persuaded of the desirability of changing its range of products.

There are two ways of encouraging producer-dominated

The Leverhulme Programme: Future Prospects

establishments to be more adaptable to the needs of society. Much of the debate of the Leverhulme study centred on these two opposing models, one which would involve external regulation of institutions through controls, the other which would expose them to the opportunities and rigours of the market. In the former, the external influence comes from the politicians and the bureaucrats; in the latter, the consumer, through the market, decides which institutions are going to decline and which prosper. There is something to be said for moderate versions of both. Markets can in some circumstances work rather well as resource-allocation mechanisms (this, to my mind, is a different issue from the question of who has the legal right to the income generated by the market). Central planning need not simply mean people being told what to do by uncomprehending bureaucrats. But in higher education, both markets and bureaucracies do have their dangers.

The central issue of the SRHE-Leverhulme report, the kernel to which all the proposals are in some way linked, is to find a balance between the producer-dominated, the bureaucrat-dominated and the consumer-dominated models of higher-education provision that is appropriate for the circumstances of the 1980s and 1990s.

Excellence in Diversity does not have a list of underlined recommendations. Instead, it tries to present a succinct summary of key issues and to convey, in the form of sometimes Delphic phrases, a number of radical but viable ideas to individuals and groups that will be taking major decisions in higher education during the next few years.

One basic assumption is that new developments must come from adaptation, not expansion. Another basic assumption is that higher education must remain largely within the public sector. The simple market solution of a privatised system of higher education is rejected. The main theme is an endorsement of diversity. This requires strong institutions and multiple criteria for policy formulation and resource allocation. Whether the Robbins report intended it is doubtful, but one of that report's main impacts was to focus attention on one single aspect of higher education – the provision of facilities for eighteen-year-old school-leavers. The great criterion that 'courses of higher education should be available for all who are qualified by ability and attainment to pursue them and who wish to do so' and its exegesis in terms of A-level and H-level passes focused the attention of politicians and civil servants on this aspect of higher education. The higher education component of Public Expenditure White Papers for well over a decade consisted essentially of projections of qualified school-leavers multiplied by an estimated average length of course and an estimated average cost per student. Research, continuing education and all the other functions of higher education establishments were linked to it. *Excellence in Diversity* aims to draw attention to the much wider range of functions of a modern system of higher education. In particular, it tries to emphasise continuing education, research and public service.

The strategy it outlines has eight main guiding principles:

To provide opportunities for all who are able to benefit from some form of higher education and to encourage access from a broader social spectrum than at present;

To reduce undue specialisation in secondary education and the initial years of higher education;

To create a framework within which the quality of teaching and research can be maintained, at a time when underlying demographic trends will make competition for resources difficult;

To stimulate research and the academic activities not directly linked to student numbers;

To encourage institutions to prepare realistic development plans;

To increase the capacity of universities, polytechnics and colleges to respond positively to changing academic, social, economic and industrial needs;

To promote efficiency in the use of resources;

To create a framework for policy and management studies that will help leaders of academic institutions meet the challenge of adaptation without growth.

The first of these aims, the broadening of access, is the subject of the next paper. Broader access is one of the considerations lying behind the recommendations of the report that received the most immediate media attention – the structure of courses. In some ways the proposals can be seen as an attempt to Caledonianise English higher education, thus trying to reverse what I personally consider to be a regrettable trend towards anglicisation of some parts of Scottish higher education.

The Leverhulme Programme: Future Prospects

Participation rates in higher education in Scotland remain considerably higher than in England. For this reason if for no other, it is desirable that those responsible for higher education south of the border should show some interest in what is happening in the north.

The second aim of the proposals on course structure is to reverse the trend towards specialisation. The one criticism of English upper secondary and undergraduate education on which almost all informed commentators can agree is that it is excessively specialised. Andrew McPherson and his colleagues have shown in a recent book (Gray et al. 1983) that Scotland can no longer be exempted entirely from strictures about premature and excessive specialisation. The specialisation demanded, understandably but rarely justifiably, by the specialist university departments that admit students, feeds back into the schools. Sixth formers and their teachers consider it a waste of time to do anything that will not help them to jump the hurdle of university entry requirements.

The view taken in *Excellence in Diversity* is that the best way of reversing this trend towards excessive specialisation is to dethrone the honours degree as the overwhelmingly dominant force in universities and to replace it by a different kind of degree structure which in the event turned out rather like the traditional Scottish pattern. In English terms this means a two-year pass degree. In many ways it would be tempting to go the whole way and propose a shorter period of sixth-form study in England, but this is not realistic.

Two-year pass degrees could be very widely available and therefore more accessible to adult students in particular. Some colleges of further education would be able to offer them, and they would almost certainly be able to be provided more economically than the first two years of an honours degree.

The next major issue covered in the report is the maintenance of academic standards. If, as appears likely, universities and colleges are going to be competing fiercely with each other for resources and for students, there is a danger of dilution of standards in an activity in which the quality of output cannot be immediately recognised. There is a considerable amount of evidence that this has been happening in the United States (see e.g. Freeman 1981; Trow 1981). A related concern is whether the standards implied by an honours degree are the same across the whole of higher education and whether the external examiner system is a robust enough instrument to ensure a reasonable measure of comparability between different institutions. There are two reasons for believing that the matter at least needs investigation. One is that the criteria for the appointment of examiners and the tasks they are expected to perform vary widely. The second is that there is a much wider variation between departments and institutions in the average A-level grades of entrants than in the degree classes of graduates. There has been remarkably little research into an issue that some people might consider to be critical in the light of the significance of degree classes for many of the opportunities subsequently open to graduates. A very useful pioneering study was made by Bligh *et al.* (1980). Some universities and particularly polytechnics seem to be more successful than others in turning (apparently) poor-quality entrants into (apparently) high-quality graduates. This suggests either that some popular institutions offer poor teaching, or that degrees from some of the less popular institutions are in fact of lower quality (class for class). Either is a cause for concern. Another possible explanation of this phenomenon is that A-level grades may be poor predictors of performance, or degree class may be a poor indicator of performance. Whatever combination of these explanations is correct, there is some cause for concern. Young people devote a substantial part of their lives to trying to get good A-level grades and degree classes, and there is a fairly low level above which the random element should be considered unacceptable.

Excellence in Diversity proposes that universities should in their own interests and that of their students establish an academic review body with functions broadly similar to those of the Council for National Academic Awards. Arrangements are needed to ensure, for example, that academic standards for similar activities do not diverge too widely between institutions, that students are not misled about the nature of the courses they select, that they are assessed fairly and in an equivalent manner throughout higher education, that the requirements of professional bodies are not oppressive for individual students or institutions, that criteria for student credit transfer are efficient and fair and that funding bodies are well informed about the academic merits of different activities.

The Leverhulme Programme: Future Prospects

The issue is not whether arrangements for external quality control should be established: much already exists and funding bodies will be increasingly drawn into quality comparisons between institutions. The essential issues are whether existing arrangements should be made more systematic, whether the administrative distinction between universities and other institutions should correspond to such a sharp distinction in methods of academic regulation, whether judgements about the academic quality of institutions should be made openly, and whether the regulation of arrangements for quality should be under academic or administrative and financial control.

The report touches gingerly on the issue of lifetime tenure for members of the academic profession. Among the problems of adaptation without growth is the recruitment of new staff, and the encouragement of existing staff to be adaptable and to develop new skills. The efficiency and enthusiasm of members of the academic profession must be maintained during a long period of adaptation without growth. Effective professional-development policies and open styles of management can help to maintain morale; but it is necessary to ensure that some well-qualified graduates are regularly appointed to academic posts; that all members of universities, polytechnics and colleges are able to contribute usefully to the work of their institutions; that those who occupy positions of responsibility retain their capacity to shoulder their responsibilities; that there is some mobility of staff; and that students have opportunities to benefit from the expertise of people with recent experience outside higher education.

The report concludes that lifetime tenure should no longer be the standard form of university teaching appointment and accepts that early retirement schemes, even if expensive, are likely to be an essential part of the higher education scene for many years.

A specific proposal concerns part-time staff. In many areas of study, especially professional subjects, applied science and technology and the performing arts, it is hard to envisage students receiving an adequate higher education unless they have some contact with teachers whose knowledge is practical as well as theoretical. In less directly practical subjects also, students can learn much that is valuable from those who have practised in politics, administration, industry, commerce, the media and the arts. For this reason if no other, the position of part-time members of staff needs protection, especially at a time when limited budgets make them particularly vulnerable.

A major concern of the report is to protect research at a time when budgets are stable or falling because student numbers are not growing. It expresses agnosticism about the closeness of the link between teaching and research. There are some complementarities in both personnel and equipment, which make it convenient for some kinds of research to be undertaken in the same institutions as some kinds of teaching. Obviously the happiest outcome for all occurs when excellent research workers are also excellent teachers. However, good teachers can be poor researchers and vice versa; and teaching and research can compete for the time of staff and for equipment and facilities. A clearer conceptual separation of the teaching and research functions would help to protect research. The report recommends that university funding should distinguish between undergraduate teaching and general support of scholarship on one hand and postgraduate teaching and research on the other. Research council funding assumes that research projects in universities will be able to make use of basic facilities and staff financed through the UGC grant. However, the UGC block grant makes no explicit distinction between research and teaching components. There is a danger in a time of declining student numbers that institutional rigidities will result in funds intended for research providing a cushion protecting universities from the need to respond to changing patterns of student demand. The unearmarked research funding received by universities is one of the main sources of the sense of injustice felt by many public sector institutions, both because of the apparent prestige it implies and because of the advantage it gives to the universities in competing for research funds. It is impossible to tell whether similar levels of resources are in fact being provided for similar activities in universities and the local authority sector. Identification of research and teaching budgets would protect research and help to bring about a sharper focus of the national research effort. It would also enable the true costs of different institutions to be seen more clearly.

This discussion of research leads directly to a more general

The Leverhulme Programme: Future Prospects
discussion of funding mechanisms, which is the subject of my later paper (p.260).

The proposals of *Excellence in Diversity* and *Response to Adversity* are designed to take advantage of the opportunities given by the falling numbers of school-leavers to develop a system of higher education that is responsive to changing social and economic needs while maintaining quality and academic integrity. It would, I think, be a healthier system, equipped to meet the challenges of the twenty-first century.

REFERENCES

Bligh, D., Caves, R. and Settle, G. (1980) A-Level Scores and Degree Classifications as Functions of University Type and Subject, in *Indicators of Performance* (ed. D. Billing). SRHE, Guildford.

Department of Education and Science (DES) (1972) *Education: A Framework for Expansion*, Cmnd 5174. HMSO.

— (1978) *Higher Education into the 1990s*. HMSO.

— (1983) *Future Demand for Higher Education in Great Britain: Report on Education No. 99*. DES.

Farrant, J. (1981) Trends in Admissions, in *Access to Higher Education* (ed. O. Fulton). SRHE, Guildford.

Freeman, R. (1981) Response to Change in the United States, in *Higher Education and the Labour Market* (ed. R. Lindley). SRHE, Guildford.

Fulton, J. (1968) *The Civil Service*, Cmnd 3638. HMSO.

Gray, J., MacPherson, A. S. and Raffe, D. (1983) *Reconstructions of Secondary Education: Theory, Myth and Practice Since the War*. London.

Robbins (1963) *Report of the Committee on Higher Education*, Cmnd 2154. HMSO.

Royal Society (1983).

Society for Research into Higher Education (SRHE) (1983) *Excellence in Diversity*. SRHE, Guildford.

Trow, M. (1981) Comparative Perspectives on Access, in *Access to Higher Education* (ed. O. Fulton). SRHE, Guildford.

Williams, G. (1983) Preparing for Adaptation Without Growth, in *Yearbook of Social Policy 1983* (eds Jones and Stevenson). London.

Williams, G. and Blackstone, T. (1983) *Response to Adversity*. SRHE, Guildford.

ACCESS TO HIGHER EDUCATION IN BRITAIN

TESSA BLACKSTONE

A policy on access to higher education must answer several questions: access on what criteria, for whom, to what, and paid for how? This paper begins by examining the present extent and pattern of participation in higher education in Britain and compares it with some other economically advanced countries. It then considers some of the policies which will be needed to accomplish an extension of access to a wider range of students and a higher proportion of eighteen- to twenty-five-year-olds than at present.

The participation rate of young people in higher education was the dominant issue confronting the Robbins Committee twenty years ago. Competition for higher education had been growing more intense in the late 1950s. The number of places available was increasing more slowly than the number of school-leavers with appropriate qualifications. It became clear that the situation would worsen as the post-war bulge reached the age of eighteen in the mid-1960s, and the chance of obtaining higher education was likely to be considerably lower for this cohort than for those that preceded it. To many commentators at the time this seemed inequitable. However, most of the Robbins debate was conceived in what now seem narrow terms. It was about young people attending degree level courses. There was little consideration of mature students, different patterns of provision or alternative entry qualifications.

The debate also focused on responding to a particular conception of demand – two A-levels and a desire to proceed to higher education. The Robbins Committee projected what that demand would be between 1961 and 1981, as it happens remarkably accurately despite having substantially underestimated it up to the early 1970s. It then proposed that the system should be expanded accordingly. Many of the assumptions of that period are no longer valid, and new policy questions arise. Should the same criteria continue to apply? Should demand be stimulated by changing policies at various levels to try to bring more people into higher education? Should the

Access to Higher Education in Britain

pattern of demand be changed? Should student numbers be constrained to enable higher education provision to be based on criteria other than meeting student demand? These are some of the questions that the Government faces today.

The percentage of school-leavers entering higher education nearly doubled in the twenty years between 1960–61 and 1980–81, from 6.9 to 12.5 per cent. However, it was not a steady growth. The age participation rate had already doubled by 1970; it reached a peak of 14.2 per cent in 1972–73 and then fell away. During the 1960s the proportion of eighteen-year-olds achieving two or more A-levels rose less rapidly than the number of places. Since 1970 the number of places has grown less rapidly than the number of eighteen-year-olds obtaining this minimum entry qualification. There has thus been a decline in the proportion of qualified leavers going into higher education from 1968 onwards. The participation rate for women has been lower than for men throughout the period. By 1980–81 it was 11.0 per cent compared with 13.9 per cent for men. The gap narrowed a little in the middle part of the period only to widen again more recently.

International comparisons of higher education provision can be misleading, and care must be taken in interpreting them since we are not always comparing like with like. British higher education is particularly difficult to place in an international perspective. The boundary between higher education and what in Britain we call further education is not drawn in the same place in all countries. For example much of the work of the two-year colleges in the United States and Japan would in Britain be called non-advanced further education. Few other countries make our sharp distinction between full-time and part-time students. Thus, many British part-time students probably ought to be included in international comparisons. Yet it is likely to be misleading in the other direction to include all of the 50,000 students on evening-only courses and all of the 60,000 on Open University courses with the same weighting as full-time students.

Nevertheless it is interesting and legitimate to compare education with that of other economically developed Western countries. Briefly what emerges when we do is that Britain can be seen as coming towards one end of a scale in which rigorous selection for full-time and part-time day study is accompanied by a high probability of obtaining a degree. At the other end of the scale come the open access countries, where only one in four or fewer of those who qualify for entry to higher education emerge with a degree (Cerych 1982). Many of the recommendations of the Robbins Committee which shaped the expansion of British higher education in the 1960s and early 1970s were based on the belief that winning is more important than taking part, and that the high success rate of entrants to higher education with few students dropping out or failing justified restricted access. Some people take the view that this still provides the best guide to policy in the 1980s and 1990s as well. However, the question of the right balance between a system in which some higher education is available for many and one in which much higher education is available for a few needs frequent re-examination. In the interests of greater social equality and the promotion of a rather less elitist system there is a good case for policies aimed at increasing participation even if this is not accompanied by a proportionate increase in the number of people who emerge with a university degree of the traditional type.

The high success rate of students in British higher education is clearly related in part to the higher selectivity of the system. It is also associated with relatively high levels of expenditure. A higher proportion of national income is devoted to higher education in Britain than in most other countries. Again there are problems of interpretation, arising largely from the relatively generous provision of maintenance grants to British students. If these are excluded entirely the British figure falls to about the European average. However, all European countries provide some subsidy to students, often in the form of subsidised facilities; so again, to deduct the whole of grant expenditure is misleading in the other direction. The general picture seems to be that Britain devotes a larger share of its national income to higher education than most other industrialised countries, but not much more.

Overall, higher education in Britain caters for fewer students at greater resource cost than most of its European neighbours with the notable exception of Holland. This generous treatment is associated with extremely favourable staff–student ratios and high success rates at least for full-time students. This has been praised on the grounds of the traditional standards

Access to Higher Education in Britain
and superior quality of British higher education. It has also been justifiably criticised on the grounds that it concentrates resources on a small section of the population at the expense of others who are denied access to post-secondary education opportunities.

In England especially, secondary education for many pupils is a series of examination filters out of which the student emerges at eighteen as an embryonic specialist in a narrow range of subjects. In Scotland students' experiences are a little broader though in recent years not very much so, as an important recent book shows (Gray, McPherson and Raffe 1983). For the socially unrepresentative minority who are successful, this is followed by three or four years of intensive full-time study. The initiation into adulthood of the sons of the wealthy has expanded to cater for the sons and daughters of a slightly broader section of the population. Rationing of places through ability to pay has been replaced by rationing through ability to succeed in a certain type of secondary-school examination.

Farrant (1981) has produced a valuable review of the evidence on changes in the composition of the student body between 1960 and 1980. He shows that the social group which benefited most from expansion was what may loosely be called the lower middle class – that is non-manual groups such as clerical workers. Their participation rates more than doubled between 1961 and 1967, and the probability of a child from such a family entering higher education rose from 50 per cent of the middle class average to 80 per cent. The relative probability of higher education for young people from manual workers' families changed little, from 16 per cent of the middle class average to 19 per cent between 1961 and 1980. There is thus still an enormous gap between these social classes. However, different types of higher education do cater for a rather different clientele. Part-time higher education, which is concerned mainly with occupationally related courses, does attract a higher proportion of students from manual working class backgrounds. The proportion of full-time university students who are from working-class backgrounds actually fell between 1956 and 1980. The proportion of the population in manual occupations also fell slightly between 1961 and 1981, and there was probably some shift of working-class students towards the expanding public sector. However, the overall picture is clear. The expansion of full-time degree courses was associated with some broadening of the range of families which typically send their children to higher education, but this shift made no significant impact on the barrier which separates white collar from blue collar families.

Social class is not the only source of variation in participation rates. There are major regional differences as well. Farrant shows that, after adjusting for the social class composition of the population, university participation rates in Scotland are 26 per cent above the England and Wales average, whereas for the North of England region they are 21 per cent below. The same difference between Scottish and English participation rates remains if all higher education is included. There are substantial, though less dramatic, disparities in other regions, with Wales in particular having higher-than-predicted participation rates.

The chances of women entering higher education have always been less than those for men. Their participation did start to catch up during the 1960s but suffered disproportionately following the closure of Colleges of Education during the 1970s. Overall, in 1980 a woman had about 80 per cent of the chance of a man of entering full-time higher education compared with a relative figure of 90 per cent only three years earlier. Women have, however, made some apparently permanent gains in at least some of the high-prestige courses. The chance of a woman entering a university course increased from 41 per cent of the male figure in 1956 to 68 per cent in 1980, and there were a number of significant shifts in individual subject areas. For example, in 1956 the probability of a woman undertaking medical education was less than one-third of that of a man; by 1980 the figure was over four-fifths. The reduction of teacher training places in the mid-1970s seems to have pushed some young women to take more A-levels and aspire to university courses. But on balance the net effect was a slight worsening of the relative participation rates of women compared with men. The failure to improve the overall participation of women during a period when the levels of female employment, notably of married women, have greatly increased and legislation has been passed both making discrimination on the grounds of sex illegal and establishing the right to equal pay is a disappointing outcome. Mature students

Access to Higher Education in Britain
are far more likely to be found in the public sector than in the universities apart from the Open University. Amongst full-time undergraduate entrants, 13 per cent in universities and 37 per cent in the public sector were aged twenty-one or more. This is related largely, but not entirely, to the much higher proportion of part-time entrants to the public sector (53 per cent of entrants compared with 2 per cent in the universities). In fact the proportion of part-time places in universities has actually declined over the last twenty years. The Open University has, however, demonstrated that there is a demand for part-time higher education amongst adults and that they are capable of studying at a high level even if they do not have the normal university entry requirements.

We know less about participation from ethnic minority groups. None of the official statistics gives any indication of the extent of their participation. However, it is clear from casual observation that many of them are poorly represented throughout higher education. A special survey conducted on behalf of the Rampton Committee in six local education authorities shows the low proportion of children of West Indian origin entering higher education, 2 per cent, compared with 9 per cent of the Asians and 8 per cent of the other leavers in the six education authorities reviewed. The six authorities chosen for the survey, presumably on the basis of high concentration of population from ethnic minorities, also had low overall proportions of school-leavers entering higher education – about 8 per cent compared with about 13 per cent of all school-leavers in England. This evidence is a fragment and we must hope that despite all the difficulties further reliable evidence will be collected. Without it it is hard to substantiate fully the case for policies that are almost certainly urgently needed to improve access to higher education for ethnic minorities.

The decline in the birth rate between 1964 and 1978 has dominated educational policy-making at school levels for some years. Recently it has been the focal point of much of the present concern about the future of higher education. The size of the eighteen-year-old age group will fall by over 30 per cent between 1983 and 1996. Since this follows a ten-year period of stagnating participation rates, there are fears that the decline in the age group will be associated with a corresponding decline in the number of students.

If age participation rates did not increase from 1981 onwards and if mature students, overseas students and post-graduate students kept at their 1981 levels, there would be about 110,000 fewer full-time students by the mid-1990s. This corresponds to the closing of about sixteen average-sized British universities or most of the polytechnics. There are various reasons for raising the age participation rate. The first is based on the fact that the birth rate fall from 1965 to 1978 was concentrated in working-class families. The proportion of eighteen-year-olds from middle-class families will therefore rise, probably causing some rise in overall participation rates and possibly, according to Farrant (1981), by about 12½ per cent amongst young people. This might save about six universities. Another university would be saved if women's participation rose to that of men. Alternatively, if the participation rates for England and Wales rose to those in Scotland a further five or six might be able to continue. Finally, if overall participation rates rose to the present middle-class average there would be a rise of over 140,000 in student numbers, allowing for the creation of about 25 average-sized new universities.

We could make similar assumptions about the number of mature students and the number of postgraduate students, remembering that the proportionate changes in these would need to be much greater in order to counteract the effects of the fall in eighteen-year-olds.

It is, however, unlikely that the kind of changes in participation rates required can occur without substantial changes in the patterns of provision. I have mentioned that working-class students and older students are more likely to attend part-time courses different from the standard degree pattern. It is a reasonable inference that significant increases in the number of such students will not be possible without increases in the provision of such courses. In discussing the prospects for mature students it should be noted that 70 per cent of mature new entrants to higher education are in their twenties and 40 per cent are under the age of twenty-five. The potential population of mature students of the present type will therefore follow demographic trends similar to the eighteen-year-old population.

Higher education institutions as a whole face, therefore, the challenge of adaption without much growth. They will have

Access to Higher Education in Britain

change forced upon them as large-scale excess capacity begins to emerge and will have to adapt to attract new types of client. Obviously a few institutions could survive and prosper by continuing to offer the traditional pattern of courses. But this would be a risky strategy for the majority.

Many of the changes which would reduce inequality of participation must start back in the early years of secondary education. Young people with a sense of academic failure from their early teens are unlikely to prolong their education. My concern here, however, is with measures that can be taken by or on behalf of higher education institutions.

The first, and in some ways simplest, change would be in recruitment policies, particularly in the universities. In the past the A-level requirement for entry including the specification of grades has been essentially a rationing device where many institutions have had more applicants than places. How good a predictor A-level grades are for later performance has been frequently questioned. In some subjects such as mathematics and modern languages the correlation between A-level success and degree performance is reasonably high. In others, such as the social sciences, it is low (Entwistle 1973). In such subjects where it is low there is a good case for relying less heavily on A-levels as a basis for admitting students. Even where it is high, the correlation is far from perfect and there should be less insistence on these qualifications. There is a case for some positive discrimination by admitting students with different kinds of educational background on different criteria.

Whilst a national examination at eighteen provides a useful measure of student attainment for employers and higher education institutions, it should not be the *only* criterion for admission to higher education. Fulton (1981) rightly argues that institutions should admit a significant proportion of their students on other criteria. Fulton and Gordon (1979) show that many young people potentially able to benefit from higher education still leave school at the age of sixteen, particularly amongst those from working-class backgrounds and correctly maintain that means-tested Educational Maintenance Allowances should be available for this group. However, whatever reforms are introduced at the secondary school level, it seems likely that there will still be talented young people who leave school at the earliest opportunity. Some may get technical or other qualifications in further education. Others may have only CSEs and O-levels but have gained appropriate work experience. These qualifications should be considered as acceptable alternatives to A-levels and not just for mature students. The rapidly growing network of training and educational opportunities for early-school-leavers makes a more flexible approach to higher education entry even more desirable.

People who wish to return to education in their twenties and thirties or even later should be given greater encouragement. They should be encouraged not only because technological change leads to the need for education and training later in life but because, on grounds of equity, people who did not have the opportunity of higher education earlier should be given it later. It also needs to be provided because mature students can bring to a university course much useful experience and insight which they can share with younger students and staff to the benefit of everyone. One way of encouraging them is to make the barriers to entry less formidable. This means making many more courses available part-time and taking into account experience at work, other qualifications and performance on aptitude tests. One beneficial result of the population decline is that higher education institutions are likely to do more to market their courses than they have done in the past. The principles and practice of 'outreach' used in adult education could well be extended and should apply to young people as well as older potential students (see Labour Party 1982). For example, representatives of universities, polytechnics and colleges should visit further education colleges, trade union colleges, evening institutes and centres for ethnic minority groups to inform as many people as possible what is available and to encourage them to apply. The notion of an active recruitment policy is one that all institutions should be encouraged to adopt.

The second change that is needed is in the types of courses which are provided. More provision for remedial or access courses is needed. These should prepare the student who has not obtained academic qualifications by providing advice on study skills, the use of libraries, essay writing and oral debate and discussion. Courses of this kind exist in further education; for example, the successful Open College Federation of the North West is based on this principle. Such schemes need to be

Access to Higher Education in Britain

expanded and made available for all or parts of degree courses as well as for preliminary study. If we are to encourage more ethnic minority group students, we should be more imaginative in putting on courses which are of special interest to them, as has happened in the United States (see Trow 1981). There is also a need for shorter and less specialised courses, which are less daunting to prospective students than many current honours degrees (see Williams and Blackstone 1983).

Opportunities for credit transfer should be extended. A great deal has been talked about credit transfer in recent years but little has been done. British higher education institutions have been hesitant to accept students who have completed a part of their course elsewhere. The diversity of course structures and narrow interpretations of institutional autonomy have made progress difficult. For adult students it is particularly important that there be more flexibility. Many will be married and will have spouses whose need for occupational mobility will take precedence over their husbands' or wives' courses. Some may need to interrupt their studies for financial or child-care reasons. Others may find the possibility of taking a degree in two or three parts with gaps in between less daunting than the present system. There are sometimes academic advantages if students are able to obtain course credits in institutions which have strengths in particular areas. However, without encouragement from the centre, reform seems unlikely. The Toyne Report recommended a national information service on credit transfer possibilities (Toyne 1979). It is to be hoped that the present pilot scheme will lead rapidly to a nationwide system of credit transfer.

In conclusion the case for broadening access is powerful. Fulton and Gordon (1979) found that 36 per cent of the 'highly able' sons of manual workers intended to enter higher education, compared with nearly double the number (70 per cent) in the same ability category for middle class boys. A failure to increase the participation rate means the socially marginal students are less likely to find places in higher education. These include those from state schools, without a long tradition of academic sixth-form education and sending pupils on to higher education; and older students, particularly those without conventional qualifications. However, many institutions, particularly the universities, tend to make safe rather than risky choices. This means young candidates with high A-level grades who come from 'good' schools. A climate of stagnation or contraction does not encourage experiment or innovation. In turn, this means that new courses which might attract different kinds of candidates may not be introduced. Demand from groups who are potentially able to benefit but who are not attracted by the present pattern of course provision would then remain depressed.

However, the decline in the number of eighteen-year-olds in the next decade provides an opportunity for government and for higher education to introduce reforms previously difficult because of pressure of numbers. Access should be broadened because many more people could successfully pursue courses and because there will be long-term social and economic benefits. More effort should be made to recruit students from working-class backgrounds, ethnic minorities, women and older people. To achieve this up to a quarter of students should be selected on criteria other than A-levels.

Rates of unemployment are considerably lower for graduates than for less highly educated people. Even if employers recruit graduates for jobs which earlier would have gone to less-well-qualified people, this should not be regarded as undesirable. Better educated employees *ought* to be capable of higher analytical skills, better communication, more imagination and creativity and hence more confident innovatory skills. There is little cause for confidence that scientific, technological, administrative, managerial and creative jobs are being done as well as they might be in either the public or the private sector. Whilst the market for graduates may be stagnant at present, as the recession recedes the demand for qualified manpower will start growing again. Because the 18- to 21-year-old age group will decline sharply in the next decade, any increase in the amount of graduate employment would require substantial increases in participation rates.

The value of higher education is not, however, narrowly economic. It is too easy in a period of economic depression, when political attention is dominated by the problem of creating material prosperity, to neglect the cultural and purely intellectual benefits for individuals and for society. Certainly higher-education institutions must be partly instrumental. They exist to serve society. But a significant part of that service

Access to Higher Education in Britain
is the improvement of intellectual, cultural and moral life. One of the responsibilities of the higher-education system is to spread its messages as widely as possible. British higher education, with its concentration on a narrow range of courses that appeal to a narrow segment of the population, is failing to do this. It is, however, my belief that it can and should rise to the challenge of widening access that it faces.

REFERENCES

Cerych, L. (1982) *Recent Trends in Higher Education*. OECD (mimeo).

Entwistle, N. (1973) Sylbs and Sylfs; Labelling and Libelling Students. Lancaster University Inaugural Lecture.

Farrant, J. (1981) Trends in Admissions, in *Access to Higher Education* (ed. O. Fulton). SRHE, Guildford.

Fulton, O. and Gordon, A. (1979) The British Pool of Ability; Will cash reduce it? *Educational Studies* 5(2).

Fulton, O. (1981) Principles and Policies, in *Access to Higher Education* (ed. O. Fulton). SRHE, Guildford.

Gray, J., McPherson, A. and Raffe, C. (1983) *Reconstructions of Secondary Education: Theory, Myth and Practice since the War*. London.

The Labour Party (1982) *Education after 18: Expansion with Change*. London.

Toyne, T. (1979) *Education Credit Transfer: Feasibility Study Final report*. Exeter.

Williams, G. and Blackstone, T. (1983) *Response to Adversity: Higher Education in a Harsh Climate*. SRHE, Guildford.

OF THE EXPENSE OF THE INSTITUTIONS FOR THE EDUCATION OF YOUTH

GARETH WILLIAMS

It is appropriate for an erstwhile economist to pay tribute to one of the immortals of the pantheon of talent that has been associated with Edinburgh University during its first four hundred years. The essay whose title I have borrowed was published by Adam Smith in 1776 in Book v of *The Wealth of Nations*. It is not only the title that is apposite to many current concerns. Adam Smith raises issues that will be very much in the minds of anyone who is responsible for the leadership of universities and colleges as they confront challenges during the next decade that are as severe as any during the past four centuries.

Smith identifies three ways in which 'institutions for the education of the youth' may receive their income. First they can be financed 'from the interest of some sum of money allotted and put under the management of trustees for this particular purpose'. Second, educational institutions can be subject to the authority of, and by implication financed by, what Smith describes as 'an extraneous jurisdiction'. Third, they may depend on the 'fees or honoraries of the scholars'. There is, of course, no doubt which Smith thought best suited to 'direct the course of education towards objects . . . useful, both to the individual and to the public'.

His views of the first is well known – at least amongst economists who write about university efficiency, and the responsibilities of higher education to society. 'The endowments of schools and colleges have necessarily diminished more or less the necessity of application in their teachers. Their subsistence . . . is evidently derived from a fund altogether independent of their success and reputation in their particular professions.' If the university teacher 'is naturally active and a lover of labour, it is his interest to employ that activity in any way from whch he can derive some advantage rather than in the performance of his duty from which he can derive none'. 'In the University of Oxford, the greater part of the public pro-

Of the Expense of the Institutions

fessors have, for these many years, given up altogether even the pretence of teaching.'

Smith was, of course, not the only observer to notice the sloth and apathy of eighteenth-century Oxford. Edward Gibbon, for example, 'tells that his tutor neither gave nor sought to give him more than one lesson' (Rae 1895, 20). However, Smith was the first to conclude that 'the stagnation of learning which prevailed in the wealthy universities of England was due at bottom to nothing but their wealth, because it was distributed on a bad system' (Rae 1895, 21).

Smith's strictures on 'extraneous jurisdiction' over the resources of higher education institutions are less frequently quoted but no less pertinent. 'If the authority to which he (the teacher) is subject resides, not so much in the body corporate of which he is a member, as in some other extraneous persons – in the bishop of the diocese for example; or the governor of the province; or, perhaps in some minister of state – it is not indeed in this case very likely that he will be suffered to neglect his duty altogether. All that such superiors can, however, force him to do, is to attend upon his pupils a certain number of hours, that is, to give a certain number of lectures in the week or in the year. What these lectures shall be must still depend on the diligence of the teacher . . . An extraneous jurisdiction of this kind, besides, is liable to be exercised both ignorantly and capriciously. In its nature it is arbitrary and discretionary, and the persons who exercise it, neither attending upon the lectures of the teacher themselves, nor perhaps understanding the sciences which it is his business to teach, are seldom capable of exercising it with judgement . . . The person subject to such jurisdiction is necessarily degraded by it, and, instead of being one of the most respectable, is rendered one of the meanest and most contemptible persons in the society. It is by powerful protection only that he can effectually guard himself against the bad usage to which he is at all times exposed . . . whoever has attended for any considerable time to the administration of a French university must have occasion to remark the effects which naturally result from an arbitrary and extraneous jurisdiction of this kind' (p.248).

Smith's preference, of course, was for those universities, presumably Scottish, in which 'the salary makes but a part, and frequently but a small part, of the emoluments of the teacher, of which the greater part arises from the honoraries or fees of his pupils. The necessity of application, though always more or less diminished, is not in this case entirely taken away. Reputation in his profession is still of some importance to him, and he still has some dependency upon the affection, gratitude, and favourable report of those who have attended upon his instructions'. Smith was probably influenced by his experiences in Edinburgh as a successful public lecturer whose income depended almost entirely on what he could earn from his students. In contrast to England, higher education was very popular in the Edinburgh of the eighteenth century. 'As the lectures of the professors are open to everyone and the expense of attending them very trifling, it is in the power of almost every tradesman to furnish his son with that instruction which is most adapted to his taste and capacity' (E. Topham: Letters from Edinburgh. Cited in Fay 1956).

We have, of course, moved on a bit since Adam Smith's day. Specialisation and the division of labour have outgrown the pin factory and now dominate our universities and colleges as well. Adam Smith's first course of lectures during his Edinburgh period was on English literature and these were followed by a series on jurisprudence, a chair in Logic and an important book on moral philosophy before he finally turned his mind to economics. It is doubtful whether anyone whose career today followed such a path would be considered academically sound.

Building Blocks for a Model of Academic Organisation:
Disciplines, Bureaucracies, Colleges, Markets

Many writers today put the discipline at the centre of academic life (see, for example, Clark 1983). It is the discipline, a shared approach to an area of knowledge, which integrates individual fragments of knowledge into a coherent teaching and research programme. A discipline, like a church or a political party, imposes rules on its disciples. Those who are more practised or skilled in the discipline acquire authority over other adherents who are less experienced, less dedicated or less able to comprehend its mysteries. Pressure for some measure of regulation of discipline-based academic activity arises from three sources: definition of boundaries, regulation of relations with other disciplines and interpretation to the rest

Of the Expense of the Institutions

of the world.

There is a need constantly to define and re-define the boundaries of a discipline. Many people who devote their lives to the pursuit of intellectual activity feel more comfortable if the bounds of their concerns are defined and shared with others. The discipline of the discipline can be more readily enforced if there is a clear understanding of its scope. The invisible college of scholars serves a purpose in many respects similar to the annual conferences of a political party or the great Councils of the Church. Doctrine is defined, problems are thrashed out and authority is established and transmitted. Those who claim to be mathematicians have the assurance that others see them as mathematicians. This is, of course, particularly useful to young people trying to establish an academic career.

Relations between disciplines need regulation. This is often a matter of competition for resources. Members of a discipline support each other against outsiders. When resources are scarce exponents of embattled disciplines will often withdraw from exposed positions into territory that is known to be defensible. More generally, however, the boundaries between disciplines are fluid. Any discipline is composed of many 'schools' or sub-disciplines. The map of knowledge is like a weather map of constantly shifting isobars rather than the contours of solid geological features. Without regulation there can be demarcation disputes, which cease to be mere intellectual games when significant resources or the careers of individuals are involved. It is widely believed that interdisciplinary research proposals which have to go before several different subject committees have less chance of success with research councils than those which are squarely within a recognised area of study.

The disciplines must also be interpreted to the outside world. Which problems, for example, are susceptible to the approach of a philosopher, which to a chemist, which to the two of them cooperating with each other? However, the aspect of academic coordination that is most important in the outside world is the regulation of what is taught to students under the labels of the various disciplines. At its simplest, students and those who will employ them afterwards, need to have some assurance that, for example, what they learn in acquiring an economics degree in one department at one time bears some relation to a similarly named degree in another department at another time. Public concern about academic standards is often a concern that this is not so; and whether the concern is justified or not, its existence implies that some aspects of regulation of the disciplines are not being properly performed.

Nowadays we would call Adam Smith's extraneous jurisdiction a bureaucracy. Centralised management supported by an effective bureaucracy can protect academic activities by ensuring that resources are adequate. It can also ensure rapid response to a changing environment. Capacity for change is not always a virtue, however. The process of debating changes and trying to build coalitions to promote them is a valuable part of the process of selecting ideas. Rapid changes of direction in an institution concerned with knowledge that is as yet unknown can be a fruitless pursuit of will o' the wisp. Certainly institutions of higher education must adapt, but this does not mean swaying in every gust of wind. Part of the social function of higher education is to help society decide which changes are worthwhile.

As Adam Smith hinted, the relationship between managers and managed in a bureaucracy tends to be one of conflict. Students, teachers and research workers bend the rules to serve their academic interests, and managers make new rules to close what are seen as loopholes. If professional expertise is concentrated near the base of the bureaucratic pyramid the rules themselves must be largely dependent on the consent of those to whom they apply. If this consent is not forthcoming the organisation risks fragmenting into competitive interest groups. In an academic institution this may result in staff adopting the methods of industrial confrontation, or it may mean fragmentation by subject and discipline, with loyalty given to departments or research centres rather than to the institution.

In contrast to the academic employees of a bureaucracy, the members of a college take their own collective decisions, which have an authority legitimised by consensus, or at least compromise, amongst those to whom they apply. Collegial styles of management are possible only in institutions which have considerable discretion over resource allocation. As Adam Smith noted it is endowments or similar funding mechanisms that makes colleges possible. Dons are freed from de-

Of the Expense of the Institutions

pendence on consumers of their services on one hand and controlling authorities on the other. There are reasons to suppose that any organisation which depends on high-level professional skills can operate most efficiently if there is a substantial measure of collegiality in its management procedures. However, the argument is not all on one side. Vested interests can cloud professional judgement and vested interests were obviously pervasive in eighteenth-century Oxford for example. Despite Adam Smith's strictures and numerous Royal Commissions and Committees of Enquiry into the Universities of Oxford and Cambridge, the collegial model of university management proved durable and formed the basis of most university charters and influenced the financing of universities in Britain at least up to 1981.

The problems of consensus-building in a college have been illustrated often in academic novels. The departmental meeting, the college council, the senate, are standard literary setpieces. Constructing a consensus is time-consuming and erratic in its outcomes. It can sharpen conflicts, or it can lead to mutual toleration of incompetence and to a neglect of the views of those who are not part of the consensus. If differences of interest and opinion are wide, it is probable that even though compromise is reached many individuals and groups remain disaffected. Compromises can often be reached only when they do no damage to any existing balance of interests. Change almost invariably affects this balance and is therefore impossible. This is particularly debilitating when lack of overall growth means that expansion of some activities can occur only if there is reduction in others. This suggests that in an environment where adaptation is necessary, collegial forms of management are most likely to be successful in institutions which do not comprise too wide a range of interests. The greater the variety of interests the more it is likely that compromise can be achieved only around the existing balance of power and the more likely it is that some individuals or groups will see themselves as being in conflict with the institution as a whole.

When resources are not increasing, styles of consensus management must adapt. Where innovations do not damage the vested interests of others, consensus can mean simply the aggregation of individual claims on resources. When resources are limited, consensus decisions must be consciously collective. They must be taken in the light of a responsible assessment of their possible implications for everyone in the institution. Collective decision-making in a period of adaptation without growth requires active management both to ensure decisions are taken and that once taken they are implemented.

The weakness of bureaucratic and collegial models of organisational behaviour have led some observers to follow Adam Smith's example and propose the market as a way of avoiding the fickleness of the one and the inertia of the other (see, for example, Lindley 1981; Wagner 1981; Morris and Sizer 1982; Shattock 1983). The intellectual attraction of the market is that resource-allocation decisions are apparently taken out of the hands of both politicians and of academics. They are determined instead by many independent decisions of consumers of academic services. Advocates of the market claim that it avoids the difficult technical problem that the outputs of higher education are almost impossible to define and measure. 'Output' becomes what consumers are prepared to buy. Effectively the power, which is in the hands of the politicians and administrators in the bureaucracy and in the hands of academics in the college is possessed in the market by students and consumers of other academic services.

One issue is the extent to which it is desirable that such power should be in the hands of individual students. If higher education were simply bought and sold, only students with substantial incomes would be able to afford to buy it. That is easily overcome through subsidy. More generally, students' lack of information and the difficulty they have in reversing decisions once they have taken them casts doubt on the efficiency of a higher-education market. If markets are to operate properly, consumers must be well informed about the likely outcomes of their purchases, the effects on the decisions of one individual must be independent of decisions of other individuals, and consumers must have the opportunity of learning from experience. In higher education choices by any individual student are made once only and are usually irreversible, the ultimate outcomes are not apparent for a considerable length of time, and they are strongly affected by decisions taken at the same time by large numbers of other students.

In *Access to Higher Education* Martin Trow, drawing on United States experience, has pointed to the dangers of inadequately informed students being courted by institutions whose survival depends on success in the market.

Take, for example, the elaborate, indeed sometimes desperate, efforts of many, especially weaker, institutions to recruit students, whether for their tuition fees or for the enrolment-driven formulas by which most public institutions are funded. Most institutions do not confront the question of whether the strenuous recruitment of some of these students serves the interests of the students as well as those of the institution. Sometimes the justification for these activities draws on the widespread American belief (only now beginning to be questioned) that, on the whole, people ought to get as much formal education as you can persuade them to sit still for; sometimes this is combined with the market's classic disclaimer of moral responsibility – *caveat emptor*. But whether the market is for warm bodies to meet budgets, or for black or brown bodies to meet affirmative-action targets, it is clear that there is not a perfect correspondence between the interests of the recruiting college or university and the recruited student. Important moral issues arise in this area. One can question the institutions' responsibility in recruitment for what might be called 'consumer protection', or, after students have been admitted, for providing counselling and other support services. The 'revolving door' has moral dimensions, as well as academic and financial implications, for colleges and universities. Grade inflation and the lowering of demands and standards to attract students are among the other pathologies of colleges and departments that are acutely threatened by the decline in enrolments and of the fear of administrative action or budget cuts. There are similar dangers on the research side. (Trow 1981)

Some of the weaknesses of a free market can be ameliorated by interventions. Financial support for needy students reduces the inequity of dependence on family income; public funds can avoid the problem of support for basic research. Advocates of the market claim that the provision of advisory and counselling services independent of the institutions would enable students to make better-informed decisions about choice of courses. However, even proper counselling cannot completely overcome the problems of the irreversibility and interdependence of individual decisions about higher education. It is unlikely that higher-education provision entirely determined by the wishes of large numbers of individual students would meet their real long-term needs, or those of society as a whole, better than a system in which critical decisions are taken by political bodies on behalf of society as a whole or by the academic bodies with access to expert knowledge of the processes involved.

Matching Academic Co-ordination to the Allocation of Resources

Becher and Kogan (1981) distinguish between four structural levels within higher education – individuals, basic units or departments, institutions and central authorities. Next they 'separate two components in the everyday life of the academic world which are not in practice sharply distinguished. The first of these relates to the monitoring and maintenance of values within the system as a whole'. This they designate the 'normative mode'. It involves academic authority, resource allocation and legal authority. 'The second in contrast, refers to the business of carrying out the practical tasks at different levels within the system'. This they call the 'operational mode'. The distinction is broadly between activities concerned with carrying out teaching, research and public service and those which create the conditions in which they can be carried out effectively.

It is possible to conceive a higher-education system with no formal organisation. Individual students would purchase the time of individual teachers through individual negotiations. However, as soon as several students wish to pursue coherent programmes of study with the help of several teachers there must be academic coordination, and there must be some form of financial control. There are two basic elements that determine academic structures. One emanates from the organisation of knowledge and the other derives from the provision of resources. Academic organisation and funding mechanisms overlap; resource allocation should be informed by academic criteria and no academic priority can be independent of resource availability. However, resource allocation and academic coordination are different functions, and different criteria are needed to evaluate each.

Of the Expense of the Institutions

Academic coordination is rooted in the processes of individual learning. Appropriate organisational forms are determined by the nature of knowledge and, in general, they are more robust the nearer they are to where learning takes place. Departmental and quasi-departmental structures are durable because these basic units are where individual teachers and students interact. Institutional and inter-institutional arrangements are more heterogeneous, and their forms depend on custom, inertia, interplay of interests and bureaucratic convenience.

The opposite is true of resource allocation. Its viability derives from capacity to generate income. In publicly financed higher education this means proximity to representative political power.

Amalgamating these two elements, we arrive at two fundamental organisational structures in higher education. One is the basic unit or small group of individuals able to interact with each other to produce coherent disciplinary programmes of study. The other is a funding mechanism with the political power to determine priorities for resource allocation.

Intermediate mechanisms of regulation are determined largely by context. Their function is academic coordination and resource planning. If learning processes come first, initiatives derive from individual students and teachers, and are integrated by departments and institutions and other intervening agencies till they aggregate at the national level into a higher education policy. This is fine provided the political authorities are willing to make the necessary resources available. Conversely, if higher education is structured so as to respond to political priorities, the process is reversed. Funds are passed down a hierarchy in such a way that the learning processes undertaken accord with government views of national interests.

Sizer (1982) refers to 'top down' and 'bottom up' models of higher-education planning to describe a similar distinction. Burgess (1982) refers to an 'autonomous' and a 'service' tradition in higher education. The former is firmly discipline-based and originates in the activities of independent individual scholars. The latter derives from views about the needs of society and leads to policy-making mechanisms in which outside pressures take priority. A related distinction is that between disciplines and domains of knowledge. Disciplines are rooted in the epistemology and structure of knowledge, while domains depend on the way the external world is organised. Thus, disciplines demand that the organisation of academic affairs be rooted in the nature of knowledge itself and hence develop out of the internal life of institutions. Domains derive from 'problems' and their motive force is ultimately the needs of the real world. The relative position of the academic and the politician is different in the two cases.

The university or polytechnic or college is primarily an administrative unit – a convenient grouping of basic units. It does not have the intrinsic claims to existence of either the basic operating units beneath it or the funding bodies above it. It is essentially the first of a number of resource allocation bodies that link the basic units to the sources of funds. The institution offers an acceptable focus for outside pressures mediating national social and economic needs in accordance with agreed academic purposes.

As an administrative entity a university is subject to three forces. First, it is a haven for the individual scholar and should provide an atmosphere conducive to free enquiry and professional autonomy. Second, however, the general consensus of academic opinion within the university sets bounds to the activities of the basic units and the individuals within them. Third, the university is a significant channel for contact with the outside world. The university or polytechnic or college should combine these three pressures into a corporate identity which defines the place of that particular institution in the spectrum of higher-education activities.

The House of Commons Select Committee (HC 1979) recommended that each institution of higher education should prepare for itself a statement of its present position within the spectrum of higher education and the position it aspires to hold five and ten years hence. In a higher education system which has in recent years been showing many signs of demoralisation, the process of preparing such development strategies would involve an assessment by the members of each institution of its fundamental purposes and its place in the spectrum of higher education. A candid appraisal of its comparative advantages and disadvantages in each of these activities in a long-term perspective would be invaluable for any college or polytechnic or university.

Such statements of long-term policy would also define the institution for students who are considering entering it. The prospectuses of polytechnics, colleges and universities are showing an increasing resemblance to promotional material rather than offering students a reliable basis of information for selecting the courses which would be appropriate for them. It is not without significance that in many institutions students themselves are preparing alternative prospectuses to counter some of what they see as the misleading propaganda of official information. Obviously, formal statements of development strategies could not replace college prospectuses, but the prospectuses themselves should be written in the light of clearly defined objectives that each institution has set itself.

Long-term development plans need to offer both stability and a capacity for evolution. They should be subject to review from time to time. Certainly every institution ought to take a penetrating look at itself at least once every ten years. Statements of development plans should not in themselves prevent institutions from engaging in other activities, but they should provide a background against which proposals for new initiatives can be assessed.

So far I have attempted to derive a role for the institutions from the need to nurture the professional work of individual scholars and the basic units in which they work. The other fundamental feature of academic authority, is the allocation of resources according to legitimately established priorities. This discussion must start with government which in England comprises both central and local government. In Scotland local government is much less important. Government has a significant interest in the overall shape and nature of higher education. It must decide how much priority to give to higher education compared to other branches of education and other items of public expenditure. However, higher education comprises a wide range of activities, and it is also appropriate for government to establish broad priorities amongst these.

The prime concern of government should be the efficient use of public funds. However, the concept of efficiency is a difficult one, particularly in higher education where output is not clearly defined or measurable. At its simplest, it carries an implication of avoidance of waste. Few people, even amongst the most ardent supporters of academic freedom, would deny the right of government to discourage waste and misuse of public funds.

A more ambiguous concept of efficiency arises from notions of cost-effectiveness and value for money. It is appropriate for central government to influence unit costs. It is quite proper for the state to keep public expenditure costs under review, and to make specific enquiries when there is, for example, *prima facie* evidence of significant differences in the costs of apparently similar activities in different institutions. Either institutions can justify the differences on the grounds that their apparently similar activity is in practice different or they risk losing funds to other institutions able to carry out similar activities more efficiently. In the long run, institutions should have an incentive to concentrate on areas where they have a price or quality advantage. The only outside interference need be in those areas of apparently unjustifiably high costs.

The most controversial concept of efficiency is that of higher education as a whole in producing a pattern of output that maximises the benefits from the resources devoted to it. This is the most difficult area in which to define the proper roles of political and academic authority. Would there be net benefits if resources were taken away from theoretical physics and devoted to mechanical engineering? The most that can be said *a priori* is that there will be differences of opinion. It is hardly likely, for example, that physicists will have exactly the same opinion on the question as engineers. In my opinion a proper role of the political authorities is the allocation of resources between such broad areas of activity after open consultation with those who have an informed contribution to make. Political authorities in a publicly financed system of higher education have a responsibility to decide through the evaluation of political priorities the total amount of resources to be devoted to each of the major programme areas in which higher education is involved.

Models of Higher Education Funding

A financing mechanism is both a means of allocating resources so that learning can occur and a channel for messages between providers and users of finance. Budget estimates and accounts of expenditure are among the most useful indicators

Of the Expense of the Institutions

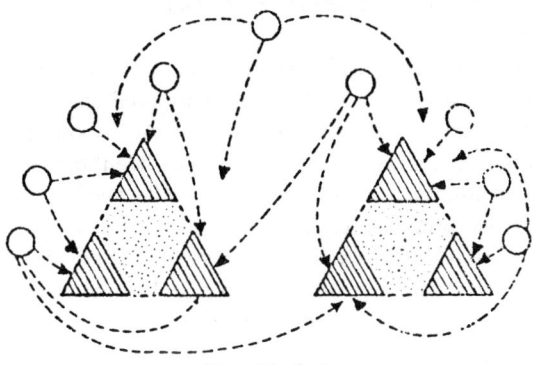

Free Market

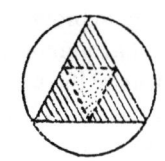

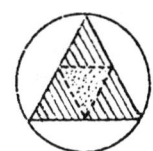

Collegial

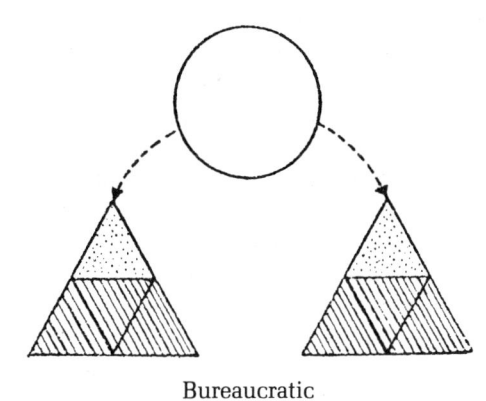

Bureaucratic

Key

◯ Sources of finance

🔺 Operating units in institutions

🔺 Administration of institutions

------▶ Flows of finance to institutions

of the intentions and performance of a higher-education institution.

The diagram shows three possible arrangements for the finance of academic institutions and predicts some likely effects of each. They correspond to Adam Smith's three models. Our concern here is not with distributional efficiency in the economy as a whole but on the effects of the financing mechanisms on the organisational behaviour of universities.

The first is the 'free' market. There are a variety of sources of finance and the basic units sell services to them. Each basic unit receives income from several sources and each source of finance purchases services from more than one university. No single external agency can control the activity of any university and no purchaser of academic services is dependent solely on what any one university is willing to provide. The market decides and provides the focus for the monitoring and maintenance of values. Within the university the basic units have considerable power. Central bodies exist to service the income-earning basic units. We would expect such institutions to be keen to attract students and to disseminate considerable information about themselves and to respond continuously to changing circumstances.

The second model is the college which has its own independent source of finance and therefore has no need to respond to external pressures. Priorities are determined by the academic preferences and values of university members, usually expressed through bargaining and the building of coalitions. Administration is largely a matter of holding the ring while consensus is reached. Students are admitted on terms set by the university which is likely to have an interest in limiting numbers and admitting only those who conform to its ethos.

The third model is the 'extraneous jurisdiction' which is likely to lead to bureaucratic organisational behaviour. A single external funding agency allocates funds to many institutions and has monopoly power with respect to any one of them. Naturally it wants to ensure that resources are efficiently allocated in accordance with its own priorities so the funds tend to be allocated to the administration at the top of the organisational pyramid, and these are passed down to basic units according to fixed bureaucratic rules. At each level the superordinate body is able to exert powerful influence over the

Of the Expense of the Institutions

behaviour of the subordinate body. The administration is powerful and carries out most of the normative control of monitoring and the maintenance of values. Basic units are weak and exist to carry out the practical operational tasks of the institution.

Of course none of these models exist in the pure state but a casual comparison between the operations of an Oxford College, a Central Institution or Polytechnic and the University of Buckingham, suggest that there is some relationship between mechanisms of finance and the organisational behaviour of academic institutions.

The Finance of Higher Education in Britain
in the 1980s and 1990s

Nearly all the finance of higher education in Britain today derives ultimately from central government – or to be more accurate from those who pay taxes to central government. For a variety of historical and political reasons which it is instructive to reflect on, but form no part of the present paper, the arrangements by which this central government finance finds its way to those who actually undertake learning, teaching and research follows two very different channels.

On the one side there is the public sector, organised on different bases in Scotland and England, but in both countries clearly recognisable as corresponding to the bureaucratic model. Funds are made available to a powerful administration. The 'Directorate' of a polytechnic never fails to bring a slightly patronising smile to the lips of even sympathetic university observers. The polytechnic or central institution is subject to a web of extraneous jurisdiction, financial regulations, course controls and conditions of service to force each lecturer 'to attend upon his pupils a certain number of hours and to give a certain number of lectures in the week or in the year'. It is part of my case that such arrangements take away a sense of responsibility from the skilled professionals who carry out teaching and research and result in considerable inefficiency in resource allocation. A well-informed observer within the public sector who arrives at a similar conclusion is Pratt (1982).

On the other side of the so-called binary line are the universities. They receive just as high a proportion of their income from central government, but on very different terms. The

275

Gareth Williams

financial mechanism which developed through the operation of the University Grants Committee had the function of bolstering the collegial principle. In crude terms until the mid-1970s universities received a guaranteed income from central government and were given only the most generalised advice about how to spend it and were subject to very little monitoring to see whether funds were allocated according to this advice. Certainly the central authorities have come to exercise considerable control over universities' capital expenditure during the past quarter of a century. Part of the case being made in this paper is that in a period of adaptation without growth the government and the UGC no longer have this lever of control.

The University Grants Committee is, with some justification, a hallowed institution. It has been much admired and widely copied in many countries. Essentially it is a mechanism for transferring public funds to the universities without subjecting individual universities to the rigours of detailed political accountability. It has preserved for British universities a 'collegial' model of finance despite their almost total dependence on central government funds. Its essential features are, first a membership that is predominantly academic and second, recurrent grants to universities that are not earmarked or monitored to see whether the actual expenditure of recurrent funds has corresponded to what was assumed when the grants were made. The critical question for the future is whether these arrangements are sufficiently robust to cope with the inevitable stresses of the next two decades. Should the structure and membership of the UGC be altered, and should it change significantly its methods of allocating funds?

The UGC is in many ways one of the last bastions of the traditional British ways of managing affairs through gentlemanly conduct and fair play. Its legal basis is tenuous, yet it has responsibility for institutions that are at the very centre of the intellectual life of the nation. Its members are appointed by the Secretary of State for Education and Science, but there has been a strong tradition that they will be broadly acceptable to university opinion. It allocates well over £1,000 million each year yet its staff is small, and, apart from the Chairman, its members devote only about one-fifth of their time to UGC business. It claims to understand university thinking, yet most of its full-time staff are career civil servants. Its members are appointed

Of the Expense of the Institutions

in their individual capacity and are concerned with the interests of all universities, yet most of them spend four-fifths of their time working in a particular university. In the past the UGC has surmounted these paradoxes and created a university system that has worked well even though it has sometimes been criticised for being slow to respond to changes in the economic and social climate. However, the UGC conventions have evolved over a long period of university expansion during which public funds available to universities have increased year to year. The doubts which the Association of University Teachers and some vice-chancellors have begun to express about its ability to meet the challenges of the 1980s and the 1990s are likely to become more and more insistent.

During the course of the next ten years the following main changes are likely to prove to be necessary: (i) placing the UGC on a proper statutory basis; (ii) the appointment of several full-time members with functional responsibilities in broad subject areas; (iii) the appointment of part-time members who are in some way representative of the main groups with an interest in higher education – for example, the Vice-Chancellors' Committee, the Association of University Teachers, other unions with an academic membership, employers' organisations and local authorities; (iv) a substantial increase in the number of staff who have significant experience of academic administration within universities.

There are doubts also about whether the UGC's methods of allocating recurrent funds can cope with the pressures of the 1980s and 1990s. When universities were expanding, the UGC, and through it the government, was able to exercise considerable influence on the pattern of university development through detailed control of capital expenditure. It did not matter much if recurrent grants were allocated on a quasi-collegial basis since the availability of buildings and equipment determined the essential pattern of university development.

It is doubtful whether the convenient fictions of the quasi-collegial model can be sustained during the next decade. The absence of the levers of capital expenditure and increasing budgets means growing pressure from government for the UGC to earmark increasing proportions of its recurrent budgets and to be selective between institutions. This can be damaging for academic freedom, and with the present size of the UGC support staff it will almost certainly be arbitrary, unfair and inefficient; even if it is not, those institutions selected for unfavourable treatment will proclaim loudly that it is.

Neither the bureaucratic procedures by which public sector institutions are financed, nor the quasi-collegial model of university finance is likely to be adequate for the 1980s and 1990s. The key to the finance of higher education during the next two decades may prove to be a simulation of the market.

The UGC will fulfil its historic functions of protecting academic freedom and encouraging efficient resource utilisation more effectively in the future if it cooperates with other funding agencies in a move away from its quasi-collegial model of resource allocation towards a simulated market model.

Instead of there being a total higher-education budget subsequently divided amongst institutional claimants, expenditure under main programme heads should be determined separately by government and allocated to the institutions through separate funding modes. There need be no higher-education budget as such, though obviously for statistical purposes it would be possible to aggregate expenditure under the several headings. The political and other criteria for determining the appropriate level of resources would be different for different types of activity; and so would the appropriate machinery by which the funds found their way to the basic operating units. Mechanisms and funding criteria which are appropriate for high-level research, for example, may not be the same as those which are appropriate for continuing education; yet both are legitimate activities of higher-education institutions.

Two objections are sometimes made to the creation of a variety of mechanisms through which public funds can be channelled to a particular public service. One is that since all the funds derive ultimately from government, the machinery for their allocation makes no difference to their total amount: a multiplicity of funding mechanisms merely leads to bureaucratic complexity. The other objection is that such machinery is merely a way of obfuscating the lines of accountability, to enable professional academics to evade political scrutiny. The first argument is wrong: the second is correct but misconceived.

The first objection is wrong because 'government' is not a

Of the Expense of the Institutions

unitary body taking simple decisions. Government is a tangle of competing interests, each only partly understanding the implications of the decisions it takes, and applying different criteria to different aspects of its responsibilities (see, for example, Kogan and Boys 1982). There is no reason why a decision about the overall size of a higher-education budget should have the same outcome as separate decisions about each of the different activities that comprise higher education. There is no doubt that a 'political' division of the higher-education budget into a number of major problem areas would be advantageous to some activities and detrimental to others compared with a block allocation according to 'academic' criteria. However, there can be little doubt that in a period in which the traditional higher-education population will decline sharply, the net effect of applying a variety of political criteria to basic resource-allocation decisions would be more advantageous to higher education as a whole than the continuation of arrangements which essentially link finance predominantly to the single criterion of traditional student numbers.

The second objection is correct because a variety of mechanisms of finance will increase the independence of institutions. The aim is to free universities, colleges and polytechnics from dependence on single sources of finance. However, this need not reduce their total accountability for the public funds they receive. Institutions should certainly be answerable for what they receive *via* different routes, and they would find it difficult to obtain resources for activities that lay outside their agreed development strategies unless they could demonstrate good reasons for them. What they would not be, is accountable to, and dependent on, a single omnipotent outside funding body.

John Pratt has proposed the interesting idea of 'problem budgeting'. 'First, problems should be identified and expressed in terms external to the educational system. Second, funds should be allocated in relation to the importance of the problems. Third, choice between alternative solutions (activities) could be based on comparative cost effectiveness of those activities. Fourth, the evaluation of the system should relate its overall effectiveness in solving the problems to the costs of doing so' (Pratt 1983). This concept has considerable promise in the conditions likely to confront higher education during the next two decades.

Institutions with a substantial measure of independence from direct control by both central and local government, but which have financial incentives to respond to changing social and economic needs, are the key to a higher-education system that is able to offer excellence and diversity in the 1980s and 1990s. There will have to be some regulatory mechanisms coordinating their individual endeavours so as to protect students and academic standards from possible damaging effects of inter-institutional struggles for survival and to guard against inefficient use of resources such as wasteful duplication or gaps in provision. Each university, polytechnic and college should have an explicit academic development plan which is formulated within the institution but agreed by relevant funding bodies in accordance with their perceptions of national and regional needs. The plans would be essentially similar to the quinquennial plans universities prepared for the UGC before the quinquennial grant system collapsed in the mid-1970s. However, in a period of adaptation without growth it will be necessary to include the whole range of institutional activities, whereas in the period of expansion it was possible to concentrate mainly on incremental resources and new activities. It will also be necessary for the UGC and the National Advisory Body for Local Authority Higher Education to monitor the patterns of actual expenditure more carefully than has been done previously.

Leaders of academic institutions are subject to four pressures: i) teachers and research workers with professional expertise; ii) agencies responsible for the implementation of national and local policies; iii) students, who are the main consumers; iv) employers of graduates and users of research. Any mechanism of institutional finance reflects these pressures. It is a compromise between them. There is a compromise between the claims of academic freedom and the claims of elected governments to establish priorities and require accountability for the use of funds. There is a compromise between the desire of institutions for guaranteed funds to enable them to plan rationally according to their own academic criteria and the wish of external funding bodies to use financial incentives to encourage particular kinds of response. A balance

Of the Expense of the Institutions

between the pressures can best be achieved, and the independence of institutions safeguarded, if they receive their income explicitly through several different routes.

Each institution whose primary activity is higher education should be entitled to receive core funding in the form of a general grant through the appropriate funding body in accordance with its agreed development plan. Guaranteed core funding can be seen as reflecting the professional interests of members of academic institutions, allowing them to allocate resources according to their institution's own academic priorities. The appropriate level of core funding will vary between institutions depending on their circumstances. The higher the level of its core funding, the more an institution will be dependent on this single source of funds, the less incentive it will have to initiate responses to changing circumstances and the shorter the period for which the core funding can be guaranteed.

A second component of institutional income should be the full-cost funding of specific teaching and research programmes and projects. This may be seen as reflecting the priorities of bodies responsible for national and local policy. Funding agencies should earmark funds for designated programme areas and institutions involved in the provision of higher education should be entitled to bid for them. As well as being for specific purposes, programme grants would differ from core funds in being of shorter duration. Institutions would be inhibited from relying too heavily on programme grants for fear of over-exposing their financial position. For example, they would be unwise to make academic appointments with lifetime tenure on the basis of programme funds.

Local authorities should be able to make programme grants to both public sector institutions and universities. Some provision for locally based programme funding could be made in the block rate-support grant. Such local authority programme grants might become the dominant form of finance of higher education courses in institutions with a small proportion of advanced-level work. Some funding bodies, for example the Research Councils, would probably adopt primarily the programme funding mode, while the UGC would probably allocate a relatively small part of its total funds in this way. However, since programme funds would be a powerful instrument for the encouragement of adaptation and innovation, it is desirable that the UGC set aside a significant part of its funds for special programmes. Given the greater variety of provision in the public sector and its greater need to respond quickly to local needs, the National Advisory Board and its Welsh and possible Scottish counterparts would probably reserve larger shares of their allocations to the programme funding mode.

The third constituent of the income of institutions should reflect the priorities of student customers. The Robbins Report argued for the maintenance of a significant fee component in the income of institutions. The Committee regretted the decline in the proportion of university income derived from fees, considering it a source of strength that public finance should come through more than one channel, and arguing that up to a point it is better to subsidise students than institutions. Robbins recommended that the level of fees be revised so that they met at least 20 per cent of current institutional expenditure. There remains a good case for student choice influencing but not dominating the orientation of higher education institutions. In the late 1970s student fees did reach the levels suggested by Robbins, and it is a pity that this policy was subsequently reversed. Individual universities, colleges and polytechnics should be entitled to retain fee income.

The fourth source of funds reflects directly the interests of employers and users of research. Income can be earned from full-cost courses and from research, development and consultancy for industrial and commercial enterprises and central and local government. A limited involvement in such income-earning activities will be valuable to many academic staff, broadening their range of experience at a time when mobility will be low. Income can also be earned from the hire of facilities such as buildings, sports amenities and computing facilities. Institutions should be allowed to retain income earned from such sources, although core funding bodies might wish to set an upper limit.

The key element in these proposals is the notion of core funding, guaranteed for long periods but needing to be supplemented to a significant extent from other, less secure sources. If an institution failed to supplement its core income to the necessary extent, the core funding body would be obliged to consider whether to reduce the amount of core funds or

Of the Expense of the Institutions

whether there were good reasons for raising the core funding percentage. Where institutions exceeded their target supplementary income they would be eligible for, but not have an automatic right to, increased core funding.

The main aim of the mechanism is to encourage institutions to seek outside income where possible and to reward them for doing so, but not to make them so dependent on market pressures as to squeeze out academic activities by staff and students which are intrinsically worthwhile but have little likelihood of appealing to immediate market or policy interests. The non-core sources of finance – programme grants, fees and earned income – would have a multiplier effect on the amount of core funds to which an institution was entitled, unless the core funding body explicitly decided otherwise. This is the reverse of the mechanism developed by the UGC in the 1960s whereby institutions which are able to generate earned income are deemed to have less need of UGC funds. This remains the rationale by which the UGC penalises universities for enrolling students in excess of the UGC targets.

A key question is the proportion of their incomes that institutions should be expected to derive under each heading. It is unlikely that it could be precisely the same for each institution so the appropriate core funding component would need to be the subject of individual negotiations and to some extent trial and error. In 1979/80 the general component of the total income of British universities amounted to 63 per cent, fees from students 13 per cent, funding of specific programmes 13 per cent and other earned income 11 per cent (Shattock 1983). There have been many changes since then and UGC initiatives such as restructuring money and 'new blood' money would certainly come under the heading of programme grants. Home student fees have gone down as a result of the government view that it is difficult to cash-limit them. (There is, however, no real reason why student fees should not be cash-limited within reasonable bounds. Forecasting student numbers one or two years ahead can be done reasonably accurately – a high proportion of the students are already in higher education. It is much easier than forecasting expenditure on unemployment. If it were felt that precise annual cash-limiting was essential, the student fee component and the programme grant component could in the short term come under the same cash-limited budget head.) A target for the higher education system as a whole which would give due recognition to the four sets of pressures I have identified might be: core funding 50%, programme funds 20%, fees 20%, earned income 10%.

The mechanisms by which governments allocate funds make a difference to the overall size of budgets. Government is not a homogeneous single-minded bureaucracy; it is a complex network of interacting interests and pressure groups. Both the overall amount and the pattern of public expenditure on higher education would be different with the mechanisms being proposed here, almost certainly to the long-term advantage of higher education both quantitatively and qualitatively. Certainly it would help to maintain the autonomy of academic institutions. The Robbins Report considered it 'a source of strength that public finance should come through more than one channel'. This is likely to be even more true in a period of severe resource stringency than it was when funds were relatively abundant.

REFERENCES

Becker, A. and Kogan, M. (1980) *Process and Structure in Higher Education*. Heinemann, London.

Burgess, T. (1982) Autonomous and Service Traditions, in Wagner (1982).

Clark, B. (1983) *Perspectives on Higher Education: Eight Disciplinary Perspectives and Comparative Views*. University of California Press.

Fay, C.R. (1956) *Adam Smith and the Scotland of His Day*. Cambridge.

House of Commons (1980) *The Funding and Organisation of Higher Education: 5th Report from the Education, Science and Arts Committee 1979-80*. HMSO.

Lindley, R. (1981) *Higher Education and the Labour Market*. SRHE, Guildford.

Kogan, M. and Boys, C. (1982) The Politics of Sectoral Change, in Wagner (1982).

Morris, A. and Sizer, J. (1982) *Resources and Their Allocation*. SRHE, Guildford.

Pratt, J. (1983) Resource Allocation Within the Public Sector, in Morris and Sizer (1982).

Rae, J. (1895) *Life of Adam Smith*. Reprinted by Augustus M. Kelley. New York, 1965.

Shattock, M. (1983) *The Structure and Governance of Higher Education*. SRHE, Guildford.

Sizer, J. (1982) Better the Dirigiste Devil We Know, in Morris and Sizer (1982).

Wagner, L. (1982) *Agenda for Institutional Change*. SRHE, Guildford.

COMMENTS BY ANDREW McPHERSON

One of the many commendable things about the Leverhulme Programme is that it is timely. The aim has been to set the agenda for policy discussion for the next fifteen years. For the past three years the Programme has rolled forward a series of discussions together with a related programme of research and enquiry in the hope that, if you like, some sort of a snowball of consensus would accumulate. I am sure that others today will express the very considerable debt that higher education owes to all involved; and I am sure also that, as time passes, their achievement will seem even more considerable then it does already.

But, if I may, I will stay for a moment with the idea of the snowball, perhaps not an entirely fanciful metaphor in a harsh climate. This is the very day on which the Leverhulme team, having rolled their snowball through the drifts of academic and policy discussion in their own back garden, finally trundle it out into the wider fields of public scrutiny, where the rougher children play. How will it be greeted now by the individual polytechnic, central institution, university and college? Will the arguments indeed persuade us all to lend our shoulders to it, to roll it forward, and to send a growing consensus bowling into the doors of Elizabeth House or, indeed, St Andrews House? Or shall we decide that actually it is not a very consolidated snowball; that it lacks internal structure; and that its constituent arguments and values show signs of falling apart into discrete lumps whose only use will be to supply material for projectiles that we can throw at each other in a boisterous but ultimately ritualised conflict of a type to which Edinburgh University of the snowball riots has been no stranger in the past?

I think it is necessary to consider the question of access in the context of the Programme's main recommendations, and I should also like to bear in mind our discussions so far. The structure of the argument that attempts to hold the consensus together seems to be this: first, the threat of the cavernously empty lecture hall; second, that we should look to what are identified as 'socially marginal groups' to fill the seats; third, that the attempt to fill the seats with a new clientele will require and also stimulate innovations in course structure, content and methods, innovations that happen also to be required on other grounds, such as the avoidance of premature specialisation; and, fourth, that a mandatory grant for 16–20-year-olds will force this on the system in the form of a two-years plus two-years structure of post-compulsory education.

I want to comment on each of these points in turn, and also to reflect on them in the light of Scottish experience. First, then, the empty lecture hall. I do not want to place too much emphasis on this, but there are already doubts that there are going to be as many empty places as was thought when the Leverhulme Programme got under way. I will not rehearse the details of the argument here. Demography is a fairly exact science and we can be sure that the number of 18-year-olds will fall by about a third between now and 1995 (Department of Education and Science 1983a and 1983b). We cannot be sure, however, that those parts of the population of 18-year-olds that produce most higher-education entrants will fall by anything like the same amount. Suffice it to say that, in its present unsatisfactory state, the argument about projections at the very least leaves some scope for some individual institutions to doubt that the climate is going to be that cold for them. For example, one recent projection shows no fall in the absolute numbers of 18-year-old candidates for university before 1990 followed by a fall of between 16 and 19 per cent by 1995, with numbers picking up sharply again in 1996 and in the years immediately following (Collins 1983, from tables 4.2A and B). Whether the author is right or wrong the very fact that his discussion is framed in terms of universities may itself be indicative of a response from higher education that is less than consensual (though the deficiencies of data on demand for non-university higher education may also have been a consideration in this instance).

So the first clutch of questions that we might discuss are: how confident are we now of the extent and duration of the fall? How confident are we that it will be evenly distributed across sectors and institutions, or indeed between England and Scotland? Is it a part of the Leverhulme strategy to frighten us into consensus; to make us more flexible by scaring us rigid?

One other point, which I will simply put a marker on, is the questionable activity of predicting student demand as though it were an exogenous variable. Student demand is not entirely exogenous and when we 'predict' it we necessarily make many assumptions about future policy and practice. Unless we discuss these assumptions as well as the narrower technicalities of prediction, we run the risk of conceding much of the argument before it is joined, whatever the prediction might reveal.

Let us, nevertheless, assume something like 25 per cent empty places. The two-year degree proposal would itself, of course, initially make this worse by emptying the 33 per cent of places in the third year (rather more in Scotland where we have both three- and four-year degrees). In what sense would an institution trying to fill perhaps half its places 'do best' to target its recruitment at socially marginal groups? Do we mean 'doing best' as a matter of values, because we believe that an egalitarian admissions policy is a good thing in its own right? Or do we mean 'best' as a matter of an institution's narrow interest in having bodies in seats, no matter whose, no matter whether or not they are 'socially marginal', provided that they are 'potentially able to benefit', or at least warm?

I wonder if Leverhulme is right that a university's narrow self-interest (by which I mean, its filling of seats, by whomsoever) is best served by the pursuit of socially marginal groups. This may seem an odd doubt to raise in view of the fact that such groups – women, the working classes, ethnic minorities and the aged – constitute the large majority of the population. Indeed, if one were to add one other group, the under-educated, one might have to admit the entire population, ourselves included, to the condition of social marginality.

Now, what has arguably motored the expansion of higher education in the last 100 years or, if it has not driven it, has been closely correlated with it, has been the expansion of the middle classes and of their growing appetite for a level of education that would keep them above the low but rising level of popular education. There is no reason to think that this process has exhausted itself (Edwards 1982). Moreover, there is some reason to believe that, the more the balloon of class privilege is squeezed smaller at the earlier or lower stages of secondary or tertiary education, the more it will expand commensurately at its later or higher stages. Hence one has the theory of credential inflation, status competition and status preservation as a partial explanation of expansion; the theory that also says, if I understand economists' language correctly, that it is possible to have a high private rate of return to education at the same time as precious little return to the public (Collins 1979). Anyway, credentials have attracted the middle classes, and the Oxford Mobility Study and also our own work in Scotland both indicate that, whilst the children of the professional and managerial classes have been mobilised into an upward curve of participation, the working-class participation rate, in Scotland and in England, is still crawling along with little sign of take-off (Halsey, Heath and Ridge 1980; Gray, McPherson and Raffe 1983).

So one could perhaps adapt the rhetorical device from Tessa Blackstone's paper on access and say: children of social class II, the managerial class, constitute about a fifth of 18-year-olds. Raise their university participation rate from 25 per cent to the 43 per cent that class I has achieved (Farrant 1981, table 2.18) and one will raise the overall age participation rate from 12.7 to 16.1 per cent. This would constitute a 27 per cent increase that would require fourteen new universities if it were to happen tomorrow.

My second main clutch of questions, then, is as follows: is the recommendation that higher education 'reach out' to the disadvantaged a purely tactical move to recruit apparently conservative institutions to egalitarian causes? Or does Leverhulme genuinely believe that there is a happy conjunction in this situation of threatened contraction between the egalitarianism of outreach and an institution's narrow self-interest in maintaining its numbers, a conjunction of interest similar to the expansionist consensus of the 1950s and early 1960s when we thought that economic prosperity and the expansion and equalisation of opportunity were mutually sustaining goals?

Now, to some extent, I think that Leverhulme's commitment has to be to egalitarianism for its own sake. I say this because Tessa Blackstone rightly asks us, in her final paragraphs, not 'to neglect the cultural and purely intellectual benefits for individuals and for society'. In other words, she asks us to see education as valuable in its own right, in absolute terms; as a consumption good, if you like, and not as human capital or as something that simply improves one's position relative to other persons in the job queue. So we need a moral theory to guide the distribution of this scarce resource. But the theory that was implicit in the expansionist consensus of the 1950s and 1960s is in some disarray. I will mention two difficulties.

First, the relationship between expansion and equality is not simple, and is not linear. The pattern of the distributions of secondary education attainments across individuals within the social classes leads one to expect that, as long as entry to higher education is substantially determined by individuals' rankings on a scale of attainment, modest expansion is unlikely to change class inequalities of access to higher education, and might even increase them (Halsey, Heath and Ridge 1980, ch.8). This is because expansion of access to, say, 20 per cent of the age group may still find more middle-class than working-class applicants, or potential applicants, massed at the changing threshold entry requirement. Does not egalitarianism therefore indicate that one should entirely abandon selection for entry to higher education and not, as is suggested, retain it for 75 per cent of places? Perhaps this is what Leverhulme intends ultimately to happen. Is 25 per cent non-selected places the thin end of the wedge? Logically and morally should we not be driving that **wedge in** further? But, if it is fixed, how are we to distribute access to this 25 per cent of places? Furthermore, if most of them are to go to persons other than school leavers, will we not come to depend more heavily on public examinations in selecting school leavers for the remaining 75 per cent of places?

This brings me to a second difficulty with equality. We need a clearer account of the socially marginal applicant. As I have mentioned, women, the working class, the older person and ethnic minorities together make up rather a large share of the population; and they compete among each other. In Scotland in the 1960s and 1970s, for example, the increasing representation of women in degree-level education has displaced working-class men (those with fathers in manual employment) without enhancing the representation of working-class women (Hutchison and McPherson 1976). It has mainly been the middle class among women who have come, and come partly because they have done well in school examinations. In one sense this trend has been egalitarian; more have come to degree-level education from the socially marginal group of women. But how are we to adjudicate the claims of competing marginal groups? Part of the problem here is that the account of the marginal student is framed in terms of groups, and not of individuals. An account that would serve as a basis for selection decisions about individuals would require to treat groups as secondary, as only part of the explanation of the differential access of individuals to advantage in society. In the absence of a calculus of social marginality, admissions' decisions would be arbitrary and not self-evidently egalitarian.

The third part of the argument that links expanded access to innovation I must discuss only briefly. Yes, 'outreach' education, the attempt to create and meet new demands, will require change, and its history is, indeed, one of continuing innovation. But does this history suggest that the way to get innovations taken seriously by established institutions of high status is to link them to the low status, to the provincial and the civic, to women, the working class, the black and the aged? Could the established university (and here I *mean* university) not say to Leverhulme something like this: although you condemn specialisation at school and university you have not argued the case for reduced specialisation in its own right, but only in relation to the expedient of maintaining student numbers. Nevertheless, as one institution, we fully support your general case for diversity and innovation in the system. Our institution's contribution to systemic diversity will be to stay exactly as we are, whilst others change. Or, if we are forced to change by the change in student grants, we shall innovate with the two-year Honours degree. However, we doubt if you will force us to do this, because an Honours degree in only two years would attract many more applicants than an Honours degree taken only after a two-year general course. Our institution would still, therefore, have to select for entry, probably using school examination results. Unfortunately this would make school examinations even more competitive and more conducive to the premature specialisation which, you say, is a bad thing and a reason for your call for innovation in the first place.

So the third set of questions that we might discuss runs as follows: is the Leverhulme position that specialised courses in themselves are so bad that all institutions must abandon them? If so, why are they bad? And, if all institutions must abandon specialisation, what becomes of the principle of diversity? Alternatively, if this principle does allow some institutions to remain specialised, how are their 'backwash' effects on schools and on other higher education institutions to be contained? Or is the argument simply that numerical expedient requires innovation? If so, would we not do better to encourage the newer arrivals among higher-education institutions to do most of this innovating, to do the job that they, after all, claim to do better? Could we not then rely on the higher status of the older institutions to attract the new demands that innovation would fuel, but leave unsatisfied, if the credentialist account of the hunger for certificates is correct (Collins 1979)?

Scotland, of course, has its own experience of a curriculum structure that offers a five-subject course in the upper secondary school that links to a five-subject degree course in the non-professional faculties, the five subjects then reducing to one or two subjects at Honours level for something over half, now, of our students. I will say a little about this, because it is not well understood by the English, partly because they are not interested in it, and partly because, when they do show an interest, it is often to plunder Scottish experience for particular examples that might help grind an axe to be wielded south of the Border. Scots, I should add, are also to blame, because they have tended to confuse the myth of the system they would like to have with the reality of the system that they do have (McPherson 1983). In other words, we have not been self-critical enough and we yield too easily to the flattery of misinformed English attention.

The point about the 1892 settlement is that it combined the four-year Honours degree with the three-year General or Ordinary degree in an end-on structure. Outside science faculties, the General degree is a shallow collection of specialisms, bounded by the department and the written examination. The long-term trend, certainly in the last twenty years, is against the Ordinary degree. Students want Honours degrees and the longer course. There is competition for entry to Honours; hence certain cognate subjects in years one and two become 'recommended' in relation to particular specialisms. Specialisation creeps down. Some classes are 'streamed' for Honours or Ordinary in year one. Selection and competition further distort an already unsatisfactory structure and this has effects on the school curriculum as well (McPherson and Neave 1976; Gray, McPherson and Raffe 1983).

Andrew McPherson

What is more, social selection has been heavily involved in this academic selection. Socially marginal students, that is, women students, and working-class students, have been disinclined to take the longer Honours course (McPherson 1973). The three-year Ordinary course has, until recently, been a major channel of recruitment to that most marginal of professions, school teaching, especially in arts, but also in science.

We can therefore expect demand for the Ordinary degree to continue to decline at least until the end of the 1980s when more teachers will again be required. Now, is the Scottish experience an analogue for the Leverhulme proposal to situate the one year Honours course after the mandatory grant period, and to fund it by loans? Is there a risk that this will simply transfer social privilege to this point in the system and strengthen the already dominant cultural equation of specialisation with high social status? Is it a price worth paying for wider access at the lower, two-year level?

I also want to approach the fourth argument, concerning the four-year post-compulsory grant, through some comments on experience in Scotland. In broad terms, Leverhulme's chilly analysis of trends in access, and of its social distribution, applies to Scotland as much as elsewhere. Nevertheless, the Scottish scene is in some respects warmer and promises a thaw spreading south. Scotland's age participation rate is higher and, on a class-adjusted basis, is even higher than Tessa Blackstone's paper suggests (Farrant 1981, p.63). Much of this has to do with the legacy of the nineteenth-century university and college system which was constructed on lines similar to those that Leverhulme now recommends. The nineteenth-century model placed less emphasis on selective entry; relative to today, it gave more power to 'consumer-students' than to 'professor-producers'; it offered remedial classes; it had many points of entry and exit; its calendar was adjusted to the demands of the country working man; mature students worked their way through university; its boundaries with the institutions of teacher training were blurred by the widespread taking of concurrent courses, akin to transferable credits; and so on.

So a higher age participation rate for England and Wales lies within the bounds of reasonable human ambition and has been historically achieved, by the standards of the time, along Leverhulme lines.

Comments

Well, you might say, you can export Scotsmen, but you will have more difficulty when you try to transplant Scottish traditions to an alien culture. Nevertheless, I think it might be done. But one needs to pay more attention to one further aspect of the nineteenth- and twentieth-century Scottish model, an aspect that Leverhulme perhaps does not sufficiently consider but one again that has already been discussed; and that is the overlap and competition between school and university. One may put it in terms of developments since Robbins. In 1962–3 only 11 per cent of Scottish university entrants direct from Scottish schools entered aged seventeen, after a fifth year. The other 89 per cent entered at eighteen after a sixth year. In this sense the Scottish system at the time of Robbins operated along predominantly English lines. Also, it was homogeneous in that the universities differed little one from another in their preference for eighteen-year-olds. That situation has since changed, mainly in the 1970s. More students enter from fifth year. Also the national system is no longer homogeneous. There are now two systems in Scotland, not one. Outside the Strathclyde Region, in the East and North of the country, the English model still predominates: at Edinburgh and also St Andrews in the 1980 student entry, an estimated 10 per cent of the direct entry from Scottish schools came from fifth year, and 90 per cent from the sixth. At Dundee it was 15 per cent from fifth year; and at Aberdeen and Heriot Watt, 18 per cent. In the Strathclyde Region, however, at the University of Glasgow, 39 per cent entered from fifth year; and at Strathclyde University 44 per cent of the entry was from fifth year and 56 per cent was from sixth year. So the West of Scotland model, if you like, today stands half way between a pure Scottish and a pure English model, whereas the East and North remain substantially as they were. Stirling, incidentally, is located half-way between East and West, statistically as well as geographically: 35 per cent of its 1980 entry came from fifth year. (I owe these figures to Adam Redpath's analysis of the 1981 Scottish School Leavers Survey that we administer.)

Let me crystallise the implications of this, possibly too compactly, by suggesting that Scotland's response to demographic change perhaps should be to abandon the sixth year or, to be more precise, the provision for sixth year in the schools. To put it another way, ought we not to recognise that universities are in direct competition not only with other sectors of higher education, but also with the schools? The arguments for abandoning sixth year are, first, that entry to higher education from fifth year would both reduce the cost to the individual of post-compulsory education and also increase life-time earnings. It would therefore be popular. It would also be an act of positive discrimination, working in favour of individuals from poorer homes but without invidious attempts to give privileges to poorer groups. Moreover, it works. No-one here today, I think, will tell us that the standard of degrees given by the Universities of Glasgow and Strathclyde is inferior, nor that their graduates are immature. Third, only if we get all our students in at seventeen will the argument for the four-year Honours degree remain cogent in a period of financial stringency. Fourth, the schools are struggling anyway to retain sixth year; and it is always easier, I am sure you will agree, to kick a man when he is down. Finally, the man is threatening to get up. Since 1968 the schools in Scotland have had the audacity to annex to themselves part of the function of liberal education as Lyon Playfair, John Stuart Blackie, John Burnet and many others would have understood it. The Certificate of Sixth Year Studies was designed to help pupils develop self-sustaining intellectual interests for their own sake. An important part of this design was that the Certificate was not intended to count as a formal qualification for entry to higher education or to the labour market. It marked an attempt to return to the nineteenth-century conception of the 'examination' as teaching and learning.

There would, it is true, be costs, and the loss of liberal provision in the schools would be one. But what could be more persuasive than an act of positive discrimination, applied universally and without invidious distinction, that would increase access without jeopardising standards, would serve each university's narrow self-interest, and also give all Scottish graduates the competitive edge of entering the labour market a year earlier than their English counterparts? After what the Indian Civil Service examinations did to Scottish students (Davie 1961), this small advantage is the least we can ask in return. What a snowball of consensus we shall have here, and what a throng of graduates on the road south!

And what, finally, does this mean for England and Wales

and, in particular, for the proposal for the four-year post-compulsory grant? It seems to me that the tidiness of the proposal for a two-year degree rests on the assumption that A-levels will always be taken by eighteen-year-olds. But why should they? The Leverhulme argument seems to be that school qualifications are a poor indication of potential for higher education. So why should the innovating higher-education institution not 'cut and run', to use the language of the moment, admitting its school candidates at seventeen years, one year after O-levels, and concentrating its innovatory energies on the demonstrably soluble problem of assisting younger students to an Honours-degree level? If the history of abortive school examination reform in England and Wales in the last twenty years shows that the universities have jealously guarded the A-level, think how much more jealously they will guard the Honours degree.

So my final questions are these: why has Leverhulme launched its republican assault on the inner citadel of the Honours degree when the A-level is more vulnerable? Why is the only 'boundary' Leverhulme does not want to reduce that between the English sixth form and the many other evolving forms of post-compulsory education?

REFERENCES

Collins, P. M. D. (1983) *Demographic Trends and Future University Candidates: a Working Paper*. The Royal Society, London, April.

Collins, R. (1979) *The Credential Society: an Historical Sociology of Education and Stratification*. London.

Davie, G. E. (1961) *The Democratic Intellect: Scotland and Her Universities in the Nineteenth Century*. Edinburgh.

Department of Education and Science (1983a) Future Demand for Higher Education in Great Britain, in *Report on Education 99*. DES, London, April.

— (1983b) *Statistical Bulletin 6/83*. DES, London, April.

Edwards, E. G. (1982) *Higher Education for Everyone*. London.

Farrant, J. H. (1981) Trends in Admissions, in *Access to Higher Education* (ed. O. Fulton). Society for Research in Higher Education, Guildford.

Gray, J. M., McPherson, A. F. and Raffe, D. R. (1983) *Reconstructions of Secondary Education: Theory, Myth and Practice since the War*. London.

Halsey, A. H., Heath, A. F. and Ridge, J. M. (1980) *Origins and Destinations: Family Class and Education in Modern Britain*. Oxford.

Hutchison, D. and McPherson, A. F. (1976) Competing Inequalities: the Sex and Social Class Structure of the First-year Scottish University Population 1962-1972. *Sociology* 10(1).

Leverhulme Programme of Study into the Future of Higher Education (1983) *Excellence in Diversity: Towards a New Strategy for Higher Education.* Society for Research into Higher Education, Guildford.

McPherson, A. F. (1973) Selections and Survivals: A Sociology of the Ancient Scottish Universities, in *Knowledge, Education and Cultural Change* (ed. R. Brown). London.

— (1983) An Angle on the Geist: Persistence and Change in the Scottish Educational Tradition, in *Scottish Culture and Scottish Education 1800-1980* (eds W. Humes and H. Paterson). Edinburgh.

McPherson, A. F. and Neave, G. (1976) *The Scottish Sixth: A Sociological Evaluation of Sixth Year Studies and the Changing Relationship Between School and University in Scotland.* National Foundation for Educational Research, Slough.

COMMENTS BY SIR KENNETH ALEXANDER

At the outset I would like to say how glad I am that the Open University was mentioned; we can learn a great deal from its experience. By way of passing birthday greeting to the University of Edinburgh, I remind myself that it was an MA (Ordinary) graduate of this University, Jenny Lee, who played a major part in creating the Open University. I sat under her on the Advisory Committee of the University of the Air and I know just how important her contribution was, which may say something also about the ordinary MA – that that academic experience stimulated her to feel strongly about the need for an Open University. This Seminar is very well-timed. It brings out very, very sharply in my mind that while we have been talking here now for four days about the pressures from outside on the universities and on higher education generally, the world outside is engaged on a general election campaign in which higher education is playing hardly any part at all. I think that it is important for us to be aware of this disinterest; it explains why we are talking here as though we were victims and not leaders of opinion and people of influence. It is ironic, I think, that education, despite the cuts and all the public discussion that the cuts have generated, is being so little discussed at the present time. If we were primarily concerned with autonomy, we might take some comfort from this disinterest, but we would be very foolish to do so. The election manifestos make it clear that autonomy is not the issue; the extent of government influence is, and the only issue is what form that influence shall take. Part of the reason for that is that the universities, and possibly other sectors of higher education also, are regarded as insufficiently tough-minded, influential or even clear-headed to have much attention paid to any resistance which they offer or could offer.

I would like to comment briefly on what we have heard from the Leverhulme spokespersons. First of all, I want to say how much I admire the experience, the intelligence and the social concern that has gone into these reports and the contribution thus being made to thinking about higher education. Because, as we have been told by Professor Williams, some of the messages are delphic or coded, I cannot be sure that I have interpreted them all correctly. I am least satisfied, I must confess, with what Leverhulme has said and what we have said here about the purposes of the universities and of higher education. There are waves of fashion within academia, periods when people debate nothing else than our purposes and periods when we accept that what is being done is too obviously 'a good thing' for purpose to be debated at all. Following the Robbins expansion and the indigestion that was a consequence of that, there was a period of calm which has now been disturbed, mainly by external questions being asked and pressures exerted, frequently by Government. The current debate about purposes has not been self-generated in the main.

Harold Silver argued, I thought very powerfully, that if we ignored as he implied we did, the needs of society and thereby failed to find satisfactory answers to society's problems, then in due course other answers will be thrust upon us. He was followed by Sir Stuart Hampshire who counter-argued that too much emphasis should not be placed on what he described as 'society round the corner'. Too much emphasis on 'society round the corner' would diminish the quality of what students could do with their time in higher education. Here we have two very different views, both still alive and kicking within the system. We have been told about similar views alive and kicking in every century of the four through which this University has lived. It is against this background that I shall comment on what Leverhulme has to say about the objectives

Sir Kenneth Alexander

of higher education. Four of the eight aims which Gareth Williams spelled out are concerned with objectives. The first of these is the egalitarian aim and I find it very difficult to think about this aim and to understand what has been said about it without biology and psychology to guide me. Are we talking about equal opportunity for people of unequal quality or are we talking about equal opportunity because we believe there is more quality around than gets opportunity (this is my own view)? We have to be clear about this before we discuss this issue of equality. Professor Saul uses the word 'elitism'. Higher education is about intellectual elitism and if we are frightened to admit this, I do not believe we can ever get the objectives right or discuss the objectives openly. We have to draw a distinction very clearly between intellectual egalitarianism and social egalitarianism – the two things are quite different. The trouble is that many people have believed, and may still believe, that by getting the educational part right, greater social equality will necessarily follow, a view which I think is totally misguided and confused. Far too much weight is placed upon the social change that can be achieved through education, with the result that far too much pressure is placed upon the educational system to move away from what is its primary purpose, to produce an intellectual elite. One of the ironies of this is that very often the people who argue most for educational opportunity on egalitarian grounds are also often the same people who strongly defend the differentials in society which arise out of limited educational opportunity. We cannot have it both ways, in my view, although from time to time I have found myself trying to. Speaking here as an educationist, and not as a social reformer, I want to emphasise the importance of intellectual elitism as a purpose of higher education, an objective which in my opinion ought to have been brought out in the Leverhulme report, always assuming that its authors also accept that this must be so.

The other references in the report to objectives concern the need to respond to changing needs, to be adaptable and to reduce undue specialisation about which we have heard a great deal. The two-year degree course was suggested as one way in which undue specialisation might be reduced. We have already heard comments upon the possible financial implications; I do believe there would be enormous pressure for (in

English terms) four-year Honours courses if a two-year first degree were the norm. The claim that a two-year first degree would be cost-effective would then be invalidated. I also find it difficult to accept that the proposal for a two-year degree course should be interpreted as a compliment to Scottish traditions and a move towards what has been called here the 'Caledonianisation' of higher education. If the linked proposals of a basic two-year course and possibilities of credit transfer between institutions are taken into account, I suggest that the outcome is more likely to be what I would call the Frenchification of higher education, a standard state-system spread throughout the land, which may bring some advantages to the French but would reduce diversity which I believe is what we need more of, rather than risk more standardisation. I do not want to defend specialisation, and would like to have less of it, but Adam Smith (who was mentioned by Gareth Williams) used to write about what he called 'unintended consequences' and I am rather afraid that in the attempt to use a two-year modular first degree, to help reduce specialisation, the unintended consequence might be to increase standardisation and reduce diversity. There is certainly a risk of that. On specialisation, Stuart Hampshire made a very valid point, I thought, when he told us that in the natural sciences there was a law of increasing specialisation and it could not be denied. In my view, this makes the need for breadth all the more important.

There are three ways in which this can be achieved. First, by squeezing some humanities elements into all courses, no matter at what expense to the degree of specialisation in the sciences and technologies. This has been called 'the solution of the 50s and 60s', but that is no reason for dismissing it, or for failing to return to it to make a more determined effort to apply it. Secondly, by ensuring that students specialising in the arts and humanities have some grounding in the sciences and in scientific method. Mathematics, psychology and biology would seem appropriate subjects for this purpose. Thirdly, by ensuring that the position of the humanities, arts and social sciences in higher education is not sacrificed to make room for the increased attention that must be paid to science and technology. We need that balance. It is quite mistaken to believe that by more efficient technology we can, by increasing

Sir Kenneth Alexander

material prosperity throughout our world, solve the more deep-seated problems of social and international relations.

Here, at Edinburgh University, it may not be necessary to quote David Hume, but if we are to perpetuate and strengthen the 'democratic intellect', it is necessary to recall its Scottish origins:

> It is evident that all the sciences have a relation, greater or less, to human nature – and that, however wide any of them may seem to run from it, they still return by one passage or another. Even *Mathematics*, *Natural Philosophy* and *Natural Religion* are in some measure dependent on the Science of MAN; since they lie under the cognizance of men, and are judged by their powers or faculties. (*Introduction to Treatise on Human Nature*)

Harold Silver emphasised the influence which students can have on course content. My experience is that students want a combination of the vocational and what is often described as 'the academic'. The young have wide horizons, and I am confident that if they could exercise greater influence on the characteristics of the supply of higher education, the influence they would exert would be to ensure that values as well as vocational relevance were effectively represented.

There is not time to comment on the many other important issues raised in *Excellence in Diversity* and discussed at this most timely Conference. In singling out a few on which I have a different view from the Leverhulme spokespersons here today I hope I have not given the impression of being in fundamental disagreement with much of what has been written and said by them. Their work will, I believe, prove most valuable in the process of re-thinking which must guide the adjustment which the institutions of higher education must now face up to. I am sure we are all grateful for that, and for the opportunity provided to us by the University of Edinburgh to discuss these matters in some depth at this Conference.

COMMENTS BY S. B. SAUL

I shall concentrate solely on the last part of Professor Williams' paper dealing with the method of funding, though I would like to say that I felt the first part of the paper contained many wise things. But we have to talk about money, and money is important; for example, Professor Williams was saying earlier (in answer to something I said) that the proposal for a two-year degree is very flexible, and he talked about the possibiity of having a four-year honours history degree arising from it. That would be ideal, but who is going to pay for a four-year history degree?

I do very much agree with Professor Williams that although we are concerned with the efficient allocation of resources, it is fatally easy to think that the market mechanism is going to bring this about. The essential requirements of the market, as he has said, perfect mobility and perfect knowledge, are conspicuous by their absence and for the most part the commodity that we are selling is an elitist one – and I am using elitist in the very widest sense – and not a commodity which seems likely to preserve its image in the face of very sharp price competition and some kinds of aggressive selling. I think it is interesting that where overseas students are concerned, universities have certainly been very wary of price competition. Very few of them have been prepared to charge fees above the minimum or, if they have gone above the minimum, it has been by such a small amount that it does not really make any difference. They have also been aware of what happens in price wars and have urged the government and the UGC to preserve the minimum. I wonder whether those who are very much in favour of market competition really know what they are looking for? It does seem to me, if I may say so (and it neither applies to Edinburgh nor to the University of York), that several institutions have hardly enhanced their reputations as academic bodies by the way they have been chasing any foreign student, and particularly any American student, who can sign his name on a cheque.

Coming to the 50/20/20/10 division of funding Professor Williams' discusses on p.284, my problem here is that some of the definitions were understandably not completely precise, so that sometimes I am not really clear what the different forms of expenditure are. Even so, I cannot see that what he suggested is really very different from what exists at present. What about the 20 per cent on research and programmes? My university would not find any difficulty at the moment in saying that it was at 20 per cent and I guess Edinburgh would probably find itself a little higher. Now if the average some years ago was 13 per cent, then that obviously means that there is a very great range throughout the whole system of earnings on research grants and also to some degree on programme funds. I do not think that is necessarily a bad thing. A higher level of research grants enhances the reputation of a university though, as Professor Williams said, under the dual support system there is always a danger that research grants are in danger of bankrupting the rest of the university. So if Professor Williams' idea is to include dual support, i.e. getting rid of the dual support grant and putting that support into the 20 per cent, then I would not have thought the 20 per cent is a high figure at all. In fact it is quite a low figure and I would suggest the next stage of the report should take up the dual support question in some detail – I think it was a serious omission in this paper. Professor Williams also offers the possibility of the funding body granting extra support and thereby encouraging new initiatives with a high level of research and programme income. But the funding body may also compensate for the shortfall in ths area, though I cannot see any good reason why it should, given that there is core funding for normal student teaching – but I may have missed the point.

Then there is the matter of fees; on the face of things the 20 per cent seems to be a large and variable item, but of course it is not, because whatever Robbins may have felt about universities keeping a larger share of fees, in fact during the great boom, the total number of students was closely related to core funding and physical capacity; as Professor Williams said, there was no great margin of flexibilty available. In any case, even under the present system, the core-funding body must inevitably assume that there will be a substantial level of students in order to justify the core funding at all. Given then that we already have a certain amount of fees which are part and parcel of the core funding, it is really only at the margin that there is going to be any flexibility as regards numbers of undergraduates. One must then ask what sort of margin are we talking about: 2, 3, 4 per cent, that sort of order? I was also wondering what is the incentive to go for extra students in those circumstances, because the fee, if I work out Professor Williams' figures correctly, is expected to be perhaps a third to a quarter of full-cost funding. Now unless the marginal cost is that far below the average cost, it would not pay to have any extra students. I cannot understand where the financial incent-

Comments

ive lies. I can see that flexibility over fee income arises from many of the activities Dr Blackstone was talking about which are additional to normal graduate and undergraduate work – part-time arrangements, special courses for mature students, and continuing education in general. But those fees come to us anyway now. One of the great shortcomings of the system at the moment is that our fees for part-time students are fixed by the UGC at an artificial level making it very difficult for us to compete effectively with other institutions. But in general it does not seem to me that Professor Williams' ideas of fees make much difference to the pattern of funding we have at the moment.

I must hasten to say that I am not one of those who believe that universities should disdain money-making – quite the opposite. I admit I have some trouble with my colleagues at York who take that view, and I am sure that the Principal of Edinburgh University has the same situation here. And I am not against the spirit that Professor Williams emphasises, especially when he is talking about his final 10 per cent. But I have to admit that I am worried by some of the notions that are coming out now – not, I hasten to say, in Professor Williams' paper – where the possibility is raised that we would move towards raising money in the market, and this would then subsidise the teaching activities of the university as a whole. I think here a problem arises: cross-subsidisation from, let us say, engineering, which can earn money in the market, in order actually to pay for the teaching of history or English would be very divisive within an institution, and I must say I would hate to see that happen.

The only other thing that I would like to say refers to the points that Professor Williams made about the UGC and its structure. I am not sufficiently knowledgeable about political mechanics to know whether they are right, but I do not believe that the UGC did all that badly in the end in responding to contraction, compared with what might have happened. In one very special sense I think that the UGC succeeded splendidly simply because when the crisis came they had the courage to do what some academics thought unmentionable, to discriminate. We will never get agreement in such circumstances that they got it right. I do not believe they were ignorant or capricious, but then my institution did better than some. Those who suffered shouted loudly; and, possibly unfortunately, those who gained were too gentlemanly to try to justify their selection. But we cannot know whether the UGC were right or wrong in those that they selected to be discriminated against, and those that they selected to be discriminated for, because we do not have the means to judge. It may be that we ought to have the means to judge, though I foresee awful trouble if every university has the right to appeal and call for a fifty-page document explaining why engineering in one university is not quite so good as engineering in, say, Imperial College.

I am deliberately not being very positive here in putting forward any new ideas of my own because I think that Professor Williams' arguments do not require any significant change and because I am not convinced such fundamental change is required. The basic elements in them as regards the core funding, the programme and research grants, and to some extent the fees, take us right back to the UGC which has to make the decisions to supplement or compensate. I am not necessarily arguing that the core funding body should work in precisely the same manner as the UGC now does and be constituted in the same manner, but I am convinced that there must be a statutory body to make much the same decisions as it has done with no mean success in the past.

REPORT OF THE DISCUSSION BY PETER SCOTT

The four-hundredth anniversary of the University of Edinburgh coincided, to the year if not the month, with the twentieth anniversary of the report of the Robbins committee on higher education. In the context of the third session of the conference, on the university in future society, this second anniversary was perhaps more relevant than the first. For higher education has reached and passed beyond the far horizon established by Robbins; it has no similarly magisterial map to guide it through the next twenty years to the end of the century. Perhaps the most important perspective for British higher education to keep in mind today is the simple fact that we are closer, in time, to the twenty-first century than to the Robbins report. Yet, as the discussion that followed the papers by Professor Williams and Dr Blackstone showed, in terms of higher education's assumptions and aspirations Robbins was

Report of the Discussion

but yesterday. Indeed the final report of the Leverhulme programme, the subject of this third and last session, takes up many of the themes of Robbins, most prominently the issue of overspecialisation of undergraduate courses.

British society, of course, is not as much in love with the memories of the 1960s as British higher education. The once confident belief that material progress and social reform could be simultaneously pursued with equal and complementary success has drained away. It has been replaced by a less-than-generous and rather myopic utilitarianism which is as apparent on the left as on the right. The result is a growing disjunction between the nostalgic and defensive conservatism of higher education and the increasingly aggressive but unsystematic invasions by lay society into territory in which not so long ago the autonomies of higher education were fully respected.

Sir Kenneth Alexander, the principal of Stirling University, emphasised this in his comments. 'If one reads some of the manifestos and some of the small print in the manifestos, one will see that interference is taken for granted now. The question is only what form shall it take rather than is it proper for us to try to exercise it. Part of the reason, I believe, is that universities at least, and possibly other sectors in higher education, are regarded as insufficiently tough-minded, influential, or even clear-headed to have too much attention paid to any resistance they can put up.'

This, then, was the rather unpromising context in which Professor Williams and Dr Blackstone had to present the final report of the Leverhulme programme. This programme has been an attempt to re-establish a dialogue that if it has not been entirely broken in the twenty years since Robbins has become faint and sporadic. Yet it is not clear that the two partners, Government, either in its own interest or acting as proxies for collective abstractions like 'industry' and 'society', and higher education are very interested in re-establishing this dialogue. The former tends to act as Sir Kenneth described, partly as an increasingly oppressive paymaster, partly as a demanding customer but rarely as the willing negotiator of a revised concordat between lay and academic society. It may not always be clear about what precisely it wants higher education to do, but it is quite clear that it has the moral as well as effective right to command higher education to do something.

Higher education for its part seems unsure about the advantages of opening a dialogue with Government on the broad issues raised by Leverhulme. Alternatively it appears paralysed by its changing fortunes, the cuts and the reversal in public reputation that these presumably represent and the rising tide of lay intervention; or resigned to a new oppositional and beleaguered role as the guardian of academic rationality in an increasingly philistine society. The outcome of these two different reactions is a strange mixture of micro-collaboration – for who can resist the temptation to dance to the latest ordained tune whether it is 'continuing education' or 'information technology' if refusal risks the undermining of a whole institution – and macro-opposition – for it is difficult to recall a period of greater mutual hostility between Government and higher education. This makes it difficult for higher education to begin and to sustain the kind of civilised and positive dialogue implied by Leverhulme.

This ambivalence about the need for such a dialogue underlay much of the discussion that followed Professor Williams' and Dr Blackstone's papers on the last day of the conference. It also influenced the attitudes of participants to the detailed proposals made in the Leverhulme report, two of which, for two-year ordinary degrees and for a rearrangement of the funding of institutions of higher education were discussed more fully than the others. In an important sense the context for these discussions had been set the previous evening, before Leverhulme had been published and its contents known, by Dr Harold Silver, principal of Bulmershe College of Higher Education, in his plenary address 'Higher Education – the Contenders' and Sir Stuart Hampshire, warden of Wadham College, Oxford, in his reply to Dr Silver. For they expressed contrasting, and perhaps incompatible, views of the relationship between higher education and society, views that must predetermine more detailed views about the Leverhulme proposals.

Dr Silver warned of the dangers of post-Robbins isolationism. 'Universities are going to continue to be drawn into debates about the relationship between their curriculum and structures and processes and methods on the one hand, and employment, the professions, the labour market on the other. If

Report of the Discussion

their autonomy appears undermined by this, then it is no good looking for solutions in Newman or Flexner. If there are traditional values that appear to be at stake, then these will need to be scrutinised and redefined, knowing how relative they in fact look across national boundaries and across time', he said. He also argued that it would no longer be sufficient to identify the wishes of students with the unchallengable values and purposes of institutions, and that universities would have to take more account of the polytechnics and other non-university colleges. What Dr Silver was arguing was not only that higher education in its relations with the state and more broadly society was being made an offer that it could not refuse — because in the end it was subject to their direction — but also that it was from its efforts to adapt to changing conditions and to meet new needs that higher education created and recreated its own dynamism as not only a social but also an intellectual institution.

Sir Stuart Hampshire took an opposite view. He argued that if higher education paid too much attention to what he called 'society round the corner', its creativity would be blunted, its horizons for future action restricted, and the quality of the experience it offered its students impoverished. He added that one of the functions of universities was to give pleasure. If students simply felt they were being prepared for niches in society, they would find that depressing. A university was a place where people should be encouraged to experiment and this could be inhibited by too insistent and too precise demands being made of higher education.

It was this clash of views that provided another context for next day's detailed discussions of the Leverhulme report. Two opposite views of the sources of vitality within higher education and so two contrary interpretations of higher education's best stance to society, one delivered by the principal of a college of higher education, the other by the head of an Oxford college (although it would be misleading to align this fissure of opinion with the binary division of British higher education). It was at this stage that the declining influence of Robbins was most keenly felt, because the true genius of Robbins was to provide a framework sufficiently broad to incorporate both views of higher education. Although substantially modified almost immediately by Anthony Crosland's binary policy and the creation of the polytechnics, Robbins established a powerful concordat between discordant views within higher education and the discordant interests of lay and academic society. Leverhulme could not hope to recreate such a persuasive concordat of views and interests. But the next day's discussions soon showed that it was a victim of our contemporary discordance.

Sir Kenneth extended Stuart Hampshire's general critique of Dr Silver's views into a more specific criticism of the Leverhulme report. He criticised its lack of clarity about the objectives of higher education and singled out for particular refutation what he saw as a strand of unreflective egalitarianism. 'In my view higher education is necessary elitist. It is about intellectual elitism and, if one is frightened to admit that, one can never get the objectives right or discuss the objectives openly', he explained. He drew a sharp distinction between intellectual and social egalitarianism but insisted that it was a mistake to believe that by getting 'the educational bit' right we could solve 'the social bit'. He also pointed out that those who supported greater educational opportunity, with the aim of promoting social egalitarianism, might also be encouraging in the same process intellectual elitism. Sir Kenneth's firm conclusion was the need to emphasise this latter form of elitism as a central purpose of higher education. Professor S. B. Saul, vice-chancellor of the University of York, broadly agreed. 'The commodity we are selling is an elitist one', he said.

This assumption, appeal even, that higher education should be let alone because only by being let alone could it fulfil its proper mission and so realise its true utility to society heavily influenced the two vice-chancellors' view of Leverhulme's detailed proposals. Both questioned the report's assertion that undergraduate courses had become too specialised, an assertion also made by Robbins, and so cast doubt on its proposal for two-year ordinary degrees as a remedy for overspecialisation. The previous evening Sir Stuart Hampshire had half-defended specialisation. He argued then that the subject matter of knowledge set certain limits on how broad courses could be made. In the natural sciences the law of increasing specialisation could not be avoided, although in the humanities divisions between disciplines were remarkably arbitrary. Sir Kenneth agreed.

Although he supported the need for breadth, he also wanted to be able to defend appropriate specialisation.

He also had more practical concerns about the Leverhulme proposal for two-year degrees. First, he believed that a broader two-year first degree would lead to 'enormous pressure' for a subsequent two-year honours course, making four years in all. This would be impossible in financial terms. Second and more significantly, he feared that Leverhulme-style two-year degrees would lead to the creation of a 'standard state system spread throughout the land', to the 'Frenchifying of higher education' rather than the 'Caledonianisation' to which Professor Williams had referred so approvingly in his opening remarks. If this happened, Sir Kenneth argued, it would not lead to a broader undergraduate education. Instead its unintended consequence might be to reduce the diversity which both he and the authors of the Leverhulme final report desired. Professor Saul reinforced Sir Kenneth's scepticism about Leverhulme's crusade against specialisation. He said that in his experience at York it was the specialisation at honours level that students enjoyed. It presented them with a challenge that made the degree worthwhile.

Leverhulme's proposal that each institution should receive 'core' funds amounting to half of the necessary income and be expected to bid for the rest by putting forward specific programmes or obtain it through higher student fees found more favour with the two vice-chancellors. Sir Kenneth believed that the wider horizons and expectations that could be reflected through student fees could be an effective counterweight to what would be the governmental and bureaucratic influences exercised through 'core' grants which would reflect a narrow definition of society's needs and indeed of the character of society itself. Professor Saul was a little more cautious. He warned against over-optimism that the market would necessarily produce a better distribution of resources. However, the Leverhulme proposals on funding would not in practice make things much different for universities. The University Grants Committee would still have to decide how best to stimulate initiatives or whether to compensate for deficiencies in other income. By receiving more of their income through student fees universities would not necessarily acquire a significantly greater margin of flexibility.

So what might be called the 'Hampshire line' on the proper relationship between higher education and society, from which flowed an instinctive scepticism about Leverhulme's detailed proposals on access and breadth, was probably the most powerful strand of opinion during the discussion that followed Professor Williams' and Dr Blackstone's papers. The fact that both the vice-chancellor respondents espoused this line, of course, was a decisive factor in shaping the discussion. There were participants, many from the wrong side of the borders (English and binary) which may have placed them at a strategic disadvantage, who held more to the 'Silver line' and so regarded Leverhulme's proposals with more favour. But the discussion of access was perfunctory and rooted in self-interest. The commonest fear seemed to be that if universities ever experienced any serious shortage of traditional students because of the coming demographic downturn, they would poach the non-traditional students for whom non-university institutions at present catered and catered better.

Dr Andrew McPherson, however, took up the incestuously entwined issues of improved access and student famine. He questioned whether universities would be best advised to try to fill any empty places in lectures halls by concentrating their attention on socially marginal groups. Would not it be better to try to raise the already healthy participation rates of the middle class to the almost universal participation rate of the upper middle class, he asked? He could have added, but did not, perhaps to spare egalitarian sensibilities, that this was precisely the recruitment strategy that has sustained higher education during the last twenty years, so why should it not be equally successful over the next twenty? Dr McPherson also argued that participation rates could most readily be increased and access widened by taking more students after only one year in school sixth-forms, the traditional pattern in Scotland which had been intensified since the 1960s especially in Strathclyde and partly because of the mounting difficulties of sixth forms. After all why mount a frontal assault on the specialist honours degree while leaving untouched the specialist A-level? The implication of his argument was that in time the reorganisation of the upper secondary school, through the Manpower Services Commission or tertiary colleges, might have a more decisive influence over the social placing of higher

Report of the Discussion

education than any internal reform.

This discussion was the Leverhulme's first outing. So it might be unfair to build too elaborate conclusions on its performance. Few of the participants had had a proper opportunity to read the only-hours-old report and the general election campaign was approaching its peak. Yet the outline of higher education's probable reaction seemed clear. For many people in universities, rather fewer in polytechnics and colleges, the case for opening up a new dialogue with Government on the agenda laid down by Leverhulme remained at the best unproven, especially as there was no convincing evidence that Government was seriously interested in sustaining rather than exploiting such a dialogue. From this nervous scepticism flowed considerable doubt about the wisdom of the detailed proposals being made in the report to improve access, reduce specialisation, and increase accountability and efficiency. Finally, even among those convinced of the virtues of Leverhulme's goals there was still uncertainty about the effectiveness of Leverhulme's means. But this accumulation of scepticism was perhaps as much a reflection of the high uncertainty of British higher education just over halfway between Robbins and the twenty-first century as of the detailed proposals made in the Leverhulme final report.

INDEX

Aberdeen University, 56, 85, 88, 120, 161, 163, 293
academic drift, 180, 183
access, see availability
accountability, 226, 276, 278-80, 311
adaptation without growth, 239-42, 245, 254-5, 266, 276, 280
adolescence, and function of a university, xi, 5, 6-10, 12-16, 18, 23-4, 26, 28, 32, 165, 231
adults in higher education, 236, 244, 248, 253-4, 256-8, 287, 303
aims of higher education, x, 4, 48-9, 297-9
  egalitarian, 250, 287-90, 298, 308
  new universities, 153-4, 157
  Robbins report, 135-6
  see also functions of higher education
Alexander, Sir Kenneth, 305-6, 308-9
Amis, Kingsley, 137, 218
Anderson, John, 170, 180
Anderson, Robert, xi, xii, 211-12
Aristotle, 39, 49-50, 55-7, 68, 100, 102-4
Armstrong, George Frederick, 175-6, 184, 204
Arnold, Matthew, 118, 120-4, 148, 151, 159, 192, 217, 222
Ashby, Sir Eric, 215
  and liberal education, 141, 158, 210, 220
  and science and technology, 133-5, 169-70, 179-80, 219
Astbury, W. T., 196-7
autonomy, ix, 113, 132, 138-42, 160, 195-6, 199, 215-17, 221, 226, 230, 232, 239, 257, 297, 305, 307
  and central financing, 269-70, 277-8, 280, 284
  civic universities, 129, 153
  Edinburgh, 14, 21-2
  new universities, 147

see also needs, social
availability of higher education, 121, 131, 136-7, 145-6, 193-4, 248-59, 285, 310-11
  and entry qualifications, 255-6, 258
  to ethnic minority groups, 253, 257-8, 287, 289
  extension of, 242-3, 248, 250-2, 257-9, 294-5; see also expansion, university
  restriction of, 250
  and social class, 181-2, 251-2, 254-5, 257-8, 287-90, 292, 310
  see also part-time study

Bacon, F., 63, 70, 84, 93, 102, 240
Bagehot, Walter, 191-2
Baker, David, 8
Barbeyrac, Jean, 102-3
Barker, Ernest, 129
Barlow Committee 1946, 197-8
Barran, Sir David, 227
Batchcroft, Master, 12
Beare, T. Hudson, 176-7
Beattie, James, 83, 88
Becher, A., 268
Bentham, Jeremy, 187-8
Bentley, Richard, 18, 70-1, 72
Berdahl, R. O., 215
Birkbeck, George, 180
Birmingham University, 121, 181, 194
Blackie, John Stuart, 294
Blackstone, Sir William, 18
Blackstone, Tessa, 288-9, 292, 303, 305-6, 310
Bligh, D., 244
Bolgar, Robert, 64
Boulliau, Ismaël, 77
Bowen, Francis, 83
Boyce, James, 195
Bragg, Sir Lawrence, 224-5
Brewster, Sir David, 204
Briggs, Asa, 137, 204-5, 207, 210
Bristol University, 129, 181, 194
Buchanan, George, 54, 62, 78, 101
Burgess, T., 269
Burnet, John, 294

Index

Busleyden, Jérôme de, 44-5

Carlyle, Thomas, 192
Carmichael, Gersholm, 91
Carter, Charles, 232
Cecil, Sir William, 9
Chamberlain, Joseph, 194
Charron, Pierre, 102
Cheit, Earl, 219
chemistry, 170
Cicero, ideas of, xi-xii, 37-9, 47, 54, 56-7, 69, 89, 91-2, 97-8, 102, 104
citizenship, ideal of, xi-xii, 97-8, 103, 116, 136
 and humanism, 37, 47, 58
civic universities, 127-30, 151-5, 157-8, 164-5, 181-2, 205, 207-8
 and innovation, 194-8, 200-1, 202
Clapmarius, A., 68
classical studies, 3, 72-3, 74, 77
 in European universities, 44-7, 65-7, 75-9
 and humanism, 37-41, 44-50, 53, 57-9, 65-7, 102-4
 nineteenth century, 117-19, 121-3, 160, 186, 190
 in Scottish universities, 13, 62-4, 82
 see also rhetoric
Clough, Arthur Hugh, 191, 193
Cockburn, Henry, 89
Colleges of Advanced Technology, 136, 152, 183, 198, 221, 225
Comenius, 64, 74
Comte, Auguste, 35, 125, 161, 192
contraction in higher education, xiii, 138, 218-19, 230, 304
control, social, as function of university, 28, 32, 106-7
 Edinburgh, 20
 Oxbridge, 6-13, 18, 22, 26-7
Cousin, Victor, 84, 99
credit transfer, 245, 257, 293, 299
culture:
 'common', 136, 142
 and idea of university, 107, 115-16, 119-26, 132-4, 150-2, 159, 161, 179, 207-8, 220, 258-9, 288-9
 two cultures, 36, 122, 147, 218

 see also liberal education
curricula, 82, 108-9, 150-1, 161, 210, 219-20, 292
 and civic universities, 152-3
 Edinburgh, 13, 19, 21, 57, 90-1, 93, 162
 and humanism, 41-2, 44-6, 50-2, 55-9, 62, 64, 68-9, 74, 77, 79, 107
 of new universities, xii, 153-5, 156, 159, 160, 164, 201-2
 nineteenth century, 118, 120, 124, 126, 163, 171, 192, 194
 Oxbridge, 8, 190-1
 USA, 176
 see also inter-disciplinary programmes

Dainton, Sir Frederick, 220-1
Davenport, Dr, 11-12
Davie, George, 161, 163, 182
Davies, Samuel, 4
degree system, 4, 6, 8, 26, 162-3, 222, 250, 257
 honours degree, 243-4
 2-year honours degree, 290
 2-year pass degree, 243, 287, 295, 299, 301, 306, 309
 3-year ordinary degree, 291-2
 4-year honours degree, 291-2, 294, 299, 301
democratisation of universities, 129, 132, 182, 188, 207
Descartes, René, 63, 70, 76, 102, 104
D'Ewes, Simonds, 8
discipline, 5-6, 32
 academic, 32, 262-4, 269-70
 Edinburgh, 13, 18, 21
 and learning, 30
 Oxbridge, reform of, 22-6, 28
 tutorial system, 6-12, 14, 16, 18
Dodds, Harold, 139
Duncan, Douglas, 62
Duncan, William, 83
Dundee University, 181, 293
Durkan, J., 54-6

East Anglia University, 154, 199
École Polytechnique, Paris, 175, 178-9, 206
Edinburgh University, 125, 215, 262, 301

313

Edinburgh University—*contd*
  and Common Sense philo-
    sophy, 20, 85, 87-91, 93
  1583-1660, 13-14, 56-7
  1660-1780, 18-22, 28, 32, 162
  see also technological
    education
egalitarianism, *see* aims of higher
  education
elective system, 19, 21
Eliot, T. S., 151, 164
elitism in higher education, 5,
  133, 137, 204-6, 250, 299, 308
  medieval, 7, 22-4, 26, 48, 107
  nineteenth century, 116, 118,
    191-3, 207
engineering, 124, 169, 170, 172-8,
  204-5, 211
  in civic universities, 182
Erasmus, x-xii, 9, 37, 51, 73, 104,
  106
  educational theory, 38-43, 47-9
  and universities, 37-8, 41-2,
    44-7, 49, 53-5, 58-9, 108
  see also humanism
Essex University, 154, 199
examinations, 4, 171-2, 194, 244,
  251, 255, 290
  Oxbridge, 24-5, 27-8, 118
  Scottish universities, 162
Exeter University, 201
expansion in higher education,
  218, 287-9
  1851-1914, 127-30, 194
  and idea of university, 128-9,
    130-4, 137-42, 149-50, 158-9,
    208
  post-1945, 130-8, 145, 147, 151-
    3, 157-8, 164-5, 197-202, 210,
    221-2, 277, 280
  purpose and effect of, 198-9,
    221-3, 230, 232, 240, 251, 297
  see also Keele University

Farrant, J., 238-9, 251-2, 254
Ferguson, Adam, 83, 87-8, 90, 93,
  96-7
financing of higher education, ix,
  130-1, 138-9, 195-7, 221, 232,
  246-7, 250, 260-2, 265, 301-3,
  306
  and academic coordination,
    268-71, 280

and bureaucracies, 241, 264,
  274-6, 278, 309
core funding, 281-4, 302-4,
  309-10
earned income, 282-4, 302
Edinburgh, 14, 19, 21, 262
and future, 275-84
and government policy, 271-2
and market forces, 241, 266-8,
  274, 278-83, 301, 303, 310
models of, 260-2, 272-8
programme grants, 281-2,
  283-4, 302, 309
student fees, 282-4, 301-3, 309
Fletcher, John, 43
Flexner, Abram, 129, 218-19, 230
Fowler, Thomas, 51
Fox, Richard, 49-50
Freeman, E. A., 190
Froude, J. A., 148, 149
Fulton, O., 255, 257
functions of higher education,
  x-xi, 3-6, 31-2, 107, 116,
  141-2, 161-2, 165, 207, 210,
  215, 230, 242, 246, 264, 297,
  307
  civic universities, 128-30
  nineteenth century, 190-2, 206,
    217
  and university expansion, 133,
    135-6, 150-1, 200
  see also adolescence; aims of
    higher education; liberal
    education; vocational
    education

Gardiner, Bishop, 9
Gaguin, Robert, 38
Gibbon, Edward, 261
Glasgow University, 56-7, 108,
  125, 162, 293-4
  engineering at, 173, 182
  moral philosophy at, 20, 85,
    90-3
Gordon, A., 255, 257
Gordon, Lewis, 173
graduate studies, 137, 225
Grafton, Anthony, 58, 101, 104-6
Grant, Sir Alexander, ix
Gregor, Ian, xii, 137, 160, 163,
  165, 209
Grotius, 69, 75-6, 91-2, 102, 104-6
Guarino, 47

Index

Hamilton, Sir William, xi, 113, 138, 160, 189
Hampshire, Stuart, x, 107, 209, 297-9, 307-9
Hardy, Thomas, 145-6
Hawkins, David, 217
Haydn, Hiram, 101
Heath, Terence, 42
Heinsius, Daniel, 67-8
Hemsterhusius, Tiberius, 72
Heriot-Watt College (later University), 177-8, 183, 293
higher education:
   diversity of, 215-16, 223-6, 231-3, 242, 280, 290-2, 299
   employers' requirements of, 226-8, 229
   history of, 216-19, 230-1
   possible future of, 218, 236-9
   roles in, 215-22, 224-5, 231, 260-71
   students' requirements of, 228-31
   see also civic universities; expansion in higher education; higher education, colleges of; polytechnics
higher education, colleges of, xiv, 216, 226, 243, 252
Hoggart, Richard, 222, 223
Hornius, Georg, 71
Houghton, Lord, 118
Hull University, 201
humanism, xi, 37-59
   Christian, 38-40, 47-9, 51, 56, 58, 102
   and early modern education, 62-9, 74-9, 101-2, 104-5
   and early modern state, 62-9
   impact on English universities, 43-6, 49-53, 59, 108
   impact on Scottish universities, 53-8, 108
   and moral philosophy, 69-70, 102-6
   scientific/technological, 123, 134, 218
Hume, David, 31, 34-6, 62, 84, 86, 88, 92, 95-7, 100, 300
Hutcheson, Francis, 83, 91-2
Huxley, T. H., 118-20, 125-6, 148, 161, 163

IJsewijn, J., 47

Imperial College, London, 128, 205
independence, *see* autonomy
innovation in universities, 3-4, 24, 133, 151-2, 182, 188-202, 204, 282, 286, 290-2, 295; *see also* tradition, place of
inter-disciplinary programmes, xii, 137-8, 153-4, 263
   Keele, 156, 158
interference, political, ix, 46, 107, 138-41, 149, 189, 197, 215, 218-19, 232, 239, 241, 271-2, 297, 305-7, 311
   Edinburgh, 22, 28, 108, 189
   historical, 260-1
   new universities, 201-2
   Oxbridge, 9-10, 22, 25-6, 28, 32, 108, 113-14
   see also autonomy; needs, social; pressures, external

Jardine, George, 189
Jefferson, Thomas, 19
Jeffrey, Francis, 33, 189
Jenkin, Fleeming, 173-5, 177, 183, 205
Jeune, Francis, 190
Jewel, John, 51-2
Jonson, Ben, 7, 59
Jouffroy, Théodore, 84

Kant, Immanuel, 34
Keele University, 119, 155-8, 164, 198, 201
Kelvin, Lord, *see* Thompson, William
Kent University, 154, 165, 199
Kettel, President, 3, 12
Kogan, Maurice, 227-8, 268

Lancaster University, 199
languages, 36
   in early modern education, 74
   and humanism, 40-1, 44-8, 54-6, 58
   nineteenth-century reforms, 118
Latin, *see* classical studies; rhetoric
Laud, Archbishop, 9
learning, Christian, 38-41; *see also* discipline
Leavis, F. R., 122, 164

315

Index

Lee, Jenny, 296
Leeds University, 181, 195-7
Leibniz, G. W. von, 70, 75
Leicester University, 201
Leverhulme Programme of Study into the Future of Higher Education, xiii, 240-6, 285-93, 295, 297-300, 305-11
liberal education, xi-xiii, xiv, 3-5, 20, 59, 107, 142, 145-7, 160-1, 165, 205, 209-11, 217-20, 294
   and new universities, 127, 132-4, 149-51, 154-5, 158-9
   nineteenth century, 114-21, 126, 147-8, 161-4, 172, 181
   see also vocational education
Lindsay, A. D., 155-6, 158, 164
Lipsius, Justus, 63, 65-8, 104-5
Liverpool University, 181, 194
Locke, John, 4, 62, 102
logic and humanism, 41-3, 49-50, 55-7, 64
London University, 127, 171, 193
Lowe, Robert, 191
Luther, Martin, 44-5
Lyons, F. S. L., xi, xii, 145, 147, 163-4, 210

McConica, James, 101, 104-6
MacLean, Professor, 4
McPherson, Andrew, xiii, 241, 310-11
management:
   bureaucratic, 264, 266, 274-5, 278
   collegial, 264-6, 270, 274, 276-8
   by market forces, 266-8, 274, 278-83
Manchester University, 127, 181-2, 194-6
Mandrou, Robert, 64
Marshall, John, 194
mathematics:
   and liberal education, 117, 160-1
   and 'new science', xii, 64, 76, 101-2
Maurice of Nassau, 66-7
Mead, Joseph, 8
Mechanics' Institutes, 180-1, 205
medical schools, 21, 82, 106, 170
Melanchthon, Philip, 42, 43
Melville, Andrew, 46, 53-7
Melville, James, 54

Mill, James, 89, 161
Mill, John Stuart, 35, 118-19, 147-8, 149, 186-7, 189-92, 217
Minogue, Kenneth, 140
Moberley, Sir Walter, 131-3, 139, 164
morality:
   and Common Sense philosophy, 88-100, 102-7
   and function of a university, xi-xii, 6, 26-7, 33, 35-6, 56
   and humanism, 69-70, 102-5
   private, 33-4
   and tutorial system, 7-9, 13, 16-18
   see also philosophy, moral
More, Thomas, 69
Morley, John, 193
Murray, Lord, of Newhaven, 197, 199-200

needs, social, 28, 109, 129, 136, 140-1, 147, 156-7, 160-2, 165, 221, 226, 230, 242, 247, 264, 297-9, 307-10
   and financing of higher education, 269-70, 280
   Oxbridge, 25
   and professional self-regulation, 240-1
   see also autonomy
Newcastle University, 181
Newman, J. H., 113, 217, 222, 230
   and liberal education, 114-19, 121, 142, 147-8, 150-1, 155
North, John, 8
Nottingham University, 198, 201
Nuttgens, Patrick, 127, 137, 204-6, 210

Oakeshott, Michael, 133, 140
Oestreich, Gerhard, 68
Ogilvie, Sir Frederick, 197
Open University, 233, 249, 253, 296
Oxbridge, 108, 202
   influence on new universities, 155-6, 157, 165, 195-6
   nineteenth century, 114, 117-18, 190-3
   see also tutorial system

part-time study, 216, 224, 249, 250, 253-4, 256, 303

316

Index

nineteenth century, 162, 181, 204
Pattison, Mark, 32, 116-17
payment by results, 19-21
Percival, J., 128
Perizonius, Jacob, 71-2
Peston, Maurice, 221, 224
Peterson, A. D. C., 218
Petrarch, 69
Phillipson, Nicholas, 101-2, 104-7
philosophy, moral, Common Sense, 83-100, 102-6
physics, 170
Pitcairne, Archibald, 77
planning of higher education, x, 138, 200-2, 237-9, 242, 269-71, 280-81
   central, 241, 277
Playfair, Lyon, 118-19, 125-7, 134, 148, 163, 207, 294
   and technology, 170-2, 173
Plutarch, 38-9
politics as academic discipline, 67-8, 89, 97-8, 190
polytechnics, xiv, 152, 175, 181, 183-4, 216, 224-5, 231-3, 275, 307-8
polytechnic schools, 174-5
Pratt, John, 275, 279
pressures, external, ix-xi, 155-6, 161, 163, 190-1, 202, 210-11, 219-21, 226-31, 269-70, 296, 298
   from Church, xi, 9-12, 17, 28, 107
   from employers, 226-8, 280, 282
   from parents, xi, 7-8, 10-12, 15, 17-18, 28, 107-8, 229
   from state, xi, 8-12, 17, 28, 107, 138-41, 232-3, 307
   from students, 27, 108, 202, 229, 266-8, 280, 282, 292, 300
   and tutorial system, 7-13, 15, 17
Preston, John, 11-12, 15
professional education, *see* vocational education
Pufendorf, 69, 91-2, 102, 104
Pusey, Edward, 187, 192

Quintilian, 38, 41, 47

Rainolds, John, 50-1, 53, 56
Ramus, 54, 55-7, 59, 64, 99
redbrick universities, *see* civic universities

reform, university:
   nineteenth century, 113-14, 117, 124-6, 189-93
   Scottish universities, 162-3, 189
regents, Edinburgh, 14, 18-19, 56
Reid, Thomas, 83-8, 93-5, 97-9
relevance in higher education, 147, 150, 157, 159, 194
religion, influence of, xi-xii, 6, 56, 187, 208
   Edinburgh, 13-14
   and liberal education, 3-4
   in Oxbridge, 7-10, 13, 17, 22, 26-7
research, 3, 114, 161, 176-7, 179, 181, 205, 242, 246-7
   in civic universities, 128-9, 131, 152-3, 164, 196
   funding of, 281-2, 302, 304
   increase in, 127
   in new universities, 155, 158
   Oxbridge, 25
   in polytechnics, 224-5
residential universities, 162, 164-5, 216
   civic universities, 130
   Edinburgh, 13, 20
   new universities, 156, 200
   Oxbridge, 6, 11-12, 17, 24
resource allocation, *see* financing of higher education
rhetoric and humanism, 41-3, 50, 52, 55-8
   preservation of, 73-9
   see also classical studies
Ringer, Fritz, 206
Robbins report 1963, 304-6
   and financing of higher education, 246, 282, 284, 302
   impact of, 130-1, 140-2, 242, 250, 308
   and specialisation, 135-7, 183
   and university expansion, 198, 202, 221-2, 232, 237, 248
Rollock, Robert, 57
Rothblatt, Sheldon, 161, 217
Royer-Collard, P. P., 83
Rudbeck, 74
Ruddiman, Thomas, 62, 78
Rush, Benjamin, 82
Rutherford, Lord, 129

Sadler, Sir Michael, 195

317

Index

St Andrews University, 56-7, 119, 125, 147, 161, 293
Sanderson, Michael, 205, 208, 217, 226
Sarbiewski, Casimir, 77
Saul, S. B., xiii, 298, 308-10
Scaliger, Joseph, 54, 63, 66-7, 71
scepticism, 35-6, 59, 102, 107
   and Common Sense philosophy, 84-7, 92, 94-7, 99, 105-6
schools, secondary, 118, 177, 242-3
   expansion of, 127, 193-4
   and higher education, xiv, 128, 163-4, 199, 251, 255, 290-2, 294, 311
   see also Erasmus
Schurzfleisch, Conrad Samuel, 74-7, 101-2
science, teaching of, 18, 183-4
   Cambridge, 205
   Edinburgh, 19, 170, 173
   and humanism, xii, 63, 64-8, 70, 77
   and humanities, 299-300
   nineteenth century, 118-20, 122-5, 161, 163, 182, 189, 194
   twentieth century, 127, 134, 201-2, 205, 222-3
Scott, Peter, xiii, 224, 232
Scottish universities, 161-3, 165, 192-3, 204, 210, 243, 290-4, 299
   Enlightenment period, 82, 90-2, 98-100
   humanism in, 53-8, 102-4
   influence of, 82-4, 188-9
   new universities, 157
   and technology, 167-70, 172, 182
Scruton, Roger, 150-1, 160-1
Seeley, John, 118
Selden, John, 75, 102
selection for higher education, 251, 255-6, 257-8, 289-90, 292
self-regulation of higher education, 239-40
Sheffield University, 128
Shils, Edward, 232
Sidgwick, Henry, 117-18, 159, 193
Silver, Harold, xiv, 297, 300, 306-8

Simond, Louis, 20-1
Sizer, J., 269
Smith, Adam, 84-5, 92-3, 96-8, 100, 190, 260-2, 264, 266, 274, 299
Snow, C. P., 122
Southampton University, 201
specialisation, xii-xiii, 4-5, 14, 136, 138, 305, 309
   in civic universities, 152-3, 164
   and liberal education, 114, 116-17, 119, 134, 147-8, 160-1, 163, 218
   Oxbridge, 190
   pressures for, 226-8
   reduction of, 242-3, 286, 290-2, 299-300, 311
Spencer, Herbert, 35, 120, 186-7, 191
staff, academic, 25, 245-6; *see also* tutorial system
standards, academic, 19-21, 24-5, 28, 136-7, 142, 146, 244-5, 247, 263-4, 280; *see also* teaching: quality of
Stevenson, John, 88
Stewart, Dugald, xii, 83-5, 87-9, 92-100
Stirling University, 154, 223, 293
Stone, Lawrence, xi, xiii, 30-6, 105, 106, 109, 162, 165, 211
Strathclyde University, 183, 293-4
student numbers:
   decline in, 15, 18, 236-8, 240, 246-7, 249, 253-4, 257, 279, 286-7, 310
   increase in, 25, 130, 136-7, 148-9, 249, 254
student participation, 221, 229-31, 236-8, 240
Sussex University, 137, 155, 156, 199-201, 211
Swann report 1968, 223, 227

Tawney, R. H., 155, 164
teacher training, 181, 216, 220, 292-3
   contraction of, 238, 252
teaching:
   civic universities, 131
   content, 30-3, 51-3, 99
   methods, xiv, 25, 157, 171, 195, 200, 223

Index

teaching—*contd*
  new universities, 154, 156-7, 201
  quality of, 16-17, 18-20, 32-3, 229, 242, 244
technological education, 118, 126, 129, 132-5, 152-3, 169-71, 175-6, 179-81, 183-4, 193, 204, 206, 210-11
  and civic universities, 182-3
  Edinburgh, 167-78
  new universities, 201-2
  role of, 218-19, 222, 224-5, 227
  technological universities, 136, 152, 179, 183, 198, 219
  see also engineering; Mechanics' Institutes
Tesauro, Emanuele, 77
tests, religious, 26, 188, 193-4, 209
theology, 106
  and humanism, 44-5, 49-51, 55, 57
  and liberal education, 114, 121
Thompson, William (Lord Kelvin), 170, 173, 182
Thomson, Thomas, 98
Touraine, Alain, 220, 227
tradition, place of, 138, 186-90, 193-4, 196-7, 201-2, 204, 307; *see also* innovation in universities
Tripp, Simon, 51-3
Trist, E., 269-70
Trow, Martin, 266-7
Truscot, Bruce, 130-1, 164
Tuck, Richard, xi
tutorial system:
  collapse of, 14-18
  Edinburgh, 14
  nineteenth century, 192
  early Oxbridge, 6-13, 14-18, 25-8, 165

United States of America, 20, 27, 31, 82, 175-7, 225, 232, 267
  academic standards in, 244
University College, Dundee, 207
University College, London, 83, 188
University Grants Committee, 113, 129-30, 131, 148, 194
  and control of higher education, 138-9, 226, 232, 304
  and financing of higher education, 275-8, 280-3, 301, 303-4, 310
  and idea of university, 218
  and new universities, 157-8, 197-202, 210, 222
  and technological education, 225

Vice-Chancellors' Committee, 138, 197-8, 277
vocational education, xi, 106, 160-2, 183, 218-20, 224
  nineteenth century, 114, 115-19, 126, 147-8, 163, 172, 180-1, 190, 194
  and student requirements, xiii, 228-9, 300
  and university expansion, 133, 136, 147, 149-50, 158-9
  see also liberal education

Wakefield, Gilbert, 17
Waldegrave, William, xiiin.
Wales, University of, 209
Walker, James, 183
Warwick University, 154, 199
Webster, John, 74
Weise, Christian, 77
West, William, 51-2, 53
Whewell, William, 117, 119, 160, 186-7, 193
Whitehead, Phillip, xiiin.
Wiener, Martin, 205-6
Williams, Gareth, xii, 297-9, 301-6, 309-10
Williams, Shirley, xiiin., 210
Wilson, George, 78, 167-9, 170, 183
Witherspoon, John, 20, 82, 88
Wolf, F. A., 78
women:
  admission to Oxbridge, 124-5, 193
  colleges for, 26
  participation in higher education, xi, 249, 252, 254, 258, 287, 289-90, 292
Woodruff, Sir Michael, 150-1, 160
Wyttenbach, Daniel, 78-9

York University, 154, 199, 302-3, 309

319